Christian Lenz
Geographies of Love

Cultural Studies | The series is edited by Rainer Winter | Volume 47

Christian Lenz (PhD) teaches British literary and cultural studies at TU Dortmund University. His research interests include cultural geographies, British horror and romantic and erotic literature.

CHRISTIAN LENZ

Geographies of Love

The Cultural Spaces of Romance in Chick- and Ladlit

[transcript]

This thesis was accepted as a doctoral dissertation in fulfilment of the requirements for the degree ›Doktor der Philosophie‹ by the Faculty of Culture Studies (Fakultät Kulturwissenschaften) at TU Dortmund University in 2014.

Bibliographic information published by the Deutsche Nationalbibliothek
The Deutsche Nationalbibliothek lists this publication in the Deutsche Nationalbibliografie; detailed bibliographic data are available in the Internet at http://dnb.d-nb.de

Cover layout: Kordula Röckenhaus, Bielefeld
Cover illustrations: Zauberschmetterling/photocase.de: Flug verpasst, 2010. margie (Margot Kessler)/photocase.de: Blaues Büro, 2015. kai/photocase.de: Guten Morgen 3, 2006.
Printed in Germany
Print-ISBN 978-3-8376-3441-9
PDF-ISBN 978-3-8394-3441-3

Table of Contents

Acknowledgements

Writing acknowledgements is always a hard thing to do. This book represents the work of quite some time and having it finally finished still feels unreal. I started my dissertation project of which this book is the ultimate result in 2008 and during the course of writing it, many people have contributed to it, challenged and inspired me. First and foremost, I want to thank Prof. Jürgen Kramer (TU Dortmund). When I presented him with the idea to write about the geographical implications in contemporary trivial literature he did not even flinch and from the start encouraged me to pursue this topic. Also, I have to thank Prof. Gerold Sedlmayr (TU Dortmund), who took on this project and was equally supportive. I cannot thank you enough for giving me the opportunity to write about a topic that is indeed close to my heart.

I owe many thanks to my colleagues and doctoral siblings, Marie Hologa and Cyprian Piskurek. Both were generous in their feedback and suggestions and I could have not asked for a better team of 'comrades-in-writing'. And, because of our very diverse topics, I have not only learned a lot about Scotland and football, I am equally grateful for the bonding of our shared years of writing our theses, which I shall never want to miss. I especially have to thank Iris-Aya Laemmerhirt, dear colleague and even better friend, because what comes after these acknowledgements is as much her work as it is mine: her countless ideas and input are immeasurable, and her support and laughter have helped me along more times than I could count. Furthermore, I would like to extend many thanks to Bianca Roters, Julia Becker, Stefan Schlensag, Mark Schmitt, Sina Nitzsche (and the Space Collective), Laurence Kane, Barbara Hamblock, Richard Bell and last, but not least, Christiane Binder. A special 'Thank You' goes to Tamara Braunstein and Dieter Hamblock for proofreading this text (all mistakes found hereafter are solely my fault…), Benjamin Lehmert for his technical expertise and Simone Waiblinger for re-creating the Geographic Puzzle for me.

As this book is based on ideas I started pursuing during my time as a student at Ruhr-Universität Bochum, I would like to thank Prof. Anette Pankratz and Claus-Ulrich Viol, without whose idea for a James Bond conference I probably would have never considered starting such a long-time project such as this which lies before you. Also, I have to thank my once fellow students Daniela Reschke, Christina Hamann, Lina Kindermann, Florian Gerhardt, Henrike and André Tönnes, Raffaela Teich, Robin Köhler, Jennifer Redeker, Katharina Kwasniowski, Verena Siebert, Sarah Göhring and Domenica Nottenkämper – who have become very good friends indeed. Yet, this list would not be complete without Claudia Rüttgers, Dennis Köchling, Maximilian Hummerich as well as Kathrin Müthing and Nils Jablonski, who were an incessant fountain of joy and reinforcement – more than I could have ever hoped for.

Of course, I am highly indebted to my family. They always supported me in my endeavours and even though they were not always quite sure what I was doing or writing, they never stopped being there and giving me everything I needed or did not even know I needed: my parents, Lutz and Heike Lenz, who always provided me with literature and never even considered that some literature might not be suitable, my sister Sabine Schneider and her family for being a constant source of support as well as my extended family: Katharina Hillebrand, Ursel Köchling, Nadine Erasmus and family and Martin Rempe – thank you all!

My heartfelt thanks go to Bastian Rothe, who survived many years of me writing this and who never stopped supporting and helping me. Your contributions to this book are beyond any words as the embraces, dinners and incessant encouragement can be found between the lines of these pages. Thank you so very much!

Lastly, I would like to thank all the people who bought and continue to buy chicklit and/or ladlit novels. Yes, these stories might be 'sort of' the same, and, yes, the endings are indeed predictable – but due to your never-ending search for love in literature, your cravings for happy endings, this book has been possible. May it help you to pursue your own happily ever after: just because it is fiction does not mean it cannot come true in real life.

Spaces of Love

> Love makes you see a place differently.
> ANNE MICHAELS *FUGITIVE PIECES*

It is Friday, 19 April 2013, close to midnight: "What am I doing? What am I doing? Why did I start all this? Why didn't I stay as I was?" (Fielding 2013: 25) Bridget Jones is back. Seventeen years after Helen Fielding's series started and seventeen years after *Bridget Jones's Diary* gave a global phenomenon a figurehead. Now, in 2013, Bridget has become older, a mother and a widow. It is safe to say that the eagerly awaited third novel about the famous Singleton was not what readers expected, mainly, because she is no longer what she used to be: "I literally *was* Bridget Jones but this character isn't like me now and that is an outrage." (Freeman 2013, original emphasis; cf. Patterson 2013) It is interesting to note that the same year, another, albeit lesser known novel was granted a sequel: Mike Gayle revisits his character Matt Beckford, and he chronicles the protagonist's days before and after *Turning Forty*. Just like Bridget's, Matt's life has also not turned out the way he planned: he is divorced, unemployed and has to move back in with his parents.

These two novels as well as the further development of their two protagonists mark a distinct cut in literary history: *Bridget Jones: Mad about The Boy* and *Turning Forty* could be considered testimonies to the end of two genres that had their heyday in the 1990s – chick- and ladlit (cf. Day and Perry 2011, Showalter 2002: 76); 'could' but not 'can'. Fielding's latest novel is a case in point:

> In all my time in publishing I have never experienced such a palpable sense of excitement and anticipation from colleagues, booksellers and friends and family as I have with the return of Bridget Jones in *Mad About The Boy* [sic]. It has been phenomenal, as are the sales we have seen to date. This is only the beginning. (Drake-Lee, qtd. in Page 2013)

It appears that fans of the novel's earlier instalments are just as eager to read the last book in the series[1]; that neither fans nor critics seem to like the novel is a different matter. Mike Gayle's novel seems to fare better with many readers considering it a good novel, whose ending is not as satisfying as the beginning (cf. *Goodreads* 2013). Regarding the aforementioned cut, however, the novels mark the transition from chick- and ladlit novels, respectively, to more grown-up territory. They are no longer concerned with problems that other chick- and ladlit characters have to face – except the search for love. This feature is the driving force behind the protagonists' actions in the two genres and their stories revolve around the 'hunt' for the perfect partner to spend their life with.

According to the Bible, when God created the world and "saw every thing that he had made, [he thought] *it was* very good." (Genesis 1: 31, original emphasis) But when he made Adam and beheld him in his Garden of Eden, he decided that "[*i*]*t is* not good that the man should be alone" (ibid.: 2: 18, original emphasis). It appears that humans, as biological and social beings, are not meant to live on their own, because "[i]solation can [...] be unbearably stressful for people" (Klinenberg 2013: 2). Scholars have different opinions as to why human beings live, for example, in family units or collectives but they tend to agree on the following: "Human societies, at all times and places, have organized themselves around the will to live with others, not alone." (Ibid.: 3)

Now, at the beginning of the twenty-first century and "at the global level[,] the number of people living alone is skyrocketing, having risen from about 153 million in 1996 to 202 million in 2006 – a 33 percent increase in a single decade." (Ibid.: 10) However, despite the fact that nowadays people have the advantage of freedom, flexibility and personal choice (cf. ibid.: 13), which is distinctly favoured by living on one's own, people are longing for a partner to share their lives with. Dating websites are a good indicator as they are booming across the globe and this suggests that romance is still very much on the singles' minds. Especially in large metropolitan areas, to which many young professionals have relocated, there is a steady demand and supply of single men and women.

These trends have been mirrored in numerous texts in many different media, but it is especially in two genres that young urban singles searching for their perfect partners are depicted: chick- and ladlit. Generally associated with British authors Helen Fielding and Nick Hornby, many countries have produced their own national variations of the rather standardised formula. These novels depict modern twenty- to thirty-somethings and their professional careers. But, most importantly, they always feature a romance plot that is the central motor of the story and the charac-

1 Unfortunately, sales figures for Gayle's novel were unavailable.

ters' lives. The stories are very often humorous, involve a lot of misunderstandings and depict a fair amount of 'will-s/he-won't-s/he'.

Due to their similar structure, chick- and ladlit novels are often considered as two sides of the same story, the female and the male side, respectively, but this is a misconception: despite their many similarities, the two genres come from different (socio-cultural) backgrounds and the characters depicted do not experience the same development – if there is any, actually. However, it is the ending that can be considered the same for the characters aspire to a happily ever after as expressed by the loving union with their perfect partner. In the following, I will argue that the two genres are indeed similar but not for the reasons that are popularly accepted.

So far, a larger comparative study between chick- and ladlit has not been undertaken, only shorter scholarly essays have been concerned with such an endeavour as, for example by Kate Dorney (2004) and Katharine Cockin (2007). Some critics have devoted themselves to analysing specific aspects of the novels but they tend to only look at the categories of consumption or construction of gender identities. However – and this is a very important point to make – this book is neither a study of gender issues nor is it primarily concerned with gender roles. It is easy to just follow the obvious route and analyse discourses of femininity and masculinity with a subject like chick- and ladlit, even in a geographical discourse: the hierarchical structures within the workplace, the role of shopping for female protagonists or the possible sexism of laddish behaviour. I decidedly claim that the protagonists behave uniformly when it comes to the geographies of their search for love. Therefore, I will approach both genres equally to gain new insights into the usage of space and place. I will comment on hierarchical structures in the workplace, but in terms of how the offices are ordered and organised and how each individual workspace is structured and laid out. In this book, I will look at shopping tours by both female and male protagonists, where they shop, and what those goods can disclose about their ideas, about themselves and their partners. The topic of cultural geography presents an opportunity to find out what links the protagonists of chick- and ladlit, their problems of modern life and opportunities which might present themselves to them. All this will be achieved by focusing on space and will inevitably touch upon gender issues, which, however, will never be the primary and sole focus. There will be remarks which point into the direction of gender-related questions and concerns but only in order to delve deeper into issues of cultural geography.

Until now, very little comparative research between the two genres has been done, and an extensive academic investigation into chick- and ladlit on a global level has not been undertaken at all. Some scholars have recognised ethnic and global varieties of chicklit (e.g. Donadio 2006, Ferriss and Young 2006a: 5-6, Peitz 2009: 29 and Pérez-Serrano 2009) and some have connected Indian to Western ladlit (Iqbal Viswamohan 2013a), but this book is the first comparative study of the various national varieties of the two genres. By adding a transnational dimension to the comparison of chick- and ladlit, it provides the first study to look at a phenomenon which has spanned the globe and created an international literary sensation.

But just like the gender constructions are taking a less pronounced role here, the different nationalities of the novels, authors and protagonists are not a primary issue either. The cultural and literary heritage is mostly British, due to the intertwined past of the novels' countries of origin, but as a result of the globalised market it can be assumed that other nations took up the 'ready-made' product and spiced it up with local phrases and reference points. The formula itself remains largely untouched, testifying to the universal appeal of the concept, which, by now, is divorced from the cultural genesis. This explains why concepts are taken up – especially in the Indian and Aboriginal varieties of the novels – that might not have originated in the countries without the presupposed success of Western chick- and ladlit novels. Although some of the books are peppered with Hindi and Aboriginal terms but very rarely whole phrases, they are written in English, favouring and supporting international sales to the diaspora as well as home markets. Especially for the latter, reading these novels, which are clearly inspired by successful novels such as Helen Fielding's or Nick Hornby's, the "This is Me!" response grants them internationality and might enable readers to feel part of the large international community of aficionados.

A third original aspect of this book, in addition to an extensive comparative study of international novels of the two genres, is that it concerns itself with a geographical focus. This is the first work that applies a cultural geography approach to chick- and ladlit novels, and furthermore acknowledges the inherent spatial qualities outside of geographical contexts as well as the spatial turn[2] in cultural studies (cf. Bachmann-Medick 2007, Dünne 2010, Hess-Lüttich 2012, Winkler, Seifert and Detering 2012). Moreover, by not focusing exclusively on one geographical aspect in novels (cf. Röll 2002), it presents a more diverse and significant contribution to the topic.

It has been observed that, "[a]s a literary form, the novel is inherently geographical." (Daniels and Rycroft 1993: 460; cf. Röll 2002: 6) Readers seem to expect from a novel that it is set in a location readers can identify as being similar to, if not the same as their own (cf. Dünne 2010: 7): by mapping a world, which can happen both scientifically and literarily, the author creates lifeworlds. These are

2 According to Winkler, Seifert and Detering, the term 'spatial turn' is attributed to Edward Soja as well as Fredric Jameson (cf. 2012: 254, 262; cf. Bachmann-Medick 2007: 284, 290-291).

constructed, socially produced spaces that present the "illusion of transparency" as Henri Lefebvre calls it: "Comprehension is […] supposed, without meeting any insurmountable obstacles, to conduct what is perceived […]. The presumption is that an encrypted reality becomes readily decipherable thanks to the intervention first of speech and then of writing." (1991: 28) People believe the words they read – or write, or speak – to have the properties to (re)create space(s) in a way that mirrors reality and thus they believe the wor(l)ds to be true. This, then, blends with Lefebvre's concept of the "illusion of reality":

> In the course of any reading, imaginary and the symbolic dimensions, the landscape and the horizon which line the reader's path, are all taken as 'real', because the *true* characteristics of the text – its signifying form as much as its symbolic content – are a blank page to the *naïf* in his unconsciousness. (Ibid.: 29, original emphasis)

Lefebvre concludes "that (social) space is a (social) product." (Ibid.: 26, 30) Being a social product means that space can be considered to be a topology, a space constituted of locational relations (*Lagerelationen*), as space between bodies of any kind (cf. Dünne 2010: 6): "In other words, […] space [is exposed] as a sign system filled with meaning upon which social reality is constructed." (Hess-Lüttich 2012: 8) Jurij Lotman suggests that only through language or acts of speech is reality constructed and he goes on to claim that any piece of art, in this case literature, is a secondary modelling system that indeed creates spaces – without language there would be no space (cf. 1972: 22-25): space is the very element of the (literary) artwork (cf. Mehigan and Corkhill 2013: 15). Lotman writes that each multidimensional world is compressed into the less-dimensional container of art, in which many signifiers, codes or points of reference might be lost due to the density – or in some cases brevity – of the piece of art the creator and audience, respectively, is able to gather: if a building is described, the authors have to be selective in their description, thus necessarily omitting or altering the reality for their text, reconstructing the pieces of information in their own words. The readers, in a next step, have to reassemble these pieces via the linguistic and semiotic signs to form the world anew in their imaginations. Readers are therefore in the hands of the author via the narrator but the construction of their worlds "allows for conclusions concerning respective effective social standards and cultural values" (Hess-Lüttich 2012: 7). And, of course, the readers, when they create the world from the words in the text, will match the authors' pieces of information with the ones stored in their memories and they will use them as the foundation to build their worlds upon. Already, this notion of space hints at a very artistic connotation and texts become an interface between various experiences and imaginations. Moreover, it points towards a plural of geographies, not one universal geography.

In this book, I follow the ideas proposed by Edward Soja in his seminal work *Thirdspace*, namely that there is an "inherent spatiality of everything [...], with human geographers [...] as critical analysts of the human condition." (2007: 264) His concept of the lived space, which he calls "Thirdspace" (ibid.: 265), complements the perceived space ("Firstspace" or the cartographical perspective) and the conceived space ("Secondspace" or topographical perspective) (cf. Soja 1996: 65, 2007: 265-266): "Thirdspace [is] the space where all places are, capable of being seen from every angle, each standing clear; but also a secret and conjectured object, filled with illusions and allusions, a space that is common to all of us yet never able to be completely seen and understood" (Soja 1996: 56; cf. Winkler, Seifert and Detering 2012: 262-263).

Soja furthers the ideas of Lefebvre, whose spatial practice and representation of space (cf. Lefebvre 1991: 33) he deemed somewhat dualist and reductionist (cf. Soja: 2007: 265). Lefebvre appears to have sought "to break out from the constraining Big Dichotomy by introducing an-Other" (ibid.: 268) and Soja's Thirdspace is "a starting point for new and different explorations that can move beyond the 'third term' [Lefebvre's 'an-Other'; C.L.] in a constant search for other spaces" (ibid.: 269-270). The Thirdspace in Soja's definition unites in itself "subjectivity and objectivity, the abstract and the concrete, the real and imagined, the knowable and the unimaginable, [...] structure and agency, consciousness and the unconscious, [...] everyday life and unending history." (Soja 1996: 56-57) Moreover, "[t]hey are the chosen spaces for struggle, liberation, emancipation" (Ibid.: 68) and

> [i]n this sense, Thirdspace (as Lived Space) is simultaneously (1) a distinctive way of looking at, interpreting, and acting to change the spatiality of human life [...]; (2) an integral, often neglected, part of the trialectics of spatiality, inherently no better or worse than Firstspace or Secondspace approaches to geographical knowledge; (3) the most encompassing spatial perspective, comparable in scope to the richest forms of the historical and sociological imaginations (Soja 2007: 269).

Soja deems especially cultural studies to have spawned "the most creative explorations of Thirdspace, and hence the most accomplished expansions in the scope of the geographical imagination" (ibid.: 270), because they are inseparably connected to art, science and philosophy (cf. Mehigan and Corkhill 2013: 7). This argument is supported by the claim that "[g]eography, of course, has traditionally been the discipline without exclusive source material, engaged in a 'borrowing' exercise" (Pocock 1981: 9). Citing, for example, bell hooks as a venerable inspiration, Soja writes that cultural studies, when engaging with (cultural) geography, can "create 'Other' spaces that are radically open and openly radicalized, that are simultaneously material-and-metaphorical, real-and-imagined, concretely grounded in spatial practices yet also represented in literary and aesthetic imagery, imaginative recombinations, epistemological insight, and so much more." (2007: 272) In Soja's opinion, disciplines such as gender studies, postcolonial studies or political studies enrich and stimulate geography and account for a truly *cultural* geography.

That (cultural) geography and literature share an intimate connection has been acknowledged by various (humanist) geographers: "We should not see geography and literature as two different orders of knowledge (one imaginative and one factual) but rather as a field of textual genres" (Crang 1998: 58). This way, the worldliness of literary texts, with their "biographical, economic, institutional [and] geographical contexts", are realised as intertwined with the imaginativeness of geographical texts, "the images [writers] express and in the way they construct, through modes of writing or composition – however empirically – particular and partial views of the world." (Daniels and Rycroft 1993: 461; cf. Pocock 1981: 12, 15) By considering the bond between literature and geography, "[a]n artist's imagination and sensitivity towards human attitudes, values, and perceptions, as well as his [and her] ability to filter the essence of our relations with nature [and the built environment] help us understand our interactions with the landscape, its cultural value, and our deep roots in the environment." (Lando 1996: 6) This argument supports the idea of the literary text as the interface between geographies, be they real, experienced or imagined. It also shows that each (literary) text is inherently geographical for a narrative must *take place* some*where* and despite not always being directly visible or obvious, a spatial dimension cannot be absent. Because a "literary product is an expression of [a] group's social structure and cultural texture as influenced by its territorial consciousness, and [its] genesis and development of any concept of territory or landscape" (ibid.: 8), a literary text carries meaning: the environment, be it natural or urban, becomes an intermediator and helps to disclose societies' attitudes and values (cf. ibid.). Moreover, "[g]eography and literature are both writings about places and spaces. They are both processes of *signification*, that is, processes of making place meaningful in a social medium." (Crang 1998: 44, original emphasis; cf. Lando 1996: 6) It appears logical to assume that "it is only through 'geography and literature' that the soul of a country and its people becomes *really accessible*." (Lando 1996: 7, emphasis added) Especially the novel appears to favour geographical components because it is characterised by the actions and developments at the stories' cores. For the progress of the novel, the author needs one or more spaces of action in which the events can be situated (cf. Röll 2002: 6). The spaces described in novels are always subjective and the characters living, performing and operating in locales will consequentially (try to) turn them into places (cf. ibid.: 7). It appears that a (cultural) geographical approach to chick- and ladlit is a most suitable indicator as to their protagonists' ideas, attitudes, fears and hopes, but also as to how they have been shaped by their respective cultures and societies.

The book is structured into two parts: the introductory chapters into the topics of chick- and ladlit as well as into cultural geography depict the current state of research and the second, larger part consists of the analyses of a corpus of various chick- and ladlit novels from England, Australia and India. Following these introductory words, the second chapter considers the geneses of the two genres of chick- and ladlit, the literary and cultural influences that favoured and furthered the production of these novels and turned them into a global phenomenon. Starting with chicklit, the roots of the genre are disclosed – from early romances, through mass-produced fantasies to the notion of romantic fiction in general. Using ideas of postmodern intertextuality, a working definition is provided and the stereotypical chicklit heroine is introduced. This section is followed by an examination of ladlit, which can look back on the redefinition of masculinity and the advent of laddish magazines such as *Loaded*. Although the novels' origins are similar, they are not identical and the much-proclaimed sameness is not as obvious as some critics suggest. Yet, I claim that the various novels are indeed very alike in their usage of spaces and places and it will be one focus of the book to prove this claim. The last part of the first chapter presents a structuralist model for a standard chick- *and* ladlit plot as well as major building blocks and stereotypical characters, which serve as blueprint for the analyses.

The third chapter introduces theories from the wide field of cultural geography that provide the basis for the analyses. After a short history of the discipline, various influential concepts are in the focus: first and foremost, the notion of space and place is explained and complemented by concepts such as Foucault's heterotopia, Gilles and Deleuze's striated and smooth spaces, wayfinding and the Actor-Network-Theory, to name but four important theories. As the characters in chick- and ladlit prefer an urban setting for their adventures, the term 'territory' is defined and the (spatial) processes that are important to learn within such a space. Of course, the theories selected and presented in the third chapter only make for a fraction of the possibilities that cultural geography has to offer. I have opted for a rather eclectic mix so as to not privilege one theory over any other. Moreover, I aim to show that theories from cultural geography can be combined quite rewardingly and thus promote the application of cultural geography to literary texts. The last part of the theoretical basis establishes a rhizomatic construction that encompasses the independent ideas used here. Through a structuralist framework the ideas are harnessed and directed towards the investigation of the cultural spaces in chick- and ladlit. In addition to proving the claim that chick- and ladlit characters use space in a similar fashion, the following analyses prove that spatial compatibility foreshadows the characters' successes or failures in their romantic endeavours. It is the starting point of the geographical exploration into one of the most fascinating, yet largely ignored genres of the late twentieth, early twenty-first century.

The analyses themselves are organised into three sections, which account for the three major anchor-points in a person's life: the home, the workspace and spaces of leisure. These analytical chapters will all emphasise the characters' relationships to spaces and places in a specific geographical context. As many protagonists visit and occupy more than one place in their respective novels, there will be many cross-references, which testify to the close bonds that exist between (fictitious) people and their spaces. Nonetheless, due to repetitive structures and contents, not all novels can be discussed in detail. But what is analysed in the consecutive chapters is almost indiscriminately applicable to all novels that can be classified as chick- or ladlit.

The fourth chapter, then, focuses on the characters' abodes, their homes. First, the concept of 'home' is considered, taking into account other disciplines such as psychology or sociology. Next, the construction of the protagonists' homes is at the centre of attention. The analysis considers the rooms the home is comprised of as well as the identities they support. The home can be a retreat from the world or a place of loneliness; however, it always mirrors its occupant. Consequently, the homes of the respective partners likewise signify their compatibility with the protagonists – or, in some cases, their incompatibility. Within this context, an important feature to establish a feeling of home is the urban family, a group of friends that is as closely-knit as a biological family. Advantages and drawbacks of the urban family are presented before the last subchapters explore the home as a repository for nostalgia and memories and the hotel as temporary form of the home, respectively.

These findings are followed by the analysis of workspaces and workplaces. After the introduction of important features of these locations, the analyses distinguish between open-plan offices and enclosed, private offices. What unites them, ultimately, is the notion of the prison. Characters do not feel comfortable in these spaces and are therefore going to abandon them in order to be free to find their perfect partners. A prominent part of this chapter is dedicated to Indian workplaces, for Indian chick- and ladlit novels are conspicuously concerned with their protagonists' working lives. The various working spaces include both open-plan and enclosed offices but are further complemented by professions outside offices as well as the office-cum-home. To conclude this chapter, the Indian practice of arranged marriages is taken into consideration and is regarded as a business transaction, hence turning the private home into a business space.

Having dealt with the most important anchor-points in chick- and ladlit, the sixth and final chapter is about spaces of leisure. It is subdivided into three parts: the first is comprised of spaces of consumption and the identities that can be assembled via products or even bought like commodities. Employing the notion of the habitus, it will be emphasised that characters buy (into) a certain lifestyle and try to create a space in which they can become a product for their perfect partners to consume. This idea leads to the second part, the spaces of clubs and parties. Looking at how the carnivalesque and the spectacle are created in liminal spaces, the club proves to be a more limiting territory than the party but both spaces are united in the fact that they must be left if the single wants to become part of a couple, as only this form of living represents and resides in the normative centre. The last part of this chapter investigates leisure spaces such as bars, pubs, cafés and restaurants. They are characterised by their neutrality, which means that they can be accessed by everyone. This in turn presents both advantages and problems as the characters have to find out.

The conclusion of this book summarises the argument and revisits the hypotheses that chick- and ladlit are very alike in their usage of space and that according to theses narratives only spatial compatibility will guarantee a lasting love relationship. Furthermore, it regards the genres from a critical point of view and evaluates the idea of understanding 'love' as a commodity.

Sprightly Ladies and Lost Boys

"Oh! it is absurd to have a hard-and-fast rule about what one should read and what one shouldn't.
More than half of modern culture depends on what one shouldn't read."
OSCAR WILDE *THE IMPORTANCE OF BEING EARNEST*

DEAR SIR OR MADAM...

"It is a truth universally acknowledged, that a single man in possession of a good fortune must be in want of a wife." (Austen 1967: 15) This is the famous beginning of Jane Austen's 1813 novel *Pride and Prejudice*. This novel is not only one of the first texts that can be considered the foundation of chicklit, and serves as the intertextual background of Helen Fielding's *Bridget Jones's Diary*, it also displays the many constitutive elements which are now considered vital for romantic fiction. In fact, Austen's characters as well as her usage of 'diversions' or misunderstandings have been so influential for romantic fiction that they are still visible in chicklit more than 200 years later. In addition to Austen, the mass-produced fantasies of prolific publishing house Mills & Boon were crucial to the development of chicklit. Without these publications, certain trends and images would not have entered the public consciousness and influence romantic novels worldwide.

But Jane Austen's *Pride and Prejudice* is not the only important literary reference. Whereas women in romantic fiction, including chicklit, (stereotypically) dedicate most of their time and energy to finding and charming the eligible bachelor, the men in contemporary ladlit have a different 'founding father', namely Peter Pan, the boy who never grows up. In J. M. Barrie's 1911 novel *Peter and Wendy*, the beloved fictitious character revisits his childhood friends once more after they have returned from their adventures in Neverland. Peter is given the choice to stay with the Darlings but is not too keen on the idea, which his friends' mother proposes. Instead he exclaims: "I don't want to be a man. [...] Keep back, lady, no one is going to catch me and make me a man. [...] I shall [always] have such fun." (Barrie 2004: 144) Like Peter Pan, the heroes of ladlit are afraid of growing up, a concept they associate with responsibility, a dreary job and a wedding band – hence the phrase "Keep back, *lady*, no one is going to catch me and make me a *man*." It is especially the notion that a 'proper' relationship will be the end of the youthful shenanigans which the lads fear because it would mean that they have to face the reality of being a man with obligations and duties. Indeed, ladlit is highly influenced by the 'dispute' over what a 'man' is: the socio-cultural creation of two types, namely the 'new man' and the 'new lad', has had a huge impact on both the cultural depiction and formation of masculine sensibilities and thus their literary representations. The former is the understanding and sensitive partner but the latter is the fun-loving, responsibility-shy boy in the disguise of a man.

The two genres of ladlit and chicklit gained extreme momentum in the 1990s and have since accumulated a huge following. Their readers tend to devour every new novel that comes out and which is advertised and marketed under the label of one of these genres. But instead of claiming that chick- and ladlit are merely two sides of the same coin, I argue that they come from different backgrounds and do not just approach the same topic from two different sides – in chicklit, the male perfect partner to the heroine is *not* a lad and in ladlit, the female perfect partner is *not* like a chicklit protagonist. But the genres' motifs and motives are directed at the same outcome – the formation of a union – and this can be proven by looking at the characters' spatial behaviour and practices, their geographies as well as the ideas and concepts they connect to spaces and places. Therefore, it is proposed that the two genres *are* similar, just not in the way that publishing houses like their customers to believe.

CHICKLIT

Dismissing chicklit seems to be very easy. After all, many people have commented on the very formulaic and, indeed, rather repetitive plotlines of this form of romantic fiction. Therefore, "criticism of popular feminine narratives has generally adopted one of the three attitudes: dismissiveness; hostility – tending unfortunately to be aimed at the consumers of the narratives; or, most frequently, a flippant kind of mockery" (Modleski 1982: 14; cf. Cockin 2007: 108). Acclaimed writer Dame Beryl Bainbridge managed to embrace all three of these attitudes when she was asked to comment on chicklit and labelled it as "a froth sort of thing. [She continues to claim that as] people spend so little time reading it is a pity they perhaps can't read something a bit deeper, a bit more profound, something with a bit of bite to it" (qtd. in Ezard 2001). And Nobel-prize winner Doris Lessing wondered why these "instantly forgettable books" are actually read (ibid). It seems that these writers regard the very successful chicklit novels – in 2003, *Bridget Jones's Diary* had already sold over 15 million copies around the globe (cf. *The Independent* 2003) – as too low-brow or 'pop' for their readers' own good. "It has become part of contemporary 'common-sense' that romantic fiction is a 'formulaic' 'trivial' and 'escapist' form read by 'addicted' women" (Hollows 2000: 70; cf. Anderson 1974: 14, Gray 2000, Bly 2005, Montoro 2013: 198-203). Some critics, however, do not follow suit entirely and rather see the chicklit phenomenon as proof of a new development:

> I would argue that chicklit represents a revival of the middlebrow, and that the perceived danger of chicklit lies in it being fiction read by those who *should be reading something else*; the guilty pleasure of the middle-class, party-educated female reader who is too hip for Mills and Boon[1] and too dumb for Virginia Woolf. (Knowles 2004: 2, original emphasis; cf. Pérez-Serrano 2009)

Yet the literary quiz *The Write Stuff* on Radio 4 (the show aired 19 February 2003) clearly shows that audiences do understand both genres as they "were asked to perform a pastiche of Virginia Woolf writing Chicklit" (Whelehan 2004: 5). The quiz foreshadowed and surpassed Knowles's negative comment, because the contestants were indeed very able to write adaptations of the highly praised author and the widely-read chicklit novels (cf. ibid.). This does not only show how splendidly the two seemingly antithetical styles can be merged but also that reading highbrow literature, which Woolf's narratives are generally identified as, does not exclude one from indulging in novels that are able to "rais[e] a smile now and then" (Colgan 2001). Jenny Colgan, who is a very successful chicklit authoress, responds to Bainbridge's slighting comment and firmly states that "[y]oung women aren't stupid. We [and she wholeheartedly includes herself in that group; C.L.] do actually know the difference between literature and popular fiction. We know the difference between foie gras and Hula Hoops, but [...] sometimes we just want Hula Hoops"[2] (Colgan 2001).

1 Whelehan also commented on the (potential) readers: "What chicklit provides, fundamentally is the post-feminist narrative of heterosex and romance for those who feel that they're too savvy to be duped by the most conventional romance narrative" (2004: 7).

2 Although Colgan defends chicklit as well as her own and other women's attraction to this genre, she still adheres to the binary of good literature (high-brow) and pop-

Regarding the term 'chicklit', Imelda Whelehan finds the

epithet [...] interesting and provocative. It manages to insult women at the same time as it reminds us that the act of reading is just as gendered now as it ever has been, in addition to alerting us to the fact that having 'women's books' as a category can be positive for women readers as well as continuing to be a useful marketing category in publishing. (2005: 171)

Her comment exposes the dual identity of both the term and its signified genre: both empower females and simultaneously relocate the power of denomination elsewhere, by claiming the right to call their readers 'chicks' and alluding to the 'frothiness' of their nature as well as marketing novels under the headline 'chicklit' and thus manipulating readers' perception. Most scholars attribute the term 'chicklit' to Cris Mazza and Jeffrey DeShell, who used the term in 1995 for their anthology *Chick-Lit: Postfeminist Fiction*, albeit ironically (cf. Mazza 2006: 17-19, Ferriss and Young 2006a: 3, 9, Pérez-Serrano 2009).

Historically, the term 'chick' was first applied to children or young girls in the fourteenth century and has since undergone a change from a term of endearment to denoting promiscuity in women and pointing towards "a liberated or independent female" (Mills 1989: 47). Today, the term is a contested one: some scholars are of the opinion that "the term chick implies women who are not intellectual, who are child-like, and concerned with trivialities; women who are defined according to youth, sexual status and attractiveness." (Gormley 2009) Other critics object, and claim that the term, previously considered derogatory by second-wave feminists, now stands for "solidarity and [...] empowerment" because "women of the third wave seek to reclaim and refashion their identity through terms considered unacceptable by the previous generation." (Ferriss and Young 2008: 3) The implications and allusions of chick(s) have been considered by Diane Goodman, who has pondered the differences both of spelling and pronunciation:

Chick-Lit. A hyphenated word. If you say it as a spondee, accenting both syllables equally, it's a very hip term – confident and cool: this is "lit" by chicks. Read it.
If you say it as a trochee, accenting the first syllable, you get a term even more reductive than the slang term Chick that replaced Broad and Babe in the evolving spectrum of demeaning endearments. What you get is a baby chicken.
If you remove the hyphen and say it as one word real fast you get a more powerful meaning; this is especially true if you ignore the first three letters. (1996)

---

ular fiction (low-brow). Additionally, she excludes male readers of chicklit. Thus, her 'brave' defence leaves a bitter aftertaste.

As Goodman's final assumption is indeed the most empowering, I will use the spelling 'chicklit'. This term evades the notion of the novels being literature only for "hip" chicks, as Goodman's first notion proclaims, or that they are about protagonists who behave like chickens, which are "not known for [their] great intelligence" (Mills 1989: 47). The same spelling will be applied to ladlit later on, in order to stress the semantic equality between the two genres and to allude towards the similarity that will be highlighted. Additionally, by using neither hyphens nor blanks but writing it as one word, the same spelling forms a united front against disdaining critics of the two genres[3].

When one tries to pinpoint the origin of chicklit, many readers and scholars believe Fielding's bestseller to be the first novel of this genre:

> In the beginning there was Bridget. That's not entirely true – there were Chick Lit books in circulation in England for some time before anyone realized a trend was starting – but by all accounts, the Chick Lit wave started with a British invasion, spearheaded by one plucky young 'singleton' by the name of Bridget Jones. (Yardley 2006: 6)

Although much is owed to *Bridget Jones's Diary* – Suzanne Ferriss and Mallory Young claim it to be the "urtext" (2006a: 4) – there has indeed been a tradition leading up to the famous Singleton. Elena Pérez-Serrano (2009) makes a good case for Marian Keyes's *Watermelon* (1995) as the first chicklit novel because it was published one year before Fielding's bestseller. While this is correct, it does not take into consideration Fielding's debut novel *Cause Celeb* from 1994, which is also part of the chicklit canon. Additionally, it cannot be disregarded that Candace Bushnell's *Sex and the City*, which also came out in 1996, the same year as *Bridget Jones's Diary* and which also started as a newspaper column, is as influential as Fielding's novel (cf. Whelehan 2005: 18). Like *Bridget Jones's Diary*, Bushnell's text has seen further cross-medial adaptations – both as a TV series (1998-2004) and in the form of two movies (2008 and 2010) – while the original novel was inspired by Edith Wharton's novels from the early twentieth century (cf. Smith 2008: 3, 10) and Mills & Boon's American sibling Harlequin[4]. However, Imelda Whelehan warns that "[i]n reality, this work of fiction [*Sex and the City*] has very little in common with any contemporary British chick lit, except that subtextually the women are all shown to be desperate to have a meaningful relationship." (2005: 206-207) The most striking differences can be found in Bushnell's heroines who are far more cynical and the fact that her novel is more about depicting the deadened

---

3 Despite my choice of spelling, I will use other scholars' spellings in quotes.

4 For a more detailed history of chicklit in America, Caroline J. Smith's *Cosmopolitan Culture and Consumerism in Chick Lit* (2008) is recommended.

New York high society. In contrast, chicklit heroines like Bridget Jones are sympathetic and likeable and therefore the British Singleton can be regarded as more influential in depictions of global chicklit than *Sex and the City*. With regard to Indian and Australian chicklit, it can be assumed that publishing houses realised the potential that lies in a national variety of this genre and 'jumped the bandwagon'. As mass-produced fantasies were already available in Australia and Indian author Shobhaa Dé was successful with 'bonkbuster' novels (cf. Kasbekar 2006: 93, 100), the way for chicklit was paved and a readership established. Publishing chicklit thus seemed to be the next logical step in generating a new market and a new possibility to increase the publishing houses' profits.

It is hence important, before actually delving into the description and analysis of the genre (and, inevitably, characterisation of) chicklit, to consider the genesis of the genre[5]. However, as Rocío Montoro cautions, "the genre's precursors now appear to be only tangentially related to Chick Lit, primarily because these novels have tended to be seen in isolation and not as part of a specific narrative genus." (2013: 6) Looking at what could have led to the 'existence' of chicklit, many ancestors can be considered and obtaining a trustworthy maternity test becomes a challenge. By classifying the origins of chicklit as identified by scholars (cf. Paizis 1998, Whelehan 2002, 2005, Ferriss and Young 2006a, Harzewski 2006, Wells 2006, Gormley 2009, Montoro 2013), two important strands appear, namely the (broad) genre and tradition of the romance and, in particular, the books published by Mills & Boon: not entirely separable, these two main sources paved the way for chicklit (cf. Smith 2008: 4).

Starting with the first of the two roots, the term 'romance' as denominator for the genre has changed over the decades: "Chick Lit is sometimes seen as a revamped version, a rebranding, or (for some) simply a renaming, of other more traditional forms of popular writing, namely *romance* or *romantic fiction*." (Montoro 2013: 7, emphasis added; cf. Anderson 1974: 13) With regard to the former term, it is possible "to give some weight to the claim that romance is one of the oldest and most enduring of literary modes which survives today" (Radford 1986: 8). In literary history,

> *[r]omance* is a term that has been used at different times to refer to a variety of fictional works involving some combination of the following: high adventure, thwarted love, mysterious circumstances, arduous quests, and improbable triumphs. The term *romance* derives from

5 Radford defines genres as "contracts between a writer and his/her readers [or audiences], and the conventions which go with [the contract] obviously differ according to the conditions of class, ideology and literacy in different social formations" (1986: 8).

the French and was first used exclusively to refer to medieval romances (sometimes called "chivalric romances") written in French and composed in verse. (Harzewski 2006: 31, original emphasis)

Montoro adds that, diachronically, 'romance' "refers to narratives that contain heroic, fantastical or supernatural deeds, sagas and tales." (2013: 8) As these definitions show, a simple classification seems out of the question and "the only continuity is in its term: there is no historical relationship between Greek 'romances', medieval romance, Gothic bourgeois romances of the 1840s[6], late nineteenth-century women's romances and mass-produced romance fiction now – except the generic term" (Radford 1986: 8). It appears that "chick lit seeks to unite readers across genres lines, by grounding themselves in nineteenth-century, heroine-centred literature" (Smith 2008: 2). 'Romance' is a form of "non-mimetic prose narrative focusing on *emotion*" (Radford 1986: 8, emphasis added) and the driving force of these texts still echoes in contemporary romances and romantic fiction: texts produced under the label 'romance' wanted to engage their readers in an emotional narrative and did not – originally – display any "interest in character or [...] the plausibility of events" (Williamson 1986: 2): "The fundamental characteristic of romances is structural not stylistic [...], but to be romances they must have, or adapt, a particular story structure. Romances classically have a tripartite structure: integration (or implied integration); disintegration; and reintegration." (Greenblatt et al. 2012: 141) Romances were to "provide examples of heroic virtue for readers to imitate." (Reeve, qtd. in Harzewski 2006: 32) Therefore, 'romance' and 'romantic fiction' share the qualities of emotions and imitable behaviour and attitude, but whereas the (classical) romance focuses more on quests and morals (cf. ibid.), romantic fiction – or what is considered romance now – is "the happy resolution of a heterosexual romantic relationship [that] forms the backbone of the narrative" and which results from the "sentimental nature" of romances (Montoro 2013: 103, 7; cf. 9). The term 'romance' "has changed, and to some extent deteriorated, so that today it conveys a variety of different ideas to different people." (Anderson 1974: 13) Eventually, the love story became more pronounced, leaving out the "heroic tales of the past in favour of distinct contemporary components" (Montoro 2013: 8) and therefore

6 For example: Chariton (*Chaereas and Callirhoë*, 1st century A.D.) or Xenophon of Ephesus (*Anthia and Habrocomes*, 2nd century A.D.) through to the Gothic romances, most prominently associated with Ann Radcliffe (*The Mysteries of Udolpho* (1794) or *A Sicilian Romance* (1790), which already carries the genre allocation in its title) (cf. Anderson 1974: 13-14).

[t]he romance novel is a work of prose fiction that tells the story of the courtship and betrothal of one or more heroines. All romance novels contain eight elements: a *definition of society*, always corrupt that the romance novel will reform; the *meeting* between the heroine and the hero; an account of their *attraction* for each other; the *barrier* between them; the *point of ritual death*; the *recognition* that fells the barrier; the *declaration* of heroine and hero that they love each other; and their *betrothal*. (Regis 2003: 14, original emphasis)

These eight elements can then be found in examples from the beginnings of the novel – Richardson's *Pamela* (1740) – through to *Bridget Jones's Diary*'s source, Jane Austen's *Pride and Prejudice* (1813) (cf. Harzewski 2006: 32, 41, Wells 2006: 51-2, Harzewski 2011), up to recent examples, though the betrothal in contemporary times is toned down (cf. Ferriss and Young 2006a: 3, Wells 2006: 50). Nevertheless, "[t]wo basic elements comprise every romance novel: a central love story and an emotionally satisfying and optimistic ending" (Romance Writers, n.d.; cf. Gray 2000), which follows complications that have arisen in the plot (cf. Montoro 2013: 9). Again, this is a feature that can be traced back to the early forms of romance: "The broader modal commitment of romance to 'comedy' (a story with a happy ending) also has classical roots. Romances are 'comic' stories but not because they make us laugh but, rather, like Shakespeare's comedies, they make us feel good through happy endings." (Greenblatt et al. 2012: 140-141)

Daniel George writes that "[r]omantic novels are novels which deal with love rather than sex [and] are written with *humour* that does not depend on impropriety" (qtd. in Anderson 1974: 273-274, emphasis added). This inclusion of humour links the (literary) romance strongly to the cinematic romantic comedy, because the romantic comedy – just like the (modern) romance novel – has "as its central narrative motor a quest for love, which portrays this quest in a *light-hearted way* and almost always to a successful conclusion" (Jeffers McDonald 2007: 9, emphasis added; cf. Mortimer 2010: 5-6). Moreover, "the romantic elements [outweigh the] comedic elements" (Rubinfeld 2001: 70), clearly suggesting a strong link between romance, romantic comedy – sometimes even termed "chickflick" (Mortimer 2010: 1) – and chicklit (cf. Ferriss 2006, Smyczyńska 2007: 24-31, Smith 2008: 12-13, 43, 74-100). The romantic comedy – again, just like chicklit – traditionally ends with the union of the central couple and in order to fashion this union as the end of a tumultuous process, this type of movie takes (at least) one of the following plots to keep its viewers interested:

the couple [is] separated in the initial stages [of the plot], only to be reunited by the end [...]. [T]he couple [experiences] love at first sight yet [is] unable to be together, due to factors beyond their control. [...] A third significant model is that of unrequited love. One half of the couple realises their love for the other early on, but the other half is slow to recognize and return their love, often having to lose the wrong partner in order to be ready for the right love [...]. Another identifiable narrative is that of the couple who are at war with each other from the start but come to recognise their love for each other as a result of various misunderstandings and complications. (Mortimer 2010: 5)

These dynamic plots and complications (cf. Paizis 1998: 5) are themselves taken from texts predating romantic comedies or cinematography in general, for example Shakespeare and his comedies, which feature romances and happy dénouements (Mortimer 2010: 10; cf. Deleyto 2009: 31-38). But the bard is not the only one – Paizis states that "[t]he antecedents of modern romantic fiction in Britain can be traced back to the eighteenth century via *The Heir of Redclyffe* by Charlotte M. Yonge, *Jane Eyre* [...] to Samuel Richardson's *Pamela*." (1998: 29; cf. Webb Johnson 2006: 143) In this context, especially the relationships and romances Jane Austen has depicted in her novels are adapted and mirrored in contemporary chick-lit (cf. ibid., Harzewski 2006: 41): "Anyone familiar with Jane Austen's oeuvre will immediately recognize in chick lit a kindred wit, the same obsession with choosing a mate, and a shared attention to the dailiness of women's lives." (Robinson 2009; cf. Ferriss 2006: 72) It is especially the endings of her romantic stories and the happiness the couple experiences which are said to account for the great satisfaction of reading Austen's novels (cf. Hardy 1984: xiv). The emotional dimension is paramount to Austen's novels and, equally, the motor for contemporary romantic fiction and chicklit.

Since the days of classical Greek or Arthurian romances, the concept has changed according to the societies and times and, as already alluded to above, by now, people tend to use 'romance' and 'romantic fiction' synonymously. Although this is a simplification, which both Rocío Montoro (cf. 2013: 103) and Paizis (1998: 182) acknowledge, I will adhere to the modern concept of 'romance' – love is supreme, yet there is a possibility, but not a necessity, of toned-down quests – which segues into the more general idea of 'romantic fiction'. Due to the criteria illuminated above, chicklit can be seen as standing in the tradition of romance, but the influences go further than that. Texts which deal with the union of a (hetero-sexual) couple are just as likely to borrow tropes and motifs from romantic comedies, which makes the term 'romantic fiction' the superordinate category under which romances, romantic comedy and chicklit can be classified. Therefore, "[t]he significance of romantic fiction, as a cultural phenomenon, cannot be exaggerated." (Paizis 1998: 1)

However, it is not only romances that have left their traces in and on chicklit. Other scholars, especially Imelda Whelehan, do see further literary works as predecessors and influences on chicklit, but it appears that most critics agree that chicklit is part of the (hi)story of 'women's literature' (cf. Peitz 2009: 33-34). This can be seen in Whelehan's suggestion of tracing chicklit back to two rather different 'ancestors': firstly, she names the feminist consciousness raising novels, which emphasise "their link to the practices of Second Wave feminism" and whose "narrational style [...] draws the reader in, encouraging us to feel that we share these experiences rather than viewing them from a distance." (2005: 8) The narrative style, married to the emotional subject of the search for love, bridges the distance and results in a feeling that one reads an account of someone who is like the reader. Secondly, Whelehan refers to the 'bonkbuster'[7] or 'sex and shopping' novels of the 1980s as important forerunners: "The new woman of the 1990s and beyond found in *Bridget Jones's Diary* and subsequent chick lit offerings both a warped reflection of the glossy *Cosmo* woman and the rebellious daughter of the bonkbuster heroine." (Whelehan 2005: 175) It is the "confessional tone, the use of self-deprecating humour, and the focus on the quotidian" that suggest an ancestry between, for example, Erica de Jong's *Fear of Flying* (1974) and *Bridget Jones's Diary* (Whelehan 2002: 19-20; cf. Gormley 2009). But it is acknowledged by both Whelehan (2005) and Gormley (2009) that in contrast to bonkbuster heroines, chicklit protagonists lack direction and their main goal is the search for love, as opposed to a counter-reaction to oppression and a heightened sense of sexuality, again highlighting the idea of romance over any other goals and aspirations[8]. Nevertheless, the many sources from which chicklit draws its inspiration, plots, motifs and motives account for the time of origin of chicklit, namely postmodernism (cf. Wells 2006). As the late twentieth century favoured intertextuality (cf. Belsey 1994: 31-32, Whelehan 2002: 18-20, Smyczyńska 2007: 20-23), issues of identity (cf. Ferriss and Young 2006a: 2-3) and the idea of consumerism, both intradiegetically and extradiegetically (cf. Pérez-Serrano 2009), became increasingly important: chicklit "is adept at revealing and/or reflecting the society that produced it, interfacing with the dominant ideologies of the time and period, and challenging, rather than deploying, the ideologies transmitted by women's magazines, self-help books, romantic comedies, and domestic-advice manuals." (Smith 2008: 16) Juliette Wells summarises the question of the ancestry or connection between romances and chicklit as follows:

7 In India, the 'bonkbuster' is strongly associated with (in)famous writer Shobhaa Dé, the "Maharani of Muck" (Kasbekar 2006: 93). She is one of India's bestselling authors and secured her place in Indian literature for bringing this particular genre of literature to her country in the late 1980s as well as helping Mills & Boon to find their 'desi' readership (cf. ibid).

8 Chicklit heroines might not be as sexual as bonkbuster protagonists, but they certainly have progressed from the chaste and 'virtuous' women of the eighteenth- and nineteenth-century novels (cf. Wells 2006: 51).

> Chick lit departs from its predecessors [...] in several ways: its emphasis on the role of sexual adventures in the romantic quest; the nature of the conclusion to the romantic plot; the importance of the heroine's experiences in the world of work and her evolution as a professional woman; the delight and consolidation the heroine finds in herself, particularly in consumer goods; the privileging of entertainment value, particularly humor, over any challenging or experimental content or style. (2006: 49)

Although one might think that love – one of the grand narratives as explained by Lyotard (cf. 1984: 509) – might be ridiculed in contemporary, postmodern romantic fiction, it remains remarkably untouched in almost all novels: "Every chick-lit novel centers on a love plot" (Wells 2006: 49). On the contrary, whereas the heroines are sometimes exposed as inept (cf. ibid.: 52), narcissistic and weight-obsessed (cf. Umminger 2006: 240) to generate comedy, the pursuit of love is taken seriously. Therefore, after all the trials and tribulations the heroine had to endure and master to get her perfect partner, chicklit affirms love and the quest for it as possibly the only worthwhile constant in the heroines' and consequently chicklit readers' lives.

The other important and highly influential basis that inspired chicklit is the history of the mass-produced fantasy[9] and its chief publishing house, Mills & Boon[10] (cf. Montoro 2013: 4). Mass-produced fantasy has a strong connection to the tradition of romances like Austen's *Pride and Prejudice* (cf. Whelehan 2005: 185) and can also be classified as romantic fiction (cf. Montoro 2013: 103-104). In 1908, Gerald Mills and Charles Boon founded their own company after having worked many years for another publishing house (cf. McAleer 1999: 11-35). At first they published "in a form and at a price that was within the reach of a wide readership. [...] Mills & Boon seemingly published anything it could lay its hands on" (ibid.: 17). It was a trying enterprise, for Mills and Boon had to face up to a financial crisis in the 1920s, Gerald Mills's death in 1928 and the restructuring of the company following that tragedy (cf. Dixon 1999: 17, McAleer 1999: 84-112, Mills & Boon

9 This term was used if not coined by Tania Modleski in her famous study *Reading the Romance*. However, she employs the term to refer to the books by publishers Harlequin and Mills & Boon, Gothic romances and soap operas (cf. 1982: 11-34). Additionally, Pamela Regis accuses both Radway and Modleski of examining too narrow a sample (cf. 2003: 5-7).

10 "Ninety years after its founding, Mills & Boon is one of only two British publishers to have become a household name in Britain and throughout the Commonwealth" (McAleer 1999: 2). "Mills & Boon" even made it into the *Oxford English Dictionary* and means "romantic, story-book"; a testimony to its cultural importance (*OED*: "Mills & Boon").

United Kingdom). It was only in the 1950s that they concentrated solely on romances. But already in 1957 Mills & Boon established a relationship with publishing house Harlequin (cf. Paizis 1998: 13), bringing out a Mills & Boon novel in North America (Anne Vinton's *The Hospital in Buwambo*). This was the starting point of a long business relationship during which each company published in the other's market and finally merged in 1972. Today, Mills & Boon operates as part of Harlequin Enterprise (cf. homepages of Mills & Boon United Kingdom and Mills & Boon Australia). In 1998, 200 million paperback novels were sold in over 100 overseas markets and Mills & Boon books have been translated into 26 different languages. In the UK alone, four out of ten women read Mills & Boon and one book is sold every five seconds (cf. McAleer 1999: 2-3, Mills & Boon United Kingdom)[11].

With regard to the content of the mass-produced fantasies, Mills & Boon chronicler jay Dixon distinguishes between three variants: the country novel, the city novel and the exotic novel[12] (cf. 1999: 5). The first is set, as the name implies, in the countryside and thus evokes images of Jane Austen's novels, the second usually employs London as its main place of action and the third is set abroad in countries of the British Empire, which was still thriving in the 1910s to 1930s. Over the years, the heroine and the hero changed from hapless governess to independent career woman, from aristocrat to Latin lover, respectively, just as the plot lines have been altered to cater to readers' needs. Here, positively-minded critics see a great divergence from the prejudice "that 'Mills & Boon' books are all the same'" (ibid.: 8), because "[t]hroughout the century, plots [and characters] have changed to meet readers' changing expectations, showing that Mills & Boon authors respond to an audience which is far from passive and unrequesting [in their consumption]" (Auchmuty 1999: xi). Joseph McAleer takes a similar approach and adds that, because of its close observation of its readership, Mills & Boon books can be "a valuable source for the social historian of the twentieth century" (1999: 4). A good example is the mid-twentieth century inclusion of the soldier's wife in the Mills & Boon portfolio, who has to deal with Britain's housing shortage and the psychological effects of WWII on her husband (cf. Dixon 1999: 3). Thus, it can be seen that it is not all "girl meets boy, they encounter problems, girl runs away, girl returns, all is miraculously explained away, and marriage ensues" (ibid.: 1). But "[t]he novels have their limitations, of course. Conservative in many ways, they are

11 Actually, McAleer states that every *two* seconds a Mills & Boon book is sold. Apparently, sales rates have declined since his 1999 book.

12 There used to be a fourth category, the society novel, but it "disappeared [as an independent 'genre'] around the time of the First World War" and most of its features merged with the other, remaining variants (Dixon 1999: 5).

also homophobic and racist" (Auchmuty 1999: xi). There are characters that are not Caucasian but they are always connoted as 'Other', as is the case with the "exotic books" of Mills & Boon. Regarding the categories of sex and gender, only female and male or feminine and masculine, respectively, belong together – confusion is neither expected nor allowed.

Interestingly enough, these problems are mentioned only in passing, but are never properly discussed by either Dixon or McAleer[13]. What they do acknowledge, however, is the notion and function of escapism. The guidelines for "aspiring Mills & Boon authors" state the following:

> We're in the business of providing entertainment, a short foray into the emotions. Our readers don't expect to read about the sort of petty worries they can encounter any day of their lives, such as an overdue library book, or the sort of serious problems which cause too much heart-ache or anguish. We're talking about escapism. But escapism must be based on reality. (Qtd. in McAleer 1999: 2)

For a TV special celebrating Mills & Boon's centenary, *How To Write A Mills & Boon* (first broadcast 2 November 2008), presenter and author Stella Duffy has met with women who claim to be passionate readers of these mass-produced fantasies. The women say that they started reading these novels when they were still in school and never stopped reading or loving the books. One interviewed woman has even spent "somewhere in the region of £20.000" on them – and is not yet 'satisfied'. This is in line with Janice Radway's 1984 study *Reading the Romance*, for which she interviewed and analysed the female readers and connoisseurs of mass-produced fantasies in the (fictitious) American town of Smithton, who started reading these books at all ages (cf. Radway 1991: 56)[14]. These women have hardly anything in common except a similar lifestyle – as suburban wives and mothers – and their love for mass-produced fantasies, proving that "romantic fiction has been seen [...] as an 'imaginary community' of women sharing 'utopian' dreams" (Hollows 2000: 68; cf. Radway 1991: 144-145). The utopian dreams manifest themselves quite distinctly and can be subsumed under the term 'escapism'. As the Smithton women "referred constantly and voluntarily to the connection between

13 Yet feminist and gender critics comment on these problems ever so often (cf. Stacey and Pearce 1995).

14 This study by Radway deals with an American readership and the author herself is wary of applying her findings to other romance readers (cf. Radway 1991: 48). However, her book is regarded as a model of interdisciplinary insights (cf. Wood 2004: 147) and as it is considered one of the most important scholarly texts for the analysis of mass-produced fantasies, Radway's ideas will be employed here.

their reading and their daily social situations as wives and mothers" (Radway 1991: 9), it becomes obvious that there is a strong connection between the life they are living and the life they would like to lead. Radway ascertains that the women use the novels as a means to escape their "daily social situations" although they are quite reluctant at first to use that word – escapism: "Who ever turned to romance in quest of truth? Romances are precisely fiction, and pulp fiction at that. They are mass-produced fantasy, after all, no more than a form of harmless escape." (Belsey 1994: 31) It can be observed that "[r]omances are texts that, through a social fantasy (experienced as active desire), fill in the 'lack' in women's lives" (Ebert 2009: 100). This lack has been characterised as a "lack of [both] attention and validation" (Dubino 1989: 107). Consequently, "it becomes clear that romance novels perform [a] *compensatory function* for women because they use them to diversify the pace and character of their habitual existence" (Radway 1991: 89, emphasis added). Radway goes on to explain what she means by compensatory fiction: "romances can be termed compensatory fiction because the act of reading them fulfils certain basic psychological needs for women that have been induced by the culture and its social structures but that often remain unmet in day-to-day existence as the result of concomitant restrictions on female activity." (Ibid.: 112-3)

Ordinary life "is apparently the last thing romance readers want to confront in their spare time." (Gray 2000) This is especially true for historical books in the oeuvre of mass-produced fantasies, which are set in a different time and place – far removed from the readers' own reality. Radway identified the value of compensatory fiction as being twofold: on the one hand, the female reader identifies with the heroine of the story and thus experiences the protagonists' emotional nurturance 'first-hand'. She wants to be swept away and find herself in such a boundlessly loving relationship in which only she and her handsome hero exist – no cleaning the house, feeding the husband and the kid(s) – just like the heroine of her beloved books. On the other hand, the simulated travel to other countries and times pose a great attraction for the women who never have visited the Scottish castles of medieval times and therefore the readers deem historical books 'educational'[15] (cf. Radway 1991: 109).

15 "[A]nything the readers learn about the fictional universe is automatically coded as 'fact' or 'information' and mentally filed for later use as knowledge applicable to the world of day-to-day existence" (Radway 1991: 109). The female readers claim that all authors research their facts very meticulously and therefore they take the "information" which they get from the books to be true. The fact that one author might have taken another author's "facts" and included them in her books does not cross their minds. Yet this is very possible as most authors of the mass-produced fantasies

Escapism from one's own life – which in the reader's opinion might have fallen short in one way or the other – does pose the biggest difference to chicklit novels. Whereas the Smithton women try to experience a time, love or even life they dream of, chicklit 'addicts' do not have the feeling of "I wish that were me!" but rather recognise themselves: "This is me!"[16] (cf. Whelehan 2002: 55, Vnuk 2005, Freeman 2013). This generalising reader response is said to be a feature of chicklit because "[f]or the fans, it is claimed that chick lit reflects the experiences of contemporary young women" (Gormley 2009; cf. Ferriss and Young 2006a: 3-4, Smyczyńska 2007: 8, Peitz 2009: 13, 41-42, Montoro 2013: 58-69, 136-197). The first exclamation is phrased to highlight the impossibility of the statement and points to a longing for a different life – decidedly and especially not the one the reader is leading right now. The latter exclamation, however, clearly states a strong identification with the novel's heroine, because this reader does not dream or wish to be different, but appears to be in the same position as the fictitious character – at least she believes she is: "one of the most powerful features of chicklit [...] is that it seeks that identification which doesn't simply come from empathy with the central female characters, but rather in understanding the world they inhabit, and actually accepting that women's lives are governed by quite different realities" from those fans of Mills & Boon read about and dream of (Whelehan 2004: 7). Whereas the Smithton circle – as representatives of the stereotypical reader of mass-produced fantasies – was composed mostly of stay-at-home mothers or part-time working housewives, who wanted to experiences a different life and (a different) love in their books, the readers of chicklit novels do not feel the need to read about lives they might have led, but want to read about lives that are close to their own. They long for stories about "the personal, social and professional lives of young women working in cities" (Smyczyńska 2007: 23) – stories they are likely to experience

---

started out as readers themselves – and therefore (re)produce empty signs without even being aware of it.

16 If one looks at online reviews of chicklit novels the phrase "This is me" does occur quite frequently. For example: "*This is me* only a lot worse – phew!" in the review of Kinsella's *Confessions of a Shopaholic* (Rogers 2007, emphasis added; cf. Van Slooten 2006: 220). Generally, readers tend to identify with the heroine but, at the same time, contrast themselves with the fictitious persona. Here, the reviewer claims that she and Rebecca Bloomwood, the heroine of the novel, share many similarities but she has not yet reached the spending level of the "shopping-addicted" heroine. Andrea Ochsner also found in a survey that readers responded similarly to ladlit novels (cf. 2009: 161, 164-166) and although she does not specify the sex of the respondents, it can be assumed that the "This is me!" response to ladlit comes from males.

themselves[17]. The readers of these novels do not want to be closed off from the world they live in but embrace it fully, which is another reason why their affirmative exclamation "This is me!" is not formulated in a conditional sense. Imelda Whelehan, writing about *Bridget Jones's Diary*, claims that the success of that novel – and consequently of the whole genre – is based on the fact that

> Bridget is a kind of "everywoman" of the 1990s. Bridget's life, aspirations, and consumer tastes to a large extent reflect the tastes, trends, and popular cultural milieu of glossy women's magazines and popular television in the mid 1990s, and this is what makes her so instantly recognizable to so many readers who have the same cultural diet. (2002: 12-13)

It is not that the heroine – in this case Bridget Jones – presents an ultimately perfect, fairy-tale-like 'Other', but is rather 'one of us', an "everywoman" as Whelehan says. Rosalind Gill and Elena Herdieckerhoff even proclaim her an "icon, a recognisable emblem of a particular kind of femininity, a constructed point of identification for women" (2006). Although, interestingly, the heroine's problems can be described with the same notion of "girl meets boy, they encounter problems...", chicklit authors manage to ground their novels in a time and place that is familiar to its readers which makes the identification process easier and the heroines more approachable: these women *do* struggle with life's "petty worries" like programming one's video recorder or having drunk too much at last night's outing with one's friends.

In the following, chicklit will be juxtaposed with books companies like Mills & Boon publish in order to establish a definition as to what 'chicklit' is (today). And almost instantaneously, Katarzyna Smyczyńska points out a problem when it comes to defining the genre: "Numerous novels by young female [...] writers, which have been published worldwide from the 1990s onwards, have tended to be labelled chicklit, thus stretching the convention's boundaries and making it increasingly difficult to define" (2007: 7; cf. Ferriss and Young 2006a: 5-7, Gormley 2009, Montoro 2013: 12-13). Of course, given the enormous success of the 'first' chicklit novel, Helen Fielding's *Bridget Jones's Diary* in 1996, publishing houses were keen on 'discovering' similar stories and flooded the book market with novels they labelled with the same profitable denominator.

There are many varieties of definitions of 'chicklit', but what they all share are the three features of chicklit being "novels written by women, (largely) for

17 Of course, despite the fact that "the novels directly [appeal] to women in their mid-twenties to early forties, [they] also [gain] fans in men and women of all ages" (Whelehan 2002: 13), which can be said for the mass-produced fantasies only very cautiously.

women", featuring "predominantly young, single, urban, female protagonists" and are usually clad in "bold, pink or pastel-coloured covers with cursive fonts and line drawings" (Gormley 2009; cf. Montoro 2013: 1-3, 28-50). It is especially the latter marker – the novels' "clearly marked jacket designs" (Gill and Herdieckerhoff 2006) – which is important for marketing and thus sales, because the archetypical jacket design is "virtually always exploited as the first point of contact between readers and works." (Montoro 2013: 3)

With regard to defining the archetypical protagonists of chicklit novels, a good starting point comes from Joanne Knowles: "Chicklit commonly focuses on a young woman (let's say under 40) who is prone to some form of relationship angst, steeped in consumer culture, and is seeking fulfilment in life, often in the shape of consumer or romantic gratification and preferably both." (2004: 2; cf. Webb Johnson 2006: 142, Peitz 2009: 29, 38-41) Moreover, Montoro has stated that "the original Chick Lit novels tend to prefer a woman who is white, middle-class, heterosexual, young and single" (2013: 3; cf. Smith 2008: 2). Pérez-Serrano further recapitulates that "[t]he genre revolves around a specific type of fictional character: a thirty-year-old, white, middle-class, educated, single woman" (2009) and Ferriss and Young concede "that the overwhelming majority of chick lit continues to focus on a specific age, race, and class: young, white, and middle." (2006a: 8) Apart from the fact that chicklit revolves around the lives of single women, the two aspects that are repeated are "white" and "middle-class". Not only does the stereotypical protagonist have a comfortable position in society, she is also comfortably white. That the latter is no longer the case this book proves by including Indian and Aboriginal chicklit characters, whom Vnuk (2005), Ferriss and Young (2006a: 5-6), Pérez-Serrano (2009), Gormley (2009) and Peitz (2009: 29) would call heroines of 'ethnic lit'. The middle-class aspect, however, prevails, possibly so as to help readers to "feel straightforwardly identified given their shared profile" (Pérez-Serrano 2009)[18].

Before the characters in their comfortable middle-class urbanity can enjoy being united with their Mr Right, chicklit heroines have to brace themselves for various kinds of problems in both their private and their public spheres. Furthermore, these spheres usually come into contact and, more often than not, intertwine and cause additional problems (cf. Smyczyńska 2007: 57). Readers experience these conflicts in their daily lives as well, which is reflected in the novels: "Some novels labelled as chicklit, far from being light-hearted relationship stories, in fact tackle serious social and personal concerns, such as family disintegration or the problem of sexism in the workplace" (ibid.: 30), like Rajashree's *Trust Me*, which depicts abortion, sexual harassment and exploitation. But by the end of the novel, hero and heroine are happily joined in a union – and the bleakness of some of the novel's issues is

18 More on the "comfortable position" of chicklit heroines follows in chapters 5 and 6.

(temporarily) forgotten: "Romance novels end happily. Readers insist on it. The happy ending is the one formal feature of the romance novel that virtually everyone can identify." (Regis 2003: 9) Here, Smyczyńska disagrees: "Perhaps the most evident shift in narratives [from mass-produced fantasies to chicklit] is visible in the endings, none of which promises the union of the heroine and her potential partner" (2007: 56). Yet, the novels close with exactly that – a *union*. Instead of a 'happily ever after' (read: marriage), the heroine in chicklit settles for 'happy for now and hopefully ever' (cf. Wells 2006: 50, Ferriss and Young 2006a: 3). The heroine is quite content that she has 'bagged' the handsome stranger or eligible, formerly aloof bachelor. She might continue to fantasise about a fairy-tale wedding, yet her living in big cities has taught her that it is not (going to be) easy. Already finding her perfect partner has proven a thorny road, usually spiked with relationship angst and consumerism bordering on the pathological (cf. Knowles 2004: 2). The chicklit heroine is never fully convinced that she and her soon-to-be boyfriend will be united. Deep inside, she is highly insecure and compensates for that by shopping or going out with her friends.

Psychologically speaking, this type of novel presents the readers with a side of themselves that is overtly neurotic, insecure and impressionable. Yet, this is never done in a way which suggests ridicule of its heroine or readership. Instead, the comic elements, which make chicklit novels "light-hearted, humorous stories" (Smyczyńska 2007: 23), tend to balance this rather dark side of the heroine and "[t]he humour is often of a self-depreciating kind – things go wrong for the chief characters, wild coincidences happen, and this mocking or ironic tone [of the novels] maintains that [...] neither the heroine nor the author is taking herself seriously" (Whelehan 2004: 7; cf. Harzewski 2006: 38). Not only do the sense of humour, clumsiness or naiveté of the heroine level the dark with the light sides of the novel (cf. Peitz 2009: 53), they also make the identification process easier because the humour is transported through "wisecracking characters or ridiculous situations, usually involving work or dating." (Vnuk 2005) The stereotypical chick-lit heroine "has some idealistic romantic aspirations and beliefs which often give rise to comedic moments; comedy in turn, is further exploited as a means to disguise their protagonist's shortcomings and some of her many flaws as well as to downplay the general vicissitudes of her life." (Montoro 2013: 3) Moreover, Smyczyńska argues, "[w]hile to readers they appear to be packed with acute critical observations and convincing portrayals of their own experience, chicklit fictions have often been accused by feminist critics of breeding backlash rhetoric, disguised in stories about successful women and postfeminist girls *par excellence*." (2007: 24)

As has been stated above in connection with Mills & Boon, feminist critics have made many lunges at the genre of mass-produced fantasies and chicklit. They are eager to find fault and agree that these novels 'suffer' from "derogatory, condescending overtones" and employ "stereotypical notions of neurotic, insecure, shopping-obsessed and husband-hunting feminine identity" (ibid.). Yet, chicklit – and ladlit for that matter – can be regarded as an important contribution to the literary canon because these novels "rework and document certain aspects of the lives and dilemmas of modern women [and men]; they are therefore convincingly 'realistic'" (ibid.: 58). By employing the literary equivalent of Hula Hoops, to borrow Colgan's phrase, they present their readers with a modified, nonetheless easily decodable image of themselves. Especially the romantic plotline, though still figuring prominently if not primarily, has adapted to the new developments women have undergone:

> Love at first sight and the final union with the male character is no longer the woman's destiny: the characters are not so much preoccupied with "love" as with the aim of finding a Mr. Right[19], by no means at the price of rejecting other pleasurable aspects of life. Finally, the novels generally emphasise the value of female friendship and female support, even though they do not rule out female rivalry. (Ibid.)

This also points to another important feature of chicklit in comparison to mass-produced fantasies. In the latter books, there are not many characters: the main protagonists, who will inevitably be smugly enveloped in their 'happily ever after' at the end of the book, and only very few other characters who are presented in the form of "abstract foils [and] embody those features of the female and male personalities that must be eradicated if women and men are to continue to love each other and fill one another's needs" (Radway 1991: 131). These characters are constructed through binary oppositions and clearly mark themselves off as the wrong way to pursue a loving relationship (cf. ibid.: 132). The heroine is presented as virginal yet spunky – a term the Smithton readers employ fairly frequently (cf. ibid.: 125), independent but looking for a nurturing husband; the female rival is also looking for a husband but wants him to finance her luxurious and lavish lifestyle. She has slept with many men in order to get what she wants, which marks her as dependent on others. The hero, on the other hand, is set off against the equally handsome, yet effeminate man who is not masculine enough to nurture the heroine as well as a rival who is not attractive and constantly employs force towards women, whereas

19 The use of the indefinite article "a" is quite important: contrary to the romantically inflated fairy tale concept of the 'one and only perfect man', chicklit heroines are quite content to settle for 'somebody close to the perfect man'. This is in line with the aforementioned notion of 'happy for now and hopefully ever'. See also Montoro's usage of the phrase "*a* prince charming" (2013: 3, emphasis added).

the hero only does so because he has misunderstood the heroine. In contrast to the villain, the hero stops this violent behaviour the very instant he becomes aware of his error[20]. As this short summary of Radway's findings has shown, the minor characters only function as threat or comparison and further – or postpone – the books' romantic plots' developments.

In chicklit, the situation is slightly different: here, there are also rivals and fairly one-dimensional characters but the heroine's friends fulfil a more important function, that of the urban family (cf. Whelehan 2002: 14): "The heterosexual family is not a natural unit in chick lit, which substitutes [...] a new 'urban family' of friends and neighbors" (Ebert 2009: 105). As the heroines nearly always leave their families behind when they move to the city, they have to adapt to new rules and 'schedules'. Similar to the mass-produced fantasies' motif, "[t]he heroine's social identity is thrown into question" (Radway 1991: 150) and the female protagonists need others who help them in their development of a 'new' identity – or regain their old one. In the mass–produced fantasies this task usually falls to the hero, who establishes the heroine as his wife. In chicklit, the hero is imperative to the romantic plot, but the urban family takes it upon itself to inaugurate the heroine into the city. Like her, the protagonist's friends have come from a different town, are in similar relationship situation and share the heroine's interests, like shopping or consumption in general. They contribute prominently to the heroine's way of living and thus influence her directly and indirectly. Consequently, their idea and use of space is as important as the main protagonists'.

To conclude, chicklit is rather a conglomeration of different aspects and codes and the boundaries of which remain fluid instead of fixed: "When analysing the phenomenon of the novels' popularity, it is important to acknowledge that what is perceived as their textual 'message' has been influenced by *historically specific cultural codes*" (Smyczyńska 2007: 40, emphasis added). Chicklit not only draws from the codes established in romantic fiction and mass-produced fantasies but also from "contemporary novels and popular guides, popular TV series, glossy magazines, video clips, computer games – in other words, an innumerable number of modern artefacts of the western cultural system" (ibid.: 25). Therefore, 'chicklit' is "not a precisely ordered group of texts, but an approximation, a horizon of expectations for the readership, a series of imprecise 'echoes' between texts, one regime among others of the organisation of intertextuality and in no way privileged above the others" (Palmer 1991: 121-122). Smyczyńska advocates that

20 For further reference on the nature of mass-produced fantasies' heroines and heroes (and their foils), see Radway's study in which she analyses in detail what features make an ideal and a failed romance.

> [c]hicklit could in fact be referred to more accurately as an event, a discursive strand, syndrome, or convention, which has emerged within a heterogeneous body of other texts, not delimited by any clear boundaries, yet homogenised by means of the presence of certain regularities which have been highlighted and categorised[21]. (2007: 30)

Smyczyńska's definition is both a splendid definition and a comment on the phenomenon, marking chicklit as one step in the evolution of romantic fiction. At the same time, she acknowledges that it is not just book but an event: readers feel that they are the characters, they regard them as their fictionalised avatar, hence the "This is me!" response. Chicklit unites and merges various predecessors and traditions in its genre and although it may be light-hearted, it is definitely not "instantly forgettable" (cf. Ezard 2001).

LADLIT

Having discussed the roots and defining characteristics of chicklit, one might assume that it is going to be easier to define ladlit as it is generally touted to be "the masculine equivalent of the Bridget Jones phenomenon" (Showalter 2002: 60). Especially the protagonists of Mike Gayle's novels are marketed as "[t]he male Bridget Jones" (1999: Cover) or "Bridget Jones for the boys" (2005: Cover)[22]. But in Elaine Showalter's opinion, there are two variants of this genre and the ladlit which is closer to *Bridget Jones's Diary* marks the "low end of the market", whereas the high end is characterised by its "masterly examination of male identity in contemporary Britain" (2002: 60). She establishes thus a good variety, the high end, and a dismissible one, the low end – echoing the reservations of Bainbridge and Lessing. Showalter's sentiment is taken up by Joseph Brooker, who writes that, "as verbal craftsmen", ladlit authors such as Nick Hornby or Tony Parsons are not "fit to light [Martin] Amis's cigarette" (2006: 6), hence creating a similar dichotomy between these authors. Brooker and Showalter approach ladlit with the same bias that chicklit is confronted with – namely, being very much lowbrow and thus

21 There are variants of the genre such as Mumlit or Hacklit, meaning novels that deal with the trials and rewards of being a mother or of being a journalist, respectively (cf. Vnuk 2005, Ferriss and Young 2006a: 5-7, Peitz 2009: 28, Smyczyńska 2009: 30, Montoro 2013: 12-14). However, these variants will not be of relevance here as this book is devoted to chick- and ladlit only.

22 In turn, this strengthens *Bridget Jones's Diary*'s position as a seminal text, because it is regarded both as an important part in the literary canon and a strong sales argument.

not good literature, as Bainbridge's snubbing comment testifies to. It has to be acknowledged, though, that Showalter subcategorises ladlit novels, which will be elaborated upon shortly, but this subchapter will show that what she terms 'high-end ladlit' can indeed not be truly considered ladlit. Starting with Showalter's taxonomy of (her idea of) ladlit, a brief discussion as to why ladlit is the most fitting denominator is going to follow. Afterwards, this subchapter will focus on the socio-cultural background that resulted in the construction of the New Lad, who has been idealised, idolised and exposed in ladlit. Additionally, characteristics will be highlighted which can be found in the literary works of the international authors discussed in this book and common motifs will be pointed out.

Elaine Showalter recognises a long tradition of ladlit and Holger Kiesow agrees with her that one cannot analyse the genre without considering its history of masculinities and the predecessors of ladlit. Between them, Showalter and Kiesow map a time span of (now) sixty years of what they deem 'ladlit'. Although this tradition will be acknowledged, it should already be hinted at the fact that the genre has progressed and transformed remarkably from what Showalter and Kiesow identify as the 'first ladlit novels'. Thus, the evolution of ladlit mirrors the progress of chicklit from romances, romantic fiction, bonkbusters and mass-produced fantasies. In the following, Showalter's taxonomy of the various ladlit versions will be explained and supplemented with Kiesow's observations.

Both Showalter and Kiesow take Kingsley Amis's novel *Lucky Jim* (1954) to be the first novel that should be given the title 'ladlit' (cf. Showalter 2002: 62; Kiesow 2007: 6). Showalter actually defines the novel's protagonist, Jim Dixon (after whom she names the prototypical hero of 1950s ladlit "Laddish Jim"), not just as a lad – a denominator that "has changed its meaning in English literature" (Kiesow 2007: 4) – but as an "angry young lad" (Showalter 2002: 63). This phrase points towards the 1950s phenomenon of the *Angry Young Men*, a group of working- and middle-class playwrights and novelists whose most prominent members were Amis and John Osborne. The latter author's play, *Look Back in Anger*, is the epitome of the "anger and post-war alienation" these men felt (ibid.: 62). Similar to the play's protagonist, Amis's Jim Dixon also experiences anger and outrage but – and here it becomes apparent that one cannot lump the angry young men and ladlit protagonists together – "Jim is also a vulnerable hero, easily undermined and crippled by feelings of pity, guilt, and shame. [...] This lad is *not an angry young man* at all, not an existential rebel or political revolutionary, but rather someone who would prefer to be happy, loved, and settled" (ibid.: 64-65, emphasis added). Whereas contemporary ladlit protagonists indeed want to be loved, be it because they feel a lack of emotions as such or because they have fallen unexpectedly in love with a woman, the angry young men push the ones close to them away. Showalter identifies a correct character trait in ladlit heroes as to what they want, yet she chooses a somewhat unfitting term and example.

Her 1980s version of the lad is the "Lucky John", taken from Martin Amis's novel *Money* (1984) (cf. 2002: 65) and, just as before, she glibly extends the characteristics of the novel's protagonist to an unspecified canon of other 1980s ladlit novels[23] and deems them all anti-heroes. But the laddish behaviour alone does *not* make ladlit protagonists anti-heroical as Showalter claims. Moreover, the weakness and confusion rather depicts them as clueless when it comes to their aspirations in and knowledge of life – but contrary to the notion of the anti-hero it does mark them as likeable and comic instead of deviant or mean-spirited. This is analogous to the chicklit heroines, who, through their status as clumsy everywomen, also evoke fun which is directed at them, but at the same time create compassion and affection for the hapless women. The last 'type' Showalter identifies is the 1990s "Funny Jim" (cf. Showalter 2002: 72, 65): "Lads of the 1990s were no longer able to blame the class and caste system or the ludicrous narcissism of their fathers for their difficulties. All their problems are their own fault." (Ibid.: 73) Thus, the ladlit protagonists' own shortcomings and the comic consequences that ensue are quite similar if not reminiscent of chicklit heroines in that respect. This already marks one of the numerous strong connections between the genres and others will become apparent further down.

Before delving deeper into the subject of the actual genre, its denominator must be considered as to what name will be employed for the male novels that will complement the chicklit oeuvre. In her book *Lad Trouble*, Ochsner identifies three varieties for a corpus of novels which are deemed to be the same: *cynical young men* (Nieragden 2000), *ladlit* (Showalter 2002, Cockin 2007) and her own variety *male confessional novel* (2009). Starting with Göran Nieragden's denominator, Ochsner dismisses his definition on the grounds that the 'heroes' he categorises under that term are clearly-marked deviants of society (she cites the characters' tendencies towards murder, drugs[24] or sodomy; cf. Ochsner 2009: 31). Nieragden

23 One can argue that one character is not enough to stand in for a whole decade of literary heroes. In fact, Showalter claims the trend of ladlit has produced many different varieties but she focuses on four novels only to justify her taxonomy, two of which belong to the "Funny Jim" and only one each to "Laddish Jim" and "Lucky John".

24 Iqbal Viswamohan cites drugs as a recurring topic in ladlit (2013a: 19). The corpus assembled for this book, however, does not feature any drugs – apart from alcoholic beverages which are not on the same level as cocaine or ecstasy – thus it seriously questions whether Iqbal Viswamohan's idea is applicable to a larger corpus of novels.

claims that the male characters in the novels by Hornby, Brookmyre and Welsh can be summarised under the same title and points towards the aforementioned *angry young men* (Nieragden 2000: 221; cf. Showalter 2002). Contrary to the politically charged term of the *angry young men*, the heroes in ladlit are "too tired to feel angry anymore and have become cynical instead" (Ochsner 2009: 31). But the cynicism Nieragden emphasises, the aforementioned lack of political interest as well as the missing asocial components in their characters (taking drugs or murdering people) must lead to the rejection of his sombre classification. On the contrary, despite darker moments, the novels with male protagonists employ – like chicklit – a humorous, comic mood or tone. The lads generally miss something in their lives but they do not fill this void with illegal substances or actions. Considering Ochsner's term next, it has to be acknowledged that the novels discussed in her book are very similar to those examined here. Yet her otherwise splendidly chosen term has too narrow a focus. She traces the confessional first-person narration to the Bildungsroman and confessional novels such as Rousseau's *Confessions* and De Quincey's *Confessions of an Opium Eater* (cf. Ochsner 2009: 101-111). Whereas this history is accurate, it would limit my corpus too much. Ochsner claims that even if an author chose a reflective narration, it can still be considered a confessional novel because

> quite a number of authors of the male confessional novel […] share the profession with their male protagonist (such as Mike Gayle's hero in *Dinner for Two* (2002) in which Dave, the main protagonist, starts to work as an agony uncle, a job that has been partly pursued by his creator as well). (Ibid.: 110)

But the problems of this idea cannot be dismissed if one considers more than one novel by the same author and one needs to look no further than Gayle himself, because in his novel *The Importance of Being a Bachelor* his protagonists' professions include construction engineer and bar owner – none of these 'careers' has been pursued by Gayle. Therefore, *confessional novel* will be ruled out as denominator for this genre, leaving only *ladlit* as a suitable term. This is the most fitting title because it emphasises the strong connection between the two parts, namely the cultural phenomenon *lad* and his depiction in *lit*erary texts. Additionally, the spelling – a connection to chicklit – neither favours one part over the other, nor does it suggest that this type of literature is only for males or, more specifically, lads. Showalter's criteria, however, are too all-inclusive. One cannot compare "Laddish Jim" with "Funny Jim" as easily as she suggests or summarise both under the same name. First and foremost, the cultural circumstances which 'produced' these two protagonists are quite different and they are hardly comparable: whereas 1950s "Laddish Jim" feels "guilt, pity and shame" (Showalter

2002: 65), the 1990s ladlit heroes cannot be bothered to think that far. They are too engrossed in themselves to reflect on these feelings, because they have not matured enough to consider them.

Therefore, I will use the term ladlit throughout to refer to the novels chosen for my canon, as I deem it the perfect denominator. However, Showalter actually proclaims the end of ladlit as "the genre was showing signs of decline [by 2001], perhaps because of authorial self-consciousness about being part of a trend, and perhaps because the formula itself had become named and familiar" (ibid.: 76; cf. Kiesow 2007: 4). The way her criticism is phrased, it might just as well be attributed to chicklit[25]. Yet both genres can hardly be in decline, taking into account that authors still produce novels that can be categorised as belonging to the genres of chick- and ladlit and quite successfully so. Additionally, it is questionable if one can ever speak of decline when it comes to very formulaic genres: they tend to be more resistant than critics would like to admit[26]. Many of the two genres' novels which will be analysed later on were written after 2001 and still manage to contribute new aspects to the genre, which is why "chick lit and lad lit have [proven] to be a surprisingly long lasting phenomenon" (Cockin 2007: 120). The fact that these genres can arouse such diverse emotions is evidence of its important literary and cultural value and impact and thus proves this book right for analysing them in more detail.

At its core, a ladlit novel has a quest for love – like chicklit novels. Yet, it is only a search for a soulmate as second step. The primary aim is to find oneself first and to realise that one is too old to be a 'boy' any longer. The men, who are locked "in terminal adolescence" (Showalter 2002: 63), need to free themselves of their Peter Pan Syndrome[27]:

---

25 A similar 'death' has been proclaimed with regard to chicklit (cf. Day and Perry 2011).

26 Especially popular literature seem to be very prone to 'die' – many people have declared the death of various genres and yet people continue to buy books like mass-produced fantasies, as the conversation between Stella Duffy and the Mills & Boon aficionados has shown.

27 Sylvia Farnham-Diggory was the first to define the "Peter Pan Syndrome", which includes, among other features, the "refusal to consider entry into the world of adult plans and responsibilities, [the] refusal to 'grow up'" (1966: 51). Her ideas are taken up by Dan Kiley, who goes on to show that men suffering from the "Peter Pan Syndrome" are afraid of taking on responsibility, are lonely and display a tendency towards narcissism and chauvinism (1984: 29-34).

Peter Pan symbolizes the essence of youthfulness. [But he] was a very sad young man. His life was filled with contradictions, conflicts, and confusion. His world was hostile and unrelenting. For all his gaiety, he was a deeply troubled boy living in an even more troubling time. He was caught in the abyss between the man he didn't want to become and the boy he could no longer be. (Kiley 1984: 25-26)

Ladlit protagonists need to embrace the present with all its problems but also opportunities and find love for one's more mature stage in life and consequently the love for oneself. Showalter's "Lucky John" novel(s) – her idea of 1980s 'ladlit' – is "the apotheosis of the Ladlit genre [as] its subtextual worries about marriage and paternity" are constantly recurring themes (Showalter 2002: 63, 69). While she is correct that there are indeed questions of matrimony and fatherhood, this notion already goes one step too far. Andrea Ochsner has a better understanding of the lads' problems when she writes that

[t]he typical male confessional novel is a first person narrative written by a male author in the 1990s. It is likely to have an urban setting (London in most cases), and features a male protagonist who struggles with adulthood both in terms of *professional and private choices* he is forced to make. (2009: 32, emphasis added)

Ochsner's idea of the lads' "private choices" refers to the worries of Showalter's lads about eventually having a wife and possibly children. Indeed, ladlit protagonists oftentimes wonder whether to pursue a settled and legalised partnership or to continue concentrating "on women, alcohol [and] football" which would rule out taking the back seat and focusing on somebody else (cf. Kiesow 2007: 4). Additionally, the "private choices" with regard to the lads' love lives point to a strong notion of heterosexuality as ladlit almost always features men who might not be too sure of where they want to go in life or how to express their masculinity appropriately, but who are definitely sure about their heterosexuality – even if only that. Among other features it is this dilemma of deciding whether one ought to remain the sole focus of one's own attention or whether to shift this attention to somebody else – e.g. girlfriend, lover, wife, children – that distinguishes the lad, or more precisely, the self-centred fun-loving 'new lad' from the caring, emotional 'new man', who preceded him culturally. And it is in this development that ladlit has a significantly different genesis from chicklit as the socio-cultural background is more pronounced and influential than in the 'female' variety.

The 'new man' came into being in the 1980s in Britain, or, more precisely, the images that furthered the construction of him were produced up to 1990 (Nixon 2001: 375). Sean Nixon links the development of the 'new man' to the intensified advertising of men's images in three specific areas, namely menswear, grooming and toiletries and consumer magazines[28] (ibid.: 374). This ties in with the argument that the "style-conscious 'new man' is frequently cited as [...] a consumer-driven construction" (Benwell 2003: 18): he no longer wants to be 'just a man' but rather the best possible partner for his wife, girlfriend or lover, and it is indeed the 'new man' who is closer to chicklit protagonists than the actual 'heroes' of ladlit. Rosalind Gill attributes the advent of the 'new man' to various incidents, coinciding and intermingling. Apart from men being the focus of style magazines and the sought-after object of marketing strategists in terms of consumption, Gill points to the effects of the gay liberation movement and the new outlook on health which contributed to the construction of this new 'masculinity' (2003: 43-46). The gay liberation – additionally fuelled by the rising influence of feminist criticism – caused the male to become the centre of (marketing) attention and thus he featured in marketing campaigns and on billboards[29]. Moreover, a man had to shape up now for everybody looked at him. Therefore, he had to care for and look after himself much more than he used to: health became a more and more important aspect of his life. However, this does not only mean going to the gym to work out but rather looking after one's 'self' "as increasing numbers of people [sought] personal therapy and counselling" (ibid.: 43). It is the idea of the "whole person" or "self-actualized person" that has gained in importance (cf. Maslow, qtd. in Gill 2003: 43). Another important feature, which will surface again in the construction of the 'new lad', is the connection to feminism. Not only did the feminist movement reshape the role of women when they challenged binaries like male/female or public/private sphere (cf. Gill 2003: 42), they also helped 'new men' to break free of their restrictive roles:

> This redefinition [of gender identities by the feminist movement; C.L.] also promoted a different model of the individual, as someone connected not simply to a family but also to wider communities and to the environment. In doing so it sowed the seeds for a revisioning of traditional masculinity, and helped to create a cultural milieu in which discourses of new manhood could emerge and flourish. (Ibid.: 42-43)

28 As with the 'new man', (consumer) magazines will play an important part in the construction and affirmation of the 'new lad'.

29 In 1982, Calvin Klein created a campaign featuring a young, toned man who only wore underwear. This campaign is deemed to be "the height, the epitome of a sexual revolution, primarily for men" (Edkins, qtd. in Bowermaster 1989: 36). Although it was an American campaign, its influence – helped by globalisation and fashion magazines – made the picture and the product world-famous: man became a sex(ualised) object.

Thus, the deconstruction of gender (roles) also contributed vastly to the 'new man'. Finally, men were free of the old, 'hyper-manly' discourses that restricted them. Regarding the transition from 'new man' to 'new lad', however, it becomes complicated.

Many critics see the 'new lad' as the opposition or counter-movement to the 'new man'. Indeed, the latter has even been 'buried' in the now infamously often-quoted famous Condé Nast press release from January 1991:

> *GQ* is proud to announce that the New Man has officially been laid to rest (if indeed he ever drew breath). The 90s man [the 'new lad'; C.L.] knows who he is, what he wants and where he's going and he's not afraid to say so. And yes, he still wants to get laid (qtd. in Nixon 2001: 379).

Benwell states that the "'[n]ew lad' was a clear reaction to the 'new man', and arguably an attempt to reassert the power of masculinity deemed to have been lost by the concessions made to feminism by 'new man'" (2003: 13). Ochsner has summarised these "concessions" as follows:

> While still being married, our man in question might be a New Man, looking after his children and doing the washing-up to give his wife some space to have a professional and private life apart from being a wife and a mother. He might use cosmetics and shed the odd tear when he is unhappy. (2009: 22-23)

Yet, she continues to say that the 'new man' "also might want to do away with all that 'feminist stuff' in order to be a 'Lad', especially when he goes out with his male friends" (ibid.; cf. Nixon 2001: 380). Men knowingly employ the 'new man' 'sensitivity' and 'thoughtfulness' in order to bed women, but dispose of their caring mask directly afterwards and revert to their 'true self' (cf. Gill 2003: 48) – which would affirm Condé Nast's doubt that the 'new man' ever 'truly' existed. Rosalind Gill has therefore argued not to talk about different clear-cut – if that is ever possible – masculinities which are mutually exclusive but about 'sensibilities':

> [The clear-cut masculinity] is [...] too neat and linear a characterisation, which excludes fragmentation and division within the categories[. ... I]t is possible to see elements of different versions of masculinity appearing simultaneously in popular cultural texts – for example new man, new lad, metrosexual. To think of new laddism as a sensibility avoids these problems and allows for different formulations of masculinity to co-exist, and to see them as being reworked, recycled and used to 'kick off' [...] against each other. (2009, original emphasis)

It seems that "what we are [...] witnessing at the start of the twenty-first century is nothing less than the emergence of a more fluid, bricolage masculinity, the result of 'channel hopping' across versions of the 'masculine'" (Beynon 2002: 6) and it consequently follows that the 'new lad' is not simply "a clear backlash against the 'new man' and partly feminism" (Kiesow 2007: 20). Following Gill, it indeed makes sense to regard the 'new lad' as a sensibility, which opposes as well as shares traits from other masculine sensibilities. They are not exclusive but can overlap, however slightly or firmly. What testifies to this idea is that some of the novels discussed in this book present protagonists who struggle *because* they do not have a clear model or image to follow. Their self-perception might be highly influenced by 'new man' sensibilities but – and this is important – they will always display traits of the 'new lad'.

The 'new lad' has been – stereotypically – characterised as "hedonistic, post- (if not anti-)feminist, and pre-eminently concerned with beer, football and 'shagging' women" (Gill 2003: 37). This 'trinity' of laddish behaviour also poses the main focus in ladlit novels and many lads hail it to be the best lifestyle worth pursuing. However, it becomes clear very soon that their lives are not as carefree or easy as this threefold maxim might imply. Indeed, it usually leads to even more problems the characters of ladlit could have ever imagined. The motif of beer, football and sex is just a shiny veneer that connects them to other lads but hides deeper needs and fears in their lives. The lad's attitudes – and especially of those of ladlit heroes – cannot be described as shallow just because of the trinity as lads distinguish themselves from preceding masculinities by an "unrelenting gloss of knowingness and irony, a reflexivity about its own condition" (Benwell 2003: 13): lads pose as shallow but their shallowness is – ironically – only skin-deep. This has also been noted by Ochsner, who goes even further, stating that a "key feature of some constructions of the New Lad is the emphasis on his knowing of and ironic relationship to the world of serious concerns" (2009: 23). It is what Benwell calls an "irony-as-knowingness" (2003: 21) and it heavily depends on both the speaker and receiver of such statements to understand each other and to create a mutual basis for 'laddish mate-ness'[30]. Janice Turner, writing an article on the misogynist stance in lads' magazines, asks the male editors of these weeklies (e.g. *Zoo* or *Nuts*) whether they think the impressions they convey in their magazines are degrading: "Their response was puzzlement. 'You're just reading too much into it,' they all reassured

30 See also Stuart Hall: "Members of the same culture [here 'new laddism'; C.L.] must share sets of concepts, images and ideas which enable them to think and feel about the world, and thus to interpret the world, in roughly similar ways. They must share, broadly speaking, the same *'cultural codes'*" (1997: 4, emphasis added).

[her]. 'It's just harmless fun.'" (Turner 2005) Especially in this example it becomes apparent that Ms Turner is not "in on the joke" that is the mask of sexism[31].

It seems that the relationship between 'new lad' and magazines – just as between 'new man' and their 'manuals' – is a rather close-knit one. Whereas the latter is always associated with the glossier *GQ*[32] or *Arena*, the 'new lad' is always – but not exclusively – connected to *Loaded* (cf. Benwell 2003, Gill 2003, Gill 2009): "Loaded [sic] is a [then] new magazine dedicated to life and liberty and the pursuit of sex, drink, football and less serious matters. Loaded [sic] is music, film, relationships, humour, travel, sport, hard news and popular culture. Loaded [sic] is clubbing, drinking, eating, playing and living" (Gill 2009). What the magazine's 'manifesto' shows is that *Loaded* intends to capture and include as much as possible when it comes to a new, *manlier* lifestyle. Interestingly enough, there is no mentioning of personal grooming and consumption with regard to clothing as this is considered too 'new man'-ly, or rather too effeminate for *Loaded* and consequently for its target group: the 'new lad' (cf. Benwell 2003: 16).

Reverting to the comparison of chick- and ladlit and consequently the function of literature, the 'new lad' takes the magazines and novels as a means to justify his proposition and outlook on life. It is thus no coincident that the first issue of *Loaded* and Nick Hornby's first laddish novel *Fever Pitch* were both published within two years: the latter in 1992 and *Loaded* two years later (cf. Cockin 2007: 107). Although lads' magazines have to be taken with a grain of salt – a virtue not every male possesses (cf. Benwell 2002: 164-165) – 'lads' use them to confirm their status and (re)create a masculinity, or more correctly a sensibility of a masculinity. Ladlit is such a means which depicts the status quo of the laddish sensibility. Male readers, however, do not read the 'accounts' of Hornby, Gayle and co. in order to 'gain knowledge' about romantic pursuits. Similarly, the main incentive to read a ladlit novel is not the quest for a 'happily ever after'. Of course, the forming or keeping of a functional relationship is also on the characters' minds, but it does not always pose the sole focus in these novels. Looking at ladlit novels, one can say that the representation of a certain notion of masculinity takes its cues from current cultural trends (in this particular case, *Loaded* hit a nerve of young men who were dissatisfied with the effete 'new man') and thus creates an identity for its readers as to make the novels more appealing (which results in the production of the books

31 Creating one's own systems of signs would put the 'new lad' in a similar position as sub-cultures. Indeed, the notion of a laddish sensibility would additionally account for this idea. Yet, it does make more sense to refer to the 'new lad' (and thus also the 'new man') as a "structure of feeling" (cf. Williams 1961: 48) that has prevailed in the 1990s (cf. Ochsner 2009: 66-72).

32 Ironically, it was exactly this magazine which doubted the 'new man's' existence.

and in the consumption by their readers). In contrast to chicklit novels, in which fairy-tale elements (and the happy ending would count as such) are used, ladlit authors employ more 'realistic' notions as the 'happily ever after-ending' of the novels is not a must. It has to be said, though, that both types of novels usually end with the hero or heroine in a happy relationship but the focus lies on the lives of the protagonists themselves: chicklit heroines need their heroes to feel complete (see Smyczyńska's view of happy endings), but ladlit heroes need to feel complete in themselves – accepting a new job, new home or, more generally speaking, a new way of life – which then might include a perfect girlfriend or sometimes a wife – and in order for them to lose their Peter Pan-attitude of being an eternal boy or lad[33]. Andrea Ochsner observes that "[i]n the medical discourse, especially in psychiatry, *prolonged adolescence* is treated as an abnormality due to lack of a successful identity formation." (2009: 275, emphasis added) This prolonged adolescence means the lads "have not yet made a personal commitment to a set of beliefs or an occupation." (Heaven 1994: 32) According to Patrick C.L. Heaven's taxonomy, human beings – and he is actually concerned with teenagers – need to pass through three stages before they arrive at that of "identity achievement" which "is synonymous with maturity and, ultimately, identity formation. It marks the completion of adolescence, and signals that identity crises have been successfully resolved. Having experienced a crisis (or crises), the individual has now made a commitment." (Ibid.: 33) This suggests that most lads are 'stuck' in the stage of "identity moratorium", in which a crisis is experienced, but no "choices or a personal commitment" have been made (ibid.: 32).

The life the lad lives is characterised by a strong notion of 'easy-going-ness', which means he has not invested into something by making important choices or personal commitment(s): the lad's attitude has been characterised as being "anti-aspirational" – or as lads' magazine *Loaded* claims: "the man who believes he can do anything, if only he wasn't hungover" (qtd. in Gill 2003: 51). This notion of being in a situation which would require too much effort to evolve from is rather common when it comes to ladlit protagonists as is evident in Hornby's *High Fidelity* for example: Rob is aware of being 'stuck' but he is not 'bothered' enough to change his life drastically, i.e. leaving his unprofitable record shop and finding another more lucrative job. "In most cases [the 'new lad'] is not really happy with where he is and with what he has got, but whether he truly wants to change the circumstances he is in we can never really be sure of because he constantly makes change impossible" (Ochsner 2009: 108). Gill, comparing the 'new lad' to the strong and very masculine heroes of spy fiction, claims that the "laddish sensibility"

33 Here one can actually make a connection to initiation novels which deal with a rite of passage: the lad that finally becomes a man.

presents its readers with "a distinctly unheroic masculinity, one that is fallible, self-deprecating and liable to fail at any moment" (Gill 2009), tying it in with the lad's 'anti-aspirational' behaviour which can be read as a protecting shield – again a veneer like the motif of the 'trinity' – against any possible failure. This man is not the hero lads' magazines depict and intend to mirror for their readership to identify with. On the contrary, ladlit novels present the neglected side of the 'new lad', in which he questions himself and the life that he leads. It is true that the heroes are still interested in women, gadgets, alcohol and leisure time activities but it becomes apparent very quickly that they are not the happy-go-lucky men *Loaded*, *Zoo* or *Maxim* present in their issues. Ladlit heroes are "[s]imultaneously detached, bitter, and self-deprecating, [they despise what they are doing], but not enough to actually try to change anything" (ibid.)[34]. The reason these two types of 'literature' can still be likened is in its depiction of the lad as 'not-man'.

Furthering the notion of not wanting to go anywhere, the ladlit hero is characterised by his looking backwards, instead of looking towards the future: he yearns "for freedom from responsibility or [looks] back nostalgically to simpler times" (ibid.; cf. Benwell 2003: 14, Kiesow 2007: 4). The lad creates an image of a long-gone past that resembles the bedsit from his youth – in more than one way. Svetlana Boym has termed this "restorative nostalgia", which does not "reveal any signs of decay; it has to be freshly painted in its 'original image' and remain[s] eternally young" (2001: 49). She identifies nostalgia generally speaking as "a yearning for a different time – the time of our childhood" (ibid.: xv). The Peter Pan-like lad is stuck in his boyish behaviour and thinks he can get away with attitudes or actions the same way he could when he was about fifteen years younger, behaving as if a nostalgic notion is actually a reason for and the long-gone past can be resurrected by the denial of the present. Here, one can also find the lad's reasons for his "anti-aspirational" behaviour: he is reluctant to shoulder the blame for his life, which is not going well – most of the times both on a personal and a work-related level (cf. Showalter 2002: 73). Everything used to be much easier when one could just shrug one's problems off and turn to something else if one's initial plans did not work out. Being in their late twenties or early thirties, lads are confronted with obligations such as paying rent (rarely having mortgages), finding a suitable profession or not being able to "score women" every other night[35]. Everything they do has conse-

34 This accounts for the reason why Gill actually wonders if ladlit novels, also by their confessional tone of narrative, are not written for women instead – in order to make them understand their male companions better (2009). But as the example of Janice Turner has shown, the issue is far more complex.

35 When it comes to women, lads have to face the fact that they are not as successful and capable of managing their lives as the women are or as they would like to

quences and the heroes of these novels tend to look back nostalgically in order to avoid these truths. Adam Bachelor, one of the three male protagonists in *The Importance of Being a Bachelor*, is told by his mates – all of whom are in serious relationships – that he will never settle down with a woman because, "while the girls [he goes] out with are undoubtedly attractive and usually well turned out, none of them are exactly girlfriend material" (Gayle 2011: 13). Adam, who owns his own bar and is thus able to continue a lifestyle in which night-time activities are paramount, goes out only with women he can be sure to never see again after they have had sex. Inevitably for ladlit, he does find the perfect woman eventually and admits to be 'cured' from thinking that "this love business was [not] for [him]" (ibid.: 373-374). Mike Gayle's novel can be regarded as a 'best of' of ladlit motifs. Adam and his two younger brothers experience what Aysha Iqbal Viswamohan enumerates as being stereotypical ladlit themes: "masculine insecurities, competition at college or the work place [sic], sexual fantasies, […] relationships, heartbreaks, family issues and obsession with sports." (2013a: 19) Naturally, not every novel is able to cover all of these motifs but it is striking that all novels discussed at least have in common the themes "insecurities", "relationships" and "heartbreak", which all point in the direction of love and the thorny road to find it.

CORPUS

It is the aim of this book to prove that chick- and ladlit protagonists behave significantly uniformly – geographically speaking. As already indicated, the genres are generally treated (by publishing houses and in most non-scholarly popular culture) as if they were two sides of the same coin but the historical and cultural backgrounds suggest otherwise: whereas chicklit has a strong tradition and affiliation to romantic fiction, which also influences their retrograde depiction of women aspiring to be perfect (house)wives, ladlit looks back on the development of both magazines and the related (re-)construction of masculinity. Nonetheless, the genres are united in the oft-mentioned motor, namely the quest for love, and this quest – which itself is a nod to classical romances – is the search for Mr Right. Yet, whereas chicklit heroines seek indeed Mr Right, ladlit protagonists need to realise their own potential to become said Mr Right – it is a search for themselves, their best possible selves. The plotlines of ladlit novels which are dedicated to romance will inevitably

acknowledge (cf. Gill 2009). All of a sudden, they find themselves being superfluous in their role as bread-winners. Interestingly enough, the same women the ladlit heroes strive to go out with are depicted as rather clumsy and to an extent helpless in chicklit.

see to it that, once the ladlit slacker becomes that better person, he will become attached to the matching Ms Right.

The hunt for the characters' respective perfect partners has a significantly geographical side to it: the characters' notion of space, private and public places, territories and anchor-points play a vital role in the aforementioned search – as well as in their current unsatisfying status quo as a 'Singleton', to borrow a term coined in *Bridget Jones's Diary*. The next chapter will introduce important ideas from the field of (cultural) geography, but prior to this the corpus which will be at the heart of the following analyses will be defined, according to extra- and intradiegetic criteria. Furthermore, the formula against which all the chick- and ladlit novels can be mapped out will be introduced.

The novels discussed in this book are either chick- or ladlit novels and are comprised of the features which are elaborated on further down. All selected novels were published after 1990 because this decade marks the heyday of the two genres. As has been explained in the previous two subchapters, in the 1990s many factors came together and resulted in a cultural climate in which both chick- and ladlit were able to thrive and to attract attention. Moreover, it was in the mid-1990s that the most famous (English) novels of both genres were first published: *Bridget Jones's Diary* by Helen Fielding (1996) and Nick Hornby's *High Fidelity* (1995). Interestingly enough, both novels are not the authors' first books. Yet, whereas Fielding's first novel *Cause Celeb* (1994) can be regarded as chicklit, Hornby's debut *Fever Pitch* (1992) is generally regarded as an autobiography as he writes about *his* life and *his* connection to the lads' pastime of football (cf. Ochsner 2009: 109). Although many readers have recognised themselves in Hornby's novel – mirroring the "This is me!" response to chicklit novels – *Fever Pitch* cannot be regarded as a work of fiction and is therefore not part of my corpus.

Considering every novel written after 1990 belonging to the general canon of chick- and ladlit is nigh impossible and therefore made a selection necessary. Because of the many international varieties of the genres (cf. Donadio 2006), I limit the countries of origin to England[36], India and Australia. These countries are chosen because they share a common history as former parts of the British Empire and they are still entwined today as members of the Commonwealth, which provides a basis for an in-depth comparison. However, despite their shared past, the countries are separated by their current political, ideological and socio-cultural differences,

36 Technically, this should read 'British' instead of 'English' chick- and ladlit. However, there are so very few Welsh, Scottish or Northern Irish chick- and ladlit novels that the striking majority is actually English. I thus decided to use 'English' as denominator to signify this circumstance. Yet, with regard to India and Australia, there the writers do stem from various states which justify the broader categories.

which the novels may (subtly) address. Whereas India gained its independence from Great Britain in 1947, Australia's head of state is still the ruling monarch of the British royal family, but the continent 'down under' is governed by its own prime minister. The two countries are therefore marked as politically different from their former mother country. The inclusion of Indian as well as Australian chick- and ladlit further testifies to the cosmopolitanism of the genres and globalising market, which plays to both publishing houses' and readers' preferences (cf. ibid., Ommundsen 2011: 108-109). Moreover, looking at English, Indian and Australian chick- and ladlit, the analyses will show that the formula to which the two genres adhere does overcome geopolitical borders, and, despite localised practices and attitudes displayed in the narratives, the international varieties of chick- and ladlit prove the resilience of the formula and the genres, which are just as prominent in other countries of the world not discussed in this book (cf. Ommundsen 2011: 110-111). Yet, while the analysis of the notions and negotiations of the countries' politics and colonial past present an interesting and rewarding topic – especially in the texts by Chetan Bhagat (India) and Anita Heiss (Australia) – they will not be in the focus but only referred to when fitting.

As the comparison of chick- and ladlit from three different countries still includes too many authors, I consider only two authors and authoresses per country and genre, respectively. Because of these extradiegetic criteria, the following writers have been chosen: English chicklit is represented by Helen Fielding and Sophie Kinsella and English ladlit by Nick Hornby and Mike Gayle. The Australian novelists are Anita Heiss and Melanie La'Brooy for chicklit and Nick Earls and Matt Howard for ladlit. At the time of writing this book, the Indian authoresses have only published one novel each that can be considered chicklit, which is the reason why there are three different novelists who ensure a significant textual corpus to analyse: Advaita Kala, Swati Kaushal and Rajashree. With regard to Indian ladlit, best-selling authors Chetan Bhagat and Harsh Snehanshu are selected. To get as complete a picture as possible, all the novels from these thirteen authors are considered as long as they adhere to the genre criteria of chick- or ladlit. This is important to note because some writers have risen to fame with their chick- or ladlit novels but have since developed in a different direction and write novels which can no longer be considered to be part of the aforementioned genres. The authors might have written literature for teenagers (Hornby's *Juliet, Naked* (2009)) or they might also write poetry and non-fiction (like Anita Heiss), which are not included in the corpus as I am dedicated to the genres of chick- and ladlit only. Some novels have even garnered sequels: *Bridget Jones's Diary*, *Confessions of a Shopaholic*, *Bachelor Kisses*, *Turning Thirty* and *Oops! 'I' Fell in Love*. From these series, only the first three are looked at, in order to not over-represent one particular character's accounts.

It has been previously mentioned that novels from the genres adhere to a specific formula or "conventions of the chick [and lad] lit genre" (Smith 2008: 135) – which at the same time can be considered a litmus test as to which novel truly belongs to the genres of chick- and ladlit. With regard to chicklit, it "seems to have become a catch-all term for any text written by a female author about a female protagonist." (Ibid.: 137) This is a misapprehension because chicklit – and consequently ladlit – is only a specific form of literature and cannot be lumped together with mumlit, henlit or even hacklit. The chick- and ladlit formula depends on two main factors – the main protagonist and the plot, including its ending. There might be overlaps with other varieties such as mum- or dadlit, but they are ultimately different from one another. Throughout this chapter, many features of the two genres of chick- and ladlit have been described and put into context and due to the differences in their geneses, chicklit and ladlit have unique features which distinguish them from the other. Despite their differences within their respective genres as well as between the two genres, there are 'building blocks', which Claude Lévi-Strauss calls "mythemes" (1974: 211). They bridge the differences between the genres and make the novels comparable in a second step for they share the same parameters. Combining these building blocks or constitutive factors will result in a formula which is applicable to both genres and which ensures a common foundation for the following analyses.

In order to acknowledge the individuality of these components and the formula, a specific structuralist method is going to be employed, which Max Black termed "'range concept' or 'cluster concept'" (1992: 128). Thus, I regard both chick- and ladlit as texts which vary "from case to case in relation to different configurations of a range of basic features or constitutive factors." (Singer 2001: 44) Black cautions to look for "ranges, not classes" (1954: 28) because one specific constitutive factor (a) might look differently from another (b) or (c) but will have the same function (α) for the narrative. If one considers that function (α) might actually have a range of possibilities from (a) to (z) as opposed to a specific class, the formula can develop its full potential. For example, depending on the author, a character's insecurity has a specific function within the novel but the severity of the insecurity can range from being rather pronounced to only detectable in few situations. Therefore, the cluster method discloses the genres' narratives as "construct[s] of images and image-systems that work together to support a cluster of themes" (Anderson and Zanetti 2000: 352). What follows from this is a cluster of constitutive features which can be found in almost every chick- and ladlit novel, but the following building blocks can certainly be found in the novels analysed in this book. Obviously, the individual parameters of each feature can be slightly changed, but in general the narrative of these novels are constructed and mapped out against the following cluster[37].

First, the protagonists of the novel need to be young urban professionals. This means that they are in their twenties to mid-thirties and will pursue a career of some kind by the end of the novel. They can be – and actually oftentimes are – dissatisfied with their (low-paying) job in the beginning or, in the case of some ladlit novels, have no profession to start with, but they are going to have some career when the novel ends. The protagonists live a life which is distinctly middle-class, sometimes bordering on the edge of a working-class lifestyle. Yet, this is only important at the beginning of the novels as the protagonists might rise socially due to meeting a wealthy perfect partner but they will never end up in a lower class than the one they started out from. With regard to the feature of the 'urban', there is a slight difference: most protagonists live in metropolitan areas at the beginning of the novel and hardly ever look beyond the borders of their territory. But it can happen that, because of a change of profession, the protagonists have to leave the metropolis for a smaller town. Therefore, in contrast to the characters' profession or class, the protagonists do not need to live in a metropolitan locale when the novel ends, but they are very likely to. These three factors – age, urbanity, profession – pose the range from which the author can choose and build their characters. Of course, the characters seem always to be rather similar, but the possibilities actually suggest that approaching chick- and ladlit characters from Black's point of departure with regard to ranges, the formula can be regarded as most versatile within the specific range of parameters described here.

However, one point which is rather fixed is that the main protagonist has to be a woman in chicklit novels and a man in ladlit novels and it is their point of view which is presented. There is the assertion that novels from these two genres favour a first-person narration, which can also be termed confessional (cf. Ochsner 2009). But although this is true for most of the novels, there are exceptions which employ a figural narration or even multiple centres of consciousness, opening up the range of narrators. As long as the protagonists share the same sex, for example thirty-something Will and teenaged Marcus (*About a Boy*) or the Falks sisters (*The Wed-*

37 Black's cluster theory bears strong resemblances to structuralists Claude Lévi-Strauss's mythemes and Roland Barthes's semes. However, the cluster theory is better suited to take stock of the elements of a narrative whereas Lévi-Strauss's and Barthes's concepts are more valid when they are put into relation to each other within a certain framework. Due to this reason, the chick- and ladlit formula will be explained with Black's cluster theory and the structuralists' ideas regarding mythemes and semes, respectively, will be employed in the next chapter to explain the method according to which this book is structured.

ding Planner), the novel will be included in the corpus. However, should the narrative use oppositional sexes as equal centres of consciousness – for example Mike Gayle's *His 'N' Hers* (2004) or Melanie La'Brooy's *Serendipity* (2007) – they will be excluded for they are no longer 'pedigree' chick- or ladlit novels.

With regard to the plot, it does indeed vary from genre to genre and from novel to novel. However, there are constitutive factors which can be identified in all the novels, irrespective of the genre and author – even though it has to be said that some writers are fonder of certain features than others. As has been observed with regard to chicklit – which is equally applicable to ladlit – many of the building blocks that are related the plot can be classified according to the constitutive factors found in romantic comedies.

The most important strand in the narratives of chick- and ladlit deals with the romance, *the* defining feature of these genres. In the beginning, there has to be a definite lack of love or the assumption that there is something not quite right in the characters' present relationship, which leads to three possible scenarios when the story starts: 1) the protagonist is single, which is the most common scenario, 2) the protagonist is in an unhappy relationship with the wrong man or woman or 3) the protagonist is in a relationship with the perfect partner but due to complications they will jeopardise or even terminate their relationship rather quickly.

The conclusion of the novels inevitably depicts the union of the main protagonist and their perfect partner, the stereotypical fairy tale ending of living 'happily ever after': "Discourses of love and romance share a long association with women and the popular cultures they consume." (Isbister 2009) However, happiness is more important than marriage, as Juliette Wells observed: "Few, if any, chick-lit [or ladlit] novels end with the heroine's [or hero's] wedding; much more common are mutual declarations of love after a long and tumultuous period of *misunderstandings*, with future marriage likely but not guaranteed." (2006: 50, emphasis added) In some novels, the narrative does not close with a union as such but with the possibility of the same. Here, the genres' authors start to experiment with the cluster and divert from the overall generic formula by divorcing happiness from relationships. The characters become happy because of themselves and their achievements, their 'survival' of the "tumultuous period of misunderstandings" which, however, will always include a romance. Then again, Catherine Belsey writes that a happy ending is the most important element with regard to romantic fiction because "a satisfactory resolution is synonymous with true love." (1994: 22) This "true love" has been found in a felicitous relationship with the changed 'self': the characters have finally found (to) themselves instead of hunting for a partner, as society appears to demand. However, not being together with Mr Right is only once the case in chicklit (*Piece of Cake*). Not concluding the narrative with the perfect partner can be found in ladlit more often. It can be argued that, as ladlit is about finding Mr

Right too, the lads who finally come into their own realise their potential and experience a meta-union with themselves. The finding of the matching perfect female partner is then only a formality and can be postponed – and indeed this is done in some cases (e.g. *Ouch! That 'Hearts'*)[38].

The main part of the novel features the many trials and tribulations of the protagonists (cf. Smith 2008: 2). A first important building block for the (romantic) narrative is that of 'misunderstandings', usually between the main protagonist and the perfect partner, which have to be resolved before a happy ending can be achieved. The range of misunderstandings encompasses the three most frequently used tropes of 1) miscommunication, 2) jumping to wrong conclusions and 3) the withholding of important information. Additionally, the building block 'misunderstandings' can be repeated more than once, it can be combined with a different 'misunderstanding' and it can also be merged with (several) plotlines. The second major building block is that of 'obstacles and quests', proving that the classic romance still has its bearings on contemporary romantic fiction. Obstacles and quests are constructed in plotlines that parallel the romance plot, but the various plotlines and building blocks can naturally intertwine or cross. Nonetheless, the romance plot is the most important for the novel as it is the one strand of the narrative which guarantees a form of the happy ending[39].

Apart from the very pronounced romance plot another important factor is the working life of the protagonists: they either have a job with which they are initially dissatisfied or they lead a lifestyle that does not include a profession whatsoever. In both cases, however, the protagonists will inevitably take on a profession that does satisfy them. This shows the importance of being able to provide for oneself instead of relying on other people, which reflects back on the idea that the characters need to be happy with and because of themselves, not because they depend on others. The actual job can vary and includes professions such as account manager or theatre actor, proving that the occupation itself is unimportance as long as there is a sufficient income guaranteed. In one case, Sophie Kinsella's *I've Got Your Number*, the protagonist is indeed happy with her job, but – because of 'misunderstandings' – takes on another one for the duration of the novel. Eventually, she gives up this position again because she is not happy with it and returns to her former job which has been put on hold for the time being. However, through the interim position, she has met her perfect partner. This brief example shows that the working lives and the

38 Already, the fact that both these examples come from Indian chick- and ladlit points towards the more experimental handling of the genres.

39 Even in the novels which do not feature a romantic happy ending, the protagonists have to experience at least one (failed) romance in order to appreciate themselves and be thus happy the way they are – even if that means being single.

romances of the novels' protagonists are usually intertwined and that the protagonists are very likely to meet their perfect partners at their workplaces or through a workplace-related assignment. Additionally, the trials and tribulations as well as misunderstandings usually influence the working life too, and the end of the novel has the characters triumph in their jobs and overcome the obstacle which was a considerable cause for concern beforehand. This achievement mirrors the success of finding the perfect partner and has the protagonist come out on top in each novel.

Although not directly related to a specific storyline, the characters who surround the main protagonists are of equal importance to the various plots as they depict the society the protagonists live in. They are signifiers of the world the heroes and heroines inhabit and they can influence the romantic plot by becoming an obstacle to the inevitable union. The minor characters can be classified as 'background' or 'distractors'. The distractor characters have a strong connection to the main protagonists' love lives, whereas the background characters will only interfere in their friends' romances if the happy ending is endangered.

The background characters are mainly composed of the friends of the protagonist and they comprise the heroine's or hero's urban family: mostly, these figures are like the heroine or hero and mirror their aspirations, fears or general attitude of life, yet with slight variations and therefore present the social and cultural background of the main protagonists. They can be less neurotic and more reasonable, or they can be less responsible but more charismatic: these characters highlight one specific aspect of the main protagonist and, at the crucial moment which is usually connected to the romance plot, they will be there for their friends (see chapter 4). Lastly, the background characters can also function as role models, with the protagonists aspiring to be like them. At one point, though, the protagonists will realise that there is a flaw with their role models, which makes the protagonists realise that they must find their own way. All of the background characters are responsible for the development of the protagonists and this evolution may either happen 'outside' the actual plot and the reader gets only glimpses of the protagonists' past lives and selves or it is subtly part of the narrative which then prepares the characters for being the right partner for their respective perfect partners.

The other category, the distractors, can be further subdivided into non-threatening and threatening distractors. Distractor characters are strongly connected to the romantic plotline, which separates them from the background characters. The heroine's or hero's parents are stereotypical non-threatening distractors, who constantly pester their offspring with questions about their life in general and their love life in particular. They are regarded by the main protagonists as a test of endurance or, in the worst case, as a nuisance. Some other characters also fall in the category of the non-threatening distractors, but they are very minor characters, who may only appear very briefly and are regarded as an annoyance by the protagonists. The threatening distractors can be traced back to the romantic comedy for they are part of the foil plot. Here, four types of characters are introduced into the narrative which complicate the (love) life of the hero or heroine: whereas the hero has to stand out against "the dweeb" and "the prick", the heroine usually is at loggerheads with "the bitch" or "the temptress" (Rubinfeld 2001: 33). All these characters are strongly connected to the romance plot because they are the wrong partners, either of the protagonist themselves or of their inevitable perfect partners. The threatening distractors' presence and character traits elevate the main protagonist and make them more endearing, both to the eventual perfect partner and the reader alike. What separates them from the non-threatening distractors is that the latter are usually only disapproving, whereas the threatening variety interferes in the (love) lives of the protagonists and presents an obstacle to the course of love – after all they stand between the 'correct' partners and thus in the way of the happy ending. What is important to note is that threatening distractors are only an obstacle for a limited time, a detour, because the main focus of the romantic narrative is on the two perfect people to overcome their (initial) problems with each other. Distracting characters can be linked to 'misunderstandings' because they can actively create them or *be* them, when they for example 'block' a character. This blocking happens when a distractor is going out with the protagonist or the perfect partner of the protagonist and is thus wrongly perceived as Ms or Mr Right. But as the right characters develop feelings for each other rather quickly – although they might neither admit to them nor take them seriously for some time – they will dispose of the threatening distractors and pave the way for a union of the perfect partners.

These generic features of almost every chick- and ladlit novel show the validity and importance of the cluster-concept that favours ranges over classes. The building blocks elaborated on above are the formula according to which almost every chick- or ladlit novel is constructed. Authors use these blocks and cluster them in a way that their stories adhere to a rather repetitive formula but have individual touches. This guarantees on the one hand that readers will get a protagonist and plot they are already familiar with and fond of, while, at the same time, the ranges from which the authors can compose their novels grant them enough creative freedom to still surprise their readers.

Cultural Geographies

Space is to place as eternity is to time.
JOSEPH JOUBERT

THE WORLD ACCORDING TO GEOGRAPHERS

The relationship between people and their (created) surrounding(s) is looked at closely in geography and, more precisely, human geography which aims "to explain the spatial patterns and processes that enable and constrain the structures and actions of everyday life." (Dear and Flusty 2002: 2) Human geography is one of the two great strands of geography, the other being physical geography, which includes for example geomorphology or biogeography (cf. Kirk 1963: 359, 361). In their *Introductory Reader in Human Geography*, William Moseley, David Lanegran and Kavita Pandit characterise human geography as focusing on "the patterns and dynamics of human activity on the landscape." (2007a: 3) However, depending on the focus geographers want to apply, they would either narrow the focus on the human activity or stress the "human-environment dynamics (or the nature-society tradition)." (Ibid.) Whereas the latter deals with diverse topics such as political ecology or agricultural geography, the former aspect of human geography addresses issues such as urban geography, economic or political geography and cultural geography (cf. ibid.: 4). Especially cultural geography "concentrates upon the ways in which space, place and the environment participate in an unfolding dialogue of meaning.[1]" (Shurmer-Smith 2002: 3) Cultural geography "includes thinking about how geographical phenomena are shaped, worked and apportioned according to ideology; how they are used when people form and express their relationships and ideas, including their sense of who they are." (Shurmer-Smith 2002: 3) This confirms what Peter Jackson anticipated in his famous *Maps of Meaning* twenty years

1 See also Knox and Marston: "Cultural geography focuses on the way in which space, place, and landscape shape culture at the same time that culture shapes space, place, and landscape." (1998: 191)

earlier: "Emerging from its antiquarian phase, cultural geography has begun to assume a more central position in the current rethinking of human geography." (1992: 1) Proving Jackson's assumption correct and maybe even surpassing it, "some writers assert that the recent developments in cultural geography imply that it will soon encompass all of human geography" (Lanegran 2007: 181). This statement suggests that cultural geography already incorporates many topics which (previously) belong(ed) to human geography, albeit the broadly defined variety. It has affected human geography in such a significant way that ignoring the influence of the cultural turn on human geography means creating "sterile accounts of what [are] rich and complex human landscapes." (Hubbard et al. 2002: 59)

Raymond Williams identified culture as "one of the two or three most complicated words in the English language." (2008: 16) In his 1983 essay, he goes on to trace the term *culture* and identifies various means such as culture being a reference to "*material* production" or a reference to "*signifying* or *symbolic* systems." (Ibid.: 19, original emphases) Culture "has become a general term for the practices, symbols, and meanings that different groups refer to in claiming rights of recognition." (Oakes and Price 2008a: 4) William Sewell Jr. ventures even further when he argues that

> culture [...] should be understood as a dialectic of system and practice, as a dimension of social life autonomous from other such dimension both in its logic and in its spatial configuration, and as a system of symbols possessing a real but thin coherence that is continually put at risk in practice and therefore subject to transformation. (2008: 47)

Yet, he also states that cultures and therefore "worlds of meanings [should be regarded] as normally being contradictory, loosely integrated, contested, mutable, and highly permeable." (Ibid.) He uses the plural – as did Williams – instead of the former singular to emphasise the different co-existing and influencing cultures as well as to show that there is no *one* culture and thus no *best* culture.

Putting culture and geography together now, it should have become fairly obvious that although there are scholars who deem cultural geography separate from its human variety, the definition of culture as put forward by Williams and Sewell Jr. emphasises human agency without which 'culture' is not possible. The idea that culture and human agency are to be considered apart is connected to one person in particular: Carl Sauer, who spearheaded the Berkeley School (cf. Schein 2008: 19-21, Anderson 2010: 13-24). He was under the impression that cultural geography means that "[t]he focus of cultural geography [...] should be on the study of how culture itself works itself out across space and in place." (Mitchell 2000: 32) For Sauer and his followers such as Wilbur Zelinsky, who were highly influenced by anthropologists Alfred Kroeber and Frank Boas, it was more important to consider "cultural groups and their geographical spread as ends in themselves, rather than as means to generate theoretical posturing, empire-building, or nationalistic fervour." (Anderson 2010: 19) In Zelinsky's words:

> Obviously, a culture cannot exist without bodies and minds to flesh it out, but culture is also something both of *and beyond* the participating members. Its totality is palpably greater than the sum of its parts, for it is superorganic[2] and supraindividual in nature, an entity with a structure, set of processes, and momentum of its own, though clearly not untouched by historical events and socio-economic conditions. (1992: 40-41, original emphasis)

But considering culture as being "beyond" its practitioners has become unthinkable. Peter Jackson equally deems it impracticable and proclaims that "cultural geography needed to particularly focus not on 'culture itself' [referencing the Berkeley school; C.L.] but on 'cultural politics'" (Mitchell 2000: 42) which strongly connotes agents and their important relationship to culture instead of focusing on structure and institutions. What Jackson and others promote – by looking to the cultural studies and especially the Centre for Contemporary Cultural Studies – was a *new* cultural geography. The cultural turn in geography enriched the subject in such a productive way that "to speak of cultural geography in the singular is [...] misleading" (ibid.: 63)[3], echoing Williams and Sewell Jr.'s notion of cultures being only possible and correct in the plural. It is now possible to approach geography from such diverse directions such as psychoanalysis, gender studies, Marxism, subcultural theory and many more.

This chapter shows important connections between human, behavioural and cultural geography, as "contemporary cultural geography owes much to the behavioural and humanistic approaches which constitute the previous generations [of geographers]" (Ekinsmyth and Shurmer-Smith 2002: 19). There are, of course, many more varieties that ultimately comprise geography, and "most ways of knowing [related here to the study of geography] are partial and are in flux; they continue to change as geographers examine and re-examine their strengths and weaknesses and as new ideas come along as a challenge." (Aitken and Valentine 2006a: 3) Therefore, this book only deals with a small part of geography, namely the behavioural approach and humanism. Yet it will provide an interface – or, following Kevin Lynch, a node – to connect both cultural studies and geography in a cultural geography, in order to show that the ideas laid out here can be applied rewardingly to fictitious texts.

---

2 Don Mitchell defines superorganicism as referring "to the belief in a force larger than and relatively independent of the lives of humans themselves." (2000: 30)

3 Equally, the spatial turn in cultural studies opened up many new perspectives, too.

HUMAN GEOGRAPHY

"[F]or decades contemporary human geography has been struggling with its identity, with no clear consensus as to what geographers *are*, what geographers *do*, or *how* they should study the world." (Hubbard et al. 2002: 10, original emphasis) Yet what they agree on is that "human geographers attempt to identify the *structure* of behaviour." (Walmsley and Lewis 1993: 25, original emphasis) Geography as a discipline has come a long way in terms of what it actually *looks at*. The stages of geography and its paradigms can be summarised in their three stances towards humans and their usage of place and space. From the fourteenth and fifteenth century, respectively, up to the early nineteenth century the mapping of the world was the most important incentive of geographers – the stage of exploration: to find remaining white spots on maps in order to colour them in – literally – and thus enhance what we know about the surface of the planet we live on (Soja 1996: 76). Three varieties of geography have been identified in this primary stage: the first is 'Geography Fabulous', which "occurred in the sixteenth and seventeenth centuries, where early science combined with mythology and magic [had people] marvel at the new world of discoveries." (Anderson 2010: 14-15) This phase is succeeded by 'Geography Militant', the more organised as well as systematic exploration, and finally – and consequently – 'Geography Triumphant', in which human and physical geography were "closely aligned" and which is still reflected in the maps and encyclopaedias societies use today (cf. ibid.: 15)[4]. Coinciding with the latter part of that period is the stage of environmental determinism. Charles Darwin fuelled the notion of the 'survival of the fittest', a phrase originally coined by British philosopher Herbert Spencer, which had its repercussions in colonialism: people were not only travelling about, finding the last white spots on maps, but also wanted to establish dominion over these 'blanks' and other already 'found' places – most vividly played out in the 'Scramble for Africa'. Here, geographers strived to explore and categorise human activity around the globe which also indicates a certain leaning towards the relationship between humans and their chosen – or, in the case of the disenfranchised and forcefully relocated Indigenous African tribes, allocated – habitats (cf. Diver 2001). This form of early modern (cultural) geography "[a]ttempts to understand and map national character, travel accounts, and descripttions of the relationship between the conditions of physical world and human societies" (Oakes and Price 2008a: 5). Again overlapping with this period, geographers' interest had and still has shifted to the classification of regional ways of life, the relationship between humans and their physical environment: the stage

4 This rather empiricist notion of geography resulted in the founding of the Royal Geographical Society in 1830.

of regionalism. Hubbard et al. refer to the triad of "culture-landscape-region" here (2002: 25). These three stages – exploration, environmental determinism and regionalism – mark a change in terms of scale with regard to geography: from the world to the region, from cartography to human behaviour.

The following part of this subchapter is going to elaborate on the most important aspects of the broadly defined human geography. It is about the principles of how a geographical spot can be theorised and put into context. It will show how a location is constructed and what (power) relations play into it. Moreover, it will align the basic concepts of space and place to the theory of territories and Foucault's heterotopia, because "[g]eography is so basic that we all seem to have some idea of what it is, yet curiously, many would have trouble describing the subject to another person" (Moseley, Lanegran and Pandit 2007a: 1).

First of all, one has to understand that there is indeed a difference between *place* and *space*, two terms that are used synonymously or even confused outside a scholarly geographical context: "Though the concepts of space and place may appear self-explanatory, they have been (and remain) two of the most diffuse, ill-defined and inchoate concepts in the social sciences and humanities." (Hubbard 2005: 41) Edward Relph suggests that "space and place [are] dialectically structured in human environmental experience, since our understanding of space is related to the places we inhabit, which in turn derive meaning from their spatial context" (qtd. in Seamon and Sowers 2008: 44). Hubbard thus concedes "that both space and place are made and remade through networks that involve people, practices, languages and representations. Hence, we might usefully conceive of space and place as constantly becoming, in process and unavoidably caught up in power relations" (2005: 47).

Place "can serve as a context for action, as a source of identity, and as a focus of environmental meaning" (Entrikin, qtd.in Walmsley and Lewis 1993: 118). Yet "place has not attracted the attention [...] from human geographers who have been very largely preoccupied with the abstract, geometrical, and objective concept of space" (ibid.). Phil Hubbard et al. confirm this notion as they state that "place was understood merely as a gathering of people in a bounded locale (territory)" (2002: 16). The past tense is quite significant here as John Agnew distinguishes between three components that comprise place and which attribute a present meaning:

1. *Locale* – the settings in which social relations are constituted[5];

5 This is in accordance with Thrift's notion of locale, which he defines as "the site of the determinate working of an objective social structure." (Qtd. in Walmsley and Lewis 1993: 65)

2. *Location* – the objective geographical area encompassing the setting for social interaction as defined by social and economic processes operating at a wider scale[;]
3. *Sense of place* – the local structure of subjective feeling associated with an area[6]. (Qtd. in Hubbard et al. 2002: 16., original emphasis)

Whereas the last component is rather subjective, the other two are more objective. A locale is characterised by its social structures, everyday social activities and the (in)formal practices that are connected to it, as in a bedroom or a church (cf. Sumartojo 2004: 88). Furthermore, it should be noted that "[d]ue to the interrelated nature of social relations and place, the geographical context of a phenomenon is not static. Instead, what occurs in a place shapes and is shaped by that place." (Ibid.) This form of place, locale, is very much tied to identity and the other objective component, the location, can be regarded as the geopolitical form of a place and how a specific place of various size can be located in the network of national or global spatial structures (cf. Muehlenhaus 2008: 7-8). Sense of place, then, is defined by the "[e]motions and moods [...] held by a group of people [and it] can be explored through literature and the arts because these genres have the power to crystallize the various environmental symbols, thereby expanding and universalizing individual experiences." (Lando 1996: 5) Sense of place "determines the meaning one draws from a place and vice versa." (Sumartojo 2004: 88) Place, therefore, is not an outdated concept but was rather under-appreciated and should be regarded as "polysemous" (Hubbard 2005: 43): "A place is in fact a *centre of meaning* and it ranges in size from a rocking chair, through an urban neighbourhood, to a nation state." (Walmsley and Lewis 1993: 118, emphasis added; cf. Kaltenborn 1997: 189) This definition is also in accordance with Paul Knox and Sallie Marston, who define place as "dynamic, with changing properties and fluid boundaries that are the product of the interplay of a wide variety of environmental and human factors" (1998: 3; cf. Sumartojo 2004: 89). The dynamic qualities refer to the mutability of a place, which can be shaped and modelled according to any agent's ideas, be it one's garden or a public place built, re-modelled or completely

---

6 Vidal de la Blanche has coined the phrase "[g]enre de vie", which focuses "on the livelihood practices of a group, which were seen to shape physical [...] bonds" (qtd. in Knox and Marston 1998: 194). It thus ties in with the notion of sense of place – which, as a term, will be given preference here, for its strong connection to literature: "the pertinence of literature resides in its power to amalgamate objectivity (reality – geography) and subjectivity (culture – human nature). These two elements lie at the basis of what is called *sense of place*." (Lando 1996: 5, original emphasis) Agnew's definition is clearly influenced by Raymond Williams's notion of "structure of feeling" (cf. Williams 1961: 64-67).

re-built by a government, with or without previous public demand. Not surprisingly, then, "place has multiple dimensions" (Anderson 2010: 41) and "always mediate[s] relations, contributing [its] very materiality, [its] affective and temporal flux, to the ongoing transmission of action and the wider distribution of agency." (Duff 2014: 50) Therefore, "the essence of place lies in a largely un-selfconscious intentionality that defines places as profound centers of human existence." (Pennartz 1999: 96)

The concept of space, on the other hand, has undergone a different change. Whereas it used to be looked at as "a kind of absolute grid, within which objects are located and events occur" (Curry 1996: 5), it now has become "implicated in social relations, both socially produced and consumed." (Hubbard 2005: 42) The previous notion, which stems from a positivist (or essentialist) point of view, sees space as a location which can be described in Euclidean terms: it has an x-, a y- and a z-dimension, which can be termed "absolute space" (cf. Knox and Marston 1998: 36). The problem many humanist geographers had with this definition is that it does not take into consideration the human influence. They sought a different definition:

> space is not a given neutral and passive geometry but rather is continuously produced through social-spatial relations; the relationship between space, spatial form and spatial behaviour is not contingent upon 'natural' spatial laws, but is rather a product of cultural, social, political and economic relations; space is not essential in nature but is constructed and produced; space is not an objective structure but is a social experience. (Hubbard et al. 2002: 13-14)

This leads Doreen Massey to assume that space "is the product of the intricacies and the complexities, the interlockings and the non-interlockings, of relations from the unimaginably cosmic to the intimately tiny." (2007: 283) She concludes that "space is always in a process of becoming. It is always being *made*" (ibid., emphasis added). In her opinion, space is not static but through its intricately entwining with time and politicalisations it is ever so changing[7] (cf. Massey 2005: 9-12). Contrary to Massey, however, Jon Anderson is of the impression that "[i]t is from the *empty abstraction of space* that different cultures take and *make place*." (2010: 38, emphasis added) Although this might give the impression that one concept is elevated over the other, there is no hierarchical order and both concepts are equally important: "The ideas 'space' and 'place' require each other for definition" (Tuan 1977: 6).

---

7 Norwegian architect Christian Norberg-Schulz attributes certain characteristics to spaces: different actions need different 'characters' from spaces – "a flat has to 'offer protection', an office has to be 'practical', a ballroom 'grand' and a church 'solemn'" (cf. 1982: 14). He calls this "genius loci" – the spirit of a space (ibid.: 18) – which refers to each agent's identity in their relationship to *a* or *their* space.

Phil Hubbard invokes Lefebvre and his trialectics of space, which have been explained in the introduction, and claims that "place emerges as a particular form of [perceived, conceived and lived] space, one that is created through acts of naming as well as through the distinctive activities and imaginings associated with particular social spaces" (2005: 42). What Lefebvre means – and Hubbard espouses – is the notion that spaces become bounded or invested with meaning and thus should be regarded as a new form that is termed place.

That this distinction is contested can be seen in Michel de Certeau's theories. In his book *The Practice of Everyday Life*, de Certeau explains that "space is a practiced place." (2011: 117, 130) According to him, a "place (*lieu*) is the order [...] in accord with which elements are distributed in relationships of coexistence. It thus excludes the possibility of two things being in the same location (*place*)." (Ibid.: 117) This suggests that he regards place as a form of Euclidean geography, as "an instantaneous configuration of positions" (ibid.) and he continues to claim that for stories – of whatever kind – place is merely a locale, which can be reduced to the "*being-there*" (ibid.: 118, original emphasis). Space, on the other hand, is then defined by "*operations*" (ibid., original emphasis): "A *space* exists when one takes into consideration vectors of direction, velocities, and time variables. [...] Space occurs as the effect produced by the operations that orient it, situate it, temporalize it, and make it function in a polyvalent unit of conflictual programs or contractual proximities." (Ibid.: 117, original emphasis) He appears to incorporate elements of Foucault's heterotopia in his idea of space, which precedes de Certeau's text by almost two decades (more on the heterotopia follows below), and claims that "places [can be constantly transformed] into spaces or spaces into places." (Ibid.: 118) De Certeau chooses the word "practised" instead of "personalised" when he considers the transformation from one spatial state into the other: although he acknowledges spatial agents in so far as he needs them for the transformation, his dichotomy suggests a strong connection to passivity and activity – hence "space is a practiced place". This way, de Certeau can allow for movements from place to space and vice versa, it merely needs a relaxation from actions (space) into inaction (place) or the other way around. For the following analyses, this distinction would take away too much potential for applying the ideas of space and place, as the transformation from one state into the other is *not just* a question of (in)action. I will therefore adhere to the aforementioned idea that place is a personalised version of space, as this allows for a transfiguration even if the agent responsible for it is not present; something which in de Certeau's binary appears to be a reason for inaction.

I agree with Hubbard's idea that both space and place are of equal importance and forego any hierarchy. At the same time, I am going to follow the ideas of Anderson, Tuan and Roger Silverstone, who deem "'[s]pace' more abstract than 'place'" (Tuan 1977: 6; cf. Lando 1996: 3), which is why places "are humanised versions of space" (Anderson 2010: 38). It is exactly this human(ising) component which is ever so important in chick- and ladlit and for the protagonists' search for love: "*Places are human spaces*, the focus of experience and intention, memories and desires" (Silverstone 1994: 27, emphasis added), which echoes in Yi-Fu Tuan's idea that "[p]lace is security, space is freedom" and the latter cites the home as example because "[t]here is no *place* like home." (1977: 3, emphasis added; cf. Hubbard 2005: 43) Space is the stage and place is the setting that can be erected in the former and both are versatile as well as changeable (cf. Duff 2014: 50): "Place, in other words, always involves an appropriation and transformation of space [...] that is inseparable from the reproduction and transformation of society in time and space." (Pred 1984: 279)

The ideas about space and place find a magnificent expression in Michel Foucault's concept of *heterotopias*. A geographic locale can be described in terms of its location within a larger context – for example via Euclidean geometry or via features of cognitive mapping (more on that follows below) – and it can be defined in terms of binaries such as the private versus the public sphere (cf. Foucault 2008: 16). But, as Foucault discloses, there are "real places, [...] in which the real emplacements[8], all the other real emplacements that can be found within culture, are simultaneously represented, contested, and inverted" (ibid.: 17). His defining principles for these heterotopias are six-fold, but only the ones necessary for the understanding of the relationship between space and place shall be explained in detail: first, heterotopias are omnipresent in every culture which will never cease to produce them and, second, the function and importance of heterotopias can change over time (cf. ibid.: 18). These principles do not surprise after looking at the change of perspective in geography. Foucault's third principle, however, is a heterotopia's capability to juxtapose "several emplacements that are in themselves incompatible" (ibid.: 19), which means that one space can contain many different (and opposing) places[9] – over time (diachronic) or even at the same time (synchronic). An example

8 "The term 'emplacement' in French refers to site and location (as in parking space) or the setting of a city [...]. In English, the meaning of the term is more specific. It is used in geology and more commonly as a military term to indicate the support/ position of a semi-stationary weapon. In Foucault's text, emplacement should be considered a technical term, that is space or rather place in the era of network as opposed to extension." (Foucault 2008: 23-24)

9 In the original, Foucault adheres to the notion espoused later by de Certeau, namely that 'place' is the abstract and 'space' the personalised geographical form. Although I do acknowledge Foucault's distinction, I elected to change his idea because of the above-given reasons and to avoid confusion.

would be Piccadilly Circus: to some it is a cultural icon that is regarded as a synonym for London's close connection between culture and commerce, to some it is a meeting point, to others it is a node where they can change tubes or buses and to some it is merely one place they pass on the way to another.

Human beings tend to use places and spaces without giving the distinction too much thought, but one concept closely linked to these and which is (mostly) consciously created is that of *territory*. Usually associated with animal behaviour, a territory – or restricted terrain – controls a population's density via the species' reproduction[10]. Furthermore, a restricted area in which a species lives or operates ensures the ability to stay in communication distance as well as to promote bonding and group activities. Finally, a territory "provides individuals with a known terrain within which to learn and play" (Walmsley and Lewis 1993: 120). Transferring these functions onto human beings, they help to understand how territories influence a population's everyday life. In *Places and Regions in Global Context*, Knox and Marston characterise a territory's function as the regulation of access to people and resources as well as of social interaction. Additionally, a territory provides a focus and symbol of group membership and identity (cf. Knox and Marston 1998: 239). Ralph Taylor adds sentiments and spatial behaviour to this list (1988: 81) and states that "[t]his functioning applies largely to small groups, and the individuals in those groups, and is limited largely to small-scale, delimited spaces." (Ibid.: 1) The smaller one's original territory the greater is the probability of getting to know the people who frequently use or visit the same territory, for example a certain kind of pub. Bonding and familiarity – if not intimacy – are likely to result. Yet, in order to experience something new, one has to expand or sometimes even leave the territory. As today's technological advancements enable human beings to stay in touch more easily – via mobile phones or the internet – the communication distance does not play an important role anymore (for humans, that is). Taylor acknowledges that territorial functioning is both "socially structured or conditioned" and "socially influential and relevant" (1988: 4). Furthermore, he is somewhat cautious in phrasing his claim that "[t]erritorial functioning may play key roles in maintaining ongoing behavior patterns in particular settings or sites." (Ibid.) The analyses will strengthen this assumption by looking at specific territories Taylor already hinted at in his study. However, in their discussion of territorial behaviour, Walmsley and Lewis are critical of the usage of the aforementioned criteria of territories and cite fellow scholars who support their contentions: they claim that only

10 In biology, the smaller the region of the population the fewer individuals inhabit it as resources are limited and so is the amount of specimen that can be fed from it. Only a certain number of individuals will thrive and be able to mate with others; lesser or inferior creatures are casualties of the process (cf. Taylor 1988: 17-33).

> if a territory is thought of as the space around an individual or group which that individual or group thinks of as in some way its own, and which therefore distinguishes it from other individuals and groups, then the concept [of territory] has at least intuitive appeal in the study of human affairs (1993: 120).

Yet, in combination with the understanding and distinction of space and place, the idea of territory enables a deeper understanding of the action of people in a certain spatial context: for "territoriality operates at the community level to encourage group identity and bonding" (ibid.). The notion of territory lends itself very strongly to the identification of territorial behaviour with Agnew's sense of place. It ties in with the concepts of place and space and becomes an intersection between the two: a limited geographical field that transforms into a 'playground' for a certain number of people who create their own rules whilst being in that zone. Additionally, the territory might accommodate different groups or communities creating a hetero-topia, proving again its validity for human geography and the compatibility of spatial ideas which can be connected in order to create a rhizomatic structure. For example one vast office can house many different groups of people who might work together but are also subdivided into smaller units of inter-personal relation-ships according to their tasks as well as their members' pastime activities.

Coming back to Agnew's concept of locale, everyone who can participate in the construction of places is encompassed in the locale, which "structure [and influ-ence] individual life paths [...], provide a means for interaction, provide the activity structure of daily life, and are the principal sites in the process of socialization." (Walmsley and Lewis 1993: 65) In geographical terms, the individual that engages in and with space is referred to as an *agent*[11]. Yet, the agent can also be a conglomeration of many individuals who work towards the same goal, like a neigh-bourhood watch or a book group. Yet, geographers do not solely look at so small a group of actors on a spatial level, but also at governmental apparatuses as the "phenomenal forms of structures" (Dear and Flusty 2002: 2) which are referred to as *institutions*. The last and all-encompassing actors are *structures* which are "long-term, deep-seated social practices that govern daily life, such as law, state, and family" (ibid.). The triad structure-institution-agent represents the geographical axis

11 Agents are sometimes referred to as actors. However, in the following, 'agent' relates to a small group of individuals or even just one, and 'actor' stands for the subordinating level that is divided into structures, institutions and agents. This triad is referred to as "Process" in the geographical puzzle – which, due to overlapping concepts of a different nature but by the same name, is not going to be used (cf. Figure 3-1).

of power. It is interesting to note that humans tend to recognise power and its (ab)use by agents and institutions but they are mostly unaware of the origin of governing rituals of structure: whereas in Western cultures it is permissible to express one's deeply felt emotions or love for another person in the form of holding hands or kissing in public, such gestures are shunned in large parts of India, where it is considered inappropriate[12]. Rini Sumartojo comments that "[a]s different groups, institutions, and individuals struggle for power within society, their ability to produce and define places changes. Likewise, as different actors struggle over place meaning, the power they wield in social structures is affected." (2004: 89)

This leads to another feature of geography: the scale. One can look at locales on a *macro*, *meso* or *micro* level. Whereas the micro and macro levels are easier to exemplify in terms of the individual or family and the nation state, respectively, the meso level can range from neighbourhoods to cities to whole areas: "Many levels and scales of process are distilled or crystallized into a single locale; it is as though

Figure 3.1: The Geographical Puzzle

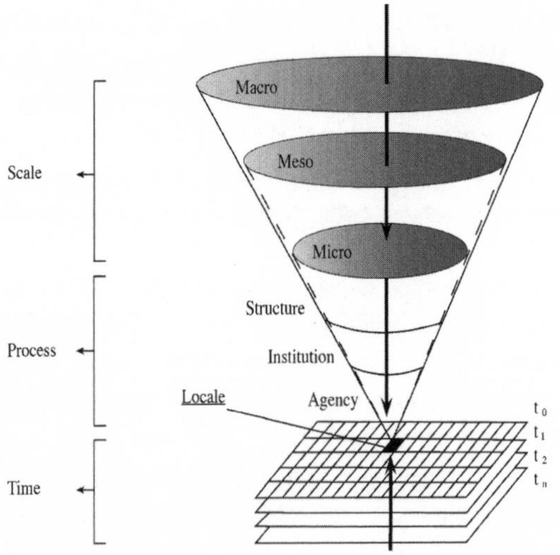

Source: Dear and Flusty 2002: 4

12 In Snehanshu's novels the public display of kissing is always connected to unease: "I moved my face ahead to kiss Tanya again when she turned her face sideways. 'Kanav, behave. It's a public place. Find a secluded place first.'" (2012: 174) Indian couples in Snehanshu's novels always have to relocate to a very private location to live out their emotions, far off the public eye.

a multitiered sequence of multiply determined events had been telescoped onto a single plane." (Dear and Flusty 2002: 3) The locale thus functions as a point of focus that helps to compare processes. Finally and logically, one can consider how the locale has been used, appropriated or created at different times throughout history[13]: for example, how has the family unit in London or Delhi changed over the decades? Combining all these pieces of information, one gets what geographers call the 'geographical puzzle' (see Figure 3.1).

As the geographical puzzle suggests, there are inherent power structures that humans tend to accept. A way to suspend this traditional belief of fixed hierarchies and to open up possibilities for analyses and insightful observations regarding texts and objects of study is the employment of the *actor-network-theory* (ANT). It does not distinguish between structures, institutions and agents, and neither does it discriminate between the varieties of "actors [be they] human, non-human[14] [or even] material [and] discursive" agencies (Bosco 2006: 136). Equally, "we have to accept that the continuity of any course of action will rarely consist of human-to-human connections [...] or object-to-object connections, but will probably zigzag from one to the other." (Latour 2005: 75) Therefore, buildings, office spaces and furniture are just as significant and equal as are their owners or users. None of the actors is more important or more influential than others when it comes to decisions and processes: "An actant [Latour's term for 'actor'; C.L.] can literally be anything provided it is granted to be the source of action" (Latour 1996: 373). A kitchen can thus acquire as much meaning as the person using it, disclosing information about that person and their lifestyle. Moreover, an actor enables other actors to transform themselves, to (ex)change signs, roles or other markers (cf. Belliger and Krieger 2006: 41) The binary structure of human and non-human, the object-subject dichotomy, needs to be re-addressed and thus no choice shall be given preference (cf. Barron 2003: 81). Moreover, this "decentred notion of agency [defines] *agency as network*. Thus, from such a point of view, things as scientific knowledge, the

---

13 Space and time have been related time and again – especially among postmodern geographers like Doreen Massey and Edward Soja, to name two of the most influential. Andrew Sayer is also of the opinion that we may look at "how the shaping of people and institutions at time *t* is constrained and enabled by their properties, which exist largely independently of the current shaping but were influenced by social forces at an earlier time *t*-1." (2006: 100, original emphasis) However, as this book deals with a certain genre of novels that are very much idiosyncratic to their time of writing, a more detailed look at other times will be eclipsed.

14 Andréa Belliger and David J. Krieger explicitly refer to the humanisation or socialisation of the machine, stressing the strong connection between humans and technology (cf. 2006: 15).

government of a nation, and even what counts as a person are no other than network effects." (Bosco 2006: 137, original emphasis) Everything that can be traced back to an actor in terms of concepts or processes is therefore on an equal level – a government is not hierarchically higher than a single person, both influence each other equally (cf. ibid.: 139). Network, however, does not necessarily mean merely connections but "[i]t's the work, and the movement, and the flow, and the changes" which are stressed by the aspect of network (Latour 2005: 143) and Belliger and Krieger agree that ANT describes neither society nor nature but a process of articulation (cf. 2006: 29).

Yet, one feature mentioned by Latour needs to be specially addressed, namely that non-human actors "have to be *actors* [...] and not simply the hapless bearers of symbolic projection." (Latour 2005: 10, original emphasis) Cameron Duff states that "[a]ctor-networks link diverse social, material, affective, symbolic and discursive entities, combining and recombining these elements in the production of dynamic, localised spaces." (2014: 50) Therefore, even if the object does not have direct agency – social force or social action (cf. Latour 2005: 70-74) – or is attributed direct agency, it is through its connection and interaction with other actors and even networks that it attaches agency to itself, either passively or actively: it can create a specific notion of space and place (anew) (cf. Belliger and Krieger 2006: 42-43).

THE BEHAVIOURAL APPROACH AND GEOGRAPHY

Before geographers – and other scientists – turned to what is now referred to as *behaviouralism* or *behavioural geography*[15] (Walmsley and Lewis 1993: 6; cf. Gold 1980: 3) and *human geography*, there were people-environment theory and positivism which focused on the "rational economic behaviour" of actors (Walmsley and Lewis 1993: 6). But, as scholars had to admit eventually, rationality is not a trait that can be applied to humans without restrictions, which is one of the main reasons why the modern varieties of the relationship between people and environment now

15 Concerning the actual term, Golledge writes that he prefers the term "behavioral research" to "behavioralism" (to him, it leads to unthinking categorisation – which, however, he does not comprehensively elaborate on) and "behaviourism" (too closely linked to Pavlov and Skinner) (2006: 75). In the following, not only will the British spelling prevail – with the exception of the usage in quotes – but the terms "behavioural research" and "behaviouralism" will be used. The term "behaviourism" is excluded because it "attempts to reduce behaviour to S-R [stimuli-response] bonds" only (Walmsley and Lewis 1993: 21).

focus on "individual decision-making units", overt and covert behaviour and, most importantly, on "how socially generated constraints influence virtually all forms of people-environment interaction, and a willingness to consider those distinctly human characteristics that lead individuals to develop an attachment to some places and a feeling of dislike for others." (Ibid.) The strongest argument that speaks against positivism and the people-environment theory as methods to use comes from Harold Brookfield, who states that "decision-makers [or actors] operating in an environment base their decisions on the environment *as they perceive it, not as it is*" (1969: 53, emphasis added). The rational homo economicus is therefore only a highly theoretical concept but hardly the person one encounters in one's day-to-day life. Shurmer-Smith also reflects on this when she talks about the cultural turn in (human) geography, which eventually led to cultural geography: "By the 'cultural turn', it was implied that the accumulations of ways of seeing, means of communicating, constructions of value, senses of identity should be taken as important in their own right, rather than a by-product of economic formations." (2002: 1) Positivism and the playing down of the importance of culture and human behaviour was eventually re-assessed – yet not abolished – and the human agent was freed from the shackles of being a rational creature that could be understood by looking at data.

Behaviouralists and followers of humanism wanted to create an opposition to the rational and empiric positivism. According to nineteenth-century philosopher Auguste Comte, positivist science is based on collected data gathered "through observation and measurement", which "assumes that the development of generalizations and deduced laws can only follow on the basis of repeated observations" (qtd. in Hubbard et al. 2002: 29). These will then be acknowledged in "accepted generalizations and hypotheses [which will be turned] into theories and laws", which, however, "can never be completely validated" (ibid.). To humanist scientists, this was too narrow an approach as "agents draw on their experiences, attitudes, and belief, as well as their moral aesthetic judgement, in making decisions that shape their environments." (Entrikin and Tepple 2006: 31) Moreover, humanist geography is about "a willingness to consider those distinctly human characteristics that lead individuals to develop a sense of attachment to some places and a feeling of dislike for others." (Walmsley and Lewis 1993: 6) Humanism argues that a greater emphasis has to be placed on human values and attitudes, cultural patrimony, the aesthetics of landscape and architecture as well as – and maybe most importantly – the emotional significance of (the sense of) place in human identity (cf. Norberg-Schulz 1982: 18, Walmsley and Lewis 1993: 16, Ekinsmyth and Shurmer-Smith 2002: 20, Entrikin and Tepple 2006: 31). Thus, scholars sought new ways apart from the notion of the "rational economic actors whose behaviour could be predicted and modelled." (Aitken and Valentine 2006a: 14)

The difference between these two approaches, behaviouralism and humanism, is based on the notion of *processes*. Golledge lists "perception, learning, forming attitudes, memorizing, recalling, and using spatial thinking and reasoning to explain variations in human actions and activities in different environmental settings" as the most important of (spatial) processes (2006: 75). These processes enable agents to engage spatially but are also important to consider on the level of structures as the formation of ideologies depends on processes: they become vital for agents' actions, especially in the creation, evaluation and re-structuring of territories. Behaviouralism intends to find explanations for these processes, whereas humanism – as the name already implies – focuses rather on the agents as such:

> humanist geographers gave [a semantic depth] to traditional concepts such as place, region, space, landscape, and nature and the extended reach of these concepts into studies of literature and art[16]. Where once these concepts referred to an underlying world of natural and cultural elements, the humanists made visible their relation to human projects and the subjects who created them. (Entrikin and Tepple 2006: 31)

Humanists believe human beings to be "determined not by stimuli as such, but by definitions of situations partly enjoined upon them through their participation in a particular society and cultural milieu" (Wapner, Kaplan and Cohen 1980: 225). Therefore, the human experience is paramount and it already hints at the importance of the connection between the cultural milieu and agency: it is about the individual('s) influence and the uniquely experienced place. Ekinsmyth and Shurmer-Smith actually deem this a problem of behaviouralism. Talking about Agnew's sense of place, they state that "it ought to be obvious that there is no single genuine essence in any place" (2002: 25): two people will not perceive one location in one and the same way. This means whenever more than one person is present at a specific location that they must create a heterotopia. Yet certain codes of behaviour, the spatial structures, came into being – how to behave in a bar or in a shop – and reduced the distance between the various perceptions within one space: agents will assimilate their perception of space to fit into certain locations or territories.

In these structures, the influence of psychology on geography can be seen and thus behavioural geography focuses intensively on cognition, perception, development, learning and ultimately on their effect on spatial behaviour of any one person (cf. ibid.: 21). To behaviourist geographers, the equation '$B=f(P,E)$' is paramount,

16 Richard Peet states that this form of second-hand experience gathered from literature is called "vicarious insiderness" (1998: 50). His positive stance towards the importance of fictitious accounts in the fine arts is a valuable contribution to the cultural turn in human geography.

"to demonstrate the way in which behaviour [B] is a function [*f*] of both the individual [P] and the environment [E]." (Walmsley and Lewis 1993: 21) This interrelation between the individual(s) and their spatial behaviour and therefore the interaction with a space is also known as *life space* (cf. ibid., Taylor 1988: 10). These interactions are possible because of the relation(ship) between two varieties of knowledge: figurative and operative knowledge. The first produces images which result from an agent's direct contact with place and is thus about perception, whereas the other has the agent structuring this information by multiple and various mental operations (cf. Moore and Golledge 1976: 6). The connection is important because agents' "perception of the world is not direct[. Thus] what [they] perceive is a mental representation of the world, which is the product of cognitive operations on sensory input" (Heft 1988: 327). The "focus should be on the way that people act in relation to the images of space that they construct [through their perception and cognition], shifting the focus from the way people dwell in 'concrete' empirico-physical space to the geographies of the mind." (Hubbard et al. 2002: 34)

When it comes to behaviour and space, emotions are a very important asset to create a bond between the two and thus create a sense of belonging. Referring both back to territories and forward to cognitive maps, Yi-Fu Tuan's concept of *topophilia* helps to connect the concepts and to create a rhizomatic theoretical construct for geographical analysis. Tuan defines topophilia as an emotion of "a human being's affective ties with the material environment" because humans feel strongly about places like "home, the locus of memories, and the means to gain a livelihood." (1974: 93) He goes on to say that "a person in the process of time invests bits of his [or her] emotional life in his [or her] home, and beyond the home in his [or her] neighborhood." (Ibid.: 99) Actually, one need not stop there: if a person has a very 'intimate' relationship to their workplace, they will experience topophilia in a similar way the football fan experiences it in their team's stadium or a very sociable person at their local pub. They feel that this particular space they are in is not only a geographical location but moreover something 'alive' that feeds positive energy back through memories[17]. What becomes clear by giving these examples is that topophilia not only references the notion of emotions but also that of nostalgia (see chapter 4). The love for a certain place – and consequentially the memories that are connected to it – has the lover ignoring or even forgetting possible cracks in

17 Of course it has to be acknowledged that topophilia is exclusively used in positively connoted contexts. A certain angst regarding places, then, has to be called topophobia, a place of conflict (cf. Muñoz González 2005: 195). It encompasses fears such as agoraphobia or claustrophobia but also more specific fears such as fearing a certain room in one's home because one has experienced traumatic events there such as child abuse.

the foundation of the perfection of their imagined space. Imagined, because topophilia is a sentiment and thus not rational, it is not constrained by laws of reality. One example are football fans who might support their team as long as they can remember but refuse to acknowledge that the team is no longer as good as it used to be. These fans will remember the "good old times" when the team actually brought the cup home and their feelings when the important goal was achieved, the smell of a particular kind of food or the chants by the whole fan block and thus remain faithful to their team[18]. The happiness of these fans is strongly tied to the place where they experienced this feeling of bliss – namely the stadium. It also accounts for a certain kind of allegiance to that place, no matter what (cf. Tuan 1974: 100-101). Ralph Taylor attaches a different term to this phenomenon, namely *centrality*: "*Centrality* focuses on the importance of the setting as a supportive context for daily functioning. [...] Centrality is not a characteristic of a place; it is an attribute of the *transactions* between an individual (or group) and a place: it is an aspect of person-place bonds." (1988: 10, original emphasis) Although Taylor stresses the bonds between a person and a location as well, his concept of centrality is less emotional and more productive than Tuan's topophilia. It is more rational and recognises nostalgia but does not rely on it as heavily. However, it is a very thin line that separates the two.

COGNITIVE MAPPING AND WAYFINDING

Despite the fact that it is only a fraction of the whole that is behavioural geography – and cultural geography for that matter – the notion of wayfinding and its contributing features will shed a new light on the subject at hand. Wayfinding with the help of (constructing) cognitive maps is always happening in each and every person, both consciously and subconsciously. Analysing how a character (or real person for that matter) structures, finds and establishes their way around a certain environment is essential to realising a person's cultural geography. Therefore, wayfinding will be discussed here and a special emphasis will be put on the creation of cognitive maps.

Arthur and Passini define *wayfinding* as "problem solving" and making a journey and reaching a destination as primary wayfinding goals (cf. 1992: 25, 27). The two components, problem solving and the undertaking and completion of a journey, have a strong connection which is not entirely obvious in an instant, though. Whereas the second part is rather self-explanatory, the first alludes to the processes people have to undergo or undertake if they can no longer find their way

18 I am indebted to Cyprian Piskurek for this insight.

around an unknown environment. Arthur and Passini continue to differentiate spatial problem solving into three subcategories: *decision making*, *decision executing* and *information processing* (ibid.: 25). Regarding the first two components, if one finds that one is lost, one has to come to a decision what to do next on a geographical level – namely, where to go next or whom to ask for directions in order to select "paths from a network" of possible routes (cf. Golledge 1999: 7). This "development of a plan of action" has to be put *into* action. The third part, information processing, is "understood in its generic sense as comprising environmental perception and cognition, which, in turn, are responsible for the information basis of the two decision-related processes" (Arthur and Passini 1992: 25). A journey is always inherent in every movement a being undertakes and wayfinding is usually only ever 'possible' the first couple of times one makes such a journey. After a while certain ways will become part of a routine, and the decision-making processes will decrease until they seem to have disappeared, which they have not – they have merely been internalised to such a degree that they need no more deliberating about.

In this case, one constructs what is known as a *cognitive map*: "a representation of a set of connected places which are systematically related to each other by a group of spatial transformation rules" (O'Keefe and Nadel 1978: 86), whereas Gary Allen simply states that a cognitive map is a "knowledge structure" (1999: 71). It is exactly this relational structure that is of interest here. For a map which can be purchased at a bookstore is a plan on a certain scale, simplified buildings from a bird's eye perspective: the whole city in a nutshell. A cognitive map, however, is produced from a personal point of view – from 'down here' instead of 'up there'. Experiencing a geographical ambit locomotively, one establishes relations between buildings, remembers natural details, memorises pathways: "Cognitive mapping is therefore a mental structuring process that integrates into a whole what has been perceived in parts" (Arthur and Passini 1992: 23), it is what Edward Soja termed 'Secondspace' (see chapter 1), the perception of reality. Because "in Secondspace[,] the imagined geography [of the cognitive map] tends to become the 'real' geography, with the image or representation coming to define and order the reality." (Soja 1996: 79)

A cognitive map will always form itself in each person's head, only depending on how much attention that person has paid to his or her surroundings or the perceptibility of that person in general (cf. Arthur and Passini 1992: 32). However, if a space, building or location is linked to a certain experience, the cognitive map becomes not only a wayfinding device but rather a map of a person's life in a defined geographical setting. In his very influential study *The Image of the City*, Kevin Lynch reflects on exactly this connection between space, identity and the resulting cognitive map:

At every instant, there is more than the eye can see, more than the ear can hear, a setting or a view waiting to be explored. Nothing is experienced in itself, but always in relation to its surroundings, the sequences of events leading up to it, the memory of past experiences. (1960: 1)

Yet the best description of how a cognitive map has invaluable influence on our lives and keeps memories alive via a link to locations is by Will Self in his rather autobiographical essay *Big Dome*, in which he talks about his experiences and links to his native town of London:

in adult life, there is the long, long shading in of the rest, the even adumbration which constitutes regular experience. Even ten years ago, and certainly fifteen, I could patrol central London and still avoid my past self when I saw him coming in the opposite direction. I could take alternative routes to avoid the districts of failed love affairs, I knew short cuts which would circumvent the neighbourhood of an abandoned friendship, I had only to swerve to miss the precincts of a snubbing acquaintance. But now the city is filled in with narratives, which have been extruded like psychic mastic into fissures. There is no road I haven't fought on, no cul-de-sac I haven't ended it all in, no alley I haven't done it down. To traverse central London today, even in a car, even on autopilot, is still to run over a hundred memoirs. (1999: 117-118)

A person traversing streets of any kind of village, town, city or megapolis will inevitably connect certain objects – be it a house, corner or even a tree – with certain associations, connotations and memories, which has been hinted at in the concept of topophilia. And sometimes, depending on the experience, one even attributes new meaning to previously constructed parts of that map as the excerpt from Self's text indicates. A cognitive map is never complete and can always be changed and modified.

So, how does one go about creating a cognitive map – or on a more basic level – get around an unknown environment? In a first step, one has to experience the location: in case one wanders accidentally or on purpose unto unknown territory, there are four vital questions one has to ask oneself: 'where am I?', 'what is likely to happen?', 'will it be good or bad?' and finally 'what will / can I do about it?' (cf. Stea 1976: 108). The concepts, or responses, to these questions are, respectively: perception and representation, prediction, evaluation and action. These responses – and questions for that matter – must not all occur, or not even in this order, yet if they can be answered and translated into activism, they can help to both familiarise with the unknown place and even find one's way home[19]. According to Reginald Golledge there are three – rather different – possibilities of getting around unfamiliar territory: firstly, one employs active search and explores the environment 'hands on' (which is in tune with Stea's ideas), secondly, one gathers a priori information before setting out (e.g. maps, descriptions, etc.) and, thirdly, one uses controlled navigational practices – like for example (human) guides, or relies heavily on signs (cf. 1999: 8-9). In any of these cases, one has to be able to identify one's point of origin as well as one's desired destination.

Yet before one is able to construct a cognitive map, one has to realise what kind of location one is dealing with. So the second step is to evaluate whether one can actually establish a map or maybe the location cannot be 'territorialised'. In their influential as well as engaging opus *A Thousand Plateaus*, Gilles Deleuze and Félix Guattari have established two varieties of territories, the *smooth space* and the *striated space*. These spaces can be characterised as "nomad space" and "sedentary space", respectively (Deleuze and Guattari 1987: 474) and the actors' possible actions within the two spaces are of importance. Because, as the former's characterisation already implies, it is a nomad-ic space, an extended sojourn is not possible. A person traversing such a space is forced to pause only, not to build up a permanent residential property, making familiarisation and a properly helpful cognitive map hard to construct. However, the novels discussed show that a smooth space can indeed be striated, although it can be a laborious process.

In the striated (or territorialised) space, agents have marked and personalised previously unruly space and thus made it habitable. Here, "one counts in order to occupy", whereas the smooth space is occupied without counting (cf. ibid.: 477). This means that one striates the un-striated space in order to gain more and more ground and the mathematical notion implies that for each count one gains ground, which can be occupied in a second step. This is pitted against the smooth space, where one can only occupy – temporarily, as has been already stated – but cannot count as this would mean ownership, nomad space will not be subject to anybody. It has to be said that the construct of a smooth space works perfectly in theory and is still applicable to most seas and oceans. However, with advancing technology the nomadic space is increasingly reduced to a concept as it can be and has been striated in reality. Another important aspect distinguishing the two spaces is the lines which run through these spaces. These may be either vectorial (smooth space) or dimensional (striated space) (ibid.: 478). If they are dimensional, one can move about the space freely as the area determines the space, but as the vectorial already implies, in a smooth space one's movements are limited to linear movements;

19 However, it is very much possible that these responses have to be re-assessed during the wayfinding process.

otherwise one would not arrive and could get lost in that kind of space. Good examples for such spaces are the woods and the sea, respectively: in the woods, one can start to clear the trees and build a hut, which can be expanded into a village and a city, making the previously hard-to-memorise place more individual – if forcefully domesticated. Additionally, one can enlarge one's personal area and is free to go from one place to another. At sea, ships sail from harbour to harbour – establishing a dominion 'on water' is almost impossible as they have to come into port at one point[20]. Apart from cruises, ships usually seek the easiest, fastest and safest way to transverse from their point of origin to their point of destination.

Once out and having established territorialised space, people will put themselves in relation to objects and in a consecutive third step, individuals will relate these objects to one another, to form a cognitive map. Now, it has to be determined what to put in that particular map. There are four varieties of environment, two of which will be important for the proposed undertaking: the *'natural'* and the *built environment*. The other two, the *human* and the *verbal environment* (cf. Wirth-Nesher 1996: 11)[21], are not of great importance for the creation of cognitive maps as they are too inconsistent – people and words tend to move far too often and quickly, but they can be found in locations and novels frequently. They are comprised of "human features that constitute setting, such as commuter crowds, street peddlers, and passersby" and "written and spoken language [such as] names of streets and places, and any other language that is visually inscribed into the cityscape – advertisements, announcements, or graffiti", respectively (ibid.: 13). The 'natural' environment consists not only of the nature surrounding a city, but rather the nature within a city – parks, tree-lined roads – and even the weather. The natural element within a city has to be taken into consideration as sometimes, depending on sunshine or rain, some areas are closed off or even more advisable, for example recreational picnics in the park are usually undertaken during sunny days. But in chick- and ladlit novels there are very few instances in which the natural environment plays an important role. The built environment, however, is always implied, and "refers to city layout, architecture, and other man-made objects as trams, curtain walls, and roofs" (ibid.: 12). Of course, Wirth-Nesher's notion of "man-

20 Of course, oil platforms are such dominions, but even they only function as temporary habitats.

21 Wirth-Nesher identified these four environments in modern urban novels. However, the features she lists and analyses can be found in actual cities around the world. Thus, they will be included here and fused with the notion of cognitive mapping to prove that fictitious narratives are greatly inspired by and can have an equally big impact on reality.

made" is rather all-encompassing and would also account for parks or billboards with advertisement.

The built and natural environments are very interesting and important when it comes to wayfinding: in Kevin Lynch's influential study, he asked his subjects to draw a map of the city they inhabit and describe it verbally, too. He found that people tend to structure a city – and consequently their cognitive maps – with the help of five features: paths, edges, nodes, districts and landmarks (cf. Lynch 1960: 47-48), which comprise both the 'natural' and the built environments. These features are part of the aforementioned third and last step in creating a cognitive map – the categorisation of features into an organised system – and are going to be elaborated on in the following.

Paths are the "predominant elements" in any city or cognitive map as they are the lines along which one moves (ibid.: 47). Paths can be roads, pedestrian walks, canals, underground lines or railroads. They are most obvious within the city but are also present within buildings. Humans tend to form primary, secondary and even tertiary routes within a setting: a person in a building will always have a *destination zone*, in which they will execute any kind of action, which can be a shop in a shopping mall, a particular office in a company or even one's own kitchen. The primary route is the circulation between "entrance or exits of a setting and the major destination routes" (Arthur and Passini 1992: 48). The secondary routes are the ones from one destination zone to another and the tertiary routes are within a destination zone. That means that the secondary and tertiary routes can be repeated before one has to leave the building via the primary route again. If one has a job in a place other than one's home, one has to leave home to get to work (primary route), with one's office building being the destination and one's office being the destination zone. Having arrived at the correct department, one will have to pass, for example, the information desk and other offices to finally arrive at one's own office – the route from door to door within a building is a secondary route. Within the office one will move about – to one's desk, to the printer, to get coffee (tertiary routes). One also needs to see co-workers to discuss matters or move to the canteen (secondary routes to other destination zones) and once there fulfil other tasks (attend a meeting and thus getting to one's assigned chair; queue to order food and find a spot to consume it, which are – again – tertiary routes).

Edges are what people regard as "boundaries between two phases [of whatever nature], linear breaks in continuity: shores, railroad cuts, edges of development, walls" (Lynch 1960: 47). Lynch observes that people tend to neglect edges as they deem them inferior in importance but use them to distinguish certain zones or areas nevertheless. Although not necessarily mentioned as frequently as the other features, edges are as important and are likely to appear without being mentioned in the form of lacunae within any given text.

Nodes, on the other hand, "are points, [...] strategic spots in a city into which an observer can enter, and which are the intensive foci to and from which he [or she] is travelling" (Lynch 1960: 47). The agents who walk through town, no matter whether they have an aim or are just strolling about, will come to a junction and have to decide how to progress with their journey. Thus, nodes are usually associated with paths. Yet, there is also a special form of the node, which Lynch calls *core* (ibid.: 48): it is the centre of a district or area which serves also as a form of strategic spot at which one has the opportunity to choose from many paths. The best example of a network full of nodes and paths is actually the tube system of London (or, for that matter, any other urban subway train system): here, one has straight paths and frequent opportunities to change trains via nodes when two lines cross, with major cores at stations like Paddington or Waterloo.

A feature that is both found in maps and adjusted by citizens is the *district*, which can be found in the above-mentioned example of the tube map in the form of zones[22]. Each town is already subdivided into certain districts and they are given specific names which sometimes have even attracted an image or identity themselves: for example Notting Hill, the West End, Fortitude Valley or Juhu Beach. In novels, characters refer to particular districts and connote a certain income or class. Districts can also be structured by their inhabitants as already indicated. This is done by criminal gangs, for example, who divide certain areas into new districts which they will then control. Therefore, there are not only the council-promoted districts but rather personal districts which need not adhere to governmental mapping or even to other people's opinions – proving the notion of heterotopias correct, with all the possibilities and possible problems.

The last and most elaborate feature with regard to piloting is the *landmark*. According to Lynch, one never enters "within them" but rather uses them as reference points (ibid.). They can be a large building, a store or even a natural element like a mountain. The main point is that agents can relate themselves to it and thus deduce their present location and probably the path for their further journey. Landmarks as foci will "assist spatial decision making, [as they are] significant physical, built, or culturally defined objects that stand out from their surrounding" (Golledge 1999: 16; cf. Couclelis et al. 1987: 102). This salience need not be as prominent or widely recognised like for example London's Big Ben or Sydney Harbour Bridge, it can also function on the personal or micro level: one's home is a very important anchor-point when it comes to planning routes and constructing a cognitive map as it will pose as the ultimate starting point and goal. Sometimes, a person will rely

22 The example of the zone can both be a district and an edge which separates the centre of London from its various suburbs. Although not physically remarkable, people tend to distinguish between the zones in terms of identity and origin.

only on landmarks to get around a known or novel environment. This "landmark-based piloting" means that each landmark poses as an anchor-point and the route is organised sequentially, with each point leading to the next as it is mentally connected to direction and distance (cf. Allen 1999: 49).

Anchor-points and the *anchor-point-theory* play an important role in behavioural geography and consequentially cognitive mapping. Golledge has stated that "landmarks usually act as anchor points for organizing other spatial information into a layout." (1999: 17) In another essay, a distinction is made between anchors and landmarks but it is admitted that they are "closely related [...], both concepts being defined as cognitively salient clues in the environment." (Couclelis et al. 1987: 102) The major difference lies in the fact that anchor-points are always individual, whereas landmarks are acknowledged individually and collectively[23]. Anchor-points may coincide with actual landmarks but this not necessary. The anchor-point-theory relies on "environmental knowledge acquisition in which location, features, path segments, or familiar districts ['anchor'] cognitive maps and [influence] the encoding, storage, and decoding processes used when accessing stored information in a decision making context." (Golledge 1999: 17; cf. Golledge and Spector 1978: 406-411) In these cognitive maps there will be a clear hierarchy in terms of anchor-points[24]: there are anchor-points of the first order, which are the major ones like home, work or one's preferred shopping area. From these there are further paths which lead to other anchor-points, of a lesser significance, thus turning the primary anchor-points into Lynchian nodes. An example would be one's newsagent's around the corner of the primary anchor-point of 'home' or a certain dry-cleaner's that is located not in the shopping area but off the high street. In this case, one tends to turn the area with anchor-points of the first and second order into a personalised district (cf. Golledge 1999: 18). Although the node is not to be confused with a landmark or building as such, in terms of cognitive maps they function in the same way. They are points at which an individual has the choice of progressing in certain but different ways via previously established paths, or create new paths by exploring them. Anchor-points help to imprint one's own 'identity' on a previously striated space: in a city with hundreds of thousands of inhabitants, one

23 Landmarks are treated as factual knowledge of a surrounding, but anchor-points are to organise the surroundings. Furthermore, "landmarks are concrete, visual cues, whereas anchor-points may be more abstract elements that need not even be point-like (e.g. a river or a whole city in a cognitive map at the regional level)." (Couclelis et al. 1987: 102)

24 The fact that one has to be able to recognize the sight or name of a spatial cue as well as knowing where it is and interact with it on a frequent basis is a prerequisite (cf. Couclelis et al. 1987: 105).

can hardly speak of a smooth space as proposed by Deleuze and Guattari. However, anchor-points establish a personalised striated space – a place – in previously (publicly or governmentally) striated space. If one takes for example a house that is inhabited by a family it becomes clear that the breadwinner of the family will have a different personalised map than the children who might still be in school. For all of them, the home functions as an anchor-point, yet due to each person's individual usage of the surrounding area – office, school, shopping centre – each will venture in different directions and thus the anchor-point will become a node.

Golledge places the aforementioned features into certain categories in order to link them to the configuration of maps: points (places, locations, landmarks), lines (paths, tracks), areas (districts, regions) and surfaces[25]. As Kevin Lynch has observed, "[a]s the density of the image [or cognitive map] builds up, it begins to take on the characteristics of a total field, in which interaction is possible in any direction at any distance." (1960: 89) It is therefore possible to speak of a map consisting of anchor-points as the foundation of a cognitive map. Each configuration is based on such an 'anchor-point map', no matter how shortly one has been to a certain environment. If one goes on holiday, the hotel will stand in for the anchor-point of 'home' from where one goes on exploring other spots in the environment or even just the beach and back (which makes the beach another anchor-point and destination zone). The only exception to this notion is a person who continuously travels and who regards the environment (unconsciously) as a smooth space in which a lengthier intermission is neglected due to one's plans of moving on. The moment one returns to one spot and is no longer constantly 'on the road', an anchor-point has been established and the formation of a cognitive map can begin anew.

THE APPLIED METHOD

In the following the method is explained that will be applied in the consecutive chapters. It is founded on the postmodern notion that there is not one "single canon of geographical thought." (Dear and Flusty 2002: 9) This vantage point allows for the selection and combination of various approaches from within geography but also from different fields of studies. Geographers increasingly turn to and analyse "*cultural landscapes and place-making*" and put "an emphasis on the *construction of the individual and the boundaries of self*, including *human psychology and sexuality*" (ibid., original emphasis; cf. Mitchell 2000: xiv). As the ideas sketched in

25 The latter will be of no greater importance here as it is concerned with physical topography or density with regard to population (cf. Golledge 1999: 20).

this chapter have shown, cultural geography is already heavily influenced by various strands of other disciplines. Thus, it is no accident that it is referred to as *cultural* geography rather than human or behavioural geography. In the introductory remarks to this chapter the problems of distinguishing between narrowly defined human geography and cultural geography have been alluded to. Due to the cross-fertilising turns, both the cultural for geography and the spatial for cultural studies, not only the boundaries within one discipline blur, as is the postmodern fashion, but also between the various disciplines themselves. I am highly indebted to this trend, without which a text such as this would have not been possible and it is clear that this book marks another step in the process of intertwining these two academic discourses even more.

Already, the concepts and theories explained in this chapter are connected and intertwined and present themselves in the form of a method that has been alluded to before: the rhizome. Of this construct, Deleuze and Guattari write that

> unlike trees or their roots, the rhizome connects any point to any other point, and its traits are not necessarily linked to traits of the same nature[. ...] It has neither beginning nor end, but always a middle (*milieu*) from which it grows and which it overspills. [... T]he rhizome is made only of lines: lines of segmentarity and stratification as dimensions (1987: 23).

The rhizomatic structure of the method provides one with the possibility to start at any given point and follow various strands to other ideas within the construction, a specific or designated starting point is not needed. However, in order to come to conclusions and not get lost in an entanglement of theoretical ideas and concepts, a structuralist approach will help to tame the rhizome and process it into ordered channels, making it readable like a map.

The structuralist methods that will help to enable this venture are by Frenchmen Claude Lévi-Strauss and Roland Barthes[26]. They have devised a system each how to analyse stories by looking at smaller constituents that comprise any story[27]. Lévi-Strauss calls these gross constituent units *mythemes* (Lévi-Strauss 1974: 211), whereas Barthes calls them *semes* (1974: 17). Both are signifiers of a certain event, character traits or, broadly speaking, feature, which can come in many forms but will eventually follow rules. The great advantages of semes or mythemes become

26 Already the connection between Lévi-Strauss's structuralist ideas and geography has been explored in Gregory *Ideology, Science and Human Geography* (1978). However, the notion put forward by Gregory and what will be suggested here are hardly comparable.

27 The following description should be regarded as a companion piece to the cluster theory put forward in the previous chapter.

apparent, because they are not "isolated relations but *bundles of such relations*, and it is only as bundles that these relations can be put to use and combined so as to produce a meaning" (Lévi-Strauss 1974: 211, original emphasis). Just like constitutive parts within the rhizome they do not exist independently of one another. They are related, yet structuralism helps to divide them up and look at them in relation to others but also within one group of mythemes or semes. Both structuralists suggest clustering them according to their similar features in columns, creating an "orchestra score" (ibid.: 212, Barthes 1974: 29). But, indeed, there is a difference between mythemes and semes: never explicitly mentioned, Lévi-Strauss's mythemes are big building blocks that 'divide' the whole story up between them. This is also the reason why after one has structured the myth into mythemes, there are two ways to 'read' the myth:

> Were we to *tell* the myth, we would disregard the columns and read the rows from left to right and from top to bottom. But if we want to *understand* the myth, then we will have to disregard one half of the diachronic dimension (top to bottom) and read from left to right, column after column, each one being considered as a unit. (Lévi-Strauss 1974: 214, original emphasis)

At first, Barthes's semes go in the same direction: they, too, want to structure the text anew and reveal hidden meanings. But in contrast to mythemes, he chooses the words 'topos', 'utterances' and 'codes' to describe his semes (cf. Barthes 1974: 20-21), giving the impression that he works on a smaller scale than mythemes. He is more interested in the precise details, which is also supported by the idea that the voices are mere categories that can have myriads of sub-categories. The building blocks in geography are easily defined and can be extracted from the anchor-point-theory of behaviouralism: the lives of the novels' young urban professionals revolve around certain geographical locations which are their main anchor-points[28], namely the home, the workplace and wherever they choose to spend their free time: in shops, in clubs and at parties or being in places where they can have a drink or a meal.

The foundation is laid and for the next part the rhizome needs to be let loose again: chick- and ladlit narratives follow their respective agents very closely, either in the form of a first-person narration or figural narration. Yet, due to the actor-network-theory one does not need to discriminate between the various actors, structure, institution and agent as well as between the animate and inanimate objects. All will be analysed equally to reveal ideologies and to find out about simi-

28 The distinction between anchor-points is inspired by Arthur and Passini's idea of the major settings (environments) one deals with daily (cf. 1992: 77).

larities and differences, both spatial and cultural. This is done to investigate the characters' *locality*, which "is the space within which the large part of most citizens' daily working and consuming lives is lived. [...] Locality is thus a base from which subjects can exercise their capacity for pro-activity by making effective individual and collective interactions within and beyond that base." (Cooke 1989: 12) Doreen Massey's interpretation of locality sheds a different, yet complementary light on the matter: to her, localities are "nets of social relations" (1993: 148). Locality describes the idea that space is closely linked to social interaction and the relationships to other people that share certain spaces, which can be regarded on the different levels.

Now that the preliminaries of the method are made available and the rhizome has been restrained, albeit not entirely, a return to structuralism is beneficial: in Barthes's *S/Z*, he identifies five semes, which he also calls voices. Two are of greater importance here, namely the voice of the person and the voice of science[29]. The former is defined as a

> connotator of persons, places, objects, of which the signified is a character. [...] Even though the connotation may be clear, the nomination of its signified is uncertain, approximative, unstable: to fasten a name to this signified depends in large part on the critical pertinence to which we adhere: the seme [or mytheme] is only a departure, an avenue of meaning. (Barthes 1974: 190-191)

This is reminiscent of the memories Self speaks of: to him a place has certain connotations, sometimes shared by others (who might have shared that particular experience), sometimes only the characters themselves – it is always the starting point (departure) to delve into memories. It also discloses a possible ideology (cf. ibid.: 191) that the characters might not even be aware of but which is shared by their community, for example Notting Hill being a 'posh' place that has been taken over from former immigrants to Britain by rich people during the process of gentrification. The other voice, which Barthes also refers to as the referential code (cf. ibid.: 262), deals in cultural allusions and references the reader has to be aware of (cf. ibid.: 206). Again, a certain ideology comes into play here which links the two codes, the difference being that the voice of the person is strongly linked to a place or object, whereas the voice of science can also refer to more abstract concepts like the history of literature, to ethics or practical medicine (cf. ibid.: 205). Creating these voices, I will look at how characters turn spaces into places and, even more so, life spaces. This interrelation between humans, spatial behaviour and

29 The other voices are the voices of empirics, truth and the symbolic field (cf. Barthes 1974: 214-216).

consequentially places is also linked to sense of place and topophilia: what are common denominators among the characters to feel at home, how do they (spatially) choose one shop, pub or even lover over another? In order to compare and analyse these, Golledge's notion of processes is of great importance. As stated already, he lists "perception, learning, forming attitudes, memorizing, recalling and using spatial thinking" (2006: 75) as parameters to consider when analysing spatial usage. Finding semes that help to identify personal notions, ideologies (via structures and institutions) or how they influence romantic entanglements will be paramount in the following chapters.

Eventually, in order to prove the point that romantic choices are made because of spatial compatibility, the construction of cognitive maps is important. The structuralist features as identified by Lynch will help to give a first, if very cursory overview of the characters' life spaces. Nevertheless, in their very individual maps, the notions of heterotopias and territories play a vital role. Similar to districts, each person draws lines and consequentially edges differently. But, as a relationship needs (at least) two people, the maps have to be appropriated to accommodate other ideas of how a location is structured, which is where heterotopia and territories come in: for finding one's perfect partner, one needs to make adjustments, sacrifices or sometimes even the opposite, to take a stand – and these 'sparring matches' have to take place in space(s); it is even possible that some characters have to territorialise already territorialised areas anew in order to prove that they are worthy of being loved.

Where We Love Is Home

> The home should be the treasure chest of living.
> LE CORBUSIER

CONSTRUCTING A HOME

In his book *Cultural Geography*, Mike Crang writes that "[t]he creation of a sense of home [...] is a profoundly geographical construction in a [literary] text." (1998: 47) He even calls the concept of 'home' "[o]ne of the standard geographies in a text" (ibid.) and thus emphasises the necessity of the home as an interface between literature and geography. Although he continues to stress 'home' as point of departure as well as return, especially in chick- and ladlit it becomes more than just a location. It mirrors, anticipates and even foreshadows the action and emotional turmoil that lie ahead for the genres' main protagonists. It is striking that some critics talk about the home only in connection with departures and cite Odysseus as the great example linking literature, geography and (the) home (e.g. Terkenli and Heller). However, the Greek hero seems to spend more time *away* from home than being actually *there*, begging the question whether the home can be anything but a haven that one needs to leave in order to appreciate it. The main focus of this chapter is on the notion of home and how the protagonists in chick- and ladlit novels turn this particular space into a place: how do literary spatial agents behave inside homes and how do their dwellings affect the characters' search for love? Following a theoretical approach to the concept of 'home', which combines (cultural) geography with other disciplines, the first part is dedicated to depictions and organisations of dwellings. Here, the home as a mirror of its inhabitant will be focused upon. The next part emphasises the importance of spatial compatibility, which will henceforth be present in all subsequent analyses. Afterwards, four specific aspects of the home will be in the limelight: a case study on the idea of the kitchen, the importance of urban families and their meeting places, the notion of nostalgia with regard to memories and home and, lastly, the hotel as temporary home.

Starting with the theoretical background, many critics award the home a significant role within a territory – and rightly so: "Integral to the average everyday life is awareness of a fixed point in space, a firm position from which we 'proceed' (whether every day or over large periods of time) and to which we return in due course. This firm position is what we call 'home'" (Heller 1984: 239). The home can therefore be compared to the human heart[1]: it becomes the central organ which enables the inhabitant(s) to travel the whole of the body (territory) and to which they (ideally) return in order to recharge. It is after all a person's major anchor-point of the first order (see chapter 3), which doubles as a landmark within a certain geographical space of a(n in)definite size: "Home is hearth, an *anchoring point* through which human beings are centred." (Blunt and Dowling 2006: 11, emphasis added) Here, the notion of the anchor-point is heightened as the home becomes the centre of a person's life, the most important point of reference and orientation. Working with Reginald Golledge's idea of equating anchor-points with landmarks (cf. 1999: 17, Couclelis et al. 1987: 102), they both share the quality of organising (cognitive) maps and of functioning as a homing device when one practises way-finding. The home as anchor-point can be very individual, like a landmark, but unlike a landmark, it can be very abstract at the same time: one can regard a location as home, one's abode's address, but calling a neighbourhood, district or even country 'home' is just as likely (cf. Fox O'Mahony and Sweeney 2011: 4).

In her article "Where Are We at Home?" Agnes Heller tells anecdotes that question this static nature of 'home' (as house or dwelling in general). She argues that for some home is the town they were born in and to which they have a very strong connection, for others it is wherever they stay the night or can bring their cat and for others still it is the place they have spent much time in and money on in order to model it according to their dreams, convictions, abilities[2] (cf. Massey 1992, Silverstone 1994, Terkenli 1995, Mallett 2004, Blunt and Dowling 2006, Deane and

---

1 The home as heart can be linked to the function of the core, which is a node whose "concentration [is] the focus and epitome of a district, over which [the highly frequented node's] influence radiates" (Lynch 1960: 48). For the home's inhabitant(s), it becomes the most significant point of 'changing' paths.

2 That 'home' does not need to include an actual address can be seen with homeless people or asylum seekers: homeless people do not have an abode, but might consider various locales such as abandoned houses, bridges or cardboard boxes 'home'. Emigrants' homes, on the other hand, might exist but in a location they are no longer able to access, because they are located in countries they had to flee from or their homes have since been destroyed (cf. Ahmed 1999). These "dwellings and experiences […] may appear 'unhomely' since they do not correspond to normative notions of home." (Blunt and Dowling 2006: 26)

Schuch 2010): "the sense that we are at home is not simply a feeling but an emotional disposition, a framework-emotion that accounts for the presence of many particular kinds of emotions like joy, sorrow, nostalgia, intimacy, consolation, pride, and the absence of others." (Heller 1995: 5; cf. Putnam 1999: 144) The emotional side to 'home' therefore becomes a very important one, especially when one looks at the state of relationships and the quest to find love: "[the] home is a place invested with special social meaning and significance where particular kinds of social relations and activities are composed, accomplished and contextualised. Peace and tranquillity may pertain for some times but conflict, violence and tension are also characteristics of home." (Saunders and Williams 1988: 82) Echoing these ideas, Alison Blunt and Robyn Dowling further elaborate on them by stating that 'home' becomes "a *spatial imaginary*: a set of intersecting and variable ideas and feelings, which are related to context, and which construct places, extend across spaces and scales, and connect places." (2006: 2, original emphasis; cf. Tuan 1977: 166) For these critics, 'home' is less of a location than a heightened locale. 'Home' is a concept, which "carries a heavy ideological burden [...]; it can be seen as part of an ideological trinity: 'family,' 'home,' and 'community'." (Munro and Madigan 1999: 107) 'Home' becomes the centre, the most important anchor-point[3], of a person's life, and this home can take a flexible shape, size or constitution – it can embrace one's family (micro level), but also the human environment of a community (meso level) or even the whole country (macro level). This is also acknowledged by Terkenli, who states that the various "concepts of home increasingly shed their spatial character [e.g. location-al; C.L.] to become contingent on flows of information, exchange of ideas, long-distance connections, and proliferations of lifestyles." (1995: 324) 'Home' is both a concept and an emotionally charged version of dwelling space, an interface. Martin Heidegger, in his essay "Building, Dwelling, Thinking", makes a distinction between the first two concepts which will be helpful here. He writes that "[d]welling and building are related as end and means." (2012: 22) Though separated in this distinction, Heidegger does not see these concepts as mutually exclusive, far from it: he deems them reciprocally determining. The building[4] makes dwelling possible, but at the same time it is the

3 Even if the feelings or experiences should be of a negative variety, the home still becomes a very important anchor-point. It influences/influenced the person in such a way that it might impress itself very deeply in that person's psyche. This might result in a feeling of topophobia.

4 I am aware that Heidegger is mixing two kinds of words here, as he distinguishes between the verb and the noun of building and dwelling. However, I believe that it does make sense to be able to use them interchangeably for the purpose of summarising his argument.

wish or need to dwell which enables (the) building. The home as an interface becomes the articulation between the physical manifestation of the building – in variable forms: house, flat, caravan, etc. – and the idea of dwelling, living and belonging: the emotional attachment that "is at the core of how people situate themselves in the world." (Putnam 1999: 144)

Emotions turn 'home' into a heavily invested place (human) beings mould from space in order to live or be: "Home is a construct. It is a place not a space. It is the object of more or less intense emotion. It is where we [as people; C.L.] belong. […] Home, substantial or insubstantial, fixed or shifting, singular or plural, is what we can make of it." (Silverstone 1994: 26) 'Home' as centre or core of a territory "confers three substantial benefits on its occupants [which are] identity, security, and stimulation."[5] (Porteous 1976: 383) Porteous's triad will serve as the foundation for the analysis of 'home' as an interface between the novels' protagonists and their surroundings, friends as well as potential lovers and partners. Identity, security and stimulation inform the protagonists' actions and how they perceive their dwelling as well as how they *are perceived* through their abode by other characters. But it should be understood that 'home' is not an essentialist concept: "Places do not intrinsically have home-like characteristics (safe, secure, welcoming, etc.); we develop these feelings for places over time." (Duyvendak 2011: 37) Human beings can turn a space into a place and turn a place into a home, but this is not a transformation which happens naturally.

Starting with the first part of the triad, identity, it proves to be crucial for humans as their identity tends to develop in accordance with their home: whereas Jaime Horwitz and Jerome Tognoli cautiously "speculated that not only do people's concepts of home change but that their experiences of homes were differentiated by their developmental needs[, that] homes 'fit' differently at different times in their lives" (1982: 335), Theano S. Terkenli is more confident. He proclaims that "[t]he concept of home alters with the passage of time and the accumulation of age. The process unfolds within an individual's lifeworld and lifetime" (1995: 330). What Terkenli means is that the first 'home' of humans is their mother's womb which

5 This triad varies depending on the critic: Massey speaks of stability, oneness and security (cf. 1992: 11), Saunders and Williams of privacy, privatism and privatization (cf. 1988: 88-91). However, I will concentrate on Porteous's triad because homes do not necessarily present 'oneness' (Massey) as homes can consist of outsourced rooms (which will be explained further down) and Saunders and Williams emphasise the private sphere too much, which is too closely linked to the home as prison. I deem Porteous's definition the most fruitful for it acknowledges the different ways in which the home can present itself and become a connection to the outside world.

they have to leave due to – literally – outgrowing it. Following a juvenile period in their parents'/parent's home(s), humans tend to move out and on into their own or shared residencies. Each experience one makes not only adds to one's personal growth but can also be traced via souvenirs in a person's home[6]. It can therefore be said that the home is constantly worked upon by making additions, subtractions, but also by influences from family, peers, strangers. It expands till it inevitably shrinks with old age when the geriatric body restricts movement and this process culminates in death which physically dissociates the body from the home (cf. ibid.). Hence, it mirrors the dweller's identity as they might change their 'home' according to their changing needs and tastes. A slightly different account is given by Margaret Jane Radin, whose theory's "core [is] the idea that an individual's attachment to a particular property, for example their home, may be so strong that the particular property becomes constitutive of their personhood." (Qtd. in Fox O'Mahony and Sweeney 2011: 3) She suggests the idea that a home is not only constructed to fit the resident, it is essential in creating the resident's identity, posing as a double-foil: the home mirrors the dweller and vice versa. Thus, Blunt and Dowling's statement "[h]ome does not simply exist, but is made" (2006: 23) has to be expanded by claiming '... and makes the dweller just as much.' This idea emphasises that "defining a 'home base' is one of the multiple facets of the structure of each period in adult life." (Levinson, qtd. in Horwitz and Tognoli 1982: 336) It ties in with the constant accretion of 'home' stated above as each expansion or, more generally, alteration results in a re-evaluation of the understanding of one's abode. It might not always mean a bigger change to one's previously established concept or definition, but it can lead to the realisation that 'home' is indeed anything but a space one likes to return to and which is then abandoned in search of new territories to call home. Sometimes, one outgrows one's home and needs to venture out to seek a new space that can accommodate one's evolved self.

Looking at the home concerning the aspect of security – the second of Porteous's features – it means that one's abode is the place which also functions as a retreat in which one can feel safe and unchallenged from the outside world. Living in or even owning a dwelling "can [...] provide a sense of place and belonging in an increasingly alienating world" (Mallett 2004: 66; cf. Duyvendak 2011: 27) which strongly suggests an aspect of security attached to the notion of 'home'. Of course, living in and, to an even greater extent, owning a home has strong connections to consumption, status and class. Belonging and knowing where one belongs can attribute greatly to one's sense of security as it means that one does not need to trouble oneself with questions like 'where do I sleep tonight?', 'where

6 The souvenir can be either a mere memory or an embodiment of any kind that links a thought to this object.

can I keep my memories so that they are safe from others?' and many more. That these fears are not entirely new can be seen in the following quote by Victorian poet John Ruskin, in which he addresses the notion of security as an important aspect of 'home':

> This is the true nature of home – it is the place of Peace; the shelter, not only from all injury, but from all terror, doubt, and division. In so far as it is not this, it is not home; so far as the anxieties of the outer life penetrate into it, and the inconsistently minded, unknown, unloved, or hostile society of the outer world is allowed by either husband or wife to cross the threshold, it ceases to be home; it is then only a part of that outer world which you have roofed over, and lightened a fire in. But so far as it is a sacred place, a vestal temple, a temple of the hearth watched over by Household Gods[7], before whose faces none may come but those whom they can receive with love, [...] – shade as of the rock in a weary land, and light as of the Pharos in a stormy sea; – so far it vindicates the name, and fulfils the praise, of Home. (1865: 147-149)

Additional to the features of "Peace" and love (cf. Archibald 2002: 6), which account for a certain (positive) sense of place, Ruskin especially stresses the idea of the home being a stronghold against the "injuries" and "anxieties" one has to endure. The home is presented as the safe haven against the 'cruelties' that one might be confronted with outside one's abode. The metaphor that the home is a lighthouse, which guides the dweller back to their secure stronghold, evokes again the idea of Odysseus lost at sea: just like him, humans tend to cherish the idea of having a sheltered place to call home. It is thus rather fitting to term the space of one's dwelling a "pocket of local order" (Hägerstrand 1985, Ellegård and Vilhelmson 2004: 283). The pocket is a "specific defined section of time-space [...] endowed with particular infrastructure [which] has a more or less formal system of regulation to facilitate the execution of [...] activities" (Lenntorp 2004: 225). It can be established at any location that supports an infrastructure which leads to the (successful) completion of projects or activities, which it shields "from destructive outside-world influences." (Ellegård and Vilhelmson 2004: 283; cf. Pennartz 1999: 98-101, Mallett 2004: 63) Additionally, this space needs to be a locale one can return to, thus ruling out 'one-off' locations. The pocket can be a well-connected workplace, a fully functioning camper van or, as Kajsa Ellegård and Bertil Vilhelmson argue, home. People can create their own (life)world within the proverbial 'four

7 The notion of the "Household Gods" can be linked to Roman goddess Vespa but also – and indeed more fittingly for Victorian ideology – to the 'Angel in the House', which is "the ideal of womanhood in the age of Queen Victoria [...] – the selflessly devoted and submissive wife and mother." (Hoffmann 2007: 264)

walls' and thus be the kings and queens of their own life. However, "the space of the house does not become a place of 'home' until people have gone through the process of placing and ordering furniture and other objects." (Hui 2011: 69) Whatever the place eventually looks like, the more it reflects its inhabitant(s), the more likely they are to feel secure and at home.

The act of constructing a home for oneself or for one's family is therefore imperative to stimulation, the last of Porteous's aforementioned features. Home is a space that furthers the creativity that finds an expression in the projects and activities, which can produce diverse results such as crafts projects, tending to plants and gardens or manufacturing goods but also attitudes and ideas. Ellegård and Vilhelmson (2004) mention activities ranging from watching TV and reading to preparing dinner or engaging with the other people living in the home. The activities one engages in inside one's home are shielded from the outside, the aspect of security, and therefore the dwellers might actually indulge in practices or activities they assume the outside world would not support or deem appropriate. The stimulation dwellers experience can also be found in the place itself, for example in the look of the various rooms. It can lead to realisation of one's dream house.

The notion of stimulation is also a major bone of contention for some feminist geographers as they deem the home to be a space of submissive female work (cf. Blunt and Dowling 2006: 15), which is not dedicated to stimulation in terms of leisure and pleasure. There is even recourse to Odysseus by citing his faithful wife "Penelope[, who is] sitting by the hearth and [is] weaving, saving and preserving the home while her man roams the earth in daring adventures"[8], as the prime illustration of the exploited female (Young 1997: 134; cf. Crang 1998: 48). These women cannot engage in practices that are not directly related to making the home more comforting and welcoming for the male. The home becomes a workplace and as such does not pose an antipode to the actual office (should there be one), just as it does not primarily promote a space of one's own, to paraphrase Virginia Woolf. Doreen Massey writes that "[t]he construction of 'home' as a woman's place has, moreover, carried through into those views of place itself as a source of stability, reliability and authenticity." (1994: 180) This idea of the connection of the female to 'home' introduces a positive idea but ultimately exposes the home as the only place in which a woman is able to achieve Massey's three sources. Additionally, women appear to achieve these sources for husbands and children and hardly for their (single) selves. That this is not an archaic sentiment can be seen in Daniel

8 This is actually an oversimplification as Odysseus spends as much time at war as he is trying to get home. The adventures he experiences might sound thrilling, yet the underlying driving force of the *Odyssey* is the hero's wish to return home.

Miller's *A Theory of Shopping* in which he reflects on the connection between consumption and the home:

> By experiencing their daily shopping as the provisioning of a household, and only separating themselves out as recipients for special 'treats', [women] can use this normative structure of shopping to reconstitute themselves as a *variant of the household*, rather than an individual. Shopping is directed to the household itself that *simply happens, for the moment, to have only one person in it.* (1998: 121, emphasis added)

Miller characterises women "as a variant of the household", and goes even further by stating that there should be more people than just one woman living it: in his opinion, women are merely waiting for the man to turn them from house-women into house-wives. I share the concerns about Miller's opinion with feminist critics (cf. Reimer and Leslie 2004: 192), especially as Miller's phrasing has misogynist tendencies. The idea that the home is said to be a female space can be traced back to the opinion that it was considered to be a woman's *only* space: "Stemming from such varied sources as de Tocqueville and Engels, the logic of separate spheres asserts that in contrast to the public (male) sphere, women's sphere was private, the realm of the domestic and the sentimental", which leads Elizabeth Klimasmith to conclude that "[c]onsidered spatially, the women's sphere *was* the home." (2005: 7, emphasis added) According to her and other feminist (cultural) geographers, women used to suffer under the clear distinction of the public (male) sphere and the private (female) sphere: "The attempt to confine women to the domestic sphere was both a specifically spatial control and, through that, a social control on identity." (Massey 1994: 179) Yet, at the same time, it appears that the domestic sphere holds great potential for stimulation, in this case for the woman as writer[9]: "Since domestic space and the novel have paradoxically constrained and liberated women's ways of knowing, writing, and being, the encoding and decoding of house and novel and domesticity as the sphere of women are integral to an understanding of this symbiosis." (Mezei and Briganti 2002: 844) The home can thus present itself not only as a stimulating location that furthers the creative output that is directly visible in the purchasing or arranging of furniture or the creative vision of the garden, but also in the literary description and furnishing of novels which will be shown in this chapter. "Home, then, is a manifestation of an investment of meaning in space. It is a claim we make about a place. It is constructed through social relations which are

9 There are of course other examples of what has been produced by stimulated females in the sphere of the home: Margarete Steiff created her famous toys in her home which doubled as (work)shop, Emily Blackwell turned a home into a hospital and Frida Kahlo painted most of her famous self-portraits at home.

both internal and external and constantly shifting in their power and significance." (Silverstone 1994: 28) Women and their relation to space have undergone significant changes which are reflected – and sometimes even contested – in chicklit novels.

HOME AS MIRROR

Turning to the home in chick- and ladlit, it becomes clear very quickly that it is one of the most important features in the protagonists' search for themselves and their perfect partners. As most of the narratives are written from a first-person point of view, they reflect the characters' inner, mostly unacknowledged selves, including their dreams, desires, fears and problems: "We create our immediate environment and then contemplate it and are worked on by it. We find ourselves mirrored in it, see what had been not yet visible, and integrate the reflection back into our sense of self." (Yandell 2006: xv) Possible as the integration may be, it is also a process which hardly ever happens consciously in the novels. Many of the characters only realise their lack (of whatever kind) in their geographical sphere by trying to add to it and find that they do indeed need to work on their locale which equals their selves. In the following, the analysis will concern itself mainly with two novels and will look at the construction of homes in *About a Boy* (ladlit) and *Bridget Jones's Diary* (chicklit) because, from them, the most important motives in the two genres with regard to the home can be deduced. The insights gained from these two novels can be applied to almost all the other novels in the corpus. Moreover, in the following subchapters homes in other novels will be looked at and thus complement this first foray which has been made with Hornby's and Fielding's novels.

The first home to consider is that of Will Freeman (*About a Boy*), who is a confirmed bachelor and believes that he has everything under control. He is the sole centre of his life and his idea of home mirrors this belief perfectly. During a visit to friends of his, Will observes with horror the omnipresent

> [c]*lutter*! Will's friend John's house was full of it. John and Christine had two children – the second had been born the previous week, and Will had been summoned to look at it – and their place was, Will couldn't help thinking, a *disgrace*. Pieces of brightly coloured plastic were strewn all over the floor, videotapes lay out of their cases near the TV set, the white throw over the sofa looked as if it had been used as a piece of gigantic toilet paper, although Will preferred to think that the stains were chocolate... How could people live like this? (Hornby 1998: 15, emphasis added)

Will's idea of a perfect life is equated with a perfect home, which is clean and stylish. He cannot deal with "clutter" and thinks that people who do not have their home under control are equally unable to control themselves or their lives (cf. Hornby 1998: 17)[10]. Being in his friends' house, Will's concept of 'home' mirroring or indeed metonymically re-presenting one's self has him come to the conclusion that, as John and Christine's home is characterised by clutter, Will can no longer be friends with them. He wants his life in order and his perception of John and Christine's clutter is reminiscent of an illness: Will does not want to 'catch' his former friends' new way of life, which is representing responsibility for another person. To him their previously compatible spheres no longer gel and a separation of spheres and thus lives is inevitable. Will wants to keep his clutter-free, responsibility-shunning life his Peter-Pan-persona is a signifier for. The fact that he deems the cluttered home a "disgrace" points towards Will's idea of a disturbed pocket of local order (cf. Putnam 1999: 146): John and Christine's home is no longer under their jurisdiction, their security and stimulation – in Will's mind – have been compromised and can only reflect their degradation, their fall from grace. This 'grace' is only *his* standard, though. His life – and consequently the usage of his home – is likened to a specific concept of Will's own making: "You had to live in your own *bubble*. You couldn't force your way into someone else's, because then it wouldn't be a *bubble* any more." (Hornby 1998: 70, emphasis added) He deems himself a solitary individual and is only 'visiting' other people's lives and homes. Yet, the moment these visits tend to intrude on his bubble, by getting drawn into other people's lives for example, or have ceased to be fun in the sense of watching a real-life drama[11], he stops coming to these other locales. John and Christine can no longer lead a detached life like Will does: their clutter means – for Will – that there will be constant 'baggage', in the form of children. For a shallow character like Will, oneself is enough and thus taking care of himself is reflected in taking care of his solitary bubble, his home. As his friends have to care for little children and their spouses, something had to give and it is the self-centred attitude Will is able to maintain, his Peter-Pan-persona, that is now absent from John and Christine.

10 Will transfers his idea of clutter to everyone else around him. John and Christine might have had a disorganised lifestyle before, yet it is only when the children arrive that Will starts to 'realise' the clutter, thus equating children with the disturbance of the balance.

11 Due to a chain of accidents, he is present when Marcus finds his mother, who has just attempted suicide, as well as when she is reanimated in hospital. Will remarks drily that "[i]t had all been very interesting, but he wouldn't want to do it every night." (Hornby 1998: 71)

To Will, his home is not only his place but it is the centre of a bubble of indefinite size, his territory. He regards his surroundings as his personal TV, in which a performance is daily aired to humour him – he just needs to engage the TV set, by going outside and watching others. Will is not fazed by anything, merely amused. This ideology of disengagement is presented in one rather striking incident: "When [Will] got home, he put a Pet Shop Boys CD on, and watched *Prisoner: Cell Block H* with the sound down. He wanted to hear people who didn't mean it, and he wanted to watch people he could laugh at." (Ibid.: 98) The two activities are not compatible, the acoustic and the visual signals that are filling his home must result in Will not being able to concentrate on both at the same time. It demonstrates that he is not interested in the content of the texts but in the spectacle that can be created with them. The laddish behaviour and attitude of 'not meaning it' is emphasised here, too: not only is Will hardly ever capable of 'meaning it', he treats humans and events as 'things' he can use in any way which pleases him. He does not want clutter in his home or life because that would mean that he would have to deal with the realities of life and start to reflect on certain parts of his life as well as potentially re-think his priorities. Additionally, Will and his bubble are 'light' in the sense that they are not dragged down by clutter, they are airy and fleeting. One cannot tie down a bubble, just as Will cannot and will not be tied down whilst being in this bubble.

The reason Will is not going to be able to keep up this solitary existence in his bubble is the infiltration of his home by young Marcus, who uses Will's self-inflicted bubble of insular existence to hide from bullies and thus the reality of life, doubling Will and his usage of his home. Now, Will has to deal with another solitary mind in his bubble:

> When Will had conceived his fantasy and joined SPAT [Single Parents Alone Together], he had imagined sweet little children, not children who would be able to track him down and come to his house. He had imagined entering their world, but he hadn't foreseen that they might be able to penetrate his. He was one of life's visitors; he didn't want to be visited. (Ibid.: 101)

This quote shows that Will lives in a fantasy world in which he is able to "imagine" things. It was only a matter of time until his bubble had to burst. The invasion of his bubble marks the beginning of cluttering Will's glossy fantasy existence. Therefore, Will is wary and tries not to engage too much with Marcus, lest he encourages the boy to come even more frequently. But it is exactly this idea of being alone together – mirroring the motto of Will's 'self-help group' – that has Marcus feel safe and welcome. At the same time, Marcus's visits result in Will opening up to other people: he becomes more deeply involved with Marcus and the boy's family situation, which is a first step into re-assessing his bubble idea. It exposes another quality of the bubble, namely that it is highly fragile, always prone to bursting and giving itself up to its environment.

When Will meets Rachel at a party, he realises for the first time that he might be actually too shallow for another person. It appears that his bubble and thus usage of home and life have prevented him from growing up, from being a man Rachel could be interested in: "Because the thing was that when this Rachel woman sat down next to him at dinner she was interested, for the first five minutes, before she'd worked him out, and in that five minutes he got a glimpse of what life could be like if he were in any way interesting." (Hornby 1998: 180) This event marks the first time that Will doubts his strategy of cherishing his clutter-free life inside a bubble when he engages with a woman. He realises that he more than 'likes' Rachel. Previously, Will has always been very suspicious of falling in love because friends of his who were in love "could no longer control themselves, or protect themselves, [they were] people who, if only temporarily, were no longer content to occupy their own space [...] to make them complete." (Ibid.: 179) Will is afraid of compromising his solitary bubble, which he deems the inevitable consequence of falling in love and 'meaning it'. This complements Rachel's initial reading of Will as his laddish behaviour of 'wasting time' on subjects is rather unfit for her. Will's pop-cultural knowledge marks him as a solitary man, for he likes to enjoy activities alone at home, combining the features of security, stimulation and identity of Porteous's triad. As a single mother, Rachel wants a man in her life who is not afraid to share his space, and Will derives most of his identity from his solitary bubble.

His home thus needs to be penetrable and a first step has been made by Marcus. Without the boy, Will would not be able to realise that "[h]e wanted Rachel to be his wife, his lover, the *centre of his whole world*" (ibid.: 197, emphasis added). The bubble begins to dissolve and Will starts to think on a larger scale now: instead of remaining on a micro level that clearly is under his control (till the advent of Marcus), he opens up and sees beyond his nose and realises that there is a whole world to be had. This idea is verbalised at the end of the novel when Will is compared to "a chick whose egg had been cracked open" (ibid.: 281). The fragile, transparent bubble has been transformed into an incubator and Will 'hatches' from behind a wall that has been shielding him off. The fact that an egg shell is opaque means that the translucency of the bubble had been an illusion: Will could not see what was really 'going on' around him, a metaphor supported by his perception that his surroundings are there for his amusement only. Rachel's affection and the relationship to Marcus have turned him from a lad into a man. This development of the lad who comes into his own can be observed in many ladlit novels: the idea of opening up one's place and not be averse to the idea to develop the place into a heterotopia is part of the central narrative which drives the lads to man up and be there for their eventual perfect partners.

In *Bridget Jones's Diary* the reader is invited into the home of a single female chicklit protagonist. Bridget's home is an environment which is comprised of different locales and which, on closer inspection, expresses a strong connection to the outside world – unlike Will's disengaging bubble. This relationship with the outside world is referred to by Bridget's fear of "dying alone and being found three weeks later half-eaten by an Alsatian." (Fielding 1998: 20; cf. 33) Bridget and her friends struggle with the constant angst of not being able to perform as well in society as they could have (or is expected of them) and thus die without a partner. Due to their Singleton status they feel the constant need to establish a connection to the outside world. The fact that this anxiety of dying alone is an urban (singles') myth somehow does not penetrate their ideology as they constantly put themselves in the position of the lonely person – thus they 'agree' to and even espouse the marginalised position they are constantly pushed into by non-single characters. Although Bridget does not gain as much stimulation from her home as Will, ultimately both characters derive a large part of their identity from their homes. Moreover, as both genres have a strong romance plotline, this identity is always aimed at being attractive to the opposite sex: chicklit heroines use their homes to make themselves appealing to men and ladlit protagonists need to leave their bubbles behind and brave the outside world. In the former case the home 'constructs' the identity, in the latter case the home obstructs it. With regard to *Bridget Jones's Diary*, two spaces typically associated with women will be examined in the following part of this subchapter: the kitchen and the bathroom. In these spaces Bridget tries to present herself as a homemaker and constructs a 'beautiful body', respectively.

Starting with the kitchen, Bridget is unable to manage the space of her flat or think of a proper way to host a party in order to accommodate both her friends and her own expectations. The kitchen proves to be too defiant a space for Bridget: she can access her kitchen but has no idea or skill to penetrate and striate it. It is not a space in which Bridget excels, as her repeated failed attempts at meals prove. Her flat thus does not really comply with the idea of stimulation as she appears incapable of commanding her kitchen to produce some variety of food: "[I c]annot go on. [I h]ave just stepped in a pan of mashed potato […] forgetting that kitchen floor and surfaces were covered in pans of mince and mashed potato." (Ibid.: 82-83) It seems that even simple dishes – here: shepherd's pie – are beyond Bridget's capacity. Moreover, she is more interested in the image she can present, namely posing as a "brilliant cook and hostess." (Ibid.: 82) There is no other way but for her to fail in her endeavour. Her kitchen does not provide her with any kind of stimulation which also reflects on her identity: she is no brilliant cook and her qualities as hostess are equally questionable. Bridget cannot come to terms with the fact that having a kitchen does not automatically mean that it provides her with the identity of a cook or homemaker. Her lack of culinary skills is both subversive and affirming gender stereotypes at the same time: Bridget is depicted as a woman who has never needed to cook or to provide a home for a husband, she has always had a career to consider. Her inability to compose a meal thus signifies her freedom from traditional norms. But Bridget wants to be able to cook and thus to be able to provide for a family. This is evident when she practises cooking with her urban family from which she hopes to graduate to her own biological family (see chapter 4). To make matters worse for her, she is constantly juxtaposed with her married friend Magda.

When her birthday dinner inevitably falls through, it ends in a place where professional chefs can produce edible food – namely a restaurant: "It turned out Magda had booked a table at 192 and told everyone to go there instead of my flat [...]. Magda said they had had a weird, almost spooky sixth sense that the Grand Marnier soufflé and frizzled lardon thing were not going to work out." (Fielding 1998: 84) Not only is Bridget overrating her skills in the kitchen, her friends – and especially her married friend Magda – are aware of this fact. This assessment by Magda clearly elevates her over Bridget: the housewife is presented as far more capable than Bridget, as she anticipates and averts the crisis Bridget produces in her kitchen. The novel appears to imply that only married women can be good homemakers or housewives. Single women, however, are not able to operate kitchen devices or to create a tasty meal for they spend most of their time in bars, not cooking. It thus comes as no surprise that the party convenes at a bar, thus establishing a connection between the kitchen-wise useless heroine and her perfect housewife friend. However, whereas the perfection of the housewife is never questioned, her happiness is. One striking example is Bridget's mother, who, after years of looking after her husband and children, decides "to change things a bit and spend what's left of [her life] looking after [herself] for a change." (Ibid.: 54) But at the end of the novel her 'escape' from her former life fails and she is reinstalled in the home. Bridget's mother wants more from life but the narrative seems to state that the housewife cannot exist outside her home[12].

---

12 The concept of the housewife is ridiculed in La'Brooy's novel *Love Struck*: here the main protagonist's sister is described as "a bit like Martha Stewart and has the added complication of being a Virgo. This has its positive side, as she does lovely domesticated, outdated things like making her own Christmas cards, and she always has fresh potpourri and vanilla-scented candles on her polished wooden kitchen table. It can also have its negative side, as she has a manic, anal-retentive approach to housekeeping that borders on the clinically insane." (2003: 23) Additional to the fact that the sister is regarding her home as more important than her boyfriend or family,

Following the kitchen as a signifier of the (im)perfect housewife, the bathroom is under scrutiny now, as a place to beautify the woman. Bridget is leading a lifestyle that is centred on the body and her never-ending quest to manipulate her body according to beauty ideals so as to attract an eligible bachelor:

> Being a woman is worse than being a farmer – there is so much harvesting and crop spraying to be done: legs to be waxed, underarms shaved, eyebrows plucked, feet pumiced, skin exfoliated and moisturized, spots cleansed, roots dyed, eyelashes tinted, nails filed, cellulite massaged, stomach muscles exercised. [She concludes:] Is it any wonder girls have no confidence? (Ibid.: 30).

Most of these tasks are taken on in the bathroom, making the place more a beauty salon than a room in which one showers or uses the toilet. In chicklit, the single female's bathroom is a place of manipulating the body, of shaping it into a version of femininity which hopefully appeals to men. Bridget even compares the process of pre-date preparations with farming and harvesting: it becomes a full-time job and thus there is no time to be lost in the bathroom that is not dedicated to the body. The bathroom might be within the female's flat or house, yet most activities in this space are dedicated to men and therefore it becomes a male place as well. It fuses these two spheres in the manner of the heterotopia for it houses two different notions – the actual locale and the one that is shaped by the ideology of the perfect female body. However critical Bridget actually is of this strict body harvesting, she still follows this 'beauty' regimen. The beauty dictate exposes the bathroom as another room that is first and foremost dedicated to her hunt for Mr Right – just as the cooking was meant to pass her off as a homemaker, or rather good wife and mother. She bows to the 'naturalised' ideology of a woman needing to look beautiful, and the lifestyle magazines Bridget reads only further encourage this belief (cf. Smith 2008). The bathroom, or more accurately, the body farm therefore establishes a connection to the outside world as all the efforts which are undertaken in private will be exposed to the public afterwards[13].

---

already the description of her positive features hint at a "domesticated" and "outdated" person: this woman is not able to live outside the security of her home which enables her identity of the perfect housewife.

13 A similar process of preparation can be found in Indian chicklit novel *Piece of Cake*, proving that the genre's topics, motifs and motives are transnational despite the different cultural contexts. Main protagonist Minal uses her home as beauty salon to dress up for a date with a neighbour of hers and another time to attend a wedding. The latter is never described, merely the preparations for it, elevating the act of beautification over the act of getting married. The preparations for the party to

It has been observed by critics that "[t]he house is an extension of the person; like an extra skin, carapace or second layer of clothes [...]. House, body and mind are in continuous interaction" (Carsten and Hugh-Jones 1995: 2). Linda McDowell goes even a bit further and claims that "houses are often thought of as bodies, sharing common features and fates which affect the sense of self." (1999: 93) Applying these thoughts to Bridget's flat, it suggests that indeed her place is more directed towards attracting the outside – in the form of single men – instead of using her home as a secure place in which she undertakes activities for herself: she wants to impress with her cooking and harvests her body to be considered attractive by men. None of these practices are adopted for herself as they always carry the connotation of public visibility. Additionally, through her attempts in both these spaces to present herself as a different person from who she really is, Bridget tries to convey the impression that she is able to regulate both spaces and therefore herself. This is supposed to show her as being in control (of herself) and that she is not a liability when it comes to being presentable – as she wonders at a book launch (Fielding 1998: 98-104). The result, however, is not as convincing as she has hoped. The home becomes a mirror of an idealised self that fashions Bridget as the perfect, yet docile and domicile woman. Her 'uselessness' in the kitchen and her behaviour in the public sphere, which includes drinking too much alcohol and smoking cigarettes, expose this image of the good (house)wife as being far from reality. The kitchen is abandoned and the day-long preparations at the domestic body farm are juxtaposed with unrestrained behaviour by getting drunk at bars. Bridget is aware of the social pressure on women and observes that "one must not live one's life through men but must be complete in oneself as a woman of substance." (Ibid.: 31) However, she will undergo the same procedures of do(mi)cile femininity time and again, and therefore she renders this statement useless – not least because only a few hours later Bridget doubts herself and wails: "What's wrong with me?" (Ibid.) If she does not change her spatial behaviour of her home

---

which Minal's neighbour is taking her cost her "eight thousand and six hundred rupees [...] and sixteen mindless hours" (Kaushal 2004: 109) and include a visit to an official salon for a makeover. Although she lists the costs, she never complains. When she dresses up for the wedding she comments on the fact that she looks like a "mannequin" (ibid.: 190). In both cases she becomes a hypertrophied version of femininity, but when a date is involved, Minal accepts her objectified status: at both events Minal presents herself as a different person from her 'everyday-self' but only in connection to the wedding that she has to attend does she regard her hypertrophied self as "disgusting" (ibid.), because the event is not directly associated with an eligible man.

and thus her idea about herself needing to be appealing to men, she will not to be able to shed the shackles of these self-doubts in relation to men.

Whereas the interior of Bridget's flat is more characterised by her actions – or mishaps – the street she lives in is described in another way. It is constructed in opposition to the spaces of Smug Marrieds – the antipodes to the Singletons. Although not clearly demarcated as only inhabited by Singletons, the space of Bridget's street is described in a way that suggests that it is not a place for families or happily married couples[14]. When Magda finds out that her husband has cheated on her, she furiously drives to Bridget's flat, but once there her car's burglar alarm goes off and Magda is not able to turn it off again. The alarm announces Magda as an intruder into Bridget's locale, as further emphasised by her smug-married lifestyle: "Magda is very posh. Our street is not very posh. It is the kind which still has posters in the window saying 'Free Nelson Mandela'[15]." (Ibid.: 109) Because the spheres of Singletons and Smug Marrieds hardly ever mix – save for social events which have Bridget always feeling inferior and humiliated (see chapter 6) – the advent of a smug(ly) married person must be introduced with a loud noise. This hubbub signifies that someone who does not belong originally – as Magda is married – is intruding into the space of the street and that something horrible has happened which demands attention: Magda might separate from her cheating husband, exposing marriage as a potentially flawed concept. Previously, Magda has been portrayed as the capable, efficient housewife and as superior to Bridget's bumbling, inefficient Singleton. Now that Magda's status as a married woman is in danger of being degraded to divorcée and Singleton, she needs Bridget's help and expertise. It is more remarkable that married people experience a crisis than if the same happens to Singletons, because their relationships are deemed unstable anyway until they 'put a ring on it' as all the married couples in the book repeatedly say. The uninvited intrusion thus needs to be announced in order to mark the crossing of borders. Magda visits a space that is characterised by inefficiency (Bridget's culinary disaster) and singledom. The constantly sounding alarm can therefore be regarded as a marker for an alternative reality Magda is experiencing: the street of Singletons is like revisiting a past when she was without a husband, a version of life she does not regard favourably as her constant distress during her stay shows. It can be assumed that the alarm has been dormant as long as the idea of Magda's marriage was untainted. Now in the Singleton space, Magda becomes as inefficient as the streets' residents and can neither control the alarm nor switch it off. Only

14 Bridget's neighbour flirts with her and kisses Bridget only to reveal immediately afterwards that he is married (cf. Fielding 1998: 110-111).

15 For more information on the poster, see Lenz 2013a.

when her husband comes can the alarm be silenced again. Magda decides to forgive him for his affair and she returns home to be the 'happy' housewife once again.

SPATIAL COMPATIBILITY

The homes of chick- and ladlit protagonists help to construct their identity: how they approach certain topics or problems, how they are connected to the outside world and that they want to be part of a couple – even Will's home, because his abode is intruded into by Marcus and 'cracked open' by Rachel. But in order to become part of a couple, usually a lot of 'wrong' people have to be dated – (hopefully) with "[m]inimum time, minimum fuss"[16] (Earls 1998b: 90) – and eventually they meet the one, their perfect partner. The question of belonging is therefore reassessed and the subtle mechanisms of spatial compatibility are sounded out – without the characters even being aware of it. In the following the process of how spatial compatibility functions will be explained with examples from *About a Boy* and *Bridget Jones's Diary*, in order to complement the previous discussion.

In *About a Boy*, Will meets Rachel at a New Year's Eve party and is instantly smitten with her. Even days after their first meeting he "remembered every single detail that Rachel had offered him that first night." (Hornby 1998: 202) He creates a cognitive map of her and her interests which has him feel inferior and shallow in comparison. As has been alluded to before, Will believes he does not offer any interesting points of contact for Rachel. Until, that is, he invents a son and arranges a playdate for 'his' boy and Rachel's son. He convinces Marcus to pretend to be his offspring for the day of the play date so that Will can see Rachel again. When they arrive at Rachel's house, Will is panic-stricken:

> Rachel lived just up the road from Camden Lock, in a tall, thin house full of books and old furniture and sepia photographs of dramatic, romantic Eastern European relatives, and for a moment Will was grateful that his flat and her house would never get a chance to meet, current north London seismological conditions prevailing. Her house would be warm and welcoming, and his would be cocky and cool, and he'd be ashamed of it. (Ibid.: 202)

The first, most obvious difference noticeable is that Rachel lives in a house, whereas Will calls a flat his home. This already indicates that Rachel's dwelling is designed for a family, not for a solitary person. This actually confirms that her

16 Although this quote is connected to the slacker lifestyle in general of *Bachelor Kisses*' protagonist Jon Marshall, he applies the same mantra to his relationships, too.

favourite topic at their first meeting is also 'family': the spatial dimension mirrors her ideas about her identity as a family person, which is further heightened by photographs of relatives. In contrast to Will's home with its veneer of coolness, which masks his lonely existence, Rachel's home signifies 'family' by having pictures of relatives and by living together with her teenage son. This is in stark opposition to Will's home, as he first pretends to have a son (see chapter 6), and then can only present a surrogate son with Marcus: Will's 'family' home is a fraud. Whereas Rachel's abode is described as "warm and welcoming", Will's is just the opposite – every bit about it saying 'Peter Pan': "cocky and cool", clinging to 'eternal' youth and the attributes Will associates with this kind of lifestyle. The notion of two different worlds is literally mentioned and spatial compatibility seems out of the question. Yet, it is the last sentence that foreshadows a romantic coupling. Rachel's home signifies a state of mind and relationship that Will realises he wants to achieve because of her. Mirroring his discovery at the party that his solitary existence is lacking in substance, Rachel's home demonstrates this again on a spatial level. Will's bubble increasingly loses its appeal and he much more prefers the warmth and welcoming aspect of Rachel and her home to his stylish, yet laddish and 'frozen' life.

In order to change, he even considers becoming just friends with Rachel as his previous relationships were not lasting or, indeed, emotional as far as Will was concerned. He generally wants to become a better a person so that even if Rachel rejected him on the grounds that he is still too shallow, he hopes that in time a woman like Rachel might find him appealing for more than a 'fling'. Therefore, to prove to himself that he can be a more respectful and mature person than his current laddish incarnation, Will is willing to grant Rachel as much space as she needs, as long as he can maintain a certain form of closeness to her, both in a locational and metaphorical way. Just as he has experiences with Marcus, he slowly comes into his own, which means he starts to 'grow up', and realises that he is actually changing his perception of women as "he had never had any kind of relationship with some-one he hadn't wanted to sleep with" (ibid.: 231). Rachel stands out from his previous affairs, because now Will longs for a life with her, instead of just a night.

When Will enters Rachel's place, the house as genuine family home, it proves to be a further step towards his change of heart: Will craves a real family and belonging. His attitude has changed and it is only in Rachel's territory – both her home as well as her direct vicinity – that this epiphany could have happened. Her home aids in constructing, or rather re-assessing Will's identity and it is here that he feels secure about admitting his feelings for her. It is hence not surprising that the novel closes with Will and Rachel united. The spatial compatibility is achieved by him growing up into a mature adult and being comfortable with this development: "Will has lost his shell and his cool and his distance, and he felt scared and vulnerable, but he got to be with Rachel" (Hornby 1998: 286). He even takes out Marcus and Rachel's son most Saturdays and therefore behaves more like a father to the two than their actual dads. Will is still a bit unsure how to live outside this shell – an armour which protects the soft inside from the dangerous outside world – but it is his connection to Rachel and thus family that has him become confident that he will succeed.

Rachel, however, is only one person who is responsible for this change of heart of Will's, the other being Marcus. Towards the end of the novel, Marcus gets into a spot of bother on his way to his real father in Cambridge, and Will has to come to the rescue. At this point in the story, Will has met Rachel already and his sense of family has been awakened. The situation that presents itself to Will on his arrival – Marcus and his friend have been taken into police custody – triggers feelings which echo those of Will's at the beginning of the novel regarding clutter: "Will couldn't recall ever having been caught up in this sort of *messy, sprawling, chaotic web* before; it was almost as if he had been given a glimpse of what it was like to be human. It wasn't too bad, really; he wouldn't even mind being human on a full-time basis." (Ibid.: 272-273, emphasis added) Whereas the notion of clutter used to be connected to losing control and in a consecutive step to a definite change in personality of the clutter-affected person, here it suddenly does make sense to him: clutter, or in this case the "messy, sprawling, chaotic web", is connected to humanity and being alive by not holding back and embracing the chaos. The situation that this thought is uttered in is that of a family crisis – interestingly of Will's 'adopted' family of Marcus – and Will realises that he cannot remain in his bubble: before he met Marcus and Rachel, he was happy to look at things from a safe distance within his bubble. But now, after he has become engaged in the others' lives and has become an important part in them, he would not want to miss it for the engagement has changed him. After what he has been through with Marcus and after he has been enlightened by Rachel as to the possibilities of his own humanity, Will finds that he needs to break out of his solitary bubble. Will realises that a messy web of clutter is good and that it can signify a happy, if chaotic family.

Turning from ladlit to chicklit, the last subchapter has established that Bridget Jones's abode is a place that has very strong ties to the outside world, because Bridget wants to be recognised as a good homemaker (which fails) and as an attractive woman (by turning her bathroom into a body farm). In the following, the living spaces of the two men in Bridget's life will be analysed: Daniel Cleaver's flat and Mark Darcy's house. These two spaces allow for a deeper insight into their characters and foreshadow their (in)compatibility with the novel's heroine. Eventually, Bridget is going to form a loving relationship with Mark and this result can already be deduced by looking at Bridget's final visit to Daniel's high-end flat:

By the time I [Bridget] got to London and off the motorway [...] I thought, instead of going straight home, I'd go round to Daniel's for a bit of reassurance.
I parked nose to nose with Daniel's car. There was no answer when I rang, so I left it a while and rang again [...]. Still no answer. I knew he must be around because his car was there and he'd said he was going to be working and watching the cricket. I looked up at his window and there was Daniel. I beamed at him, waved and pointed at the door. [...] Why hadn't he answered the door the first time? [...] Suddenly it hit me like a thunderbolt. He was with a woman. [Bridget finally gets into Daniel's flat and starts looking around, trying to not alert him; C.L.] Daniel was staring at me as if I was mad, so I couldn't go and check the bedroom. Instead I locked the loo door and started frantically to look around for things. I wasn't exactly sure what, but long blonde hairs, tissues with lipstick marks on, alien hairbrushes – any of these would have been a sign. Nothing. Next I quietly unlocked the door, looked both ways and slipped along the corridor, pushed open the door of Daniel's bedroom and nearly jumped out of my skin. There was someone in the room. [...] It was Daniel, defensively holding a pair of jeans in front of him. [...] 'After you,' said Daniel, pushing me out and shutting the door so I had to walk ahead of him back into the kitchen. As I did so I suddenly caught sight of the door that led up to the roof terrace. [...] I dodged past [Daniel], opened the door, ran up the stairs and opened the hatch out into the sunlight. There, spread out on a sunlounger, was a bronzed, long-limbed, blonde-haired stark-naked woman. (Fielding 1998: 172-178)

Two rooms are awarded greater importance in the scenario described above: the bathroom and the bedroom. Both are very private rooms as they serve to 'cater' for human bodily functions, the bathroom to clean oneself and to use the toilet and the bedroom to sleep and to have sex in. It is striking that the living room is only mentioned in passing and signified via one piece of furniture alone – the couch – and the kitchen is not searched by Bridget at all. The couch is Daniel's place for relaxation on which he watches cricket matches, even when he is at Bridget's home, and does not care about anything else, not even women (ibid.: 149). The kitchen is neglected by Bridget on purpose: throughout the novel, this space is associated with homemaking and family. Bridget assumes that if Daniel has an affair, he would not regard her as potential wife – a position Bridget thinks she can lay claim to. She reckons that Daniel would only engage in a sexual affair and thus, the other woman has to be in a room not associated with homemaking.

Having a closer look at the description of the bathroom, Bridget cannot help but search for insignia of femininity. If the kitchen is the space which connotes homemaking and thus an advanced point in a relationship, the bathroom is the space in which a first foray into establishing a serious relationship is achieved. In this room one can start to striate one's partner's personal space. But females should beware as *Cosmopolitan* cautions because leaving "[a]n unsolicited toothbrush or other toiletry will give him the impression you're moving too fast — and may freak him out." (Heitman n.d.) What the magazine article advices its (female) readers to acknowledge is that leaving their personal items at his place can be regarded as a hostile takeover of both the male's space and the male himself. Bridget, an avid reader of magazines such as *Cosmopolitan*, was not able to striate Daniel's flat which would mean that if another woman succeeded in striating and consequentially taming Daniel it would degrade her. She starts searching for signs of another female in Daniel's bathroom in order to calm herself that she is not that insignificant to Daniel's life. She is not exactly sure what she is looking for, but her list – toothbrush and hair brush – point towards items needed to rearrange one's appearance after it has been dishevelled, for example after having had sex. The fact that she associates long blonde hair with the affair is also quite interesting as the readers never get to find out what Bridget looks like but blondes are usually connoted with sexiness and glamour, which are attributes Bridget does not associate with herself. And, of course, when she finally sees the other woman, she *is* indeed blonde.

The other room which is investigated in more detail is Daniel's bedroom and in fact she finds a naked person in there – although it is Daniel. The bedroom, as already stated, is stereotypically associated with sleeping and sex. The fact that both Daniel and Bridget are not exactly comfortable with her walking in on him shows the awkwardness of the situation. After all, they already had sex and have seen each other naked. Now, however, in a context which is not related to sex, the space of blissful intercourse has become a space of dressing. Additionally, a line has been established and Bridget has crossed it: nakedness is only accepted in a room that clearly connotes sex – when both are naked – but not whilst the notion of sex is not on offer. The incident shows that the two of them are not a proper couple, something Bridget has always assumed previously and talked about with her friends and family. The structure of the bedroom is obeyed by both characters without ever having talked about it before: either they can have sex, or it is exclusively Daniel's room to which Bridget can lay no claim. Daniel only shares his bedroom with Bridget to have sex in, and this clearly establishes him as the more dominant and powerful in their 'relationship'[17].

---

17 In *Cause Celeb*, Rosie Richardson experiences an equally negative sharing of space and place. Her problem is that she has always adjusted her life (and life space) to her boyfriends but her relationships never ended well. When she brings her new boyfriend Oliver to her flat, she is rather excited as to his opinion for she deems her place "Parisian" and fashionable (Fielding 2002: 33). But he ridicules her taste in furniture as well as her style of furnishing her flat and does pick her place and consequently her self to pieces. The spatial incompatibility can be further seen in the depiction of a rather typical night. After Oliver has come to Rosie, he has sex with her and falls asleep immediately afterwards (cf. ibid.: 63). The bed as a space for

The other important fact that can be gathered from this short excerpt is that of spatial hierarchical power. In the beginning, Bridget has to ring Daniel's flat and has to wait for him to buzz her in. He is clearly in charge, supported by the spatial image that she is standing down there, literally beneath him at street level, while he is up in his flat: a hierarchical structure. The situation is comparable to fairy tales in which the princess can generally be found locked in the highest tower, but she has not the power to buzz someone in: Prince Charming has to fight his way in and rescue her. In the novel, 'princess' Bridget has to beg Prince Charming to let her in – again rendering the princess powerless to enter spaces or make them accessible. Bridget was not able to striate Daniel's flat whilst they were seeing each other, she did not "leave stuff" at his place and now he even keeps her waiting a rather uncomfortably long time. Daniel's flat proves to be a very smooth space to her and the fact that there *is actually an affair* tells Bridget that, spatially, she need not try to striate Daniel's flat and life anymore.

Finally, Bridget figures out that the only place the affair can hide in has to be on the roof and she starts climbing the stairs. Stairs can be an indication of hierarchy and labour as it can be tiring to climb stairs whereas descending stairs is rather relaxing. Here, it mirrors Bridget's endeavours and labour to find out what is occupying Daniel's mind and flat. Bridget climbs the stairs and finds another princess in the metaphorical tower: a blonde, stunning and naked woman. If one considers the stairs as a metaphor, they symbolise Bridget's efforts to be Daniel's ideal woman, attractive, suave and above all comfortable in her nakedness, a goal she tries to achieve with the help of her body farm. But the place Bridget wants to hold – namely on the pedestal as Daniel's ideal woman – is already occupied. Daniel already has this perfect woman, and all Bridget can do is arrive too late only to remain on the stairs whereas the blonde woman lolls in his sunlounger.

The spatial actor Bridget has to realise that she cannot penetrate Daniel's space to insert herself in it and to create a heterotopia of shared places of common ideals and perceptions that signify a loving relationship[18]. On the contrary, she has to

---

recreation, relaxation and togetherness has become the epitome of their separated relationship: he intrudes into her space, takes what he wants and leaves Rosie crying as silently as possible, lest she disturbs him. He commands her and her life space as if they truly belonged to him. It becomes clear that Rosie wants more from this 'relationship' than casual sex for which Oliver (ab)uses Rosie in her bed. She is eventually able to free herself from Oliver by escaping to Africa, only to have another man having power over her bed – yet this time with her consent.

18 Even before the sunlounger incident, when Daniel has been at Bridget's flat, he hardly ever wanted to share this place with her and instead took it over and watched

labour hard to climb stairs, first to his flat and then to the roof. Daniel's flat symbolises the notion of chasing ideals which do not come from within Bridget but are accepted by her as a necessary means to attract Daniel. Although she finally makes it into his flat at great cost by behaving in as docile a manner as possible, she will still be lower in Daniel's esteem than the youthful, sexy blonde woman. The flat demonstrates in a harsh way that one is not rewarded when striving for questionable ideals as this can only lead to frustration when directed at the wrong person.

In contrast to Daniel, Mark Darcy lives in a house and Bridget is surprised that his "house [is a] huge, detached wedding-cake style mansion on the other side of Holland Park Avenue (where Harold Pinter, they say, lives) surrounded by greenery." (Fielding 1998: 227) She has been invited to his parents' anniversary and "[a]ll the trees were dotted with red fairy lights and strings of shiny red hearts in a really quite endearing manner and there was a red and white canopied walkway leading all the way up to the front path." (Ibid.: 228) Mark's habitat is located in a rather affluent district of West London, which surprises Bridget because he is richer than she had thought. Mark's mansion is also surrounded by "greenery" showing that he likes nature and does not a stay inside to watch cricket like Daniel. Moreover, Bridget states that Harold Pinter is said to live in Holland Park, lending an air of sophistication to the area. Holland Park is therefore a desirable district because of the features which Bridget notices immediately.

Moreover, Mark's mansion is an object of desire because the novel suggests that it (correctly) means that people in Holland Park are prestigious and powerful. As can be observed in many chicklit novels, the man the heroine will form a lasting relationship with is usually the most eligible and richest bachelor in the story, in this case Mark Darcy. Chicklit's stereotypical Mr Right is a modern-day interpretation of Prince Charming, who might not be overwhelmingly charming in the beginning but who certainly has a palace to marvel at. Chicklit novels seem to suggest that for all the hardships their heroines endure they must be rewarded royally and therefore only the best single man the narrative has to offer will be good enough for the female protagonists.

It is striking that in Bridget's description of Mark's house, his place appears to resemble the structure of a wedding cake. On the one hand, this reflects Bridget's obsession with signifiers and insignia for marriage, but, on the other hand, it suggests that Mark is not averse to the idea of faithful coupledom either. The house is already foreshadowing what will eventually happen, namely that Mark and Bridget

---

cricket with the blinds down, forcing Bridget either to watch the game with him – and consequentially submit to his power in her space – or not to have him around. He shut off 'their' space, whereas the bronzed blonde is clearly visible on the roof, like a trophy.

will form a lasting relationship and are going to get married. The wedding cake mansion also displays what is happening inside: Mark is celebrating his parents' wedding anniversary, thus cherishing and upholding the tradition of marriage. That is the reason why there are candles everywhere, creating a *welcoming* and *warm* atmosphere, and some are even heart-shaped, underlining Mark's romantic notion: "Next we were ushered down a dramatic curved pale wood stairway lit by red heart-shaped candles on each step. Downstairs was one vast room, with a dark wood floor and a conservatory giving on to the garden. The whole room was lit by candles." (Ibid.) The atmosphere echoes Rachel's cosy and love-ly home in *About a Boy*. It shows that gender appears not matter as much as some theorists believe. The sex or gender of a person has no direct bearing on their home but mirrors their identity. Especially the perfect partners do not use their home in a way which suggests fraud or a hypertrophied version of the person: they are usually perfect from the start. Their homes invite romantic stimulation which the main protagonists ultimately crave above anything else.

Just like in Daniel's flat, Mark's home features another flight of stairs. However, whereas at Daniel's place Bridget had to climb *up*, only to discover the perfect woman at the top, at Mark's place she is ushered *down* to meet the host. The difference is that going down stairs is generally deemed easier than going up and this further creates the impression that Bridget, going down the stairs, is figuratively lowering herself to get to Mark. It shows the host's unpretentiousness despite his obvious wealth. Moreover, Bridget is ushered down to Mark and need not wait like at Daniel's flat. After Mark has greeted his guests, he starts climbing some stairs:

> As he reached the top of the stairs Natasha [a colleague of his; C.L.] appeared in a stunning gold satin sheath, grabbing his arm possessively and, in her haste, tripping over one of the candles which spilt red wax on the bottom of her dress. [...] As they disappeared ahead I could hear her telling him off. 'I told you it was ridiculous spending all afternoon arranging candles in dangerous places for people to fall over. Your time would have been far better spent ensuring that the placement was...' (Ibid.: 227-230)

Mark's attitude towards any woman is that of respect. But although Natasha presents the image of the perfect woman visually, she even wears an attention-grabbing golden dress, she is not the woman to love: she spills the candle wax of Mark's carefully and lovingly displayed candles and complains about it. She has no romantic streak in her and tells Mark off for considering romantic gestures and emphasising coupledom, here in the form of his parents' anniversary. She is ignorant of the candles and regards them as an obstruction to her walking down the stairs. Natasha is not the lovable character she wants to convey the impression of. Additionally, by grabbing Mark's arm, she tries to establish reign over the host and his space – but ultimately fails as the short extract foreshadows. Clearly, Natasha's and Mark's ideas of romance are spatially not compatible, as she thinks the whole candle arrangement is useless frippery and does not want to use spaces the way he does. Instead of being interested in creating a warm and welcoming atmosphere for Mark's guests, her focus is on showing off herself by an unobstructed descent down the stairs and a seating arrangement to fashion herself as the perfect hostess. But as Bridget is able to acknowledge the decoration as well as the lovely garden, it shows that she is a better match for Mark. She, too, cares about her family and friends and although at times happy to be at the centre of attention, she will always support her loved ones instead of bullying them around.

Regarding the geographical structure which informs an actor's sense of place, the perfection of Mark Darcy as a suitable man for Bridget is highlighted: he creates this celebratory extravaganza to laud his parents' anniversary and with the party he visualises two issues related to space. Firstly, he cares about his parents, who have raised him and given him the best possible start in life. Yet, they are not celebrating the party at their home, which one can assume is quite large, but at their son's. He wants to repay them for what they did for him: he takes his parents in and does everything, both filially and spatially, to make this a festivity to remember. Secondly, the way he cares for and provides his home shows that he upholds the value of family, which again makes him the perfect match to marry – if one shares his values, as Bridget does and Natasha does not. Space can therefore disclose Mark's rather old-fashioned romanticised ideals about love and relationships and in a second step marriage and family. Although Bridget wants to fashion herself as a happy Singleton the way she writes her diary entries exposes her desire to be in a relationship, indicating that her idea of space and family is very much like Mark's and thus complementary, which points to spatial compatibility.

KITCHEN STORIES

Already, the kitchen has been introduced as the space in which only the true homemaker or the dedicated housewife can excel. It is a space that – as part of the home – constructs or at least enables the pursuit of a specific identity, the aforementioned homemaker. Now, a different aspect of the homemaker will be analysed, namely their connection to the kitchen as a space to love. Based on the adage that 'the hearth is the heart of the home', it means that an absent hearth or an inactive kitchen signifies a heartless or love-less owner.

This deduction can be observed in many ladlit novels and even in some of the male characters in chicklit. To many of the men the kitchen is not a room which is given much attention as most lads "eat out a lot" as Adam Bachelor in *The*

Importance of Being a Bachelor explains (Gayle 2011: 119). They have yet to realise that their current identity is not appealing to women, they are too laddish. The kitchen can thus function as a marker of this development, for example in *The Fix* by Nick Earls. In this novel, Josh Lang returns from London to Brisbane but his life is in a state of disarray. His identity as well as his love life are problematic as he cannot decide what he wants to do with his life, he holds grudges against his former best friend and he is in love with his sister-in-law. Josh, however, at least knows that he wants to stay in Brisbane and buys a flat. But the state of his kitchen mirrors his irresolution: "I want to make the right choice with the new oven[. …] I don't want to rush it. It might be smarter to do the rest of the kitchen at the same time. Renovate the lot. […] The camp stove'll be fine in the meantime." (Earls 2012: 13) The camp stove signifies his state of having a place of his own in Brisbane but not yet feeling at home. There are too many problems and issues that he needs to resolve before he can move on, buy a proper oven, renovate his kitchen (read: his life) and find love. At the end of the novel, Josh has eventually fixed these problems: "Hayley [Josh's girlfriend; C.L.] and I were both at my flat. My new oven had just been installed, and it looked shiny […]. The camp stove was sitting nearby, back in its box" (ibid.: 281). Resolving or indeed 'fixing' his troubles has him evolve and he is able to overcome his personal problems for which he is 'rewarded' with the love of the perfect woman and a new kitchen.

This example only allowed a short glimpse into the kitchen and its function as a metaphor for the construction of identity and its status as signifier for love. Therefore, when a whole novel is dedicated to this specific space, it cannot be neglected. This is the reason why, in the following, the chicklit novel *The Undomestic Goddess* with its depictions and functions of kitchens will be in the focus. It emphasises the re-construction of the heroine's identity and attitude as well as being the space in which the meeting with the perfect partner is foreshadowed and begun.

Samantha Sweeting is experiencing the ultimate nightmare: having been a lawyer at a top London law firm for seven years and about to be made a partner, a small mistake of hers results in her losing the firm a multi-million pound sum and her job on the same morning. Panic stricken because her whole cosmos has been brought down, she boards a train to Gloucestershire and, through a series of coincidences, ends up being the new housekeeper of Trish and Eddie Geiger. However, since Samantha used to spend all her waking hours at the firm, she was never able to prepare food, clean and iron clothes or hoover a carpet and is thus not prepared for the tasks now set for her:

OK. I can do this. I can make a few sandwiches. [After some time, failing to cut the bread evenly and to spread jam on the wonky slices:] It's a total disaster. Jam is oozing out of the cracks. It still isn't completely square.

I've never seen a more revolting sandwich in my life.
Slowly I put the knife down in defeat. So this is it. Time for my resignation. As I stare at the jammy mess I feel strangely disappointed in myself. I would have thought I could last a morning. (Kinsella 2006: 101-102)

This short passage demonstrates a hubris that is not uncommon in chicklit[19]. It can be observed that the general notion of work in the kitchen and food-related matters are deemed 'a breeze' compared to other more challenging tasks the women managed to fulfil as Samantha phrases it: "I'll busk it for a morning. It can't be that hard." (Ibid.: 87) A certain gender aspect is of course not absent here and it is noteworthy that most chicklit heroines are able to excel at work but not at home. It proves that the previously despised prison of women actually becomes a new challenge: the tables have turned in terms of what is harder to accomplish in a woman's life – a career or a sandwich.

The kitchen is an interesting space in so far as it is said to be the heart of the home and thus it becomes the central room within the Geigers' mansion for Samantha to work in: "Food, its provision, and preparation occupies the housewife's thoughts and actions for much of the day" (Hirschon 1993: 75). This idea is related to a specific group of females, namely stereotypical housewives, but the "significance of the kitchen must not be underestimated" (ibid.). The kitchen and its 'output' – food – are emphasised and elevated over other rooms which are merely meant to be cleaned or used for more menial tasks like ironing or washing.

The kitchen at the Geigers' house and Samantha's disguise as a housekeeper rely on the twentieth-century ideology of efficiency which is said to have resulted in the "link between kitchen and the image of the professional housewife" (Cieraad 2002: 263): only the efficient and consequently proficient housewife can manipulate food and kitchen tools into a wholesome, delicious meal. In the nineteenth century, Isabella Beeton was of the impression that "[f]rom kitchen ranges to the implements used in cookery is but a step. With these, every kitchen should be well supplied, otherwise the cook must not be expected to 'perform her office'[20] in a

19 Just like Samantha, Bridget Jones and *Love Struck*'s Isabelle Beckett, too, deem themselves qualified to excel at any household activity they set their minds to because they read a book about it: "Of course I can cook. Anyone who can read can cook." (La'Brooy 2003: 206; cf. Fielding 1998: 82-84, 268-271). However, it does not take long until the women's hubris is exposed and the characters' behaviour ridiculed.

20 Beeton is under the impression that cooking or working in the kitchen in general is like working in an office – thus predating feminist ideas about the acknowledgement of homely duties of women for some decades. That she was actually quite averse to

satisfactory manner." (2012: 232) Therefore, in order to be recognised as a good and consequentially efficient housewife, a woman needs good implements. The kitchen as space becomes a canvas that needs to be worked upon (or rather, in) with the correct utensils: only then is the housewife able to perform adequately. In fact, when Samantha, in an act of desperation and diversion, claims that the kitchen gadgets are not up to her 'standard', Trish orders a completely new set of kitchen items and gadgets. She wants her new housekeeper to be able to perform as well as possible and, thus, for Samantha to "be able to stun [the Geigers] with [her] cooking!" (Kinsella 2006: 185) This, however, turns Samantha into a gadget of Trish's. Without Samantha – or at least the chef-version Samantha pretends to be – Trish cannot be perceived as efficient herself: she wants to attract the envy of her friends for having such a skilled professional like Samantha, which means that she is recognised as an efficient homemaker herself. She considers Samantha a tool which can be used to turn one's home into a better version of itself, which can be seen in her sometime bewildered attitude towards Samantha's wish for privacy. Trish is willing to hand over the territory of the kitchen and supremacy in all kitchen-related matters to Samantha in order to elevate her own position *outside* the kitchen and in other spaces – for example during a charity dinner of hers.

Therefore, in this novel, the kitchen has become an interface between the private and the public. Although one considers one's home one's castle, one's pocket of local order, the Geiger residence is more than a refuge from the outside world, as it is a signifier of their owners' status. The Geigers' home is considered (by themselves) a prestigious marker of their wealth and refinement, with recently added Samantha as pièce de résistance. Samantha is to wow Trish's guests with her 'famed' dishes and to increase her employers' standing. However, Trish eventually gets more than she bargained for: the kitchen becomes a contested space that blurs the barriers, which previously separated the kitchen as part of the private home from the public outside the home. This transformation starts when Samantha finds out that she did indeed not make a mistake in her job as a lawyer but was framed and returns to London to clear her name. When that has been achieved she is offered the promotion she used to work for every day of every week, but she turns down that offer and declares to the incredulous board that she prefers housekeeping (cf. ibid.: 343-344). What Samantha has not reckoned with are journalists finding out about her snub and starting to show up at Trish and Eddie's home. To the press, Samantha is interesting because she is the lawyer who chose the job of a housekeeper and happiness over money and prestige, literally embracing her new sphere, the kitchen: "[Samantha] spread[s her] arms around the kitchen. '*This* is what I

the kitchen "and didn't go near her own kitchen if she could possibly help it", however, puts her 'devotion' to that space into question (cf. Bryson 2010: 85).

want to do. *This* is where I want to be.'" (Kinsella 2006: 369-70, emphasis added) Samantha has come to create a very strong place-person bond as well as sense of place with regard to the kitchen. Not only does she equate the activities of a place with said locale, the kitchen becomes constitutive of her identity and by her place-person bond and by her 'inhabiting' the profession, she becomes constitutive of the place, too.

The kitchen becomes invested with different ideologies: not only does it signify Samantha's happiness as opposed to her former workplace's pressure, through the media she now has to deal with either being accused of being an "antifeminist moron" or being hailed as the "saviour of traditional values" – the Victorian 'Angel in the House' – when she chose the apron over the lawyer's robe (cf. ibid.: 368-371). The kitchen develops into a space that reduces a character's personality to such an extent that the place makes the person and not the other way round. The lawyers from Samantha's former employer deem her being a housekeeper a 'travesty' and that she lives in a fantasy land, whereas Trish expresses delight and awe at having an Oxford-trained housekeeper, and the media choose either the traditional or the antifeminist version of the kitchen. It is noteworthy that, although Samantha is accused of being a traitor to the feminist cause and equally hailed as a conservative icon, she leaves the Geigers' kitchen to return to her old life as a lawyer. However, on her way back to London and her old life, she alights and turns the job down once more. Thus, the novel ends with Samantha at a train station between London (representing being a lawyer) and Gloucestershire (representing being a housekeeper). It seems that, although Samantha really enjoyed working in the kitchen, the fact that her identity is now joined to that of a retrograde housekeeper – and not that of a genuine housewife as it is not her kitchen – is not something she wants either. Kinsella shuns the accusation that women should not enjoy working in the kitchen but cannot decide where they are better suited to work (in). However, finishing the novel the way she does, the author does make one statement: namely that Samantha decides that she wants to be with Nathaniel, the Geigers' gardener and the novel's love interest, and postpones the question of her job.

This leads to the last quality of the kitchen and that is its function for the novel's romantic plot. When Samantha first starts at the Geigers', the kitchen – as well as the rest of the house – proves to be just as Augean a territory as her previous workplace, the law office. Striating the kitchen and proving to be able to perform in that kitchen, Samantha has her work cut out for her. However, she cannot accomplish the mastery of the kitchen without help. On her first day – and whilst failing to provide sandwiches for her new employers – she meets Nathaniel, who realises very quickly that Samantha is hardly able to cope with her duties (cf. ibid.: 100). But as he takes a shine to her, he wants to help her and sets her up with his mother

Iris, who agrees to teach Samantha how to cook and introduces her to other necessary household skills to perform the housekeeper's job efficiently. Iris is a very proficient cook but her kitchen is not styled in the way the Geigers' high-tech cooking centre is:

> The kitchen is at the back of the house, and is filled with light and sun. Flowers in earthenware jugs are everywhere. There's an old-fashioned range cooker and a scrubbed wooden table and a stable door opening to the outside. As I'm wondering whether I should be making conversation [with Iris], a chicken wanders in and starts scratching at the ground. (Ibid.: 169-170)

This kitchen is presented in juxtaposition to Trish's conglomeration of shiny apparatuses and top-of-the-range equipment. In Iris's kitchen, nature is 'invited' to striate the space and is not shut out by closed doors, leaving the chicken to roam freely. It will be in the Geigers' kitchen that Samantha has to excel professionally but it is in Iris's more personal and warm domestic sphere that she undergoes spatial processes. Iris teaches Samantha how to prepare and cook most of the dishes the newly appointed housekeeper boasted of being able to serve: "'Assemblé' is just flannel. […] That's souped-up shepherd's pie. We can teach you that." (Ibid.: 171) The skilled domestic cook deconstructs the 'fancy' culinary terms and exposes them as traditional recipes. Iris establishes the home with its kitchen as the space of the real, down-to-earth meals in opposition to the pretentious spaces that disguise their gastronomic roots. Moreover, she is also responsible for Samantha's (re)formation of attitudes: "Cooking [is] about tasting. Feeling. Touching. Smelling." (Ibid.: 172) Samantha is to learn to engage with her task and to explore her new territory sensually. Cooking is presented not as an exact science but as organic: "[Samantha] watched [Iris] all day, moving swiftly and precisely around the kitchen, tasting as she goes, fully in control. There is no sense of panic. Everything happens as it should happen." (Ibid.: 176)

The notion of control and precision is not to be underestimated here, as it mirrors what is dear to Samantha and what she is good at: in her law firm she was known to be always in control and she is frustrated when she realises that 'doing housework' cannot be controlled as easily – reverberating the above-mentioned hubris. Seeing Iris manipulate a territory similar to the one that momentarily defeated Samantha, the former lawyer is awestruck. What she learns in Iris's kitchen are not only household skills necessary to perform her job as a housekeeper but she adopts a new attitude, too. Working in the kitchen and relying on one's senses has Samantha stop and take stock of her life, it becomes a space of initiation. She realises that she would rather be a housekeeper and happy than a lawyer and rich but forfeiting her life. It is this forming of attitudes that is so vital when it comes to surviving in a territory: one needs to adapt to the rules and guidelines by which a territory operates and by which the other inhabitants already live and function. Of course, the same rules can be found in her former workplace but there the function of the home had to be neglected as there was no space or time to relax but merely the necessity of sleep existed, which must not be indulged in at the office.

Under Iris's tutelage, Samantha becomes a different person altogether, her old identity has been called into question and she does not even recognise the person she used to be: when she briefly returns to her London flat, she realises the "mess" she has been living in, how alienated she was even from her direct neighbours and how she has nothing in her kitchen she is able to cook with (cf. Kinsella 2006: 330-333). But she surprises herself and her next-door neighbour when she bakes a cake from scratch without consulting a cookbook and brings it to her neighbour to eat it with her. At first the old lady is suspicious as she knew Samantha to be only at her apartment to sleep and change clothes. She is even more astounded when she tastes the cake: "It's... delicious! So *light*! You really made this?" (Ibid.: 335, original emphasis) The sensation of the cake is followed by her neighbour telling Samantha that the she "used to look like [...] the empty shell of a person[, like] a dried-up leaf. [...] But now [Samantha looks] fitter, [...] healthier... [...] happy" (ibid.: 336). The kitchen – first Iris's, then Samantha's own territory – has changed Samantha's life in such a way that she even reflects the change for everyone to see. The attitude she has acquired by learning at Iris's and working at the Geigers' has filled Samantha's automaton-like, empty *existence* and it has evolved her into a happier, more fulfilled *person*. The space of the kitchen has provided Samantha with a kind of stimulation she would not have deemed possible before. Having only lived to work and bill clients, she has forgotten that she never actually wanted that job as badly as it is suggested by her lawyer colleagues but she was pushed, even bullied, by her mother. Her experience in the kitchen, taught by her surrogate mother Iris no less, enables her for the first time to assess her present and past life by relying on senses, by being stimulated by touch, feel and smell. It also has her consider her time as valuable without billing anybody and regarding other people as more than clients, colleagues or partners of her law firm.

The space of the kitchen has changed Samantha's attitude towards her work and her life tremendously. Furthermore, it is the space in which she meets the Geigers' gardener Nathaniel, who is repeatedly associated with naturalness and genuineness, firstly and most obviously in his direct relation to gardening. Secondly, he is the mediator through whom Samantha is put into contact with Nathaniel's mother Iris, another genuine person closely aligned with nature (the chicken in the kitchen). Thirdly, he owns pubs and his unpretentious behaviour – although they are his pubs, he serves the beer, too, and is very good friends with both the staff and the patrons – has him being well-liked by everyone because he is considered 'real'. The final aspect of his genuine 'natural-ness' is his wish to own a nursery in rural Cornwall where he can grow plants and trees. Thus, Nathaniel is meant to represent a personified nature[21] which woos, wows and wins Samantha. Her transition from rationality and impersonalised business suits to loose-fitting clothing and working with her hands owes much to Nathaniel. But the nature he represents is somewhat manipulated: by gardening and even more so with his nursery, he comes to stand for a reined (in) form of nature. Nathaniel plants specific vegetables and wants to grow trees on demand. Nature is but a simulacrum here, for it is a romanticised version of it. It shows that Samantha, for all her newly acquired love of the 'natural', still prefers the wild to be controlled: she never ventures out into the forest on her own and even the first time she has sex with Nathaniel it takes place in the Geigers' roofed raspberry field, meaning it is an enclosed form of 'nature'.

Nonetheless, the spatial compatibility of Samantha and Nathaniel is expressed through their shared passion for nature. Samantha's changed attitude is the result of learning to appreciate as well as to manipulate the kitchen and to produce from it, which ultimately results in praise and respect. Thus, natural produce is a vital part of this process which culminates in Samantha's changed identity, while Nathaniel as the gardener is the direct link to the natural products from the Geigers' garden. At one point this becomes rather obvious: when Samantha's employers leave for a party during one hot summer day, Samantha dresses casually and heads down into the garden. As Nathaniel usually enters the house via the door in the kitchen, it can be assumed that Samantha uses the same door to venture outside and hence the kitchen becomes the interface between the two realms of the domesticated and the natural. Observing the different natural environments, Samantha is surprised at the heat outside in contrast to the coolness of the house. This perception foreshadows the uncontrolled desire and lust which is about to take place and which is not possible in the controlled and cool atmosphere of the house from which Samantha comes – literally. What follows is a rather steamy account of a striptease whilst picking raspberries and having sex amongst the raspberry cages. Here, the connection to mass-produced fantasies becomes fairly obvious with the description of the scene:

I stand there in the heat and the dusty earth, panting and aching [for Nathaniel's touch]. And just as I think I might explode, he comes forward and bends his mouth down to my nipple, and I nearly swoon. And this time he doesn't move away. This time is for real. His hands are moving over my body, my skirt is falling to the ground, his jeans are sliding off. Then I'm

21 In terms of what Nathaniel represents, he can be compared to the Celtic deity Sucellus, the god of agriculture, forests and alcoholic drinks – for he indeed ticks off all of these boxes.

shuddering, and clutching him, and crying out. And the raspberries are forgotten, scattered on the ground, squashed, crushed beneath us. (Kinsella 2006: 259)

The scene fashions Nathaniel in the role of the rural seducer, teasing a girl who is on the brink of ecstasy, which is a typical trope of the mass-produced fantasies á la Mills & Boon. It is quite interesting that they copulate on the recently picked fruit for it suggests a union on the grounds of nature itself. The sex is the consummation of Samantha's development which is also voiced by Nathaniel, who observes that she is now "not as twitchy" as she used to be but much "stiller" (ibid.: 260, 261). She has stopped escaping from her former life and has found a peaceful place to stay. The Geigers' house and thus her new territory with the help of 'natural' Nathaniel have given her the chance to re-evaluate her life and the perceptions of it. Thus, when she gets up to return to the house – for their employers suddenly return – she bears the stains of the squashed berries on her, visually marking her as changed. Yet, the novel concludes with a partly open ending: Nathaniel breaks up with Samantha when she announces her intention to go back to London. He decides to pursue his own dream of a nursery in Cornwall, but recognizes that he cannot live without Samantha. At the same time, Samantha chooses Nathaniel over both her jobs. While the ending makes clear that Samantha and Nathaniel belong together, the question as to what territory the two will occupy – rural Gloucestershire or Cornwall – is left open. However, belonging to 'nature' is definite because of Samantha's belonging to Nathaniel, the representative of nature.

FAMILY IS NOT JUST A WORD

In chick- and ladlit, belonging is both a motif and motive that features not only in love relationships but also among family members and friends. In this subchapter, the function and importance of a concept will be analysed which is very prominent in the novels of the two genres: the urban family. Comparing it to (biological) families as well as demonstrating the connection to 'community', the defining features of the urban family will be documented. Using examples from both genres, this subchapter will emphasise the function of the outsourced meeting space, the concept of the laddish 'felix rigor mortis' and the drawbacks of an urban family.

The concept of the urban family is acknowledging that the traditional nuclear family, which is defined as "a group consisting of two parents and their children living together as a unit" (*OED*: "Family"), can no longer demand sole supremacy: there are diverse forms ranging from large multi-generational families to single parents or singles without children[22]. Chick- and ladlit reflect these changes and they have taken up the values of the traditional family unit and re-appropriated them to fit to the evolving needs and changes of the young urban professionals. The urban family does not comprise any biological children or indeed the need to share one abode, it consists of voluntary connections of indefinite number in a metropolitan territory and can be extended – or reduced – as is seen fit: "Friends really are the family you choose[23]." (Kala 2009: 116)

In her analysis of *Bridget Jones's Diary*, Imelda Whelehan comments on the importance of urban families by stating "that the functional 'family' [or urban family; C.L.] which Bridget and her friends forge suggests the possibility of a new set of relations *at least as reliable as those of blood ties*." (2002: 30, emphasis added) What Whelehan is rather careful to express can be found in almost all chick- and ladlit novels across the continents: they display sets of friends who encompass the main protagonists and incorporate them in their network of relations or create one anew with the protagonists. It does not matter whether they are male or female as all "[seek] alternatives to family for solace and coping with the disorientation of the big city" (Whelehan 2002: 19). Most urban families are introduced very early on in the novels and thus give the impression that their existence is a very necessary feature for the characters. Moreover, the existence naturalises this form of family and puts them at least on the same level as biological blood-ties families. Here, a first glimpse at the spatiality of the concept becomes apparent because their presence from the beginning means that these urban families are more advantageous to survive and better the challenges presented in a metropolitan context than a family of blood ties. This has to do with the changed circumstances that the protagonists encounter and which the blood-ties families more often than not do not even fathom for they are left behind in a different spatial – suburban or even rural – setting. Therefore, defining features of the urban family are that its members are equally alien to the locale they are now living in because they usually relocate from a smaller town to a metropolis (cf. Crang 1998: 53). However, in almost all cases the protagonist does not address this issue, it can only be deduced from the location of

22 From 1996 to 2014, the UK saw an increase in both married couples living (with or without children) in one home as well as cohabiting couples of opposite sexes. However, the number of lone parents has steadily increased to 2 million. There were 26.7 million households in the UK in 2014; of these, 28 per cent consisted of only one person (cf. Office for National Statistics 2015).

23 There is a strong connection to homosexual or queer networks of friends as Kath Weston describes in her book on lesbian and gay kinship. Drawing from personal experience, she explains that they "began to apply the terms 'family' and 'extended family' to one another." (1997: 104)

the protagonists' parents' homes, for example in *Bridget Jones's Diary*, *Manhattan Dreaming* and *Bachelor Kisses*. Even more important than the urban families' connections to their present locales is their shared outlook on life and consequentially love, which manifests itself in a spatial compatibility otherwise only found in love relationships. There are two varieties of urban families which, however, adhere to the same aforementioned features: in the first variety, the main protagonists share their homes with their urban families. This type is usually found in ladlit, but is occasionally used in chicklit too. The second variety does not include cohabitation, which is the reason why the members of this type of urban family have to create an outsourced meeting space. This outsourced meeting space is the equivalent to the shared or communal space within the flat of a cohabitating urban family. It can happen, of course, that the cohabitating characters create an outsourced meeting space as well. This case, however, merely acknowledges a larger urban family as the one which shares a space, as can be seen in *Street Furniture* and *Brand New Friend*.

A perfect example of an urban family in which all of the above mentioned factors – support, shared attitude, spatially equally foreign – are visible is Chetan Bhagat's *Five Point Someone*: here, the "troika" Hari, Alok and Ryan meet at the Kumaon hostel at the Indian Institute of Technology (IIT) for their first semester in Mechanical Engineering (cf. Bhagat 2008: 7). It is a rare case of being able to read how the urban family comes into being as most novels depict an already existing model. All men have different financial backgrounds, which range from poor (Alok) to rather rich (Ryan) but the fact that they live in adjacent rooms nullifies these monetary concerns. They all have to live in the same kind of accommodation that does not distinguish between rich and poor or castes. Living in the same accommodation makes them equals in this sense and paves the way for friendship and an urban family: they are united by being equally alien to the IIT, despite their different financial backgrounds. After some weeks attending lectures and handing in coursework, the young men realise that the system of IIT is not as fair or egalitarian as the housing. They come up with a plan to beat the system at its own game by sharing the workload instead of suffering through all courses individually, they do it communally – and by living even more closely together: "We combine our hostel rooms into one unit – one common bedroom, one study room and one fun party room." (Ibid.: 108) This idea of sharing spaces can be regarded as a mediating stage between a shared accommodation without outsourced meeting space and separate accommodation with an external meeting space: they come from the latter stage when they used to study together in special rooms but housed separately and create the former by re-allocating the rooms and their functions. They channel their individual energies into one goal, namely that of passing the necessary exams to graduate from IIT. Of course, all of them have personal goals, too, but it is the IIT degree that will get them there – or so they think. But even this illusion maintains their shared attitude concerning their urban family. As can be found in many ladlit novels, the men start to share their rooms and therefore confirm their bonds by creating an urban family. Eventually, they will even help Hari Kumar woo his perfect partner and therefore display another shared attitude as they support their best friend in pursuing his romantic dream.

Taking the example of *Five Point Someone*, one can directly link the three men's efforts to beat the system to Raymond Williams's idea of community, namely that communities are born out of the "sense of direct common concern" and that they can materialise in "various forms of organisation" or even in "an alternative set of relationships", which hints at the alternative to traditional families (1976: 76). Robert Gottlieb explains this further by writing that Williams's "direct common concern" can be expressed in, "for example, a community of values or a community of interests" (2007: 61). The strong focus of communities to share both concern and interests is therefore visible in *Five Point Someone* and the men's goal to master IIT as well as to help Hari in his romantic endeavour. Other chick- and ladlit novels with urban families display these ideas as well, for example by spending evenings with friends or by being there for them when one of the family's members is in trouble or needs help (cf. Weston 1997: 105): chick- and ladlit novels

> herald the importance of friendships, the clarity they bring, and the mistakes we sometimes make when we don't have our friends there to help us understand complicated situations. They acknowledge female [or male] solidarity and the idea of socially constructed families (versus biological ones) from which the single woman or girl [in chicklit and single man or lad in ladlit; C.L.] can truly draw her [or his] strength. (Webb Johnson 2006: 151)

With regard to Bhagat, it has been observed that he is indeed a very political author (cf. Iqbal Viswamohan 2013a), and all of his novels deal with inequality and exploitation in India. The three friends in *Five Point Someone* as well as the call centre agents in *One Night at the Call Centre* have to create a small community in the form of the urban family in order to stand up against the (corrupt) ruling power. Eventually they will triumph and Bhagat seems to educate his readership by inviting them "to identify with the underdog where, at the end, the loser takes it all." (Ibid.: 27) Bhagat's approach to forming a strong community and to overthrowing the debauched rulers shows the political side of communities in ladlit. Similarly political are the Aboriginal characters in Anita Heiss's novels, who establish visibility through community as well as safety and belonging: when Lauren (*Manhattan Dreaming*), Libby (*Paris Dreaming*) and Peta (*Avoiding Mr Right*) are venturing out of their realm they will always connect with other

Indigenous peoples and thus they create a community that becomes a small and tightly-knit urban family, which is ever so important in metropolitan contexts.

Communities and urban families are indeed different in their size and constellation, which naturally reflects on their geographical location and the choice thereof. Urban families are usually of a size ranging up to five people. Of course, on occasions such as parties or meetings in outsourced living rooms, the number increases, yet the core mostly remains stable. The reason why an urban family is not comprised of an indefinite or rather large number is the spatiality of the concept. Urban families can only truly function if all its members know one another and can interact with them fairly easily – by meeting up, going out regularly, bumping into one another. This, however, is only possible in a limited territory. The closeness of the urban family can therefore lead to a heightened emotional attachment. Their feeling of belonging is based on "deep, horizontal comradeship" or "fraternity" (Anderson 2006: 7). Benedict Anderson applies these thoughts to the nation as an imagined community, which considers the population on the macro level. Scaling it down to the meso level, communities become more tangible and are less of a thought experiment. On this meso level, one finds that community can be "associated with the desire to establish a *sense of unity* based on a homogenous group [...] or set of values" (Gottlieb 2007: 62, emphasis added). What Anderson calls "fraternity", Gottlieb terms "sense of unity": it is the notion of belonging and feeling at home. It is what, on a micro level, the urban family provides for its individual members.

Taking Anderson's idea of fraternity or comradeship even further, urban families share this quality with communities for they are based on "face-to-face contact" (Anderson 2006: 6): direct interaction on a regular basis. Urban families can only truly function if they are conducted in a direct and therefore personal fashion as opposed to members of blood-ties families, who can be phoned once a month or not spoken to at all but can still be considered family – if only in a biological sense. The ties of the urban family are not biologically binding and require effort by the various members, which makes this type more selective and hence more special for one can be (in)voluntarily excluded from an urban family if one does not respect the notion of equality. This is also in tune with John Bardo and John Hartman's ideas about community, which "can be seen as a process, not a passive, never-changing concept. It requires action, interaction, desire for continuance, social structure and social order that facilitate personal, warm relationships. It requires a recognition of a higher social order not based merely on the selfish interests of the individual." (1982: 129)

In *Bridget Jones's Diary*, the eponymous heroine and her friends constantly meet up to discuss relationship problems or "to get the weekend off to a healthy start" (Fielding 1998: 120), no matter what day. As they are not cohabiting, they need to conduct their meetings at an exterior location, mostly bars. The reader discovers that Bridget lives in Ladbroke Grove, a district of Notting Hill, and frequently patronises the bars 192 and Café Rouge, which are in the same part of London. Urban families in chick- and ladlit tend to have a relatively small territory in which they move (cf. Knowles 2004a: 38) and they hardly ever leave the territory in which their home is located. As spatial agents, Bridget and her friends have turned their territory into a life space and through their bonding and 'play' they have created a comfort zone which supports their characters and their choice of life. However, in order to construe such a life space that is acknowledged equally by all members of the urban family, they need to re-appropriate this public space. Each of the characters, or agents, has their own flat and thus private place which they have fashioned to their liking. Now, in order to establish a space in which all are equal and at no (dis)advantage, they need to find a space they can striate and make their own. The urban family generally takes bars and applies another layer to the already heterotopic bar. The reasons why pubs, bars or cafés are chosen as meetings places are that, on the one hand, they are roofed public spaces accessible for everyone and, on the other hand, there is an almost infinite amount of beverage at these places. It is in these places of leisure that the urban family can feel at home: a "home away from home available to everyone." (Earnshaw 2000: 1) The meeting space in the public sphere becomes the equivalent to the living room of cohabiting urban families and can therefore be called the *living room-away-from-home*[24]. It is a place "where individuals may come and go as they please, in which none are required to play host, and in which *all feel at home* and comfortable." (Oldenburg 1989: 22, emphasis added)

However, in contrast to the meeting space of the cohabiting urban family, the living room-away-from-home is not under the urban family's jurisdiction as they are only customers and not in any case entitled to manipulate the interior design or dictate the prices of the beverages. They are equal to all the other patrons and with their leaving their table or spot at the bar, they will dissolve the mirage of their dominion that the locale pretends to grant their customers. Yet, by constantly patronising the same locale, they start to regard their usual 'hang-outs' as 'theirs'

24 That the outsourced meeting space's openness to the public can have its drawbacks can be seen in *Bridget Jones: The Edge of Reason*. Bridget and her urban family meet at their usual hang-out, the bar 192, but then Rebecca, a woman with whom all are acquainted, comes in: "Rebecca is not exactly a friend, except that she's always turning up in 192 with me and Jude and Shaz." (2004: 34) Because Rebecca knows where to find Bridget and her urban family, she can penetrate their space fairly easily. She does not compromise the structure in general but shows that the openness of this meeting space is not as 'safe' as the living room of cohabitating urban families.

and they create a new sense of place. Urban families attribute the feeling of comfort to it and consider the living room-away-from-home a stronghold against the overwhelming city and its daily tribulations. The living room-away-from-home becomes an outsourced space which is not turned into a place by designing it as one would a flat or house, but by being there regularly. It dissolves the minute the urban family leaves the space in which the place is created, but – as opposed to any other places one thinks one creates in any bar one only patronises infrequently or only once – when members of the urban family return to the bar, the place is re-created without any loss, even when they are not sitting at the same table: "The more people visit a place, use it, and become, themselves, a part of it, the more it is theirs." (Oldenburg 1989: 41) The concept of the living room-away-from-home is comparable to an umbrella and by frequently patronising a space, the umbrella is put up. It will remain in the bar, albeit folded, as long as the family is absent and when the family comes in, it will expand and create a place within the heterotopia of the bar in which topics, problems or news can be discussed without the need to hold back – just as one would in one's own home. This also explains why members of the urban family also discuss rather private matters in these public places: the connotations of the privacy of one's own living room are extended to that of the living room-away-from-home[25]. The frequency of dwelling in bars or similar locations establishes connotations and spatial emotions (sense of place) to a table at a bar such as those one would grant one's own living room: it suggests that the home-ly features of security (the notion of the stronghold), stimulation (however alcohol-induced) and, of course, identity (that of belonging to an urban family) can be imparted on to a hitherto semi-public space. Through all these features a public space becomes the (non-cohabiting) urban family's living room.

However, there are of course drawbacks to an urban family. The two most important and most prominent issues will be explained in the following and both of these problems establish a strong connection between space and relationships. The first issue is only visible in ladlit, namely the notion of the underachieving slacker. Each ladlit novel presents a protagonist whose life has come to a standstill and in which he is very comfortable. These men can be diagnosed as 'suffering' from a condition I want to term *felix rigor mortis*, blissful paralysis: they live in shared accommodations and are happy just like that. They might have a girlfriend or not but their urban families of usually male friends give them a reason to get up in the mornings – if only to move from their bed to the communal couch to slouch on and watch TV. The fact that felix rigor mortis appears only to affect males in a cohabi-

25 It should be acknowledged, though, that this privacy is swiftly forgotten in chick- and ladlit when the topic discussed endangers the interlocutors' chances of finding their perfect partner: see chapter 6.

tating urban family points towards the activity-inducing outsourced meeting space. If the lads have to leave their flat to meet their friends, they tend to be more inclined to be active in their general attitude too. In the novel *Bachelor Kisses*, young doctor Jon Marshall has a girlfriend at the beginning of the narrative, yet she leaves him: "She says I hardly even seem to be in the relationship. She says I just don't seem to care about what happens to us. She calls me a shit, and that's fine. I probably am." (Earls 1998b: 21) The felix rigor mortis of not caring what happens is also visible in his job: Jon cannot be bothered to decide what kind of doctor he wants to be. Jon can be compared to a leaf that landed on a flowing river – he is taken somewhere, yet not by his own design but by chance (cf. ibid.: 13). His cohabitating urban family are equally 'rigor': they have the same routines of going to the same restaurants or shops at the same day, each week – a trait they share with Dec (*Street Furniture*) and Ethan (*Ethan Grout*). The lads enjoy their uneventful lifestyles. Making decisions or facing possible outcomes of the same are regarded as too stressful: "I really do wish we could relax. Things are fine as they are[26]" (ibid.: 255). This decelerating attitude is emphasised in the novels: all laddish friends of the main protagonist are underachievers and thus both legitimise this attitude and promote its validity. Furthermore, it is one of the building blocks of their urban family as it is the shared mantra of its members to 'take it easy'.

The only incentive to (a)rouse the lads into action so that they finally decide to take a leap of faith and change something is a woman, the perfect partner. In *Mr Commitment*, Duffy is afraid that when he moves in with his girlfriend of four years they might find out that they do not like living together and "it's usually when people discover they don't like living together that they split up" (Gayle 2000: 14). He regards it therefore as a wise decision not to tempt fate and not to move in with his girlfriend. However, she takes his inaction as a sign that he does not want to take their relationship to the next level and breaks up with him (see chapter 6). It is the realisation that Duffy is about to lose the love of his life forever which has him finally act. He casts off the paralysis and proves to his (ex)girlfriend that he does indeed love her and that he wants to share a space with her – meaning to move in with her and make his girlfriend his wife.

The urban families of the lads who transformed into men are equally affected by the changes the women bring about and thus they start to regard their paralyses in a similar way as the male protagonists do. If their finances allow, they move out, look for another job or start to treat others with less disrespect. Spatially, the abandonment of the felix rigor mortis results in a new-found appreciation for one's own abode (Jon) or the search for a new home (Duffy, Dec and Ethan). Like a virus, the

26 A similar attitude is expressed by Duffy (*Mr Commitment*): "Like the saying goes, […] if it ain't broke don't fix it." (Gayle 2000: 14)

felix rigor mortis had contaminated all of its members but when the 'infected' male protagonist manages to get rid of the shackles of the condition, he will decontaminate the others, too. As the felix rigor mortis tends to affect only cohabitating urban families, they do not open up their space and their locale becomes a container in which they spend almost all their life. It takes effort and willpower to leave the restrictive space and cast off the felix rigor mortis, but the reason is always the love for a woman. It is conspicuous that 'cured' lads tend to leave their repressive homes and establish new spaces of happiness.

On a more critical note however, it is not unusual that, along with the overcoming of the felix rigor mortis, the urban family is abandoned too. To refer back to the connection between communities and urban families, David Harvey acknowledges that communities are "a recipe for isolation. They isolate groups from the city as a whole." (1997: 21) This isolation can be found with urban families, too, thus being the second problematic issue mentioned above. In *Paris Dreaming*, Libby Cutmore and her two friends Lauren and Denise have always been there for one another since all of them moved from other parts of Australia to Canberra: "I knew my tiddas [Aboriginal term for sisters; C.L.] were always there. They never sent calls to voicemail if they knew it was me on the line. They always returned text messages as soon as they received them. That's what my friends were like." (Heiss 2011: 37) Now, however, her tiddas have gotten boyfriends and this changes the dynamics of the urban family. The isolation Harvey talks about is evident here: being part of an urban family means that one is always part of some larger entity so that one's territory never feels too big and oneself alone. This also explains why urban families use only a small area of their metropolises. But in case the other members of one's urban family form their own (inevitably biological) family by becoming part of a couple or marrying, the left-over member will realise their isolation all of a sudden. This isolation is but self-inflicted as the urban family used to be enough in itself. But now the single protagonists will feel alone and by not being able to fall back on other groups, for example drinking buddies or sports teams, a reassessment of the situation and the size of the territory is in order. Libby used to believe that her friends would always be there – as opposed to men – but now she realises that this might not be true after all (cf. ibid.): "The network of friends has no unity [...]. One's many friends may offer no more than a sporadic and unreliable accessibility[27]." (Oldenburg 1989: 61) The example of Libby exposes a fundamen-

27 When Bridget Jones's best friend Jude gets married at the end of the second book in Fielding's successful series, her two still unmarried Singleton friends have her declare that "although I am now a Married I promise not to be a Smug one. [...] I promise also to keep in constant contact with my best friends, Bridget and Sharon, who are living proof that the Urban Singleton Family is just as strong and support-

tal problem of urban families, namely that of being an 'Other'. Only when the former Singletons – and urban families in chick- and ladlit novels are comprised of these to an exceptionally large extent – convert into part of a couple does the isolation of the other members become apparent. Changing a phrase from *About a Boy*, they used to be Singles Alone Together, but the reality has them isolated from others and being part of a couple is a criterion for exclusion. This is also experienced by Rob Fleming in *High Fidelity*: being together with his girlfriend Laura, he finds that he ultimately likes her friends more than his and starts to neglect his mates. He gets immersed in her life and establishes his sense of belonging by being with her, losing his own friends along the way. What Libby experiences with her friends, Rob has done to his, but when Laura breaks up with him, he not only has lost his friends but also his anchor-point: "before I knew it [...], my relationship was what gave me my sense of location. And if you lose your sense of location, you get homesick." (Hornby 2010: 171) The urban family Rob might have had once and which would have given him a sense of belonging and thus home has been done away with by him by turning his back on them – very likely not even viciously. Yet, now that Laura has also abandoned him, he finds himself without any anchor at all and longs for someone – Laura, not an urban family – to provide him with a feeling of home to overcome this sense of isolation.

Harvey, following another scholar, links communities and isolation via minorities and ethnicity. In a big city an ethnic minority tends to "define[...] itself by common attributes. [And] the positive identification of some groups is often achieved by first defining other groups as the other" (Young, qtd. in Harvey 1997: 21) the result of which is the formation of a community of variable size. Disregarding the fact that Anita Heiss's heroines are always strong Aboriginal women and thus definitely an ethnic minority, one should consider another form of marginalisation which has been touched upon before: in many novels of the chick- and ladlit genres there are two opposing parties – the Singletons and the (Smug) Marrieds, to borrow terms coined by Helen Fielding in *Bridget Jones's Diary*. They define one another by not belonging to the other group – homogeneity by exclusion. Nonetheless, given the choice, all of the characters would choose being in a relationship over being a 'happy' Singleton any day, as the example of Bridget Jones shows: in another alcohol-heavy outing with her friends at a bar, Bridget exclaims "Yes! Hurrah! Singletons should not have to explain themselves all the time but should have an accepted status", only to confess not even twenty-four hours later: "Oh God, I'm so lonely. An entire weekend stretching ahead with no one to love." (Fielding 1998: 245, 246) The urban family is thus exposed as a very strong group

ive, just as there for you, as anyone's blood family." (Fielding 2004a: 402) That this is untrue can be found in the third instalment of the *Bridget Jones* series.

but, at the same time, it appears to be nothing more than a layover on the way to blissful coupledom. By creating an unflattering picture of the 'Other', namely Smug Marrieds, the authors, and here Helen Fielding is not an exception, present the Singletons as defined by the common attributes of being independent and modern, as not being stuck in traditional, even conservative values which represent rather out-of-date concepts like marriage. Yet, it has to be acknowledged that almost all chick- and ladlit novels close with the promise of a 'happily ever after' and therefore they give in to the fairy tale narrative of 'every princess needs a prince to take her to his castle' that is so prominent in romantic fiction. The urban family, which is comprised of Singletons, is indeed isolated from society and whereas it is described as idyllic and free-spirited, all the protagonists are more than happy to leave this space to join the other side, which they previously lashed out at.

There is one incident in the second *Bridget Jones* novel when Bridget's single friends Jude and Sharon meet married Magda. They meet at the single women's living room-away-from-home and, before Magda arrives, the women dissect one another's love lives. With the advent of the Smug Married mother, however, the dynamics of the group shift drastically as their attitudes towards relationships are far from compatible (cf. Fielding 2004a: 40-43). The Singletons feel protective of both their attitude and their space and are angry with Magda for intruding into both: "She can't have it both ways. She can't be in a Smug Married Family then moan because she isn't in a Singleton Urban Family" (ibid.: 43). This example combines the idea of the outsourced living room as constitutive part of the urban family with the ideology of the secure space. At the same time the single women's discussions in this space make clear that they would like to transition to a state Magda occupies, as all their topics are related to men and how to create a lasting relationship. It has to be noted, however, that, although the Singletons are appalled by Magda's comments, her suggestions and logic are presented as much more informed and reasonable than the Singletons', who shirk making their own assumptions but quote self-help books (Jude) or feminist pamphlets (Sharon).

The examples of Libby and Bridget show that urban families have many positive qualities, but being part of one is just a passing phase and although Smug Marrieds are not well regarded, the female protagonists in chicklit wish for nothing more than to belong to them. In ladlit novels, the process from urban to biological family is not always so strongly focused upon. However, the process is merely masked: considered from a spatial point of view, the lads – like the chicklit heroines – will exchange one life space for another. They will leave their laddish space, which has been characterised by the lads' felix rigor mortis, and embrace a locality that can be happily shared with their girlfriends. The difference to chicklit, then, is that in the heroine-centred novels there is no rigor mortis but a faux-felix state that envelops their urban family's locality: the heroines pretend to be happy Singletons but secretly wish for a shared space in which they can conduct their lives with their perfect partners.

In *Street Furniture*, then, three types of families are pitted against one another: the biological family, the elected family and the urban family. Declan 'Dec' McPherson has 'lost' his biological family but he is almost immediately found by another mother and her son, Smithy:

> Smithy, now seemingly un-jealous of my hijacking his family [twenty years ago], did in the early days taunt me with tales of my mother dropping me off by the side of the road and his mother collecting me like a street person finding something of mild interest while rifling through a garbage bin. Mrs Smithy, however, has always liked to tell her friends, when I am about, that picking me up was like discovering a valuable gem, mistakenly left for just a minute. She reckons she's near as stolen me. (Howard 2004: 20)

Here, Dec passes over from one household to the next and it is only in the latter that he is finally able to live in a functional family, which, biologically speaking, is not his own. The reliability of blood ties is definitely inferior to that of an elected family and, later on, urban family. Thus, when the boys are too old to still live at home they share a flat in Sidney district Bankstown. Each of them has their own room and a mutual friend, Jeff, sleeps on the couch in the living room. They live happily in a bubble that is constructed of marihuana, doner kebabs and unemployment benefits – the felix rigor mortis of a laddish urban family. Like all underachievers afflicted by this condition, they, too, have a very limited range of their territory. This restricted movement within the territory also delineates their space and indeed the edges of Bankstown are hardly ever crossed by Dec's urban family. During one of their few trips to the city centre, Jeff is accidentally killed, leaving a void both in Dec and Smithy's flat and their lives. They try to recreate Jeff with stories in order not to forget him but the unoccupied couch is too much for Dec to bear any longer. The disruption of his urban family has also created a rift in his daily routine and thus his territory: "I realise I want my days to be different [but] I still want them to end up here. Home." (Ibid.: 61). Two things are important to note: Jeff's death has a larger impact on Dec's life than the abandonment of both his parents, thus stressing his urban family's value as opposed to that of his biological family. The other insight is that when uttering these words Dec, Smithy and Jeff's pregnant girlfriend Maya are at their local pub. On the one hand, the outsourced meeting space acknowledges the presence of Maya, a sometime member of the urban family who does not live in Dec's flat. On the other hand, as Jeff used to live in the flat's living room (cf. ibid.: 104-108), this space has become 'tainted' and Dec feels no longer comfortable staying in his living room. It seems that Jeff's death has torn the curtain which shielded Dec's underachieving life in the confinement of his self-elected territory:

all of a sudden he becomes aware that there is much more out there for him to see and to achieve, least of all to meet a woman to fall in love with. Although it is usually a woman whose presence makes the lad defy his felix rigor mortis, here she is only the justification to do so: Jeff's death leads to Dec's reassessment of the happiness of his paralysis, but it is the advent of Ms Right that confirms Dec's decision to change his life. She will encourage him not to revert to his previous laddish life ever again.

Jeff's death is such an important event in Dec's life because he sees similarities to his own development: "For me, he was Jeff, not Jeffrey Acton, he'd chosen Smithy, Maya and me for his family" (Howard 2004: 56) and he reckons he knew Jeff better than the Actons knew their son Jeffrey. Jeff, both as a person and – following his death – as a concept, becomes intricately intertwined with the sofa, but it does not stop there: with him Dec also associates the living room as the centre of the house (cf. ibid.: 123) and, just like in a Chinese box, it becomes the centre of their territory Bankstown and thus the heart of their urban family, which is likened to one's world, the "other people were 'just family'." Dec boils his learned process down to one sentence: "Family might come and go but real friends are forever." (Ibid.: 50) An urban family occupies the position between leaving one's parental home and biological family and starting a family of one's own in a new home. It is a necessary metropolitan concept and it is intricately entwined with the concept 'home' as urban families tend to establish living rooms outside their own abodes. However, these urban families will never be regarded as fulfilling and lasting as biological families, which all protagonists will inevitably establish. The urban family becomes a placeholder until the protagonists have evolved enough to be independent of their respective urban families and to be recognised by their perfect partners.

THE HOME AT THE END OF MEMORY LANE

In *The Odyssey*, Homer's titular hero tries to get back home to Ithaca when the Trojan War is over and, as has been alluded to before, this takes him a while. Of the ten years he is away from Ithaca, seven are spent on the island of seductive nymph Calypso. At one point Odysseus tries to convince his captor to let him go and he evokes memories of home, which are strongly connected to his wife Penelope: "I [...] know that Penelope, however wise, cannot compete with you in grace or stature: she is not more than mortal, whereas you are deathless, ageless. Even so, *each day I hope and hunger for my house*: I long to see the day of my *returning home*." (Homer 1990: 105, emphasis added) Not only does Odysseus want to go home, he also equates his wife with the space he is longing for, he longs for his family. The home, thus, encases memories that are dear to the protagonists: "distance allows for an appreciation of home" (Park, Davidson and Shields 2011: 3). It appears that a strong connection between literature and the notion of remembering exists as "landform descriptions in literary works have often strong symbolic overtones, the result of memories, suffering and nostalgia." (Lando 1996: 3)

The term nostalgia is a combination of the Greek words *nostos* and *algos*. The first translates as "to return home" and the latter means "pain" (cf. Trigg 2006: 53). Nostalgia itself, then, means "longing for a home that no longer exists or has never existed" (Boym 2001: xiii). However, the word itself is not of Greek origin. Hinting at the connection between the past and longing as well as a spatial dimension of 'home', it was coined by physician Johannes Hefer in 1688 when he inspected Swiss soldiers who were fighting far away from their home country. Hefer found that the soldiers were unable to fight anymore after they had heard "folk melodies of Alpine valleys" or ate a dish similar to their mothers' (Boym 2001: 4, Trigg 2006: 53). Hofer recognised that nostalgia could befall anyone who has been "uprooted" (Illbruck 2012: 37-38). Yet the disease could come back at any time, as it was and still is affecting the mind rather than the body, which is why by the early nineteenth century, "[n]ostalgia was no longer regarded as a neurological disorder but, instead, came to be considered a form of melancholia or depression" (Wildschut et al. 2006: 975). Therefore, nostalgia can be understood as being composed of affective and cognitive components, the latter relating to remembering, reflecting upon as well as evaluating and interpreting things and events past. The affective component describes emotions (e.g. happiness or sadness) which are either associated with particular items and events or which are actually activated by them (cf. Kießling 2012: 31). Summarising the ideas of numerous scholars, nostalgia is a complex emotion which is based on a high-level cognitive process (cf. ibid.: 32-33).

In the following different forms of longing will be analysed in chick- and ladlit novels and they will disclose another layer of the concept 'home'. Referring back to Svetlana Boym's idea that nostalgia does not necessarily need to be directed at a concrete place, some characters long for a home they have lost, and some characters wish for a home they have never had. In the novels discussed in this subchapter the motif of longing for 'home' is predominant as well as inevitably connected to the need to belong (again) and can therefore be strongly associated with a romantic inclination.

Concerning the objects one is nostalgic about, Wildschut et al. have conducted studies and their findings state that the objects featured in most nostalgic accounts of their studies' participants are persons, momentous events and settings (cf. 2006: 977-978; cf. Kießling 2012: 44). All three of these features are distinctly shown in Mike Gayle's debut novel *My Legendary Girlfriend*, which chronicles the weekend of William 'Will' Kelly's twenty-sixth birthday. He has recently moved to London to take up a position as English teacher at a comprehensive school. But, and this is his problem, he is anything but happy: "You think I'm scared of life, don't you? Well, I'm not. I'm not scared of failure either. After all I'm a failed teacher and I haven't killed myself yet." (Gayle 1999: 192-193) He credits his failures to his 'legendary ex-girlfriend' Aggi, who broke up with him exactly three years ago and who still occupies his mind so much that Will constantly reminisces about their time as a couple. In the novel, the moment he steps into his flat – and thus leaves the worries and problems of being a teacher at school (if only for the weekend) – he mentions Aggi and how the day she broke up with him has left a lasting impression on him because "despite everything I'd done to forget the day I was born and the occasion of her dumping me, the date remained locked in a brain cell that refused to die." (Ibid.: 17) Yet, it is because of his spatial practices that he cannot forget her: in his flat, which is characterised by its out-of-date-ness and shabbiness, she is the only silver lining to which he has elevated her:

> The yellowing refrigerator in the corner of the kitchen gurgling vociferously, as if suffering from a bout of indigestion was, at a guess, probably a decade older than myself, as was virtually everything in the flat. The cooker, wardrobes, sofa-bed, carpet – the rigours of age had consumed them all to such an extent that it had rendered them useless unless you had the know-how. […] Had I noticed all that was wrong when I first saw the flat, I wouldn't have taken it […] To try and cheer the place up – an impossibly futile task – I had stuck my favourite photo of Aggi on the wall near the sofa-bed. (Ibid.: 30-31)

The photo of Aggi is juxtaposed with the decrepit state of his flat, thus heightening her status even more – by lowering everything else. Although Will says that "[h]ad [he] noticed all that was wrong" he would have chosen another flat, it is a misleading 'confession' as he proves throughout the course of the novel that he especially loves the fact that he can wallow in his misery and he manifests his discontent as 'home'. As he has no friends to visit him, the state of the flat becomes a self-referencing system for him (because it is only visible to him): he feels miserable because of his life and his flat and, in turn, his flat is so "soul-destroyingly depressing" (ibid.: 29) it reflects back on his life – the moment he steps back into the flat he feels miserable. Thus, as stated, the photo is the only good thing in and about his flat, both glossing over and representing "present fears, discontents, anxieties and uncertainties" (Davis 1977: 420).

His notion of attaching so much meaning to the photo of Aggi is rather common as studies have shown that family and loved ones "are important objects of nostalgia" and that "nostalgia can serve to redress deficiencies in belongingness" (Wildschut et al. 2006: 989, 985) or can be used to re-establish purpose and direction in one's life again (cf. Kießling 2012: 30): indulging in nostalgic feelings and emotions helps a person to cope with (previously) negative emotions and Will feels he does not belong anymore as his only anchor-point, Aggi, has left him. Dylan Trigg quotes Kant: "Homesickness [...] is the result of a longing that is aroused by the *recollection of a carefree life* […], a longing for places where they enjoyed the very simple pleasures of life." (2006: 54, emphasis added) The italicised phrase reveals a very vital factor of nostalgia: people long for a past that was – generally[28] – better. Interestingly, that past is usually one's youth, a time when one was devoid of responsibility and sorrows that afflict adulthood – "the slower rhythm of dreams" (Boym 2001: xv): "by the late nineteenth century the term [nostalgia] had merged that desire for place with the desire for childhood – imagining that place could embody the past, and that the past could be lodged in particular places." (Katz 2010: 818) It has to be noted though that this romanticising of the past is only possible because one does not live in it anymore, thus one can ignore certain negative aspects of one's past. People look to the past because they long for stability in times of turmoil which nostalgia can provide them with: "The nostalgic desires to obliterate history and turn it into private or collective mythology, to revisit time like space, refusing to surrender to the irreversibility of time that plagues the human condition" (Boym 2001: xv). This means that the nostalgic creates a place consisting of time put on halt, and the home as place of security is such a place of carefree living. Human beings tend to repress problems in order to reconstruct the nostalgic memory as perfect: nostalgia can be compared to the photography of a room in which nothing ever changes. One can enter this room (via imagination, memory or souvenir) and whilst one is there time passes by on the outside but the room itself will always remain the way it is most comfortable and comforting to the nostalgic – stuck in time: people "consume the past in the form of glossy images" (Jameson 1991: 287). The photograph will always be shiny and perfect but it is something past and more often than not an altered version of actual events and not 'how it really was'.

It is therefore no coincidence that Aggi remains in Will's flat in the form of a photo. He keeps it close to the one place in his small apartment he spends most time in – his bed. Aggi is attributed the function of guardian angel as much as a souvenir of their three years together, a period of time which he will never have again

28 Trigg also points towards a nostalgia that seeks "ruin, dissolution, or suffering" (2006: 57) which is in line with what Wildschut et al. have found: "it would be an oversimplification to regard nostalgic memories as either entirely positive or negative. Nostalgic narratives often [contain] both negative and positive ingredients (usually in that order […])" (2006: 983). This being possible or even attractive to some people, the majority of nostalgic people tend to remember the good times rather than the bad ones.

because the "nostalgia's object must *always be absent*" (Katz 2010: 817, emphasis added):

> We do not need or desire souvenirs of events that are repeatable[29]. Rather we need and desire souvenirs of events that are reportable, events whose materiality has escaped us. [...] It represents not the lived experience of its maker but the "secondhand" experience of its possessor/owner. [...] The souvenir speaks to a context of origin through a language of longing, for it is not an object arising out of need or use value; it is an object arising out of the necessarily insatiable demands of nostalgia. (Stewart 1984: 135)

This idea of the souvenir can be complemented with the notions of the virtual and the real object: the virtual, which is not corporeal but in this case the (love) story behind the picture, should be treated as affective and thus becomes "fully real [and] can be actualized as the concrete" (Shields, qtd. in Davidson 2011: 51). Therefore, "[t]hings are the concrete result of and means towards actualizing real moments, memories, desires." (Ibid.) The picture of Aggi reminds Will of his rigor mortis – felix in so far as he loves to wallow in his misery – and therefore signifies her absence, too: when Aggi broke up with him on his birthday, she told him that "[y]ou've stayed the same […], you haven't changed at all – you didn't grow with me" (Gayle 1999: 169). Aggi outgrew Will and the picture is proof that Will has still not changed: he is still infatuated with his ex and the picture-like existence which is often attributed to nostalgia is perverted here for not only has Aggi not changed in the picture of her, Will has not changed at all since he has been together with her, too. He remained in his stasis even through their break-up and now six years have passed. The picture, thus, mirrors his laddish lethargy concerning life: "Will knows that wanting back the past does not actually help to get a life and a future, but nevertheless he stubbornly refuses to take any action himself." (Ochsner 2009: 198) He cannot muster enough energy to look into other career options or a better flat but takes the path of least resistance, which allows him to concentrate his energy on wallowing in his self-pity and longing for Aggi. It never occurs to him that it is exactly this state that was the problem between them. Will resorts to nostalgia, to a time with Aggi in which he felt truly happy because otherwise he would need to address his current problems, which correspond to the most common threats to self-continuity: regression of individual roles; loss of social contacts, isolation and loneliness; existential worries, insecurity with regard to the future (cf. Kießling 2012: 56). Will falls back on nostalgia because his sense of self is threatened, yet his nostalgia and paralysis worsen his state:

29 "But at the end of the day what have I got? *Nothing but memories*. I'm twenty-six and I constantly live in the past." (Gayle 1999: 57, emphasis added)

nostalgia serves the function of protecting personal identity against threats of discontinuity. From this perspective, rather than being a pathological or immature feeling, nostalgia is an adaptive response to the basic human problem of developing a stable and enduring sense of self in the face of an often uncertain and chaotic world. Therefore, nostalgia arises from a defensive motive to avoid the anxiety associated with failing to maintain a sense of self-continuity.[30] (Bassett 2006: 2; cf. Routledge et al. 2011: 639)

Will is reluctant to accept his own part in the break-up and through his nostalgia he glorifies 'past' Aggi at the same time that he blames her for his present problems. But "Will is so possessed by his self-pity that he does not recognise the stability he gets from what he has got. [He has got] a steady job as boring as it might be and [he has got] a permanent address even if it is located in not a very sought-after area in North London" (Ochsner 2009: 200). He disregards the actual stability he has and this disregard and his self-pity create another, to him more important stability in the form of stasis, which is reflected in his flat:

30 The need for self-continuity is the driving force behind Mike Gayle's *Turning Thirty* in which Matt Beckford returns to Birmingham after his relationship to an American woman has failed. Once back, he re-assembles his old group of friends and they try to re-enact their youthful nights out drinking and partying but they have to realise that the present is not the past: "I had no idea what we were trying to prove (that we were still young? That we didn't need sleep? That we could still talk rubbish at four o'clock in the morning?) but whatever it was I suspected our constant failure was proving the opposite." (2001: 279) That he indeed came to a crossroads and used his nostalgic feelings and the attempt to re-create bygone times to gloss over the fact that he did not know what do next is addressed in the sequel, *Turning Forty*: "Safe in the arms of friends and family in Birmingham I set about trying to turn thirty without losing the plot. And it worked, up to a point. [But] there was a major complication where I briefly mistook the hazy warmth of nostalgia for something more" (2013: 16). Matt refers to the relationship he attempted with a woman who has always been there for him in the past. However, both had to realise that they were not helping each other because they only went for the relationship out of nostalgic feelings: both have recently terminated their relationships and compensate this loss by turning to each other as that has previously proved to work. But just like Will Kelly, Matt has to face the truth that nostalgia is not a good-enough reason to have a lasting relationship: at some point the present does destroy the illusion of being able to re-live the past.

I looked around the flat. Nothing had changed. N-O-T-H-I-N-G. I wasn't sure what I had expected to happen (someone to have fixed the kitchen tap? A miracle? A message from Aggi?) but I'd desperately wanted something, anything to have changed. Instead, time had stood still and waited for my return. (Gayle 1999: 140-141)

Contrary to his confession, he is able to voice what he wants – namely a better habitat and a (re)connection to Aggi. He again connects the two in a way which suggests a mutual dependency: the locale of his flat is the background on which Will projects the interrelation between a better living space or locality and the return of Aggi – the one is not possible without the other in Will's opinion.

His flat, therefore, can be compared to a self-fashioned limbo in which Will waits for something, anything to be transformed – Will himself seems unable to effect this change. He even creates an alternative reality and reckons "if Aggi and I hadn't split up when we did, we probably would've remained together. At least I hoped so. With the combined income from two professional jobs may we'd even have had [...] a smart flat in nearby Highgate, instead of a poorly decorated shoe box in Archway." (Ibid.: 171) Will is aware that this is a fantasy as he confesses just a few lines further down but he seems to punish himself with his Archway flat for being a failure. If he did not live in such a decrepit flat it would have been harder to fashion himself as the 'victim' of the break-up. He equally punishes Aggi's avatar – the photo – by installing her *with him* in the "shoe box" so that 'she' must share this depressing home with him. Moreover, the photo is his portal from his unhappy present to his glorified past, and the flat as a whole functions even as a 'dreamspace' in which he can remember the good times, mainly because he deems the present too depressing. The fact that he hardly leaves his bed for the duration of the novel gives him no option but to internalise his thoughts – it is a focus inwards as opposed to an *out*look.

Where nostalgia can be constructed as a longing flight from the ambiguities and disappointments of everyday life, remembrance faces the open negativity of the future by knitting a steady confidence in who one is from the pains and joys of the past retained in the things [e.g. memories and souvenirs; C.L.] among which one dwells. *Nostalgic longing* is always for an elsewhere. *Remembrance* is the affirmation of what brought us here. (Young 1997: 154, emphasis added)

This quote shows that Will needs to realise that his development culminating in the stasis he now mourns cannot solely be accredited to Aggi's breaking up with him as he amalgamates his nostalgic longing with remembrance. Thus, he creates a 'custom-made past'. He constantly longs for the time when they were still together and happy, even when the cracks in the perfect memory become more and more evident. In the end, he will be able to burn Aggi's photo (cf. Gayle 1999: 280) – which he had previously only doodled on, but could not bring himself to dispose of completely. The title, however, which he awards Aggi – "[s]he was my Legendary Girlfriend and I'd miss her as long as I lived" (ibid.: 176) – is eventually claimed by his new girlfriend Alice (cf. ibid.: 352). She takes on Aggi's qualities, a fact which needs to be regarded critically: Alice represents the features of Young's remembrance, representing the transition Will has undergone. But at the same time traces of nostalgia cannot be dismissed for he has known her for exactly ten years – he met her on his sixteenth birthday: echoing again the structure of having life-changing events happening on his birthday, Alice stands for the carefree life he has had when he was younger, thus Will associates a positive feeling of the past with her, too. Additionally, Young's idea of open negativity suggests that Alice might become a similar mythological icon in Will's life, as the outcome of their relationship starts because both try to cover up a lack in their romantic longing – Alice was left by her boyfriend of some years shortly before she tells Will of her "love". Alice and Will give in to their emotional need for companionship, which suggests that their relationship is based not on romantic feelings but on the need for comfort. The fact that Will repeatedly mentions the fact that his "sole aim in life [is] to find a girlfriend who would make [him] feel so secure that [he would] never have to worry about relationships again" (ibid.: 173) points in the direction that he is prepared to settle for an option which does not necessarily include too many emotions.

The epilogue in which the reader learns of Will and Alice's union is set in a non-descript room, but due to the fact that Will now allows for another being to penetrate his previously solitary confinement, represented through his Archway flat, his concept of 'home' is re-appropriated. This undefined space has become one of companionship and it has freed Will from his destructive, backwards-trained focus. Nevertheless, the lack of description of the flat (dis)embodies his and Alice's relationship: at this moment it can go either way because the space they are depicted in is so barren it can become one of misplacement, like the description of the Archway flat, or it becomes a space of happiness, which could manifest itself in a lovingly decorated flat which speaks of both its tenants' influence. The lacuna of the description thus poses both positive possibility and the potential for open negativity.

The derelict state of the home can be a very fitting metaphor of its inhabitant's troubling emotional state. Two other examples whose feelings of loss are represented in the protagonist's living spaces are Nick Earl's *Zigzag Street* and Helen Fielding's *Bridget Jones: The Edge of Reason*. In both novels, the main protagonists are left by their partners but, in the words of the former novel's Richard Derrington, they manage "to construct an entire universe in which [his ex-girlfriend or, in Bridget's case, Mark Darcy] is central, but absent." (Earls 1998a: 30) Both characters try to overcome their longing for their respective ex-partners but are unable to. This is mirrored in their abodes: Richard moved to his late grandmother's house to renovate it and Bridget has contracted a builder to add a second bedroom to her flat. Although for different reasons, both Richard and Bridget are unable to get their homes to be habitable again. Richard cannot bring himself to repair his grandmother's house so that he can hang on to memories of her. She is elevated to the image of perfect love and coupledom when Richard finds a love letter of his grandfather addressed to his grandmother in which it transpires that she has always only ever loved her husband (cf. Earls 1998a: 102-107). Therefore, the house – the spatial representation of his grandmother's love – cannot be changed by him: Richard has recently been left by his girlfriend and his failure in the face of perfect love is mirrored in his impotence to change anything at the house. Richard cannot change his surroundings to mirror his idea of perfect love – he borrows somebody else's as an overshadowing memorial. It is only when he falls in love again that he is finally able to start renovating the home, with his new girlfriend no less: he has found perfect love himself, he does not need to overemphasise his grandparents', and the house becomes home again.

Bridget's life, on the other hand, starts out well as she is in a relationship with her perfect partner. However, shortly afterwards, her life begins to experience problems and these are reflected in the actions of her builder: for example, when Bridget suspects Mark of being responsive to the flirtations of a bitch character, her builder has put up her shelves "in mad asymmetrical manner" (Fielding 2004a: 33), mirroring the unbalanced state of the relationship. It needs to be acknowledged that the problems Bridget 'perceives' are usually blown out of proportion but have negative results nonetheless. Shortly afterwards, Bridget and Mark break up. Bridget misses him dearly and this – again – is made spatial when her builder makes a hole in her wall: "Just got home from work and hole has been covered up with big sheet of polythene but no note, no message, nothing [...]. Wish Mark would ring." (Ibid.: 199) Bridget tries to enjoy life again but her desperate actions are rather transparent – like the sheet of polythene – and she misses Mark. Her home mirrors her longing for the time when she was happy with Mark, happy in her home and, most importantly, happy *with* Mark *in* her home. Eventually, they will get back together and the builder is put in jail after Mark has interfered. They continue their relationship but the hole remains, which is the reason why the novel concludes with Mark being offered a job in another country and Bridget wanting to accompany him: they can now create an entirely new space to share instead of mending a broken one.

Longing that is connected to the familial home is both an overarching motif and motive in Matt Howard's *Ethan Grout*. However in this novel, the longing is for a space and family that Ethan has *never experienced*. The eponymous protagonist has just been to his father's funeral and is now pondering the idea that he has no more family: "And now that the only person to whom I am important has gone, and I've finally realised he isn't going to be replaced by any of the folks of [my old workplace], it is down to me." (Howard 2010: 3) The phrasing of this thought is rather significant as Ethan says "to whom I am important" instead of using "who was important to me". The passive voice of the statement expresses his wish to belong, linking the concepts of family, home and security. He feels an overpowering urge to have someone else acknowledge that Ethan's presence is important to them. This need to be acknowledged and consequentially to belong is most visible in his practice of eating out. He does not cook at home – it is very likely that his small apartment does not even feature a kitchen as it is never mentioned and Ethan is not able to cook at all – and orders at a Chinese takeaway or eats at McDonald's. This practice does reflect very much on his perception of home and how he is to become Mr Right in order to attract Ms Right's attention and love. His story of eating out starts with Ethan dining at the hospital in which his father died. At the hospital canteen his dinner is accompanied by the feeling that he is "the odd one out" because he is the only lonely diner and he does not even have a reason to eat out at the hospital anymore (ibid.: 12). Even at his usual takeaway he gets the same impression: "Never once have [the employees of the takeaway] acknowledged that they've seen me before. Am I a ghost?" he wonders when, in fact, he "ate a 52 again last night. Yes, three nights in a row. Well, it ain't a record." (Ibid.: 40, 17) Eating is here reduced to a solitary exercise as well as a dehumanising experience. Ethan feels he is haunting places instead of being a recognised customer, and a very good one at that.

This ties in with – and culminates in – his visits to McDonald's, which he only patronises because, when he was younger, his father once told him that he had seen Ethan's mother in a McDonald's, watching her abandoned family (ibid.: 22). It is not explained what happened to Ethan's mother, but she never appears except in the sole 'sighting' of his father's. Ethan thus always dines in another restaurant of the fast food chain to be able see her too one day. All these food experiences characterise Ethan as a person who dearly wishes to belong to a family unit, to no longer need to eat alone, and who indirectly constructs his identity in relation to family or rather its absence. When he eats at the hospital canteen or at McDonald's he sits by himself and has to watch other seemingly solitary eaters eventually being joined by friends and families whereas he comes, eats and leaves by himself.

It is therefore striking that when he finally makes contact with 'new' family members, they invite him to dinner: shortly before his death, Ethan's father married Joy, a single mother and fellow cancer patient. Whereas Ethan usually is reduced to a ghost-like presence, he becomes the reason for this dinner when Joy calls him up to get to know her and his stepbrother Travis better. He really takes to them although he constantly feels that he cannot keep up with them as becomes apparent on a spatial level: compared to his small, single-room apartment with only one window, Joy and Travis have an "open living area", "lots of windows" and "can squeeze in just the number of people required to make a fair amount of noise." (Howard 2010: 19) Ethan himself lives on Swanston Street in Melbourne and his abode is located directly above a pub (cf. ibid.: 5, 9). He enjoys the sound from downstairs, which has him feel less alone, but he does not participate in the hubbub. Ethan rather eats his 52, watches DVDs and minds his single goldfish, which is "a little dwarfed by his surroundings" (ibid.: 9) – a description which also applies to Ethan. The description of their house and the way Joy and Travis act within it and interact with Ethan suggest that their open living area is open to him as well, their being able to accommodate many people an invitation for Ethan to regard himself not only a welcomed guest but a member of their family now. This is also due to the fact that Joy is dying of cancer and longs for Ethan and Travis not be two solitary young men who have lost both their families, but brothers who can look out for each other (cf. ibid.: 222).

Shortly after this first dinner, Ethan happens to pass by Joy and Travis's home and as he cannot bear the thought of going to his own abode where he is only feeling depressed[31], he sits on his step-family's doorstep: "They might not even be home just now, but either way it doesn't feel empty." (Ibid.: 108) The positive emotion of the first real meeting with his step-family results in the association of the welcoming feeling of belonging with the architectural structure in which Ethan has experienced the emotion. Even without living at their place, Joy and Travis's home extends their security and identity to Ethan: he feels more at home on the doorstep of two people he has just started to get to know than in his own flat. At the same time, however, he is unsure how to react to this situation. He remains on the doorstep without checking if any of the inhabitants is home for a reason: the sensation of having a family that is not primarily absent is a novelty to Ethan. He always wished for a family unit to belong so much it is comparable to nostalgia, but he has no experiences to compare his longing to.

Kießling distinguishes between two dichotomies in such a context: the first binary differentiates between one's own experiences and experiences which are handed down, and the second binary discriminates between individual experiences and collective experiences (cf. 2012: 34). In the first binary, an individual's memory can be made independently or the person can be told about particular

31 As with Matt Howard's other protagonists, Ethan is also surrounded by motifs that signify the character's sense of belonging. In *Ethan Grout*, it is Ethan's fish Mr Fantastic that lives in a self-made aquarium far too large for him alone and from his window he can see a huge billboard of his model stepbrother, who looms as a shining example and tempting image of family out of Ethan's reach.

instances and thus take them on as being 'their own'. Ethan has never had a real family to speak of: whereas his mother is entirely absent from Ethan's life, his father is more of a guest. Due to his job, Ethan's father is constantly travelling the world and only phones in his fatherly concern (cf. Howard 2010: 109-110). Ethan was an orphan long before his biological family truly passed away. He can only rely on external or handed-down experiences of what it means to be part of a family and to engage in family activities: his visits to McDonald's or the hospital canteen are the only points of reference that are given in the novel. The other binary, the distinction between experiences one has made on one's own or in a group of indefinite size, helps to explain Ethan's reluctance to ring the doorbell. In the memory of a collective, a certain experience shared by the group is likely to blur and does not necessarily reflect each individual's understanding. Ethan is unsure whether Joy and Travis feel the same way about the dinner they shared as he does – again, he has no previous memory to compare it with – and thus he does not want to potentially destroy his positive memory: as long as he does not ask Joy or Travis, he can continue to treat the memory of the evening as being regarded positively by *everyone*. The doorstep becomes a place of hesitation, a threshold: making himself known and risk talking about their dinner means that his positive experience is going to be confirmed as being mutual or it means that he is going to be disappointed as Joy and Travis do not want to repeat the evening. In the end, he leaves the doorstep without ever checking and returns to his abode, which he no longer regards as home: "I want the sensation of returning to a home that's full of family life; not just empty rooms lit up in pretence" (ibid.: 108). Ethan might have deferred the clarification of his status in his step-family but a process has already begun which can be seen in his re-appropriation of the spatial concept 'home'.

When he was young, his wish was to belong to a gang and he was told that any four persons make a gang (cf. ibid.: 24). The wish to belong to a gang is Ethan's thinly disguised desire to have a proper family and not to have absent parents, who leave their son to care for himself, and with his girlfriend Alejandra, stepmother Joy and stepbrother Travis he has finally found three other people to create a gang – or rather family. He slowly starts to enlarge his territory and to include other homes in his itinerary which by the end of the novel will have him firmly established as Travis's brother and as Alejandra's perfect partner. So when Joy inevitably dies, Ethan, Travis and Alejandra sell their old abodes and buy a bar over which they can live as a unit (see chapter 6). This might seem like a step back into old habits as Ethan used to live above a bar – which he incidentally never really patronised – but this time he does it with his new family. His locality has changed from his very small room at the beginning of the novel, which still was too large for him alone, to a family and a girl he falls in love with. Locality is the space which most of one's life is consummated in and whereas Ethan tended to order his 52 to eat on his bed, he now has a larger space and people to enjoy it with. His longing has been fulfilled and has had a positive influence on his territory.

A different form of nostalgia and remembrance in connection to one's home is presented in the novel *Remember Me?* by Sophie Kinsella. Alexia 'Lexi' Smart is out with her friends, dancing and drinking in 2004 when she has an accident and wakes up in 2007. The time which has elapsed has actually happened but Lexi cannot remember any of the events or people of the past three years. This includes her husband and her meteoric rise from Associate Junior Sales Manager to the "bitch-boss-from-hell" she apparently turned into at a carpeting company (see chapter 5).

In 2004 she used to live in Balham in a "tiny but cosy [flat], with blue-painted window frames which [she] did [herself], and a lovely squashy velvet sofa, and piles of colourful cushions everywhere, and fairylights round the mirror." (Kinsella 2008: 61) In 2007, now, she is the wife of millionaire Eric and lives in their apartment in Kensington. After she wakes up in hospital and is deemed physically fit, she is told to go home: "'Yes!' I say after a pause. 'Home. Great.' Even as I'm saying the words I realize I don't know what I mean by 'home'. Home was my Balham flat. And that's gone." (Ibid.: 98) The Balham flat used to provide her with security and an identity, a sense of belonging. Her description speaks of the comfort and stimulation she got from her flat. Additionally, she put in effort to fashion the flat according to her ideas and ideals and turned it into a place which supports her identity, a veritable life space. Now that she is told that she 'has lived' with Eric in Kensington for some years, she is lost as to what place to call 'home', because her old anchor-point has been changed and given a new address. The last three years which have not 'happened' to Lexi create a nostalgic longing for the Balham flat and therefore her past as manifested in her previous home.

When she arrives at the Kensington loft, she is awestruck as "[i]t's way *better* than [she] imagined. [...] It's massive. It's light. It has views over the river. There's a vast, L-shaped cream sofa and the coolest black-granite cocktail bar. The shower is a whole marble-clad room, big enough for about five people." (Ibid.: 105, original emphasis) What makes the description of the loft so important for this chapter is that her husband Eric constantly asks her whether she remembers anything, if her memory is triggered by a piece of art, furniture or activity. He assumes that there is bound to be some memory and sincerely seems to hope it is nostalgia as that would mean that he can reassume their marriage to which he has grown accustomed, but Lexi still cannot remember anything. In order to compensate for this lack in her history, she creates fake memories as she "can just see [her friends] Fi, Carolyn and Debs perched at the cocktail bar, tequila shooters going, music blaring over the sound system." (Ibid., original emphasis) She assumes that these events must have happened in the past as she is unaware that since her transformation, in order to become more successful, she has lost all of her old friends. Here, Lexi has conjured up an image which can be called 'faux nostalgia': Lexi produces a perfect picture of events which never happened, but just like a true nostalgic person, she edits the past into a wholesome and pleasing image. She conjures up a simulation of a perfect life – with a perfect husband and best friends – and this simulation "masks the absence of a basic reality" (Baudrillard 2001: 1736, original emphasis). Despite the fact that Lexi has lost her memory and does not know that it is not possible to have had her friends over as they ceased to be friends a long time ago, it is still faux nostalgia: she creates a likely memory by fusing past events – going out with her friends in 2004 – with present spaces – the loft – to bridge the gap that has appeared between the two statuses of 2004 and 2007, respectively. This behaviour is also apparent when Lexi is at work and thinks her friends are happy for her occupying a better position than in 2004 (cf. Kinsella 2008: 173-178). Helmut Illbruck comments on the connection between denial, fantasy and nostalgia, writing that "[i]n the absence of the real, such dreams [Illbruck refers to nostalgic images; C.L.] may be the most realistic simulation possible." (2012: 207) Lexi does exactly that: she creates an alternate reality via fake memories which helps her to adjust to and justify her present status. She does not know of the real instances which led to her being part of 'loft-style living', such as the humiliation at her father's funeral (cf. Kinsella 2008: 374).

Her home becomes the main stage for this amalgamating fantasy that results in faux nostalgia and this can be explained with Jean Baudrillard's theory of the simulacrum: he writes that "[t]o simulate is to feign to have what one hasn't. [It] implies […] an absence." (2001: 1733) Pursuing that thought even further, he continues that "simulation threatens the difference between 'true' and 'false', between 'real' and 'imaginary'." (Ibid.: 1734) Lexi's faux nostalgia simulates a friendship which has long since ceased to exist and a loving marriage which never was. The fact that she mis-creates a memory in her new home is no coincidence for the home is also a simulacrum in itself for it symbolises the fake marriage of Lexi and Eric. Jon, a man for whom Lexi intended to leave her husband, repeatedly tells her that she is "not happy with Eric" (Kinsella 2008: 197) but she remains adamant that he must be mistaken for she would never cheat on her husband. Her behaviour is understandable, as she applies past patterns of behaviour to and in new, present situations so as to keep her life's history consistent (cf. Kießling 2012: 57): the fake memories which result in faux nostalgia help to glue together the two accidents in 2004 and 2007, which frame her lost memories. The problem as Lexi will find out as her life progresses is that the fake memories, which in turn became faux nostalgic feelings, mask the coldness of her marriage and the real reasons for her meteoric rise and loss of friends. Furthermore, it means that as Lexi cannot imagine *not* being happy with Eric, who installed her in this awe-inspiring loft, she creates a nostalgic glorification based on the assumption that their gorgeous home must mean that theirs is an awe-inspiring marriage, too, equating home and identity.

Eventually Lexi has to realise that their whole marriage is an artificial veneer of success which masks the emptiness that lies underneath. She feels that something is wrong in her marriage and marital home, but resorts to faux nostalgia to gloss over the irritating edges: when being in her and Eric's flat for the first time, she "can't honestly say this place feels like home *yet*." (Kinsella 2008: 132, emphasis added) At first she is excited and compares the flat to a hotel, but hotels are not meant to be lived in, only temporary stays are possible (see next subchapter). Lexi feels increasingly uneasy in her marriage and consequently her 'home', like a visitor in a showroom, a metaphor which is supported by the cameras and screens that are put up everywhere in the loft. Additionally, she is reprimanded when she leaves her things lying around and whilst having sex for the first time after she has returned to the loft, Eric constantly asks her whether she is comfortable (cf. ibid.: 262-265). She can never relax as she could in her Balham flat. She feels as if she and Eric are constantly 'putting on a show', namely their happy marriage, which is supported by the cameras and the pieces of non-representational art they buy regularly. This feeling is repeatedly enforced by Eric selling lofts – such as theirs – and consecutively lifestyles – such as theirs: he calls it "[l]oft-style living" accompanied by "a sweeping, parallel-hands gesture, as though he's moving bricks along a conveyor belt."[32] (ibid.: 81; cf. 109, 185, 188, 293) It exposes Eric as being only interested in perfect appearances, which is also evident in his strong regulation of his body via a carb-free diet, and when Lexi accidentally destroys a piece of art at the loft, Eric writes her an invoice and makes her pay for the damage she has caused (cf. ibid.: 293, 287). The home, as Porteous defined it – via identity, security and stimulation – is not realised.

Eric is contrasted with Jon, who is the architect of the lofts Eric's company sells to the very rich. Jon does not regard the social strata they move in as perfect and tries to educate Lexi as to look behind the fake memories and faux nostalgia to discover the 'real' Lexi. The only problem is that, just like Lexi cannot remember her husband Eric, she cannot remember her lover Jon. She only feels that she is attracted to the latter whereas she cannot bring herself to feel anything for the former, although Eric appears to genuinely love Lexi – in his own way. Her husband is spatially connected to appearances: most obviously, Eric represents and sells the lofts, but also his marriage and his 'home' (to visitors and friends alike), which he tries to manipulate into a state of perfection. Jon, on the other hand, is

32 "Jon's voice is so low, [Lexi] can barely hear it above the music. 'The minute you spoke I knew. [...] Knew I liked you.' [...] You said, "If I hear that phrase 'Loft-style living' again, I'm going to shoot myself.'" (Kinsella 2008: 293)

connected to creation and vision: he is an architect and in contrast to Lexi's husband, who wants to maintain a status quo – via diets, replacing the item Lexi has broken with an exact copy or by compiling a marriage manual which has Lexi wonder that "it can't be that we're some boring old married couple and do it *exactly the same way* each time" (ibid.: 260, original emphasis), Jon creates anew. Most importantly, Jon allows her into his private space. When she visits his flat, which used to be an artist's studio, she describes it with similar adjectives she used for her old flat: "I walk [...] through an archway into a cosy sitting room. It's furnished with big, blue-cotton sofas [...] and an old TV balanced on a chair. Behind the sofa are battered wooden shelves, haphazardly filled with books and magazines and plants" (ibid.: 382). The sofa in Eric's loft does not invite Lexi to sit down and she realises that she cannot see herself represented in a flat which is supposed to document *their* life *together* (cf. ibid.: 106, 110). Thus, she is over the moon when she finds out that many of the items from her old Balham flat – and her past – have found their way into Jon's flat: "I'm suddenly seeing the other side of me; the side I thought had disappeared for ever. For the first time since I woke up in hospital I feel like *I'm at home*." (Ibid.: 383, emphasis added)

At Jon's place she can be herself, even consume carbohydrates, which is frowned upon in Eric's 'home'. For the first time since 2004 – for that is the point of reference Lexi has – she feels secure, stimulated and her identity represented: rescuing her old life via the souvenirs of the same from Eric's clean and smooth loft into Jon's sanctuary has Lexi believe Jon that she loves him. As she cannot find herself in the loft she shared with Eric for years – "I can't see that many signs of *me*" (ibid.: 112, original emphasis) – in Jon's flat the faux nostalgia vaporises and Lexi feels that there are genuine memories that are not connected to a fake veneer. Eric's loft resembles a smooth space with markers of status that come with rising in society, but it is a solitary existence as Lexi has to learn. Jon's flat is open – many flats have been put together to form his abode – and it allows bonding and evolvement. Therefore, it is no surprise when Lexi chooses Jon over Eric, and is now able to create real memories with him.

THE HOTEL AS TEMPORARY HOME

One trope which is frequently used in chick- and ladlit is that of travelling. The characters tend to go on "mini-breaks" (cf. Dorney 2004: 12), but sometimes they venture out further and longer, turning travelling into a journey to themselves and love. This part, now, considers how itinerant chick- and ladlit protagonists construct identities from smooth hotel spaces and locations which have a hotel-like character when they cross the border of their territory – known and striated – into the unknown. From now on they have to act in a smooth space, which, according to Deleuze and Guattari, lends itself only to resting, not to staying. This subchapter proves that no space is simply 'smooth' as the characters come to locales which have been visited before. Yet travellers need an anchor-point or (temporary) base from which they can operate and navigate, to explore the unknown geography and create a territory. This location functions as landmark and homing device: people can always return to their current temporary base to rest, recapitulate the day and plan their next moves. In order to be able to do so, the hotel is an important location as it can function as "the starting point [...] for new settlements" (Krebs 2009: 9). Martina Krebs relates the hotel to an outpost for the further development of land (in many different forms), but it can also work on an ideological level. The hotel follows certain structures the agents adhere to and can rely on because of previous experiences – no matter whether they have been made by themselves or by others[33] – and thus present a first safe haven in an unknown territory: the hotel – and hotel-like structures – as temporary home, which is always a constitutive element of each journey.

Peter Jones and Andrew Lockwood provide a good theoretical background for the concept of the hotel:

> Hotels today are in the business of providing space to customers in which they can eat, drink, sleep, wash, bathe, play, confer, relax, do business and a whole range of other common human activities. [...] We, therefore, have chosen to define hotel as: 'an operation that provides accommodation and ancillary services to people away from home.' (2006:1)

Jones and Lockwood evoke the notion of the canvas: the guests are able make their rooms their own, but a certain structure of the room is always given – a bed, bathroom, closet, etc. – and after each departure the room is reset to its 'original' modus, as if the guest had never been there. However, the canvas is never entirely new, it resembles a palimpsest: under each layer of white, the old picture might shine through. The idea of the heterotopia is quite rewarding here (cf. Krebs 2009: 42-43): hotels are forceful heterotopias – one cannot but create one's own place within the all-encompassing space. Each guest treats this space – to various extents – as their current, however temporary private home. The heterotopia also works both on a synchronic level – many rooms house many different people at any given

33 In *Olivia Joules and the Overactive Imagination*, the titular heroine is aware of such structures that have influenced her working-class parents during their first ever stay at a hotel, "where the guests spoke in intimidated whispers and forcedly posh accents, and her entire family would freeze with shame when one of them dropped a fork or a sausage on the floor." (Fielding 2004b: 7)

time – as well as on a diachronic, as one hardly ever gets an entirely pristine room: *Olivia Joules*'s L.A. hotel used to be a geriatric home and is now, when the heroine checks in, a hotspot for up-and-coming actors and actresses (cf. Fielding 2004b: 70).

Olivia Joules (*Olivia Joules and the Overactive Imagination*) loves hotels – this is explicitly stated. The reason for this is that there are no strings attached: one always starts afresh in each hotel (room), one is treated like a queen and she especially likes the anonymity that comes with the hotel (cf. ibid.: 6-7). These explanations actually display Olivia's general outlook on life and her affinity towards hotels mirrors her personality: the reader is introduced to her background, in which it transpires that she always depended – or had to depend – on others. But after many setbacks she creates a mantra for herself: "I'm going to be complete in myself. [...] I'm going to search this shitty world for some beauty and excitement and I'm going to have a bloody good time." (Ibid.: 14) Throughout the novel, she is only depicted once at her flat in Primrose Hill: after she came very close to dying during her travels, she returns to her London home, attributing to it a sense of security. But this notion does not hold very long and is soon replaced by the feeling of imprisonment and stasis. Her flat is described as a place where nothing changes: "All the things that Olivia loved to escape to hotel rooms to were here [in her flat]" (ibid.: 227). It is exactly this stasis which she associates with London or England in general, a life she fled from when she became Olivia Joules and disposed of her previous 'real' identity of Rachel Pixley from Worksop, whose life was destined for 'boring normality'. Thus, because of her travelling disposition and penchant for the search for excitement, she *can* only 'live' in hotels and is the nomad Deleuze and Guattari adumbrate in *A Thousand Plateaus*. She lives for the vectorial movement and for hotels, which present a faux striate-able space which in turn disguises its smoothness. Due to the nature of hotels to be 'set back' to their 'original' blank-canvas-state, she will always feel as if she is constantly starting her life anew. A fact which is proven by her infiltrating the novel's villain's island as Rachel Pixley, whose identity she uses as a blank slate similar to the hotel room: she considers her two identities (Rachel and Olivia) so strongly divorced from each other that Rachel's actions cannot be traced back to Olivia and vice versa.

The component of the smooth canvas, of course, only applies to guests of hotels. The owners and designers of said abodes have striated it previously, which can be seen, firstly, in a brief conversation between Olivia and Feramo, the novel's antagonist and owner of one of the hotels Olivia stays in, and, secondly, in the opening paragraph of the Miami Beach chapter when Olivia checks in at the Delano Hotel. When Olivia stays with Feramo in his hotel on the Bay Islands, she is invited to his personal suite to dine with him. But as she (correctly) assumes that he is an international terrorist, she does not eat any of the food offered. This leads to the problem that she is very hungry during the night and cannot get anything to eat:

> 'I'm looking for the mini-bar.'
>
> 'There is no mini-bar. This is not a hotel.'
>
> 'I thought it *was* a hotel.' (Fielding 2004b: 204, original emphasis)

This short conversation clearly shows that no matter how one tries to striate or looks upon hotels and their rooms, one is never more than a paying guest without any real claims to anything beyond what is offered, in this case the forced hospitality of Feramo's. It shows that there are two opinions about the same space, which create a heterotopia: whereas Olivia is under the impression that she is indeed staying at a hotel, Feramo makes it clear through his comment that he deems it his personal space, an extension of his home and thus his territory. The conversation ends with Feramo ordering her to leave him and to retire to her room – he behaves like her prison guard, clearly stating that he is in charge of the hotel and the rooms and spaces it consists of. Again it shows the canvas's quality of the hotel, which is no longer masked (the hotel as temporary castle to the customer-queen) and Feramo-as-owner's spatial superiority.

The second example of the smoothness of hotels is the Delano Hotel in Miami, which looks "like a designer's hissy fit on the set of *Alice in Wonderland*. Everything was too big, too small, the wrong colour, or in the wrong place." (Ibid.: 4) The hotel, which actually exists, presents itself as a wonder-full oasis located directly on the ocean. It has a distinct look which is anything but smooth; on the contrary it even evokes images from other texts: *Alice in Wonderland* is a metaphor here, for Olivia also steps out of her known – and, from her behaviour deducible, languid – realm and into the world of espionage. The Delano Hotel has a distinct look which adds to its locational quality: guests are meant to feel as if they left their comfortable zone and are now in for a completely new and somewhat outlandish experience when they arrive at the reception. This is in stark contrast to the description of the rooms: Olivia's "room was entirely white: white floor, white walls, white sheets, white desk, white armchair and footstool" (ibid.: 5), which evokes the notion of the canvas, white being the underlying base of it before one starts applying colours, with white attributing a certain image of virginity and innocence. The Delano Hotel's rooms – or those of any other hotel for that matter – can be manipulated to present a certain image after one has checked in, as these spaces do not care for past experiences or failures. Each hotel and each room, respectively, offers its guests a fresh start. The other hotels Olivia visits may look different, but the Delano is a blueprint for all 'hotels' share the same canvas quality.

Moreover, Olivia always wishes her apartment 'back home' would look like the respective hotel rooms she is occupying. Turning her London flat into a hotel room – or, at its most extreme, a white canvas – would devoid her home of any striated quality. It means that she cannot but move out again after a limited period of time as her 'home' is too smooth a space. Olivia longs for the same smooth quality of hotels in her anchor-points: she does not want to be tied down and a striated place is characterised by the quality of being the space in which one settles. This attitude attributes vagabond qualities to Olivia: "Each place is for the vagabond a stopover, but he [or she] never knows how long he [or she] will stay in any of them [...]. The vagabond decides where to turn when he [or she] comes to crossroads [...]. To control the wayward and erratic vagabond is a daunting task" (Bauman 1998: 28). Indeed, Olivia is less driven to places than floating towards them, but once her interest is caught, she will pursue her idea – as can be seen in her tracking down of Feramo. Thus, her identity can switch from vagabond to driven operator, who will only cease to be active once her task is satisfactorily accomplished. In his essay, Bauman also defines the tourist, from which Olivia incorporates traces in herself too. Having just outlined the vagabond, the "tourists want to immerse themselves in a strange and bizarre element (a pleasant feeling, a tickling and rejuvenating feeling)" (ibid.: 29), and this would perfectly fit to Olivia's approach to life. However, the tourist wants nothing to stick, degrading each experience to be ephemeral and, moreover, the tourist will always have a home to return to, which he or she needs to feel secure (cf. ibid.: 30). Whereas the latter notion is partly correct because Olivia has a home to feel secure in, if only for a very limited time, the former notion is not applicable to her and rules out that Olivia can be called a complete tourist. But rather than being a vagabond, who has a sad, somewhat lost quality, she should be called nomad, for she is voluntarily traversing the world, always on the lookout for a fresh start into a new adventure.

Olivia's love for new adventures is mirrored in her perfect partner, special agent Scott, who is characterised as the male equivalent of the heroine. Just as Olivia's identity is not bound to a specific location but rather to the qualities of the hotel as a template, the novel needs to construct the perfect partner in a way that the heroine can attach these qualities to a human in order to have a moveable anchor-point instead of a locally-fixed one. Combining the ideas that Olivia always wishes her home were like a hotel room and that perfect partners can become 'home', Scott is fashioned like a hotel room: his profession as secret agent requires him to be an unattached and equally 'unattaching' person – he becomes as smooth a character as Olivia's hotel rooms. Moreover, as he is likened to Olivia a number of times, it can be assumed that he, too, will have alternative identities strengthening the notion of him having an accommodating personality which can adapt to surroundings and people: to those who do not know him, he is as smooth as a canvas or hotel room onto which other people can project whatever they wish. It is not clear whether the two will go on missions together and therefore, they can meet up regularly (in hotels around the world) but their time together will always be limited. All these ideas strongly suggest that Scott should be regarded as a hotel room and that is the reason why Olivia feels so drawn to him: she knows that she loves hotels and now she loves the personification of these spaces. However, the problem is that one cannot stay at a hotel indefinitely as that would on the one hand violate the structure of the hotel, and, on the other hand, it would turn the visitor into a dweller which would again disturb the notion of the hotel. Transferring these problems onto Scott, it suggests that he, too, is not going to be in Olivia's life for an unlimited amount of time. His qualities endear him to her but just with all hotel experiences, there seems to be an inevitable time limit to their relationship.

The hotel's possibilities are what entice Lauren Lucas in *Manhattan Dreaming* as well. She is especially amazed by the diversity displayed at the United Nations Millennium Plaza Hotel: "I was conscious of the energy in the air. I saw people from around the globe in sarongs and saris, burkas and business suits and speaking dozens of different languages. [...] For work or pleasure, everyone in New York was like a tourist on holidays." (Heiss 2010: 97) The heterotopia of the Plaza Hotel is evident: here, everyone is different yet co-existing as tourist, or so Lauren says. A painful break-up with Adam has her flee her previous territory, which consequently is connoted with frustration and rejection, and she now regards everything exceptionally positively and the same goes for the hotel. Whereas at other times she is quick to judge and criticise people, she is now not even commenting on the burka. She is amazed by the multi-ethnicity she observes in the lobby and it gives her the impression that she will feel right at home in New York, enhancing the cosmopolitical feeling of the hotel metonymically to the whole of the metropolis. That Lauren is indeed a guest at one of the more expensive hotels in New York is not commented on. It appears that the reader is simply to take it as 'given' that chicklit characters will always be able to book rooms in the best and most exclusive hotels. Moreover, just like Olivia Joules and Becky Bloomwood in *Shopaholic Takes Manhattan*, Lauren feels right at home. Chicklit novels tend to infuse their narratives with markers of money and although these novels are aiming to achieve identification of the reader with the heroine, it is in situations like these that the notion of escapism trumps that of identification. Lauren, Olivia and Becky are to be envied and because of the first-person narrative the readers get to enter a world they might not be able to otherwise. The fact that the chicklit heroines neither flinch at the exclusiveness of the places, nor comment on the prices of the rooms attributes an air of money sophistication to them: they are destined to be located in such eminent surroundings.

The idea of hotels being temporary homes from which one striates unknown territory is complemented by an Aboriginal practice in *Manhattan Dreaming*. It creates a disembodied notion of belonging, thus presenting another facet of the 'home away from home': during the flight, when Lauren becomes a little agitated because of leaving her known territory, she resorts to listening to music on the iPod her brother gave her as a leaving present: "The sounds of Blackfellas singing about culture, land, history, relationships, politics and the future soothed me. The songs carried me to my dreaming tracks back home, and I knew they would carry me safely to America" (ibid.: 94). Lauren is not alone, despite the fact that she is physically without anybody she knows to accompany her: she is always connected to her mob, her Aborigine family and friends. Therefore, the spiritual concept of Dreaming, the Aboriginal metaphysical connection of members of one mob, produces a spatial dimension as well. It brings about a sense of place without a place to begin with, because Lauren will have the connection to her mob, for example via the 'Blackfella music' of her brother's, and will feel at home immediately:

> The Dreaming is a reservoir of Aboriginality[34] and the land is the text from which its stories can be read. [...] On the Aboriginal map a central point, or site, is always seen to proliferate and to bestow the land with such a profusion of multiple centres that peripheries cannot exist. [... N]o place or site is insignificant, because the Great Ancestors set foot everywhere and every one of the physical tracks is part of someone's Dreaming today. When 'mapping out the land,' any linear progression on the land (or in the text) will involve a circular kind of return to sacred sites that function as centres for an understanding of Aboriginality. (Rask Knudsen 2004: 7)

This placeless sense of place bears strong connections to nostalgia, the difference being that whereas nostalgia – both reflective and restorative[35] – is retrospective, this variety is not limited to a certain direction and can signify "present and future, not just the past" (Heiss 2010: 71). The three temporal levels are interlinked and present Lauren with a help- and guideline. Just like Heiss's other heroines, Lauren's Indigenous identity is very important: one is never lost, making one's Dreaming the ultimate homing device, which, however, brings *home to you* instead of the other way around. Therefore, she creates a heterotopia wherever Lauren goes as she has

34 Aboriginality can be defined as "the experience of being Aboriginal in general and [it refers] to the particular cultural legacy of Aboriginal people in Australia, past and present." (Rask Knudsen 2004: 7)

35 Nostalgia – here of a reflective kind – is presented in the little things Lauren takes with her to Manhattan as they are all related to the Big Merino, representing her mob and her Goulburn roots: a toy sheep, mink and gloves made from merino wool.

her 'home' with her in the metaphysical form of the spiritual Dreaming or the more solidified form of songs. She actually striates space with her Aboriginality and the fact that the hotel lobby presents many different nations, cultures and religions has her feeling at home because she is no longer an outsider who needs to striate alone: the hotel has been striated – synchronically as well as diachronically – and she will continue this practice by bringing her identity to the canvas of the hotel. The feeling of possibility and potential is transported and appropriated to the whole city later on as well. The hotel truly becomes her outpost to create the city anew from her point of view and Lauren's Blackfella music grounds her even when she is not located in homely locales.

However, not all hotel experiences are as positive as the above. In *2 States*, Krish Malhotra rents a room in a shared accommodation – a form of the hotel – in Chennai in order to be near to his perfect partner Ananya. Yet, already on arriving in Chennai, he feels like a fish out of water. He does not understand Tamil and gets into trouble with his auto driver and then he has to realise that his building has a strict no meat, no alcohol and no female guests rule (cf. Bhagat 2011b: 80). Delhiite Krish knew that Chennai would not work to the structures he is used to from north India, but his helplessness is an indicator that he did not expect the sense of place to be so strict and exclusive, especially the rules of his new abode, clearly marking this space as too striated: he cannot impose his own striating structure on the already existing strict one. Krish is suddenly faced with a totally different ideological concept of 'home': living in his shared accommodation in Chennai needs much more effort and consideration than he initially assumed, as he never really thought about any possible side effects of his relocation. But apart from sleeping at his place and once inviting Ananya over for dinner, which gets him into trouble because of its involvement of a girl, cooked chicken and beer (a violation of both the rule and the sense of place), he spends more time at another temporary home, namely that of Ananya's parents. He is trying to make a good impression on the parents and to get them to like him before he asks for Ananya's hand in marriage. By gently infiltrating their home, he is smoothly introduced into their family life. When Krish and Ananya were still at IIMA in Ahmedabad, they spent their time outside the classrooms mostly in his or her room in the student accommodation, which also functions as a hotel: their rooms were their strongholds against the judicious world – for they could lock out their respective backgrounds (he is a Punjabi, she a Tamil[36]) and just be themselves. It is here that they voice their thoughts and feelings without the interruption of daily life. It is obvious that their rooms function as a life space that is freed from the structure of otherwise competitive and strict IIMA. In their class-

36 This ethnic prejudice is very strong, especially in Krish's parents' attitude (cf. Bhagat 2011b: 40).

rooms they are confined to specific seats and stripped of their individuality by their professors who only refer to them by their last names which are written on their desks (cf. ibid.: 9-10). Their private rooms thus present a place they can use freely – even if they started out by studying together in them for classes. The student accommodation functions on the same level as Olivia's hotels: there is no past and although there is no room service, Krish and Ananya are the king and queen of their rooms, which can be gathered from the fact that they have sex in there whereas they cannot even kiss in their parents' homes.

Finally, Ash Lynch (*Taking Off*) is interesting with regard to the concept of the hotel as 'home'. During his trip through Europe, he stays in various hotel-like spaces which map his mental development (cf. Lenz 2013). When he and his companion Miller arrive in Amsterdam, they do not really care about where they can spend the night. They simply choose the location closest to the station so as to not have to search at all: "we go into the first place that looks only moderately sleazy, and for 90 euros per night we get two single beds in a room that seems barely big enough for one." (Howard 2008: 124) Compared to Olivia's rooms, this one has similar canvas-like qualities of being a pseudo-smooth space, but the characterisation of being very small, not exactly clean and its explicit reference to the uniformity of the hotel's other rooms seems to hint at a lessened possibility of striating it the way Olivia is able to. One is always subconsciously reminded that one's stay at a hotel is only temporary and there will be other guests when one leaves the place. The 'classic' hotel, meaning the one which one checks into, is a misleading illusion: although Ash and Miller's room appears to be less able to provide space for individuality, it only provides *less space as such*. Individuality is never truly achievable as it is only temporary and within the limits of the locale and its features and thus the classic hotel emerges as a mirage which is chosen exactly for its smooth qualities: in a city which is unknown the space is already striated by others but entirely smooth for the new arrival. The hotel perverts this notion, for it is as striated as the city, even more so – by the personal choices of owners and designers – but it pretends to have a smooth surface (the room), which is much more easily striateable than the city as it takes up to no effort to check in to it. In addition, it even 'wants' to be easily accessible as a hotel is a commercial venture. The hotel therefore not only pretends to be an oasis to rest, it even appears to be smoother than it actually is.

Nevertheless, when Ash and Miller start to move and explore Europe, their temporary homes change in direct relation to Ash's attitude and mind-set. From Amsterdam and the "moderately sleazy" hotel, they 'graduate' to a private flat in the midst of Berlin. Although they have never met the owner of the flat before and only know him through a mutual friend, Ash and Miller are handed a spare key so that they can come and go as they please. What is even more, only a few days later,

Jarmo, the owner of the flat, leaves his home to go on a holiday and Ash and Miller have the flat all to themselves (cf. Howard 2008: 198-199). Regarding the function of this 'hotel', Ash is not able to striate this place as much as he could in a real hotel as the owner has furnished his personal living space the way he feels most comfortable with. However, this exposes the illusion of the smoothness of the hotel room, for one would not start redecoration or rearranging furniture in a hotel room either as it would only be temporary. Yet the Berlin flat fulfils all the main purposes of resting, refreshing and being an anchor-point of the first order. It depicts a change in Ash's mind-set as he set out from his home, which was a prison-like substitute for a real home[37], stayed at a hotel, which was spatially limited, and is now in a home that does not even pretend to be smooth. Therefore, the flat is no illusion of striate-able space which Ash cannot penetrate but another home, literally away from home. Similarly, Ash has started to enjoy life and experiences new things in Amsterdam and in Berlin he explores the city on his own and he goes out to gay-S&M-underground clubs as well as getting immersed in the offering of local history and culture:

> It's fast becoming tradition that, whenever Miller gets laid or waylaid, I take the opportunity to do that other touristy activity of sightseeing, given Miller's aversion to checking in with history. [...] Jarmo has lent me a travel guide to Berlin and I use the map to help find the closest subway station, which I take to get me to the Brandenburg Gate – apparently the symbol of Berlin. (Ibid.: 184-185)

Berlin as an experience furthers the development which has started in Amsterdam: the flat becomes more personal, but still remains a hotel-like locale. When the owner leaves, the flat becomes a proper home-away-from-home and similarly, Ash explores the city on his own but only when Miller is otherwise engaged. Ash is not yet confident enough to go out on his own and leave Miller behind instead of the other way around.

When Ash and Miller arrive in Athens, they briefly stay at a pool hall, which they look after as the owner has to leave suddenly. As with Berlin, they are allowed to stay without having met the owner previously. This time, they even work there and the pool hall presents yet another form of the hotel, one in which the patrons have to work to justify their stay – they become the (temporary) owners of a hotel-like space. To the other patrons, the pool hall is just that, a place to pass some time at, but for Ash and Miller it takes on the quality of a home-hotel-hybrid (for they sleep and regenerate there and can feel secure). At the same time, their power,

37 Ash once had great plans to move out from home but due to the death of the parents stayed with his sister and her husband in their parents' house (Howard 2008: 133).

however finite, makes them managers and hosts to others (even creating security). The process that is most important to consider when it comes to Ash's hotel experiences is that of forming attitudes. Before taking off, Ash just knew a very limited territory and the structures governing it were rather depressing the space's actors. Therefore, the 'home' in Amsterdam initially only presents another version of the same prison: the facts that it is small, causes unease and that he has to listen to Miller having sex with various women more or less next to him have Ash realise that life is passing him by. But the advent of his perfect partner Cali, the deepening friendship with Miller and the new one established with a man he met on their travels have Ash realise that the size of his territory is up to him, which he explores with frequently increased independence. It is not only a spatial territory here, but also one of the mind: Ash has to learn to embrace the new, stop thinking and over-analysing and enjoy himself (cf. ibid.: 114). Living in other peoples' homes or simply in the moment provides a valuable lesson for Ash which has him acknowledge the possibilities that awaits the one who starts looking past the edges of one's cognitive map. And it is the realisation of this spatial practice which leads him to Antiparos and Cali (see chapter 5).

Regarding the novels, the characters can be put into certain categories: Olivia grew to love hotels – even falls in love with the personification of this space – whereas Rebecca, Lauren and, to a certain extent, Krish merely use forms of the hotel as stopovers before they continue to another more long-term abode. Ash, however, graduates from one temporary home to the next until he finds spatial compatibility which marks the end of his hotel-hopping. All of the characters have to realise that hotels are not meant to be stayed in indefinitely but only support a break in-between journeys. What is more, hotels or forms of hotels refuse to be part of the characters' locality in that they do not become a space in which social relations can be pursued. If there is no way of 'docking' on to a person or space, a lasting relationship is not possible. Therefore, almost all characters that spend time in hotels will eventually move into more permanent residencies, places they are able to striate and to live in with their respective partners.

IDENTITY, SECURITY AND STIMULATION

"The concept of 'home' embraces both a physical and a social space; the house itself is home, as are the social relations contained within it." (Munro and Madigan 1999: 107) This quote encompasses many of the ideas laid out in this chapter: 'home' is but a whole network comprised of people, sense of place(s) and processes and it is not just a geographical address. Using again the example of heroic Greek seafarer Odysseus, 'home' is more than his palace on Ithaca: it is equally his family, wife Penelope and son Telemachus, as well as the triad Porteous establishes, namely identity, security and stimulation. Of course, for three years, Odysseus's ship was his home and his crew his family, and for seven years he was in the arms of nymph Calypso – but he has never stopped yearning for his *true* home, the one he established on Ithaca with all that it entailed.

This chapter has shown that 'home' can be both a locale, a setting that enables certain informal activities, and a concept that requires emotions and people. As the tone of chick- and ladlit is hardly ever bleak, all the characters can call a specific abode their home, be it a shared accommodation, a (rented) flat or a house of their own. All protagonists have an abode to which they can return. These homes are mirrors of their inhabitants and support the activities undertaken within the security of the four walls. This means that the home can be considered the spatial signifier of a novel's main character: it represents its dweller or it can reveal a character's true colours even if they would like to present themselves as somebody different. Examples of the latter are chicklit characters like Bridget Jones or Minal Sharma (*Piece of Cake*), who in their bathroom-turned-beauty salon want to create a different image of themselves to be attractive to eligible men, or ladlit characters like *The Fix*'s Josh Lang or Benjamin Duffy (*Mr Commitment*), whose messy flats disclose to the avid observer that their lives are not as 'cleaned up' as they would like others to believe. The home becomes a space in which the characters expose their real identities, their selves which are not manipulated so as to be perceived as desirable, competent or composed.

Likewise the home can document a character's evolution as he or she starts to re-arrange their home or even move somewhere else as their current locale does not support the changes which have started to manifest in the character. *Street Furniture*'s Dec McPherson (ladlit) or *The Undomestic Goddess* Samantha Sweeting (chicklit) can no longer remain in their flats as their lives have been turned upside-down by the death of a very dear friend or a job-shattering mistake at work, respectively. Their homes cease to present them with the security, identity or even stimulation to brave the crises in the locales the characters inhabited when their disasters struck. The home is a very flexible locale but if the connotations of the space are too much to bear, a move is the only option and the next home can be appropriated so as to represent the altered state of the individual.

Furthermore, not only does the characters' home expose their inhabitants, the same is true for the protagonists' perfect partners. Being aware of what one wants or needs in a person clarifies the process of finding a compatible person, but even if one is not able to see directly what a character is like, their homes foreshadow the eventual outcome: the stairs in both Mark Darcy's house and Daniel Cleaver's flat already indicate the men's attitude towards women (*Bridget Jones's Diary*) and a young woman's derelict house tells protagonist Jon that he needs to take care of her and that she is more of a daughter than a perfect partner (*Perfect Skin*[38]), giving just two examples from each genre. From the (potential) partners' spatial behaviour as well as the design of their abodes one can deduce their attitudes and compare them with those of the heroine or hero of the novel as in the aforementioned examples from chick- and ladlit. Realising a character's identity through their locale, the protagonist can achieve spatial compatibility with their perfect partner, and their ideas about and perception of space signify that the two characters will fit together. This chapter has shown that a house is generally associated with family, constitutive of the same or the wish for one, whereas a flat is connoted with single life. Moreover, the space of home needs to be shared and not dominated by one partner. A shared home mirrors a shared life and this idea is expressed by finding spatial compatibility with one's perfect partner.

A negative example will prove how important this spatial compatibility is. In Mike Gayle's novel *Wish You Were Here*, Charlie Mansell is left by Sarah, his girlfriend of ten years. They have been living together in Charlie's flat for most of this time and now she has moved out, taking with her all the pieces of furniture she bought during their time together: "given the deal when Sarah had moved in […] was that she would (with my blessing) systematically eradicate the flat of every single item of [my old] furniture and replace it with things that worked and looked nice […] the flat was now, inevitably, empty." (Gayle 2007: 15) It transpires that Charlie's identity has been constructed by Sarah through *her* furnishing *his* flat. She has taken away his "decrepit" furniture and replaced almost the entire 'inside' of Charlie's flat (cf. ibid.). The fact that he gave his blessing to this process shows that he was not yet ready to be a man, Sarah mainly managed to eradicate the outward signs of it but the felix rigor mortis is still there: he cannot be bothered to choose a (life) style for or by himself. As Charlie is totally dependent on her to look after him (cf. ibid.: 84), now that she has left, she has created a void which exposes the lack of identity and with that also of security and stimulation. The fact that Sarah is able to hollow out Charlie's flat and therefore his identity, which the abode mirrors, points towards a lacuna existing in Charlie as a person and which Sarah had been able to gloss over, if only temporarily and outwardly. She did not create a heterotopic space in which the two protagonists' identities were able to express themselves properly but overwrote the heterotopia by creating *her* place and allowing him to live in it, too. When Sarah changed Charlie's flat, she consequentially overwrote his identity as well which means that theirs was not a reciprocal relationship. There was no spatial compatibility to begin with, and no matter how long they had

38 Some of the examples given in this conclusive section have not been discussed in this chapter. However, they function according to the same formula and motifs explained here. This proves once more that chick- and ladlit are very formulaic genres.

been going out or would have been together – happiness has been but a mirage, bound to fail and leave Charlie without any anchor-point to call home. He loses his identity along with his sense of security and stimulation as soon as Sarah and the furniture exit his flat and life and he has no idea what to do next in the immediate post-Sarah time.

In addition to the locale of the home, this chapter has also looked into conceptions of the same. It specifically regarded the people with whom a character can turn a space into a place, or any location into a home as well as consider nostalgic notions of 'home'. What unites both these issues is the idea of belonging and, in a second step, family. Almost all characters left their home towns and moved to a metropolis in order to pursue a career, hence the description of chick- and ladlit characters as young urban professionals. The characters had to leave their biological family behind but quickly accumulated a circle of friends, their urban family. They present the protagonist with a sense of *security* – one is not alone, *stimulation* – one has others who one can go out with or talk to and *identity* – one belongs to and is a valid metropolitan member of an urban family. This specific type of family is a voluntary construction and not as fixed as a blood-ties family. This means on the one hand that the urban family is usually closer, as its members constantly see or at least contact one another in order to re-affirm their bond. On the other hand, it requires specific spaces in which the members can convene. The urban family that lives together, for example the men in *Street Furniture* and *Five Point Someone* or the women in *Confessions of a Shopaholic* and *The Wish List*, will have a living room in which they can meet and thus have a common and shared space to confirm their belonging in. However, if the urban family entails non-cohabitating members or if the urban family does not share a dwelling, such as the friends in *Not Meeting Mr Right* or *Turning Thirty*, an external meeting space has to be found. Urban families outsource a part of their home in which to convene and this is the living room-away-from-home. This space functions just like a 'normal' living room in one of the character's personal locale but here it has the added benefit that it emphasises the equality of the members. In these outsourced meeting spaces the characters can 'practise' spatial compatibility as they need to create a shared heterotopia which will later on prove elemental in the construction of a shared home for the protagonist and the perfect partner. However, this also exposes the urban family as what it really is – a mere layover on the way to another biological family, namely the one the characters want to establish with their perfect partners. Many protagonists have an urban family even before the novel begins but in the course of the romantic process, they become less important and are reduced to the background or even the past in some cases: in *Brand New Friend*, Rob chooses his girlfriend over his mates and *Paris Dreaming*'s Libby, who is initially frustrated that her tiddas are too occupied with their boyfriends or spouses, finally moves to Paris and does not return when she has found her perfect partner there: "I am exactly where I should be" (Heiss 2011: 313).

The other issue with regard to belonging is expressed in forms of nostalgia. The past is glorified because it usually means a time in which the protagonist was in a happy relationship and this relationship is then connected to the home in various ways. 'Home' becomes a container for the longing to belong. The state of the mostly deficient home – it is too small, too old or too messy – is a form of stimulation to lose oneself in the wish for the past in which the life of the character used to be better, such as *My Legendary Girlfriend*, *Zigzag Street* or *Bridget Jones: The Edge of Reason*. However, it does not necessarily need to be a turn to the past in order to long for a better life: in *Ethan Grout*, the protagonist wants to have a family unit and he taps into the collective memory of his society as he has never had a family to speak of. Ethan feels helpless in many situations as he does not know how to react to or in specific situations but can only recall images or behaviour he has seen other people create or engage in. The home of his (step-) family is therefore a contested ground as Ethan would like to belong and be accepted into this family unit but is constantly unsure how to react. Were he more adapt at reading spatial signs, he would have known that his stepfamily is open-minded and loving and wants to give Ethan the home he so dearly longs for. Whereas Ethan has no memories to compare his new experiences with, Lexi in *Remember Me?* has forgotten them. Following an accident three years of her life have been wiped from her memory and she now tries to find her way around an unfamiliar environment her husband claims she has been happy in. But Lexi never feels at home, she does not experience the sensation of belonging and in her need to overcome this problem, she covers up the lack of real memories with fake ones. These 'events' never happened but as Lexi deems them likely she just creates these fake memories in order to fall back on them and to find a footing in this unknown life of hers. She creates an identity that she thinks fits the home the man who claims to be her husband brings her to. That this identity is as fake as her new memories is apparent very soon as Lexi does not feel happy – read: secure and stimulated – in the loft. Only when she enters the flat of another man does she have this sensation and it transpires that Lexi's perfect partner is not the one she married.

Lastly, the home is a necessary location not only in one's known territory but abroad, too. Having a temporary home in the form of hotels or hotel-like dwellings enables humans to feel (temporarily) at home in the unknown, to rest and to consider one's next steps. These homes are like canvases and thus one feels stimulated to consider the hotel room one's own. That these palimpsestuous canvases are merely thinly disguised mirages might be problematic but it can also enable a re-invention of one's identity which was no longer supported by the static abodes in one's original territory (*Manhattan Dreaming*, *Shopaholic Takes*

Manhattan, *Olivia Joules and the Overactive Imagination*). Two novels, *2 States* and *Taking Off*, even present both problems and opportunities of the hotel-as-home. However, what all characters have to realise at some point is that hotels are not meant to be stayed in permanently, the time-limiting aspect a defining feature of these locations. Even hotel-loving Olivia Joules moves from hotel to hotel – she is as powerless as other guests, be they tourists, vagabonds or nomads, she cannot lay claim to these locations. All characters will have to create or move to static abodes they can call home if they intend to keep their perfect partners. Spatial compatibility cannot travel indefinitely. Olivia is bound to find out what Lauren (*Manhattan Dreaming*) learns when she re-appears in *Paris Dreaming*: she returns with her boyfriend to her Australian home town and 'home', despite feeling comfortable in hotels and being constantly connected to her ancestral locale through her Dreaming. The hotel is too smooth in its pre-striated identity.

The home, then, plays a substantial role in the characters' lives as the triad of identity, security and stimulation informs their sense of place and belonging. 'Home' with its many dimensions and facets is an important factor in chick- and ladlit: the shared usage of the concept signifies that the triad of identity, security and stimulation is important in the construction of the home as well as of the dwellers themselves because the home mirrors the dweller. Additionally, features of 'home' can be attributed or outsourced to other spaces and the people inhabiting them. If one achieves spatial compatibility with these other characters, a relationship ensues. The home as anchor-point is an important destination, it usually marks the beginning and end of each journey, and it is usually the centre of the characters' locality. 'Home' has proven to be a multi-layered space in chick- and ladlit. Moreover, it has been shown that the home-ly spaces the various characters inhabit are used in a very similar way, regardless of the country of origin of the novel: "where we love is home, home that our feet may leave, but not our hearts" (Holmes 1878: 272).

Work Placements on Three Continents

> You don't have to be mad to work here, but you do have to be on time, well presented, a team player, customer service focused and sober!
> RICKY GERVAIS *THE OFFICE*

GOOD JOB!

Not every person is as lucky as Will Freeman (*About a Boy*): "He earned more than forty thousand pounds a year [...], and he didn't have to work very hard for it; [in fact, he did not have] to work *at all* for it" (Hornby 1998: 13, original emphasis). Living off the royalties of a Christmas song his late father wrote, Will does not need to go into an office to earn money. For most people, however, places of work present one of the major anchor-points; they are, after all, the locale "[w]e spend more time in [...] than any other place after our homes[1]." (CABE and Davies Yeang 2005: 8; cf. Vischer 2005: 3) Francis "Frank" Duffy even claims that, of all buildings, "[o]ffices in particular reveal the values of those who build them and *work in them*." (1980: 255, emphasis added) Many chick- and ladlit novels present their protagonists in connection to their field of work and in their workspaces and thus characterise them in a specific way.

---

1 Will Freeman does not have a profession in the traditional sense but he regards his lifestyle as his job: he deems his life so important that he allots time slots to his activities. On the one hand, this is aligning him with professionals like lawyer Samantha Sweeting (*Remember Me?*) and spin doctor Josh Lang (*The Fix*), who both divide their workdays into specific time portions which they are able to bill to their clients. On the other hand, it enables Will to fashion his leisure time as a profession, seeing himself as the most important client: "Life took up so much time, so how could one work [...]?" (Hornby 1998: 80)

This chapter focuses on the office as a workspace and it starts with the history of this particular locale: from its beginnings as a space within public houses as clerical work was deemed inferior to manual labour, via the places that have been created because of the increasing necessity to give accountants and clerks their own space to the latest developments, such as hot desking or cloud working. Especially the open-plan office and the enclosed office are of importance as they will be the spaces occupied in the respective novels. Moreover, almost all chick- and ladlit characters who are depicted in an office or working environment closely associated with an office work in white-collar professions. The novels present a professional cosmos in which the office is a fashionable space for smart people in smart outfits. However, that this smartness of the workplace is merely a veneer which masks the unhappiness of the workers is one of the focus points of this chapter: some characters have to realise that the careers they have pursued are not what they ultimately want and that a change of the profession or workplace can bring happiness and might also lead to a meeting with the perfect partner.

The analyses are divided into two sections: the first section looks at the construction and usage of specific forms of offices, whereas the second is concerned with a specific workspace context. Starting the analyses with the open-plan office, it will be put into the context of Taylorism. It will be shown that although Taylorism is dismissed as inhumane, the principles of its robotic-like worker are still very much in practice. The open-plan office encourages workers to be on their best behaviour as they are reminded that they are replaceable and constantly monitored. This type of office is juxtaposed with the enclosed office, which, however, is just as doubtful a surrounding as the open-plan office. In the enclosed office, imprisonment is a prevalent theme and this form of the office stifles the characters' development and personality.

The second section of this chapter looks closely at various Indian workspaces. It brings together call centre agents and workers on Bollywood movies with characters who occupy managerial positions in the tourist and food industry: Indian chick- and ladlit present spaces of (white collar) professions that are enabling the characters to be part of both a rising middle class and a rising economy. Additionally, arranged marriages as well as marriage advertisements will be considered as they play an important role in the lives of these Indian characters and convey important ideas about love as a business (opportunity).

A BRIEF HISTORY OF THE OFFICE

The earliest purpose-built offices can be found in Florence – the Uffizi. Devised and commissioned by Cosimo I, the first patriarch of the de Medici in the sixteenth century, he wanted "to increase [clerical workers'] efficiency by [seating them] close to each other, and to have them where he could see them and the public could find them[2]. [And yet offices] for private companies would not be found in purpose-built buildings for another 200 years." (Vischer 2005: 11-12) In the nineteenth century, coffee houses or public houses were the first spaces to double as offices (cf. Duffy 1980: 259, Sundstrom 1986: 26), hinting at the heterotopic quality of these spaces of leisure: "In its earliest form the office was simply a place where lawyers, brokers, merchants, bankers, and the like conducted their business" (Pile, qtd. in Sundstrom 1986: 26). Soon, it was acknowledged that "space is one of the raw materials needed for work" (Fischer 1997: 45) and offices were granted their 'own' spatial existence (cf. ibid.: 44, Vischer 2005: 12).

From the mid-nineteenth century and at first predominantly in larger cities, office buildings became contested sites "because of [the] competition for the increasingly expensive space in business districts." (Sundstrom 1986: 27) For example, the buildings on Wall Street were the only locations stockbrokers would rent in New York City and therefore developers tried to create as much office space from the buildings as possible (cf. ibid.). Occupying single rooms at first, businesses started to expand horizontally before long[3]: they "would expand sidewise, knocking passages through the walls of the adjacent structures, and sometimes this process would go on, through house after house, until an entire block front of buildings had been drawn together into one intricate warren." (Logan 1961) This horizontal expansion is attributed to the fact that most businesses were located on ground level to guarantee main accessibility to visitors and – depending on the business – customers. Famous examples of businesses occupying a whole block are department stores like Macy's (New York) as well as Harrods and Selfridges (London), which are first and foremost offering goods for consumption but include offices in their structures as well. "But eventually there was no place to go but up." (Sundstrom 1986: 28) Three developments initially made this rise into the sky possible and helped the office tower to establish its place: new technology (the elevator – from freight hoist to people carrier), new materials (replacing iron girders with structural steel in the building structure) and new modes of transportation (to make an inner-city location attractive) (cf. Vischer 2005: 12, Sundstrom 1986: 27-

---

2 These twin ideas of communication and control can be observed in many texts and will eventually give rise to the open-plan office.

3 Of course, there are examples of buildings being built especially for commercial purposes as well. See Duffy (1980) for a survey of early nineteenth- to late twentieth-century office buildings.

29)[4]. From the 1880s onwards, with the first office tower erected in Chicago, the sky became the limit.

In the early days of the vertically expanding office buildings, the workers suffered from bad working conditions, such as poor light and bad ventilation, restricted access to restrooms and even faulty chairs (cf. Sundstrom 1986: 29-32). In New York, it was even tried to ban "preternaturally tall buildings" because it was feared that the skyscrapers caused malaria (cf. Logan 1961). But from the beginning of the twentieth century, clerical work had gained in importance due to an emphasis on "tertiary products [such as] governmental and other personal and intangible services" (Fisher 1936: 494; cf. Vischer 2005: 14). Office workers were recognised as valued employees and from the 1930s onwards working conditions considerably improved (cf. Sundstrom 1986: 32).

Today, the "space a company designs for itself is increasingly an expression of its identity, as well as communicating its image" (Vischer 2005: 8). Office buildings like the Gherkin (London) or the World Trade Center (New York) – now Freedom Towers – are not only workplaces, they are icons (cf. Duffy 1997: 14) and sometimes signify a story of their own. The names these buildings are given are just as important as their location because the "office tower is the pinnacle of expression of today's cultural values: the importance of jobs, the predominance of big business in the economy, and the significance of money." (Vischer 2005: 8) The office building becomes an investment both fiscally and ideologically. The most recent office buildings emphasise "organic and futuristic shapes instead of geometrical linearity. [...] Instead of the rather daunting, square, multi-storey buildings of the past, office blocks and administrative buildings now come along more knobbly and coquettish" (Hologa and Piskurek 2013: 93). Managers want their workers to identify with their company by way of identifying with the building and it is hard to imagine a particular skyline without certain (office) buildings which have become integrated both into the general cityscape but also in the people's minds as 'belonging there'[5].

4 Another problem which had to be solved was the question of light: due to the mushrooming of skyscrapers they eliminated one another's source of light – the sun. Yet, in the 1930s electric light was introduced and windows were no longer of greatest importance (cf. Shultz and Simmons 1959). Today, there is a return to natural light and many of the latest buildings (of starchitects such as Norman Foster) use glass to cover whole facades (cf. Hologa and Piskurek 2013).

5 There was a whole campaign against Norman Foster's building at 30 St Mary Axe which came to be known by the name of "the Gherkin". By now, it has been embraced as a vital and iconic part of London (cf. May 2003).

The evolution of the office and indeed the office building is a global one: especially Europe and the United States of America have developed and evolved workspaces and through a constant progress of inventions and ideas – such as the telephone, the elevator or the typewriter (cf. Sundstrom 1986: 33) – they have contributed greatly to the change of the office. This development generated two major strands of office building in the late 1970s-1980s: whereas the Northern European variety favoured buildings which cater for their end users' needs (e.g. highly cellular offices and group rooms for ten to fifteen people or social centres), in North America or Great Britain "standardized models of the speculative office building, designed for unknown tenants, [for example] the central core skyscraper or the groundscraper-plus-atrium" (Laing 1997: 35-36), were preferred[6]. Yet both systems have their flaws and especially the Northern European variety can only be maintained by rich organisations. Furthermore, in the times of globalisation and outsourcing, the concept of the office building has been brought to other countries and has been implanted into local economic structures. However, they mostly function according to similar spatial structures and implement them even if the

> North Americans – and the British – have always tended to overestimate efficiency and glorify cost minimization. [...] The northern Europeans [...] have generally preferred effectiveness to efficiency and, operating within a social democratic climate, have tended to put far more emphasis on using office space to support staff morale and thus to add value to organizational performance. (Duffy 1997: 47-48)

Duffy concludes that both these two general trends – stressing efficiency or effectiveness – have their advantages as well as shortcomings and only a balance between the two is the "most profitable route of all." (Ibid.: 48) And it is the space of the office which mirrors these trends.

Offices – as workplaces – come in different shapes and "[f]or a long time the dominant administrative model for the office environment was the enclosed office: one or several desks in a room surrounded by four walls and a door." (Fischer 1997: 46) Nowadays, this type of office is usually associated with a certain hierarchical position for the size of the office and unchallenged dominion over the territory connotes success – the private office (cf. Sundstrom 1986: 287). A person occupying such a private, enclosed office is deemed superior and, with regard to (managerial) tasks within a business, more important:

> Until recently, the office was a private enclosed space or room in which employees carried out their work in relative isolation – with the degree of isolation increasing with seniority in

6 For a concise survey of the traditions of office buildings, see Duffy (1997): 19-43.

> the company. Office size and location in the building, as well as furnishings and desk accessories, communicated the status of the employee in the company. Historically, employees at relatively unimportant levels in the organization did not have a room, they only had a desk and chair; and it was only as they moved up to more senior and responsible positions that a room was allocated to them. (Vischer 2005: 1-2).

Jacqueline Vischer describes the predominant office floor in which the higher (managerial) employees occupy an enclosed (private) office whereas the lower (clerical) members of staff have to share a workspace[7]. This second form of the office is the *open-plan office*, which can be found in many companies – and indeed in many of the novels discussed here. The open-plan office was and still is embraced by companies because it "enable[s] organizations to house workers in spaces that [promote] inter- and intra-team information sharing and interaction, by locating individuals proximally to one another and removing physical walls and obstructions" (Davis, Leach and Clegg 2011: 205). Originating in the USA in the 1920s, the open-plan office was thought to further productivity because of the possibility of the standardisation of work processes and workers alike (cf. Baldry and Barnes 2012: 232). However, it appears that "Europe was generally reluctant to adopt the 'American open plan [sic] office [...]. This was partly a result of higher energy costs for air conditioning and lighting but more importantly was the result of cultural differences." (Laing 1997: 28) Shying away from the closeness of workers that an open-plan office entailed, European offices were "narrow in depth and cellular in plan, with small offices served off a central corridor." (Ibid.)

But in the 1960s, a German consulting firm developed the concept of the *Bürolandschaft* (office landscape), which takes its cues from the open-plan office and allows no private offices, not even for managers (cf. Duffy 1980: 257-278, Sundstrom 1986: 36, Laing 1997: 28-29). The major difference, however, lies in the 'organic-ness' in comparison to the American open-plan office as it does away with straight lines and a grid-like floor plan for workstations. The introduction of carpets and plants – both of which invoked the connection of office (built environment) and

7 Vischer actually claims that even managers have to 'occupy' an open-plan office since the end of the twentieth century, by being directly located in an open-plan office or by having to work in a glass-walled office – an aquarium – into which everyone can constantly look and which is thus negating the previously awarded privacy of the higher positions (cf. 2005: 1). Yet, if a company deems itself traditional or has a traditional(ist) clientele, they are more likely to grant their employees enclosed offices with windows. Vischer names universities, banks and law firms as belonging to this group (cf. ibid.: 3). However, even these businesses are changing their outlook on space equalling seniority.

landscape (natural environment) through incorporating elements which divert from or soften the office floor – relaxed the otherwise often strict office atmosphere: "architecture came to be seen as a determinant of social interaction instead of a context for it. Social psychologists had found physical proximity associated with conversation and friendship, and had concluded that architecture could mold patterns of social interaction" (Sundstrom 1986: 253). The open-plan office, which can be found today, is a further developed form of the *Bürolandschaft*, which has been taken to North America, re-appropriated and has eventually been re-introduced into Europe under the old moniker: "casual meeting places and coffee bars on the floors were dropped, clerical workers remained in the large open spaces while managers retreated once more to their private enclosed offices." (Laing 1997: 29) The office floor has evolved once again and now houses a combination of open-plan offices and enclosed, private offices, forming a spatial unit which could be termed a hybrid office floor. Additionally to the aforementioned advantage of quicker communication between workers in an open-plan office – "[p]rivacy was subordinated to convenient conversation and circulation of paper" (Sundstrom 1986: 253) – the *Bürolandschaft* (and the evolved form of the open-plan office) repeals hierarchical markers of status and "creates an egalitarian system with equal working conditions for all employees." (Hedge 1982: 520)

It should be exactly these (presumed) advantages – no markers of status, easy mobility and the possibility to have conversations (both of which result in a noisy and unsettled atmosphere; cf. Lee and Brand 2005: 324) as well as a lack of psychological privacy – that showed that the extremes to which the open-plan office has been taken do have their drawbacks: "Now everybody knows everybody else's business[. …] It actually starts to create a level of tension in an office that never existed before. People can't focus on work because they're on top of each other." (Needleman 2009; cf. Hedge 1982: 521, Sundstrom 1986: 40, Davis, Leach and Clegg 2011: 198-201) Mirroring Cosimo I's ideas for the Uffizi, the open-plan office grants managers "the twin advantages of economies of space (a reduction in 'unproductive' built features such as walls and corridors) and an enhanced visual surveillance of employees' performance" (Baldry and Barnes 2012: 232; cf. Boje, qtd. in Hedge 1982: 519).

Very recently, the evolution of the office has seen the reduction of "the amount of personal, or what [what can be called] 'me' space" (Polucci, qtd. in Needleman 2009): workers increasingly have to do and work with less space, which, in an open-office, they already share with many other colleagues. This policy of reduction has also spawned new spatial practices such as "hot desking" or "hoteling", providing a workstation on a 'first-come, first-serve' basis (cf. Vischer 2005: 71, Davis, Leach and Clegg 2011: 206-207): "It is not necessary to provide one workplace for everyone. So-called non-territorial office worlds have become a fixed factor established in many companies" (Bauer et al. 2012: 34). These practices present the hybrid form between the office worker and the teleworker or telecommuter, who is "working from an off-site location" or "who [is working] from home part- or fulltime during normal business hours" (Aronoff and Kaplan 1995: 16). The non-territorial office pays tribute to "highly mobile and nomadic work patterns" which emerge due to "extended and erratic periods of working" as well as an increasing "use of multiple shared group work settings", "diverse task based spaces" or "varied patterns of sometimes high density space use" (cf. Laing 1997: 25-26). Although not as visible in the earlier chick- and ladlit novels, the authors have picked up on these new developments lately and in *Turning Forty*, main protagonist Matt Beckford cannot call a workplace his own anymore but is "visiting offices across Europe and Asia." (Gayle 2013: 22)

The workplace has been shaped as much by societal changes as by technological progress. In the beginning of the office at the turn from the nineteenth to twentieth century, the typewriter was responsible for a "standardized paper size, which led in turn to standardized means for printing, binding and storage" (Vischer 2005: 12) and in the late twentieth century the computer changed everything (cf. Bauer et al. 2012: 8). With the advent of this technological tool offices have been transformed in terms of pace and interconnectedness (cf. Sundstrom 1986: 32-33). Whereas theoretical texts written in the 1980s were not entirely sure what to make of the new technological additions to the workplace, the Fraunhofer Institute has found that the workstation is now characterised by "digital networks and the use of mobile devices [which allow] the majority of people to gain independence for the organisation of their work and the place and time allocation of office and knowledge work[8]." (Bauer et al. 2012: 8) Today, the "battery power [of notebooks and tablet computers] and wireless network connections mean that traditional desks are not a prerequisite for work at all – coffee tables, touch-down spots, or even just an individual's knee can be sufficient." (Davis, Leach and Clegg 2011: 204) This has been anticipated by Duffy, who said in 1997 that "[m]uch office work can now be done in ways that are mobile, peripatetic, even nomadic." (46) It is in tune with the idea that the stereotypical signifier of the workstation, the desk, is no longer needed to represent a workspace because the "work*space* is no longer a work*place*." (Skinner 2012, emphasis added) Workspaces are not as limited or enclosed as workplaces tend to be, because "[s]uccessful businesses are reducing their dependence on expensive office property and enabling a mobile workforce to be productive wher-

8 "Knowledge work can be described as involving the application of 'theoretical and analytical knowledge,' exemplified by individuals involved in areas such as product placement or consultancy work" (Davis, Leach and Clegg 2011: 205; cf. Parker, Wall and Cordery 2001: 418).

ever they are most effective." (Ibid.) Other researchers have also found that the "[p]resence of staff in the office decreases continually." (Bauer et al. 2012: 32) Skinner sees this as an advantage because a "business is only as good as its people" (2012) and granting workers the freedom to create their own workspace away from the workplace is said to increase in the years to come.

Echoing Skinner and the increasingly less anchored workplace, Bauer et al. confirm that the spectrum of models for workplaces and thus workstations is now framed by cloud workers and by, what they call, 'caring companies' (cf. 2012: 16-18): cloud workers can be compared to freelancers, yet on a grander scale – they provide their services whilst having various qualifications (at varying levels) and they are not attached to any company. In distinction from freelancers, the cloud workers' digital network is typically part of a collective and their services are usually booked and received virtually. Most forms of contact are maintained in cyberspace, which becomes their workspace and which complements their actual, physical workstation. In contrast, the 'caring company' wants to achieve the total opposite – they favour strong ties and attachment of workers to their company and prefer long-term employees. In order to achieve this goal, they are willing to provide a new form of corporate life by granting access to health care, leisure activities and focus on the family. Caring companies try to amalgamate an employee's private with their working life and thus to create a holistic system rather than an atomised one. Caring companies want their workers to feel at home at their workstations by enabling them to adjust the desk's height or to personalise the lighting and even the climate of the workplace (cf. ibid.: 38-40). Many researchers connected the manipulation of the just-mentioned factors (e.g. furniture, noise, lighting, temperature, comfort, air quality, communication and spatial arrangements) to a higher productivity and general sense of well-being (cf. Brill et al. 1984/1985, Sundstrom 1986, Lee and Brand 2005, Hameed and Amjad 2009).

Nonetheless, "[e]ven in companies where space standards have been slimmed down and people work remotely [e.g. telecommuting; C.L.], use different desks, and come to the office for services rather than for space [e.g. hoteling; C.L.], people still manifest what appears to be a non-rational attachment to space." (Vischer 2005: 20) For all the technological advances and advantages of non-territorial workspaces, most employees seem to wish for (or even need) dominion over territory, to "to accommodate the realities of everyday life within [the office building]." (Davidson 1995: vi) And the "emotional connection" (Vischer 2005: 20) a worker has to their workspace is most visibly played out at the workstation. It might bear markers of status (like a name at the door, even a door to begin with, or a more expensive model of office furniture) or it might be adorned with artefacts of the worker's own making or of their 'other life', namely that at home (for example pictures of one's family): "These markers announce a presence; they are evidence of the 'owner' who occupies the space thus demarcated. [... Yet] the clearest marker of occupancy is the *presence of a person*." (Fischer 1997: 14, emphasis added) Especially the last part shows that most human beings appear to want their presence recognised and desire a workstation within a workplace environment. Hoteling or hot desking might be the future of working, just as telecommuting and cloud work gain a stronger foothold in contemporary businesses, but so far the workstation one works at and the office one comes to (traditionally) five days a week remain an important anchor-point in most people's lives.

OPEN-PLAN OFFICES AND THE PROBLEMS OF INTERACTION

Open-plan offices, it has been suggested, "facilitate greater communication and interaction [...] and create friendship opportunities [...], leading in turn to *increased inter-personal relationships*, reduced conflict, increased job satisfaction and motivation" (Davis, Leach and Clegg 2011: 197, emphasis added). This form of the office seems to be the perfect place to get into contact with other people and to establish (first steps into) new relationships. However, as this subchapter will show, in chick- and ladlit the open-plan office is seen as a space that is unfavourable to amorous relationships as this particular variety of the office might promote communication but it definitely furthers dehumanisation, especially as the open-plan office is strongly connected to Taylorism.

In his 1911 book *Principles of Scientific Management*, Frederick Winslow Taylor laid down the foundations for what is known as Taylorism, which elevates the ideal of productivity over individuality: "What it meant was treating people as if they were simply so many units of production. Taylorism [...] led to the dehumanization of work, first in the factory and then, a little later, in the office." (Duffy 1997: 16) In a nutshell, "Taylorism [...] aims to achieve maximum job fragmentation to minimize skill requirements and job learning time" (*Businessdictionary* "Taylorism" n.d.). It was Taylor's idea that "[i]f a job that demanded a high level of skill were systematically analyzed, it could be reduced to a series of simpler tasks that could quickly be learned by less skilled workers." (Aronoff and Kaplan 1995: 59) He wanted to break down the work process and thus turn every worker who is part of this process into a cog in a machine.

Although "[n]o one today takes Taylorism seriously" (Duffy 1997: 17), Jacqueline Vischer sees the far-reaching drawbacks of this practice: "Taylor's influence continues to be felt in the planning and design of work environments to this day in the form of standardizing office space for reasons of speed, efficiency and easy substitution of one worker for another." (2005: 12-13) The connection between Taylorism and workspaces is important for this subchapter as the quality of being interchangeable with any other worker or cog in the office machine reduces individuality. Yet space can only be turned into place when personalisation is possible and pursued. In Taylorist settings, the workspace becomes a dulling instrument, turning individuals into bland workers. Similar to the felix rigor mortis, characters who experience such a *Gleichschaltung* need to abolish their synchronised (working) existence in order to find their special someone.

Taylorism is very much present in two of Matt Howard's novels, *Taking Off* and *Ethan Grout*, and in both Australian books, the male protagonists work in open-plan offices. *Taking Off*'s Ash Lynch works at "one of the nation's top three distributors of magazines" and has "worked there since leaving school." (Howard 2008: 5) Ash is a typical lad, who is stuck in a routine and thus he has spent all of his working life (ten years) in the same workspace, probably even at the same workstation, without any aspiration to rise within the company: his workspace is as much a prison as his home situation. The idea that every worker can be replaced by any other is taken to extremes at Ash's workplace:

> I take care of *InStyle*, or should I say I *am* InStyle [sic] – we often refer to each other by our magazine names, perhaps because it saves having to remember two pieces of information about any single person – their magazine AND their name. I've been *InStyle* for just about my whole time at IDS. Originally I was also Big Trucks Monthly [sic], but that name has long since been handed over to someone who cares. (Ibid.: 5, original emphasis)

The workers are stripped of their individuality, notably here in the form of their names[9], stressing the importance of productivity and brands in the corporate world. They remain flat characters for they were never three-dimensional to begin with. Ash knows two of his colleagues by their first names, because one of them is his next desk neighbour and the other is the only one who actively resists being an interchangeable cog or magazine name (cf. ibid.: 7). The setting with desks being located next to one another and the fact that the workers can be substituted for one another – their job requires the same set of skills, just the name of the magazine they are tending to is different – suggests an open-plan office. Yet it is only Ash who truly hates his existence as a cog, the other workers display at least some aspiration to 'make it' within the company. But getting promoted is not signified by a corner office or an equivalent, the worker in question merely gets a more esteemed magazine, which is more widely known. The company thus deprives the workers of a spatial marker to a larger or indeed more prestigious workspace by using a status marker divorced from space: the workers occupy the same workstation, yet gain a

9 By using the brand name instead of the Christian name, the company attaches a notion of the grotesque to the workers (see chapter 6).

new 'identity' in that they get a new name because they graduated to a 'better' magazine. This practice takes the idea that the workspace or "office a person occupies is not just a space, it is also a place; it is a person's place in the company" (Weber, qtd. in Vischer 2005: 19-20) and perverts it: although each worker has their own place on the office floor, it is not their particular place in the company as their work is too interchangeable and their only defining marker – the magazine they take care of – can be taken away as swiftly as it can be 'awarded'. There is no relation whatsoever between the (work)place and a worker's performance. The employees of the company have been turned into cogs which have a function but not an identity: if one worker (or cog) is absent, their job can just as well be taken over by any other worker in the vicinity. This shows that the open-plan office is a place where identities are taken away and substituted by new corporate identities which are identical in everything but the moniker. In this company, striating a space so it can become a place is impossible and reflects the disregard of the workers' identities and personalities – only their work*force* matters.

However, Ash no longer wants to fit into this system: when he has the chance to present the distributing figures of his magazine and thus his enthusiasm (and to an extent identification with his work), he simply cannot be bothered to participate in the ritualistic program enveloping the presentations of the various workers. Ash realises that he does not care anymore about his magazine, the workplace or the company he has spent all of his working life at: "I am outside myself now watching myself through other eyes – they look at me and see a loser, feel sorry for me. I clearly don't want what they have, what they strive for, what they rate." (Howard 2008: 55-56) He has had enough of being a cog in a Taylorist workplace, he wants something he cares about. The novel actually suggests that people can be happy in such a setting – as Ash's colleagues are to an extent – but such a workplace does not work for everybody. In Ash's opinion, his colleagues are weird and this also has him reassessing his status quo as he cannot converse with them properly, feeling "alienated" (ibid.: 36). Considering that the open-plan office is an important part of his territory as it is his second anchor-point of the first order (after his home), he is no longer feeling comfortable: being in a territory means engaging in the same behaviour as the inhabitants to promote a group identity. But as it is exactly this group identity which overrides his personal identity, he has no other option but to the leave the stifling territory and the dominant magazine names-cum-identities.

Ash leaves his job and travels to Europe with a friend. There he evolves and realises his potential and when he actually finds a job he is happy with, he also finds his perfect partner. Both are connected to a taverna on a Greek island in which personal contact is the prerogative and in which the work process is not broken down into smaller tasks. All the workers at the taverna have their specific tasks such as cooking or waiting, but they can help with other tasks if needed. The taverna is presented as a heterotopic workplace in which its workers are working together as one team instead of a group of depersonalised employees at their designated desks: "It amazes me that there's always someone around to make sure this place opens on time and runs smoothly, but without a roster or any apparent fuss. Haven't they heard of stressed managers and grim-faced clock-watching? Total anarchy." (Ibid.: 260) Ash associates the feeling of anarchy with freedom and happiness, the robotic work processes of the magazine distributor with immurement and unhappiness. In the taverna, the whole family of workers have a meal before they open the restaurant and Ash reminisces about the forced business lunches he had to attend at his old company which were compulsory so as to force bonding (cf. ibid.: 263). At the taverna it happens naturally and the employees would come to 'work' even if they did not get paid (cf. ibid.: 261). Moreover, the taverna is fashioned as a place connected to nature whereas the open-plan office is anything but natural. Taylorism is presented as a malady which has infected cities and their populations: one is only there to function and to work but not to enjoy life. Ash realises that he wants his work to be part of his life, and not that his work dominates his life and personal interactions. Furthermore, it is this feeling of being whole, of not being just an anonymous cog in an impersonal machine, which gives Ash a space and a workplace to identify with. It is only now at the taverna that he experiences the feeling of belonging with regard to a workplace. At the taverna, everyone is treated as part of their family as exemplified in the communal lunch before opening up for business. They support each other and might even fill in the positions of others – like Ash and his travel companion for the owner's son and his best friend who want to travel to Australia – but they retain their personality. The notion of a heterotopic workplace prevents the taverna from turning into a Taylorist workspace because of the diverse tasks the workers can undertake if they wish so and because of the supportive and personal surroundings. Moreover, it is at the taverna, when Ash has regained his sense of self and identity, that he falls in love with his perfect partner. The taverna as a workplace has given Ash a positive sense of place and by being happy and having finally found his place in life – literally – he becomes the perfect partner to the taverna's owner's daughter, linking happiness with what one does, oneself and love conspicuously.

A similar situation is presented in *Ethan Grout*. Here, the eponymous protagonist has quit his job in a workplace similar to that of Ash's, because, just like Ash, Ethan did not really feel he belonged and had been appreciated. He finds a new job with The Book Place, where he is in charge of buying fiction – that he has no idea about fiction or next to no conception of books in general is of little importance to his boss (cf. Howard 2010: 34). When Ethan is introduced to his new workspace he describes it as follows:

I look to my left and there lies a football field of cluttered office furniture – with people fossicking through it as if at a tip. I'd already forgotten what working looked like.
Down the left side of the vast space is the passageway that allows you to enter the maze on the right at whichever juncture takes your fancy. Within the maze most of the desk arrangements are pod-style – three people per pod, each looking inward to the pod's centre. The internal sides of each pod's three equal segments are framed by flimsy felt-covered barriers, low enough so you can communicate to your pod-colleagues without meerkating too awkwardly. I can see many of the barriers have photos of loved ones pinned to them, as you'd expect to see on the walls of a prison cell. (Howard 2010: 43)

The office floor is occupied by the workers of the various teams that are employed at The Book Place – however, their team leaders occupy their own enclosed offices, presumably at the end of the corridor. This corridor seems to be a relic of the cellular office structure which was used to connect all the small cells the workers occupied in predominantly Northern European office buildings. The actual office space Ethan is going to work in is an open-plan office par excellence: a pod consists of small entities of three desks, three low walls surrounding each workstation and the office floor as such appears like a maze. Especially the mentioning of 'maze' and the association with 'tip' betrays the workspace's heritage as that of the organic *Bürolandschaft*: it gives the impression that the workspace developed uninhibitedly. However, it might be more organised and thus closer to the open-plan than Ethan is able to fathom from this first impression: he admits that it has been a while since he set foot into an office space. The explicit mentioning of the low barriers testifies to the open-plan office's idea of easy and quick communication. This is also directly proven when Ethan's guide introduces him to his new workspace – by shouting over the barriers: "'Everybody, this is Ethan.' […] *Everybody* says nothing." (Ibid.: 44, original emphasis) It is striking that the guide only introduces Ethan to his colleagues but not the other way around and that there is a certain lack of interest as to his persona and as a new colleague. This is the first indication of the level of the workspace's anonymity which will be addressed shortly.

In the last sentence of the above-mentioned description of Ethan's workplace, two ideas are contrasted – namely making the workstation homely by attaching personal signifiers to its barriers and referencing a prison. The former is due to the photos which are put up that remind one of the loved ones one had to leave behind (at home). Yet, this practice of "sustaining and conveying social and personal identity within an otherwise bureaucratic anonymity" through putting up pictures (Baldry and Barnes 2012: 229) has it limits. Ethan is present when his guide – even before introducing his pod – reprimands another colleague by saying to him: "Don't treat this place like your home." (Howard 2010: 42) The guide makes clear that 'home' and 'work' are very distinct and separate spheres, exposing the personalising practice of using photos to make the workspace more homely as a childish exercise: it appears to humour workers rather than to allow them to striate or productively engage with the workspace. This, as the reader gets to find out later, is rather ironic for this reprimanded colleague of Ethan's does actually *live* at the office floor, having furnished the space "behind the computers [with] a fully stocked clothes rack, loads of boxes, a mirror, a pile of shoes, even a hook with a towel hanging from it." (Ibid.: 80) The office building features a well-equipped bathroom so that the worker can indeed turn the office into his home – which he has done because he lost his old home, not because he particularly likes his office so much. This worker has gone one step further than just turning a workspace into a workplace: he turned it into a hybrid home – a home office which is definitely not a tele-workspace. He has effectively and efficiently infiltrated the structure of the workplace – as identified by Ethan's guide – and created a personalised life space in it. Thus, he has established a heterotopic part at the office floor that is his territory alone.

Returning to the comparison stated above, likening the open-plan office to a prison is not a coincidence. The accessibility of the open-plan office is not only given to the immediate occupants for better communication, it also helps the bosses to monitor and control the tenants, as stated in the introduction to the office. It thus invites comparisons to the panopticon, a form of a prison and visual surveillance devised by Jeremy Bentham in the late eighteenth century. In this building, the prisoners were held in small cells which were arranged in a circle. The 'value' according to Bentham lies in the fact that the prisoners could be controlled from the inside as the guards could look into the cells but the prisoners could never be sure when that was going to happen or if at all (cf. Bentham 1995: 45). It was believed that this possibility of constant surveillance leads to the correction of previously deviant behaviour, which connects the panopticon to a Taylorist workplace: "Supervision was another key feature of the office run on Taylorist principles. It was thought that people on their own could not be trusted, that without the presence of a constant watchful eye, they may revert to non-machine-like behaviour. Accepted norms in dress and behaviour naturally followed." (Duffy 1997: 16-17) Similarly, the staff of The Book Place can also never be entirely sure when one of their bosses is watching them and thus assessing their work[10].

10 The novel also features its own prison guard in form of Ethan's guide, who is a mediator between the workers on the open-plan office floor and the bosses. But even she does not realise that one of the workers made the floor his home, which puts her skills into question. However, this confirms the connection between the panopticon and the open-plan office even more: the guide behaves as if she is constantly monitoring the staff but in reality she is not, yet it keeps the workers on their toes (to a

The control The Book Place's managers try to execute is furthermore visible during the workers' lunch break – or more precisely "the enforced bonding known as lunchtime." (Howard 2010: 51) The space is described by Ethan thus:

> The lunchroom is a big space, again without windows, which has a kitchen at one end and an entertainment centre at the other, closest to the door. In the centre of the room is the massive communal table – that aims, presumably, to bring all the diners together as one corporate family. (Ibid.: 51-52)

The 'corporate family' is an indication of The Book Place trying to fashion itself as a caring company (cf. Davis, Leach and Clegg 2011). However, the fact that the bosses of the various teams are not presented eating with their direct subordinates and that the latter are indeed more bullied than encouraged to bond during lunchtime, ridicules this idea of the caring company. Plus, the way Ethan describes it, the windowless room is anything but appealing. Yet, most importantly, the lunchroom is dominated by two bitch characters who behave as if they were holding forth at the lunchroom with everyone in their direct vicinity just there to be laughed at. The two women push Taylorist anonymity to new, yet comic levels. Each person at their workplace is given a nickname which corresponds to their country of origin – or so the women think: when a new colleague is introduced they have problems for they are "as likely incapable of remembering his homeland as his real name." (Howard 2010: 71) However, none of the other members of staff seem to mind. The workers have resorted to an attitude of indifference to survive their workdays, which is even detectable in the bitch characters as the two women do not regard anybody important enough to learn anything about them. Ironically enough, the women are just as interchangeable as they do indeed look the same and behave in an entirely similar fashion. By sitting themselves at the middle of the table and behaving disrespectfully towards their colleagues, the two women signify that the lunchroom at The Book Place does not support a group identity but furthers uniform disinterest in the workplace and workmates.

The only character who is rebuffing the two women is Alejandra, but she considers it a form of entertainment during her bleak workdays more than an attempt to change the women's attitudes (cf. ibid.: 53-54; 58-59; 64-68). Ethan takes a shine to

---

certain point). A similar situation can be found in *Can You Keep a Secret?*. When the company's owner visits the office, main protagonist Emma Corrigan notices the effect her boss has on her department: "I'm aware that I'm holding my head slightly higher than usual, as though I'm in a posture class. And as I glance around the office, everyone else seems to be in a posture class, too." (Kinsella 2003: 92) Without observation the workers *do* revert to human and thus less productive behaviour.

her and he soon realises that Alejandra has established her own place, which, incidentally, is located outside The Book Place – the smokers' corner (ibid.: 68). Therefore, when Ethan has a personal conversation with her, it is outside The Book Place, either in the smokers' corner or at the café opposite their workplace at which Ethan meets his stepmother for lunch as well (cf. ibid.: 77-78). As the only merger between family and work are the pictures connoting the prison, interlinking Ethan's family with the only thing he likes about work – Alejandra – has to happen outside the realm of the workspace. Equally, love does not take place at the workplace – Ethan follows his perfect partner Alejandra *out of the workspace*. Learning from her the spatial processes of not giving in to the crushing anonymity of Taylorist workspaces or the bullying of colleagues, this forming of attitude reflects firstly on his relation to (work)space and secondly on his relationship to Alejandra. The open-plan office is not a (work)place supportive of romance as author Matt Howard has both his protagonists Ash and Ethan flee these environments, with The Book Place even collapsing as it is taken over by another company and most of the staff being made redundant (cf. ibid.: 93). Ethan even wonders if he will keep in contact with his colleagues but reasons that "[m]ost of them will no doubt slide right out of my life like hitchhikers" (ibid.: 94) as he did not transfer his connection to them outside the workplace as he did with Alejandra. Howard's novels suggest that open-plan offices, instead of making communication easier, result in a fleetingness of the workers and their interconnectedness.

Both *Ethan Grout* and *Taking Off* are examples of how open-plan offices are negotiated in ladlit. With regard to chicklit, it is striking that the office settings are not as explicit as Howard's workplaces. The three texts which will be discussed in the following tend not to elaborate greatly on the workplaces' features but emphasise equally negative aspects of the open-plan office, which are more played out on a personal level. Within a workspace context, Kerstin Fest has compared chicklit protagonists to female nineteenth-century protagonists:

> Although chick lit's main theme is arguably the heroine's search for true love, the protagonist's working life is very often at the center, too. [...] While the fact that women (at least unmarried and childless ones) work is not disputed or discussed, the heroine's femininity in the workplace is a concern. On the one hand, the heroines work in fields in which they can showcase their feminine traits: they mainly help and care for others. On the other hand, they find it hard to combine their femininity with their work. This is not only the case in novels dealing with working mothers, so-called "mommy lit," [...] but is also an issue in novels about young unmarried and childless women. The "good" woman is expected to neglect her work and prioritize her private life. Women's professional success is very often linked with a lack of femininity and presented as a threat to the heroine and to her private personal relationships. (2009: 44-45)

Fest's ideas regarding the caring aspect of females and their penchant for putting their private lives before their professional careers are true with regard to men. And while the women are able to advance their careers eventually, true happiness is still only possible with a man at their side. However, she neglects to address the existence of female co-workers who tend to pose a distraction to the women's career – just like the pursuit of love does.

Rebecca 'Becky' Bloomwood (*Confessions of a Shopaholic*), Emma Corrigan (*Can You Keep a Secret?*) and *Bridget Jones's Diary's* eponymous heroine all work in open-plan offices and are having issues with their female colleagues who occupy the respective desks next to them. The feelings of antipathy range from envy and inferiority complexes (Becky and Bridget) to downright hostility (Emma). Due to the nature of the open-plan office the women have to endure the taunting of the non-threatening bitch characters, which are very similar to *Ethan Grout*'s two blonde women. The difference is that, in chicklit, the dislike of the bitch characters is usually only directed at the heroine, not at all colleagues equally. Bridget and Emma have to suffer their tormentors because their co-workers are, in Bridget's words, "slightly senior and therefore thinking [they] are in charge of [them]" (Fielding 1998: 17). What unites the two heroines with Becky is that their colleagues function as foil characters who make the chicklit protagonists both more sympathetic to the reader and highlight their open-plan offices as (work)spaces in which they cannot 'escape' the taunting: the bitch characters bring out a facet of the characters which is anything but caring or nurturing as the novels' first-person narrative discloses their own feelings of inferiority and ineffectiveness. With regard to the colleagues' function as non-threatening distractors, this only applies to the romantic plot, because the bitch characters do threaten the heroines' ability to perform well in their jobs. Emma, for example, feels helpless when her colleague simply takes a newly arrived desk "even though [Emma herself has] got this really grotty little desk" (Kinsella 2003: 31) and Bridget is distracted by her colleague, who brags loudly whilst being on the telephone (cf. Fielding 1998: 18). Becky, however, does not have problems as such with her colleague, but feels ever so inferior to her because her colleague appears to be much more able at her job than herself, signified by her organised workstation, and because of that Becky loathes her (cf. Kinsella 2007: 6). The only way the women can escape their co-workers is either by leaving the workplace (Becky and Bridget) or with the help of a man (Emma). It appears that chicklit heroines are incapable of confronting the issues themselves and standing up for themselves.

Fest's second feature, which suggests that the women's femininity is indeed a hindrance to move forward in their jobs and careers, holds true. But Fest fails to acknowledge that not only are men the reason why the women prioritise their private lives over the careers, but they can also be the solution to the problem.

When both Becky's colleague and another female friend of hers, who is also a financial journalist, tell the heroine that they are no longer satisfied with their jobs because, as the friend puts it, they have "no aim, no game plan, [and] no prospects" (Kinsella 2007: 112), Becky is shocked: she feels the same way but so far has only ever dreamed about working at other glossy magazines or renowned newspapers and accepted the fact that journalists have to have jobs such "as the crappiest editorial assistant possible [...] because that's all they know." (Ibid.: 10) She regards herself as entirely clueless when it comes to finances, but it transpires during the course of the novel that she has actually gathered a substantial amount of financial knowledge. When she is at a press conference and talks to an unexperienced journalist she just met, she is able to explain to him the details of the financial scheme presented as well as evaluating it immediately (cf. ibid.: 109-110). She is unable to realise this because Becky regards her private life and shopping higher than her career. But eventually she manages to put her financial expertise to good use by discovering a scandal which involves a pension scheme fraud.

Writing an article for a newspaper that gets her on national television, she is able to get public relations manager Luke Brandon to admit to the wrongdoings of his client. What is important to notice here is the fact that Becky's allegations are listened to by everyone but it needs a man to tell her and the television-viewing public that she is indeed right (cf. ibid.: 275). Only when Luke admits to the failure of his client is Becky able to gain professional recognition. Furthermore, it is Luke who offers her the opportunity to leave her open-plan office and present her with a future by asking her to become a financial advisor to his company (cf. ibid.: 278). Although Becky is offered her own slot on the show in which she bettered Luke, the consecutive novels make it clear that Becky is willing to give up her career to follow Luke, who becomes her boyfriend: he enables her to leave the constraints of the open-plan office but she eventually – in the third book of the series – will give up any career of hers to be there for her perfect partner. At that time, her job as personal shopper was going quite well but she chooses to tend to her partner, who is suffering from burnout. The nurturing female has to give up her career yet again.

In contrast to her, Bridget has to rely entirely on other people to help her with her career. In the beginning of *Bridget Jones's Diary*, the heroine is working at a publishing house and although her job is never specified, she is mostly depicted lusting after her boss Daniel Cleaver instead of working: "Mmmm. Daniel Cleaver, [I] love his wicked dissolute air, while being v. successful and clever." (Fielding 1998: 18) That she considers her love life more important than her professional career is visible when she is happy that Daniel flirts with her via instant messages (cf. ibid.: 25, 44). These messages border on sexual harassment and if Bridget really wanted to be regarded as a professional employee she would not enjoy Daniel's disregard of his female workforce. The fact that the reader does not get to find out about the specifics of her work, yet about the sexual banter she is involved in, shows that her working at the publishing house is dedicated to private pleasures, not to being a career woman. It is only when her 'relationship' with Daniel reveals itself as being nothing more than sex – and indeed a sexual fantasy on Bridget's side – that Bridget realises that she needs a new job, with a new workspace which is not connected to sex at all so that she cannot be distracted. Of course, instead of changing her attitude towards work and her boss, she opts for the easier way out by accepting a job that has been arranged by her mother and that means working for a man who is the opposite of charming, sexy Daniel (cf. Fielding 1998: 197-198). It is only now, when the workspace is divorced from desire and lust, that Bridget can concentrate on furthering her career. Thus, the reader gets to find out what she does – she becomes a reporter – and whom she interviews – with varying success – which means that this job is more about her professional output rather than the hunt for a boyfriend. However, Bridget is anything but successful. Incidentally, it is through her work that she gets to meet Mark Darcy again, who helps her to her first big success as a reporter. Without the man she eventually marries, Bridget would not have become the "home news correspondent [with an] exclusive report." (Ibid.: 242)

The plot of *Can You Keep a Secret?* has heroine Emma Corrigan disclose all her secrets to her next-seat neighbour on a plane flight. Many of Emma's secrets are related to her workspace and the low position she holds. She desperately wants to make a career for herself but it transpires fairly soon that this is only the case because she does not want to be in her cousin's shadow anymore: "Another year of [...] Kerry [her cousin; C.L.] laughing at me, and feeling like a complete failure." (Kinsella 2003: 89) Emma's open-plan office workspace becomes a place of failure very early on and it is not surprising that she focuses her energy on her private life instead of her career when she is denied a promotion. On hearing that one of the company's products is going to be discontinued, she is afraid that her grandfather will not get his beloved sweets any longer: "What will Grandpa take to his bowling tournaments?" (Ibid.: 119) She convinces one of her colleagues to advertise a coupon which turns out to be a stroke of genius as the product is suddenly in demand again (cf. ibid.: 320). Due her not thinking entirely professional, Emma has managed to surprise her direct boss and is therefore able to get the promotion she longed for. It is entirely coincidental that she is able to get the promotion as it can hardly be put down to her 'eye for business'.

However, what she did not reckon with is that the man she confided all her secrets to is Jack Harper, the founder of her company: not only has he memorised all of Emma's secrets, he uses this intelligence to implement changes in his company. By doing so, he initially improves his employees' morale and their happiness to work for him. But then, he uses Emma as the quintessential everywoman for which he tailors a new product: "'She's twenty-something,' says Jack [...]. 'She works in an office, takes the tube to work, goes out in the evenings and comes home on the night bus ... just an *ordinary, nothing-special girl*.'" (Ibid.: 257, emphasis added) Humiliated in front of every colleague, Emma withdraws from Jack, with whom she has fallen in love. Eventually she forgives him and he 'rewards' her for doing so by becoming her boyfriend (cf. ibid.: 364). *Can You Keep a Secret?* displays the life of a working woman, who is rather helpless when it comes to her job and who is only useful when she puts her private life before her career: instead of divulging her boss's secrets, she looks the other way, not wanting to get revenge (cf. ibid.: 317). She discloses that she loves Jack despite his humiliation and would not want to destroy his life. And despite the promotion she eventually gets, she is only happy when she is (inevitably) re-united with Jack.

The three women never make it out of their open-plan office into an enclosed one, which would signify a rise in their careers. Although they are able to leave the positions behind that have made them unhappy, they ultimately need a man to fulfil them completely. Whereas the ladlit characters leave the open-plan office behind and relocate to more liberating jobs – Ash (*Taking Off*) works at a taverna and Ethan (*Ethan Grout*) owns a club – the chicklit heroines do not improve their station spatially. Bridget (*Bridget Jones's Diary*) moves from one open-plan office into another, and Emma (*Can You Keep a Secret?*) and Becky (*Confessions of a Shopaholic*) do not move out of their workspaces at all, merely getting a better job (title) – mirroring Ash's experience at the magazine distributor. Moreover, the latter women are only able to improve their work situation because of external influences (Bridget) and/or by acting unprofessionally (Emma). But all of the characters' happiness is tied to their respective perfect partners and in in this they are united, for the open-plan office is not the space in which they find love, they need to move beyond it – if only temporarily.

THE PRISON THAT IS A PRIVATE OFFICE

Whereas working in an open-plan office appears to be the norm in most of the novels, some protagonists have managed to have an enclosed office all to themselves. Cells, as Duffy terms enclosed offices (1997: 61; cf. Turner and Myerson 1998: 73), have the advantage that they provide high autonomy and their occupants are able to work independently. At the same time, the characters have to adjust or confront the insularity of their territory in order to work productively. In the following, three characters will be discussed in more detail, namely Dr Jon Marshall (*Bachelor Kisses*), Alexia 'Lexi' Smart (*Remember Me?*) and Richard Derrington (*Zigzag Street*). The former two have worked their way up and they have their own enclosed offices to prove it. However, they are not as happy as this presumed space of status might suggest. Richard's enclosed office, however, is a place of stagnation, as he occupies it from the beginning of the novel and it is proof of his laddish rigor mortis. The novels' private offices will be in the foreground of this chapter but the adjacent work-related spaces are under scrutiny as well here, because the combination of these spaces will present a more complete picture as to their romantic lives.

Dr Jon Marshall is a relaxed young man, who is a resident at the psychiatric ward of a Brisbane hospital. The main character in Nick Earls's *Bachelor Kisses* is a stereotypical example of the lad: he has no real goal in life, he is unsure what kind of doctor he wants to be when he finishes with his residencies and his relationships are characterised by his reluctance to commit. At his workplace, two spaces are of particular interest as they reflect his laddish-ness and love life: Jon's room on his ward, which he is awarded because of an idea of his, and the Nurses' Quarters. Jon dates nurses for a reason as he explains to his flatmate: "It's what's available. I spend my days with nurses and patients, and nurses seem to be the ethical option." (Earls 1998b: 148) Already, Jon's usage of the pronoun 'it' instead of 'they' or even a more respectful 'nurses' shows his lack of enthusiasm as well as a certain misogynist attitude towards his objects of dating and the distance to the women. Throughout the novel he dates three nurses from the Quarters and they can be characterised as prolonged affairs at best: he is never able to commit to being with them wholeheartedly. When he is seeing a nurse called Kelly, it seems that his veneer is finally penetrated but he admits to himself – and therefore confesses to his readers – the following:

> I wish I wasn't making her unhappy. Kelly, trapped in these Quarters. Trapped here with endless repeats on TV, other nurses drifting in and out. No-one she's really close to, and she's so good at being close, so unafraid of it. I can't hurt her. I don't want her to be hurt and I don't want to hurt her.
>
> I wanted to keep this [their 'relationship'; C.L.] the way it was, but she's not letting me. Not letting it go day to day. She's talking two months ahead. So much can happen in less time than that. […]
>
> I want to reach out to her now, and pull away. Not an easy maneuvre [sic] to execute. Sometimes I think I conduct most of my life in an abstract domain, as though it's only a concept. And not a very good concept, either. (Ibid.: 252)

The Nurses' Quarters are presented as a space of incarceration: Kelly cannot escape it and feels alienated in the surroundings. Jon, on the other hand, has the advantage of being able to leave whenever it pleases him. This behaviour serves his laddish attitude in so far as he knows that the nurses are limited in their territorial space and their movement is restricted to the ways between their only anchor-points: the hospital, their place of work, and the Quarters, which is the adjacent location. The Quarters are important as they play into Jon's non-committal attitude as expressed in his lack of ambition to invest in anything more stable than on a 'day to day basis'. Moreover, Jon is supposed to be available when he is at his workplace and therefore carries a beeper. This device extends the reach of his workspace and includes the Quarters into this space. He uses the beeper to extract himself from emotional situations at the Nurses' Quarters: when he is beeped he can leave without feeling guilty or sorry, abandoning yet another woman. He abuses his (work)space by regarding his girlfriends as part of work. He will be punished for this transgression when Dawn arrives at his enclosed office later on.

The impression that the hospital becomes a prison is inevitably experienced by Jon as well when he gets his own room at this workplace, which at first does not appear to be that incarcerating: Jon is part of a journal club at his psychiatric ward and when preparing to present his findings on a particular subject, he has an idea about researching the connection between melatonin and depression. Feeling very sure of himself – less so of his proposed idea actually – Jon tells his superior that they "need a room. We've got lots of articles. We've got a lot of stuff happening. We've got to have a room.[11] […] A room with a custom-made sign on the door. How credible would that be? A room with a lockable *door* and a *sign*. Credibility and mystique." (Ibid.: 192, emphasis added) Because he is only a resident at the ward, Jon has not got an office to call his own. Sundstrom observes that "[s]ymbolic properties of the individual workspace involve the display of the individual's personal identity or status in the organization." (1986: 9) To Jon, it is more important that the room has a lock and a sign than the purpose of the room itself. Towards the other residents, nurses and patients it signifies that Jon has indeed attributed more responsibility and credibility to himself and is therefore occupying a superior position within the hospital hierarchy than them: "A room sends out the right signals." (Earls 1998b: 192) Additionally, he can then claim a territory for himself: due to his position as resident, he has to visit all of the hospital's wards, he cannot successfully striate the hospital – the space of the hospital remains smooth to him. Having a room, however, means that he can withdraw to it and by shutting the door to his place can lay claim to a specific part of the ward which has to be respected by the other people of his workplace. The room would also give credibility to Jon's idea as "[p]eople would laugh at us if we didn't have a room." (Ibid.: 193) This is in tune with Baldry and Barnes's findings, which state that "[s]ignals about hierarchy are most often conveyed by the amount of *personal space*

11 Although Jon includes his boss in his usage of "we", he is going to occupy the room alone.

allocated" (2012: 237; emphasis added). Jon's importance rises analogously to his personal space that is expressed by his room.

However, the room does not turn out the way Jon had hoped, which is due to two reasons. First, Jon has no idea how he should progress with his idea and that makes his room a non-place and the second reason is the aforementioned Dawn. The room was to express Jon's progress both in medical science and hospital hierarchy but with his stagnating – if not declining – research into his topic, the room is obsolete and becomes a place of "solitary contractuality." (Augé 2008: 76; cf. ibid.: 70) It condensates Jon's life within four walls: he is unable, as a lad, to voice what he wants and where he wants to go in the future. Augé's non-place shares the smooth qualities of the de-territorialised space of Deleuze and Guattari's: one cannot stay but only rest, which compares to "non-places [because they] are there to be passed through" (ibid.: 83). The transitory aspect foreshadows that Jon must leave the enclosed office in order to move on. Nonetheless, there is a problem with Augé's idea for he claims that only if "a space cannot be defined as relational, or historical, or concerned with identity [is it] a non-place." (Ibid.: 63) But Augé's examples of non-places are exactly concerned with these three features, "albeit not in the traditional shapes" (Emig 2011: 179). Jon's office fits into this argument for it presents Augé's features but modifies them: firstly, Jon's enclosed office severs all ties to the outside and makes (love) relationships impossible, which is the reason why he inevitably has to leave it. Additionally, although the room is linked to the hospital and to Jon's research, the relations or connections to these issues are fragile. Jon withdraws from the hospital into the enclosed office and as he is unable to start on his research, the relationship to this particular topic ends at the door. Secondly, the office does not have any history in the sense of a diachronic heterotopia as the room literally comes into existence when Jon's name is put on its door. As Jon does not produce anything in this room, there is no future (output), only a 'stale' present. Lastly, with regard to identity, the office presents a vacuum for Jon as it conserves his laddish rigor mortis. It is concerned with identity but it is not one Jon feels comfortable with once locked inside the space. He tries to disassociate from his laddish self but finds himself unable to. It can be suggested that, if a space were truly concerned with identity, it would allow progress instead of preventing the same. The enclosed office manifests what has previously only been hinted at: Jon cannot find love at the Nurses' Quarters, he does not know what ward he would like to continue working at and, at home, he becomes restless. It is therefore only logical that he must go into the office because, as all his spaces have become smooth, the enclosing walls of 'his' office only confirm the imprisonment. He even stays most nights in his room, not realising that he has become prisoner and warden in one person – which aligns him with the nurses at their Quarters.

Another feature which is interesting with regard to non-places is the category of the linguistic signs, the verbal environment of the enclosed office. On the outside there is the sign which clearly marks the office as belonging to Jon and from the inside there is a letter from Edward de Bono[12] to motivate Jon. But "[c]ertain places exist only through the words that evoke them, and in this sense they are non-places, or rather, imaginary places: banal utopias, clichés." (Augé 2008: 77) The sign on the door is supposed to mark Jon's space and thus his importance due to the idea which awarded him the room in the first place. Working backwards now, as the idea turns out to be non-verifiable, Jon's importance is nugatory – what remains is the sign on the door which ultimately only marks the non-place that lies behind said door. Taking this a step further, the sign only marks the door itself and the door is (falsely) promising to lead to the creative intelligence of Jon. Here, the general notion about closed doors and signs with a name on it takes hold: to every person on the outside these are markers enough to attribute to Jon what is inevitably absent, proving that the sign on the door is ultimately misleading. The other linguistic sign, Edward de Bono's letter, is on the inside and thus generally only visible to Jon. It works in the same way as the sign on the door – this time it is there to convince *Jon* of the importance of the idea because of which he was awarded the room and which thus should attribute significance to *him*. Placing de Bono's letter in his room is Jon's attempt to striate the room and therefore to give meaning and direction to his life in general, but the letter was originally meant for this five-year-old self, showing that he has not really progressed. The letter points only backwards – as is also evident by its content – giving Jon a past outside but not a future inside the room.

In an almost ironic reversal, now that Jon has a room of his own, it is quickly invaded by a nurse named Dawn. One evening, Jon goes out with his flatmate and whilst being very drunk kisses Dawn at a club. Although Jon hardly remembers her, Dawn is under the impression that they are going out and constantly invades his room to have sex with him. These visits border on rape as Dawn abuses Jon. However, he is under the impression that if he talks to her she will realise that he does not want to have sex with her, even less be with her. These attempts remain feeble as she does not listen to him and takes what she comes for[13]. This proves again that

12 When he was five, Jon designed a rocket and his father was so impressed that he sent the plans for the rocket to Edward de Bono, an author and inventor. Shortly afterwards, Jon received the letter with the motivational slogan, which came to be his most cherished possession.

13 Dawn's visits to Jon's office for sex mirror his own trips to the Nurses' Quarters: he only goes there to satisfy his personal need for sex and nurturing but does not reciprocate the nurses' 'services'.

Jon's room is hardly his territory to command. It is no coincidence that Dawn reads out de Bono's letter: "Elemental simplicity and confidence both of which so easily get lost later on." (Earls 1998b: 286) The room and especially Dawn's presence show that Jon has lost said simplicity and confidence. Previously, Jon deemed his life perfect as his non-committal behaviour kept things – and relationships – simple and he was equally confident because he was able to convince his superiors to give him his enclosed territory. But within his room he has to realise that he cannot undertake his study. He becomes restless and unassertive, which results in Dawn being able to bully him into sex in a space Jon believed to be in control of because it bears his name on the door. It is significant that it is Dawn, who locks the door from the inside to 'rape' Jon and whilst doing so destroys his precious beeper. She intercepts his connection to the outside world and Jon's work: whereas before, Jon only had the lingering notion that he cannot conduct his study or work towards a goal, Dawn has translated this feeling into a haptic experience now and destroys Jon's already tarnished confidence (in himself) at the same time. The destroyed beeper means that Jon can no longer excuse himself from situations by pretending that he has to leave for work-related reasons. Dawn exposes his beeper as a technological extension of Jon's non-committal behaviour.

Looking at the room and Jon's chances to find happiness in an equal relationship (Kelly was inferior, Dawn is superior) which is to last, the room can be regarded as a form of limbo: it marks his stagnation – both professionally and personally. He does not know where to go, which is also the reason why he starts to stay in the room and does not return home. Yet he cannot turn it into a functioning workspace either, there is no going back. Jon has caught on to the fact that he cannot progress with his research – and to go forward, he needs a stimulus, which manifests itself in two people. The first is Jon's next-door neighbour, a fellow resident. This fellow resident has simply claimed the other room and nobody seems to mind, indicating that having one's own room is not as special as Jon thought it would be. As both men are equally incapable of leading satisfactory and happy lives, they realise they need to change: "To suggest that I'm much better at starting relationships than I used to be, but not great with what follows. It's like the room. I'm still treating relationships and room plans as though they're sufficiently unlikely to amount to anything, that I don't need to think through their implications." (Ibid.: 263) Just as in his previous 'relationships', Jon does not believe in the outcome of the research which is supposed to result from his room. He likes the idea of being identified as being with someone or as the proprietor of his own enclosed office, but both issues signify emptiness and loneliness. The room makes spatially visible what he also experienced with his ex-girlfriends: he has not got any idea what to do with them. He is like an inexperienced boy, the same boy who received de Bono's letter, who now has to perform in a grown-up world. Eventually, Jon and his neighbour need to abandon their rooms and what they signify – for Jon's neighbour it is his career as a doctor and for Jon it is his aimless life and futile study.

The second person that stimulates Jon and has him consider his (spatial) behaviour is Dr Kate Blue, with whom he falls in love. Not being a nurse means that Kate is not limited in her territory as she can go to other places than the Nurses' Quarters. Jon therefore needs to put effort in his courtship and has to leave the enclosed office in order to form a relationship with Kate. The enclosed office, though it bore his name on a sign, only imprisoned him and, despite being located within the workplace, it divorced Jon from his workspace in particular and from work in general. Although the novel ends before Jon can disclose whether he and Kate have formed a couple, it becomes clear to the reader that Jon has matured. He has realised that it is futile to be afraid of the future as well as progress and hide in his enclosed office or in meaningless affairs. Having found somebody who he can see eye to eye with, Jon is prepared to love another person fully for the first time.

In Sophie Kinsella's novel *Remember Me?* Lexi Smart cannot remember what has happened between 2004 and 2007 (see chapter 4). One day she works in an open-plan office without standing out among her fellow workers, the next she is the manager of her former friends and occupies her own enclosed office. She does not have an obvious sign attributed to that space like Jon but her superiority is expressed through her door, too, with the added humiliation of her personal assistant: "When you go into your office, [you] always slam the door. [...] *Then* [you] come out and demand a coffee. In that order." (Kinsella 2008: 394, original emphasis) The slamming of her door demands attention as the noise is heard in the open-plan office which is directly in front of Lexi's enclosed office. Demanding the coffee to be brought in afterwards shows her disrespect for her assistant, whom she is said to have treated like her personal minion. Whereas Jon had to deal with the misery of his enclosed office mostly on his own, Lexi has everybody else suffer as well. Her enclosed office's territory is therefore expanded to the open-plan office for it demands attention from anyone present and also keeps her department on their toes as she might come out at any time. Her staff are afraid of her and refer to her either as "bitch-boss-from-hell" or "Cobra" (ibid.: 241).

The identity of the 'Cobra' is of particular interest here as it becomes a 'portable enclosed office' in which Lexi feels trapped – mainly because of her 'missing' three years during which all her colleagues have turned their backs on their former best friend, whom they called "Snaggletooth", a term of endearment which refers to Lexi's teeth, which in 2004 used to be crooked. But at one point, several incidents came together that resulted in Lexi's metamorphosis from 'Snaggletooth' into the 'Cobra': "It's my dad's funeral. The bailiffs have just arrived to bankrupt us. I come across my boyfriend screwing a waitress ... and she takes one look at me and calls me Dracula." (Kinsella 2008: 374) As a result, Lexi immediately has a complete makeover done – including her trademark teeth, leaves her cheating boyfriend and takes on the mortgage her father has put on the family's home: in order to pay off this debt she has to turn around her life and become ambitious (cf. ibid.: 71-72). Cute 'Snaggletooth' is turned into a bloodsucking vampire (by somebody else), and then morphs into a poisonous snake (at her own incentive). Within this metamorphosis, the teeth serve as a connection and they are becoming increasingly dangerous on a metaphoric level as they become more perfect on an actual level.

Eventually, Lexi gets to find out that the 'Cobra' has always been only a veneer to be successful in the corporate world and consequentially to pay off her family's debt. In combination with her surgically enhanced body and tight fitness regime, Lexi has managed to construct the 'Cobra' to achieve her ambitious goal. Just like (audibly) slamming her door, the 'Cobra' is to convince people (visually) of her ruthlessness. It is the 'Cobra' who actually makes it to the upper management levels – which is an exclusively male territory, suggesting that the 'Cobra' is equally masculine. But behind the masculine 'Cobra' mask and the slammed door, (feminine) 'Snaggletooth' Lexi is still present. Yet, what this indicates is that for a female to succeed in the corporate world, she has to create a persona: "In this way the cultural preferences of bodily order are translated into material geographies: places are taken and made in line with gender roles and relations." (Anderson 2010: 157) With her unfit, snaggletoothed body, Lexi would never have been able to become successful. It is interesting that the narrative gives more explanations as to her bodily transformation and her appearance on a TV show than on her economic or leadership skills that should be necessary to occupy a senior position. Only the ambitious and thus regulated female body, enhanced with the masculine quality of ruthlessness, is able to rise in a company – the intellectual capacity, the text suggests, is less of importance than control, which is elevated to a masculine trait.

As the 'Cobra' veneer is the key that unlocked the enclosed office and which enabled Lexi to rise in the hierarchy and pay off her father's debt, she has to inhabit her character permanently – lest she should slip and by falling back into 'Snaggletooth', the lowly open-plan office worker, endanger her ambitious plan. It is interesting to note that as amnesiac Lexi does not remember said plan, she reverts to her 'Snaggletooth' behaviour and brings in muffins which are shunned by her staff:

> I've done my bit. If they want the muffins, they want the muffins. If they don't, they don't. [...] I sit back down at my desk, open a recent financial report and start running my finger down the relevant columns. After a few moments I lean back, rubbing my eyes with my fists. These figures are just confirming what I already know: the department performance is terrible.

Sales went up in the last year by a bit, but they're still far, far too low. [...] Then I put my pen down.
Why don't they want my muffins? (Kinsella 2008: 272)

The novel pokes fun at the incongruous behaviour in the office: 'Snaggletooth' Lexi, who was part of the open-plan office, tries to re-connect with her former colleagues, forgetting that her appearance is associated with that of the 'Cobra' and the enclosed office. Yet, it also shows that the border of the enclosed office and thus the management territory, represented via both the enclosed office and the 'Cobra', is not one of nurturing and caring – two stereotypically feminine qualities – which Lexi's muffin episode signifies. Anderson observes that "the identities and meanings of the places in which are bodies live are constructed [...] – the geography of the body and the geographies it inhabits are far from being natural" and they can be always traced back to "cultural values and acts of power." (2010: 153) It appears that the feminine female body is not meant for management levels or the enclosed office, because Lexi cannot control herself by focusing on the figures and constantly thinks about the muffin snub. This is later enforced when the male board of directors who initially wanted to keep masculine 'Cobra' Lexi and let go her whole entirely female department decides that her "employment should be terminated" too (Kinsella 2008: 413). This change in their opinion is brought about because Lexi wants to save her department and not increase her own salary and power, thus no longer espousing ruthless – read: masculine – qualities.

Lexi's body becomes a contested space on which two forms of workers, identified by her nicknames, are represented. However, whereas 'Snaggletooth' is an external identity to the company, which Lexi used to have before starting to work at the company, the 'Cobra' only came into being when she occupied her enclosed office and can therefore be regarded as part of the same. While Jon is caught in his enclosed office, Lexi has to struggle constantly by being imprisoned in the body of the 'Cobra' even when she is not within her enclosed office. When she is let go, along with her staff, the 'Cobra' as well as her enclosed office can be abandoned and Lexi is not sad to see both go. Eventually, Lexi sets up her own business in London and by the end of the novel she is quite successful with her start-up business. Her move out from the enclosed office into an office of her own signifies coming into her own. She could not lay claim to the centrality of the enclosed office which turns out to have been fake all along. Now, Lexi will conduct her social relations and business transactions in a territory which suits her. On a more critical level, the novel discloses that the corporate world is still a masculine territory and females cannot hope to striate it unless they are willing to adapt to male (territorial) behaviour and controlled bodies. Lexi used to be successful in her workplace, but because she only 'faked' being ruthless and controlled, she could not permanently become part of globalise corporate institutions.

The last enclosed office belongs to Richard Derrington (*Zigzag Street*). In contrast to Jon and Lexi, he has occupied his workspace from the beginning of his job as a lawyer specialising in finance. Nevertheless, his spatial experiences mirror those of the other two characters – the enclosed office has been turned from a workspace into a place of mindless stagnation, and he feels incapable of fulfilling his duties: "I've forgotten about the power station [an assignment of his; C.L.] and I'm playing Sammy the Snake on my computer." (Earls 1998a: 13) Richard feels overwhelmed with his work, which results in a numbness or even rigor mortis behind the closed door of his enclosed office: "If I was paying any less attention to my work I would probably be drooling." (Ibid.: 66) He is unable to realise that his office has become a hideaway from work, although it should be the epicentre of his workspace, but "the only observation [he feels he] can make with any confidence about [the power station assignment] is that there are far too many pages." (Ibid.: 14) He has lost control of his work and this impotency reflects upon his life as well (cf. ibid.: 67) as Richard has agreed to renovate his late grandmother's house but has nothing to show for it. There he finds a love letter and he realises the strong love his grandparents had shared (see chapter 4). The acknowledgement of his grandparents' love seems to snap something into action in Richard, for he goes into his office one Saturday night and, because nobody is there and the air conditioning is switched off, he starts to undress to be more comfortable. This striptease results in him sitting in his office stark naked and he realises all of a sudden that he is "cruising with this work. It's making sense. [He is] going to be okay." (Ibid.: 174) He sheds the confinements of his clothing, which are mandatory for his job, yet his release does not stop there: as nobody is likely to come in at this time, he dances through the hallways naked to loud music. He is finally able to leave his enclosed and restricting office for the first time and is feeling happy about it. Richard is not immediately able to start with the renovating work, which elevates it to the most difficult task, but he takes his new-found love for life, translates it into energy and uses it to escape his enclosed office. Unfortunately, his boss, with whom he has had a one-night-stand, shows up in the office and sees him. The situation gets slightly uncomfortable for the two but this incident nevertheless marks the beginning of Richard's liberation. Shortly after this night he meets a woman he is instantly smitten with and it becomes clear to him – for the first time – that "[t]his is a time for action." (Ibid.: 200) After the encounter with his perfect partner, Richard is not depicted in his office anymore: the enclosed office-prison has ceased to exist. It is never revealed whether the protagonist makes true on his promises to find a "good job, a job where [he] can do some good" (ibid.: 87) but his liberation has been accelerated by his new love and together they start to renovate his grandmother's house. Even if he continues to work in his enclosed office, he is very likely to leave his door open for new possibilities.

Mirroring the experiences of the characters who have to share an open-plan office, the enclosed office is just as restrictive and suffocating. All three protagonists, Jon (*Bachelor Kisses*), Lexi (*Remember Me?*) and Richard (*Zigzag Street*), escape the confinements of the cell-like office which "accommodate[s] individual, concentrated work with little interaction." (Duffy 1997: 63) Occupants of such offices are supposed to be in "total control of [their] physical as well intellectual environment." (Ibid.) But the examples have shown that 'being in control' has become a hollow phrase as both Jon and Richard are imprisoned in impotence and powerlessness. Even Lexi feels this by realising that all her friends and colleagues are scared of her 'Cobra' image, which complements her enclosed office and even becomes a mobile variation of it. The men and Lexi share their need for interaction as their enclosed office-prisons have cut them off from the outside and the effect this has on their mental well-being is devastating: Lexi suffers from loneliness (which is enhanced by her loveless marriage, see chapter 4) and the men fail to realise that they have created the workspace equivalent of Peter Pan's Neverland – a place where they cannot grow up. Therefore, the only way is out (of the office) and although only Jon and Lexi truly abandon the stifling confinement of their cells, Richard at least makes a metaphorical escape by stripping and leaving his office in the nude – he forsakes the sartorial signifier of his cell and therefore meets his perfect partner.

CALL CENTRES, CAKES AND ARRANGED MARRIAGES

In a 2013 interview, Indian Finance Minister P. Chidambaram said that "[p]eople should remember that India continues to be the fastest growing economy after China." (*The Hindu* 2013, *The Times of India* 2013) Over the years, the Indian subcontinent has overtaken other countries and is only second to China with regard to economic progress. This development is prominent in Indian chick- and ladlit as well. Therefore this subchapter regards Indian workspaces and explores how they are presented and negotiated. It is interesting to note that almost all these novels deal with workspaces in a prominent way and that the working lives of the Indian protagonists inform their lifestyles as well as their romantic endeavours. Work and the protagonists' relationship to work are very important features of these novels and they present an image of an India which is more than 'poised'. The novels feature a range of different professions: stereotypically 'Indian' workplaces like call centres (*One Night at the Call Centre*) or a Bollywood production (*Trust Me*) are juxtaposed with jobs such as guest relations manager (*Almost Single*), associate product manager (*Piece of Cake*) and start-up entrepreneurs (*Because Shit Happened*). What they all have in common is a strong connection between love and their respective workplaces. Most of the characters find their partners at their respective workplaces, yet all of them need to overcome obstacles beforehand that are tied to their specific professions. The discussion of Indian workspaces in chick- and ladlit will be enriched with an examination of love as an actual business and arranged marriages, which even in the second fasted growing economy of the world is an important issue.

Becoming a global player on an economic level is reflected in literature because "within the context of a burgeoning middle class and an avid consumer culture, Indian literature in English has become an important commodity to be sold, purchased, and consumed. [...] It is the third largest producer of books in English, just after the United States and the United Kingdom." (Kasbekar 2006: 77-78) In a review of Swati Kaushal's *Piece of Cake*, Nandini Lal terms the Indian chicklit novel "a desi Bridget Jones's Diary" (2004). *Desi* is an Indo-Aryan term for cultures, people(s) and products from the Indian sub-continent (cf. Iqbal Viswamohan 2013: 195) and it is implied that Kaushal has written merely an Indian version of Helen Fielding's seminal British book, hinting at the global scale of the genre. A similar comparison can be found on specific covers of *Almost Single* by Advaita Kala, which quotes the British *Independent*: "Bridget Jones dons a sari" (Kala 2009: Cover; cf. Dawson Varughese 2015). That this comparison is not as simple as it appears will be shown in the consecutive analyses: chicklit heroines do indeed tackle similar issues as Bridget Jones in that they are on the lookout for their perfect partner and negotiate their urban setting or questions of appearances. However, the novels also address a darker side of the Indian subcontinent (especially *Trust Me* by Rajashree) and the characters do not "conform to traditional stereotypes of femininity" (Gill and Herdieckerhoff 2006). Nonetheless, their usage of (work-) spaces is comparable to those of English or Australian chicklit and thus proves their 'sisterhood'. They will be complemented with the oeuvre by Harsh Snehanshu and Chetan Bhagat. Especially the latter author is – to date – enjoyed by many readers on the Indian subcontinent, which has made him "the biggest-selling English-language novelist in India's history, according to his publisher, Rupa & Company[14]" (Greenlees 2008) and whom Aysha Iqbal Viswamohan deems "the grandmaster of lad lit" in India (2013a: 20).

14 According to Iqbal Viswamohan, Bhagat's success is due to the fact that his "work was priced under Rs 100 to make it accessible to target readers, while most works by the 'elite' writers come in around Rs 500." (2013a: 21) McCrum writes that Chetan Bhagat's novel *The 3 Mistakes of My Life* sells a copy every 17 seconds (in 2010) and he attributes "[t]he key to Bhagat's success [to the fact] that he addresses the

"India has a billion people, but at night, 99 per cent of them are fast asleep. Then this land belongs to a few chosen few: truck drivers, late shifts workers, doctors, hotel staff and call-centre agents. We, the nocturnal, temporarily rule the roads and the country." (Bhagat 2007: 219) Chetan Bhagat's second ladlit novel is dedicated to one of these nocturnal workers, presenting the lives of six call centre agents. It "tells the story of globalized environment, thwarted ambitions, sexual repression, the generation gap, pop psychology, unrequited love, cultural conflict, mounting pressure of patriarchal set-ups and so on." (Iqbal Viswamohan 2013a: 24) At the beginning of the actual story[15] of *One Night at the Call Centre*, the main protagonist muses about the requirements of both his job and identity:

> By the way I am Shyam Mehra, or Sam Marcy as they call me at my workplace, the Connexions call centre in Gurgaon [a district in New Delhi; C.L.]. American tongues have trouble saying my real name and prefer Sam. If you want, you can give me another name, too. I really don't care. (Bhagat 2007: 22)

Already this testimony shows that the protagonist has to juggle two identities at his workstation: his personal self is his Indian identity, Shyam. But in order to carry out his job, he needs to become Sam. His virtual workspace is characterised by being Sam, yet without corporeal Shyam he is merely a voice: he appears to personify a neo-liberal, postmodern hybrid worker. The two identities merge at his workstation, his desk, from which he answers calls from the United States of America. The fact that the narrator would be fine with being called by any other name testifies to the fluid and somewhat artificial identity he assumes when he operates his workstation. This, however, only 'works' at the workstation. The moment he is actually not at the phone, he becomes Shyam again and calling him anything else then would be stripping him of his true identity[16]. The 'Sam identity' is a mask that needs to be put on in order to engage with other people on a global scale. Although it might appear as if American callers are superior to Shyam because he has to adapt his name – and his identity – to their (in)ability to pronounce it, it is Shyam, who is in power: the

---

everyday concerns of India's middle-class youth, in a language they can relate to, and also consciously strives for a mass appeal." (2010)

15 Like many of his other novels, Bhagat constructs his plot within a frame narrative that sees himself as a character being told of a story – the actual plot of the novel – that should be written down and published.

16 When Shyam gets ready to go to his workplace, his family wonders why he needs to look presentable when he is just on the phone talking to clients (cf. Bhagat 2007: 24). But, just like his name, his identity relies on markers – whether they are visible or not.

Americans call *him* and need *his* help, exposing their presumed superiority as misleading. The predominantly white Western world is now dependent on the former colonial country.

But Shyam never seizes this power which makes him a laddish character who feels that nobody ever listens to him (as it is said many times throughout the novel). He laments that his life is controlled by his boss Bakshi as Shyam is unable to stand up for himself (cf. Baghat 2007: 92-93). Shyam and his team of five colleagues are assigned to 'tend to' a specific clientele at their call centre which translates into dealing with "troublesome and painful customers. These [...] customers call a lot and are too stupid to figure things out" (ibid.: 47). Nevertheless, Shyam would like to be team leader and to assume more responsibility but his boss Bakshi tells him that he has not got "the 'required skills set' yet. In [his] review, Bakshi wrote that [Shyam] was 'not a go-getter'." (Ibid.: 22) Every member of Shyam's team has specific reasons for being at the call centre at night (money is just the overt reason, being able to afford a life of one's own and change one's present status the real, underlying cause), and Shyam in particular wants to become team leader so as to be able to propose to fellow worker and ex-girlfriend Priyanka (cf. ibid.: 41). He believes that his lowly status of 'mere' call centre agent is not good enough for her and her mother.

Despite not being the most assertive one, his team still considers him their leader: "As the ad-hoc team leader, I had some influence. I could approve personal calls and listen in on any line on the desk through my headset." (Ibid.: 87-88) This device with which he is able to monitor the other workers' calls is the only feature which distinguishes him from the other five workers as they are all sitting at one big desk which presents the main feature of their open-plan office (cf. ibid.: 48). They are able to see each other all the time and it is only through their headphones and their screens, which provide them with details about the callers, that they establish privacy – yet no real hierarchy. The call centre agents get along quite well and they do not understand why Shyam never stands up to Bakshi when their boss 'drops' new work on him. Shyam himself justifies his submissive behaviour by referring to the boss's promises to grant him 'exposure' and 'work experience' when he fulfils his tasks. But Shyam is actually afraid of losing his job if he stands up to inept Bakshi, who is in charge of down-sizing the call centre agents.

The novel displays features of the stereotypical workspace comedy – as usually found in TV sitcoms – by employing "characterisations and actions that undercut or even belied the 'situation' itself. [... C]*haracters* and *actions* [take] over the comedy, leaving the *situation* – [here call centre activities such as speaking with the rather stupid callers; C.L.] – increasingly in the background." (Hartley 2001: 67, original emphasis) Most of the novel's plot takes place at the agents' bay which is even described like a static TV sitcom set (cf. Bhagat 2007: 47-48). As the night progresses, the personal problems of the workers take over and display the human lives behind the voices with the American names and accents. Contrary to English and Australian examples, here the open-plan office does indeed create a bond between the workers, turning them into an urban workspace family. The reasons for this are, firstly, that they share a dislike for their boss and that they, secondly, have been working together for quite a while. Thirdly, and most importantly, communicating is the main part of their profession and thus comes easy to them as call centre agents. Therefore, the workers manage what the other workspaces are not able to implement – a bond.

One major plot line involves the inept boss of the call centre, Bakshi. Whereas the call centre agents share a large rectangular table, Bakshi works from an enclosed office which at "[t]he size of a one-bedroom flat, [is] probably the largest unproductive office in the world." (Ibid.: 204) It is fitted with a conference table and speakerphone to place calls to their headquarters in Boston as well as a "bookshelf full of scarily thick management books." (Ibid.) The management books Bakshi keeps are to give off an air of distinction and of knowledge but Bakshi has no clue about computers, despite his flashy flat screen workstation and when he speaks he uses empty managerial phrases which are useless but are supposed to mark him as sophisticated. Vroom, one of Shyam's colleagues and his friend, classifies Bakshi as falling "into the most dangerous and common category. He is stupid [...] but he is evil, too." (Ibid.: 174) Bakshi can be considered what is referred to in an Indian context as *babu*: originally a signifier of respect and loyalty, meaning father or boss, without the suffix *–ji* (*babuji*), it has a derogative meaning denoting a semi-literate native or shallow, self-important bureaucrat (cf. *OED* "Babu", Sibani 2013). The term implies a person of higher rank who lets everybody around them feel their 'importance' without doing their work properly: "The words are frequently used to describe bureaucrats [*babus*] and the bureaucracy [*babudom*], but the bureaucrats feel both words are derogatory and have a negative connotation. [...] The bureaucrats have blamed the media for corrupting the words to become synonymous with 'comfort' and 'laziness'." (Marapakwar 2012) Although not being a bureaucrat as such, Bakshi still displays many of the characteristics, especially comfort, laziness and non-literacy when it comes to technology: "I need to upgrade my technical skills. Technology changes so fast" (Bhagat 2007: 92). His evilness is evident when he passes off a website, actually Shyam and Vroom's work, as his own. It is clear that the production of this website is far away from his cognitive and technical competence. But the *babudom* is also visible in his spineless attitude when it comes to the workers of the call centre. The management in faraway Boston wants him to deal with the dwindling calls and his idea is "to *rightsize* people." (Ibid.: 206, emphasis added) He dismisses claims of 'firing' his staff and hides behind a manager-speak coinage. Yet, as he is so inept at many things,

Shyam, Vroom and the others manage to come up with a plan to blackmail him so as to lay off letting people go and to grant the two men money to start up their own business as they no longer want to be exploited in this call centre.

Bakshi does not only hide behind manager-speak, he also refuses to call his staff by their real names, instead he uses the American aliases the call centre agents assume when talking to their 'stupid' clients. It puts him on the same level as the callers and it is furthermore aligning his with the Americans' inability to work with technological devices. But the manipulation of the agents' Indian identity does not stop there because they have to use a canteen which equally does not cater to their Indian identity: "they don't serve Indian food, again for motivational reasons" (Baghat 2007: 149). The canteen, which has been renovated according to "some overpriced consulting firm (full of MBAs) [who] recommended that a bright dining room would be good for employee motivation" (ibid.). Just as in *Ethan Grout*, it appears that when such a place for bonding and motivation is featured it is ridiculed by the narrators for having sprung from the overzealous and overpriced minds of self-important MBAs who have yet to set foot in a 'real' dining room. Depriving the Indian workers of food they would like to eat does not mean that they will feel comfortable – far from it. Before the call centre agents even enter the workplace at the beginning of the novel, they deliberately stop at an all-night *dhabha*, a Punjab restaurant, to drink chai instead of the canteen's soda water and they would have had *paranthas* instead of cheese sandwiches if they had had more time. The workplace becomes an Americanised or at least Westernised space which especially annoys Vroom.

He can be considered the political mouthpiece of the author: "Bhagat is aggressive in his attacks on American politics, culture and lifestyle" (Iqbal Viswamohan 2013a: 25[17]):

> In the twentieth century, the crisis-narrative from took on a new avatar as 'inspi-lit' which came to be much in demand due to rising levels of human dissatisfaction with the acquisition of material possessions, individuals' self-directed questions about personal worth and purpose of existence, fears and feelings of inadequacy, loneliness and friendlessness, radical disquietitudes, all aggravated by the tensions of a highly technologised and urban-centred existence in a contemporary postindustrial world scenario. (Dhar 2013: 165)

One Night at the Call Centre does not shy away from ridiculing or even dismissing Western and American attitudes. Apart from operating on the basis that "the brain and IQ of a thirty-five-year-old American is the same as the brain of a ten-year-old

17 While Iqbal Viswamohan identifies and apparently welcomes this criticism, she does not go into detail as to the implications or reasons of Bhagat's anti-American stance.

Indian" (Bhagat 2007: 63), Vroom considers the Americans dangerous locusts or capitalist mosquitos draining India of its blood – its people – because India lets them: "Our government doesn't realize this, but Americans are using us. We're sacrificing an entire generation to service their call centres" (ibid.: 232). He continues and voices globalisation-critical thoughts by claiming that an "air-conditioned sweatshop is still a sweatshop. In fact, it's worse because nobody sees the sweat." (Ibid.) This is also the reason why Bakshi is able to swindle Vroom and Shyam out of the website they created in their free time: the two men are mere workers and the American bosses do not know or refuse to acknowledge their working conditions or situation or even their presence which goes beyond that of a human environment, devoid of markers of identity (cf. ibid.: 173). However, what Vroom neglects to mention is that all the workers in the call centre are somewhat privileged: "Some labour process research, particularly by Indian scholars, acknowledges the difficulty of simply describing Indian call centre workers as working class. [Most] call centre workers come from the 'creamy layers', an Indian-English term describing those of high class or caste status." (Murphy 2011: 420; cf. Ramesh 2004) All of the call centre workers presented in the novel – the main protagonists as well as the many unnamed workers who are important to Vroom's plan to scare the Americans – have to come "almost exclusively from the upper strata of society – partly because of language requirements that effectively require an English language and thus private education, and partly because of the social skills required to engage with western clients[18]." (Murphy 2011: 420) What is also important to note is that the job pays rather well. As one of Shyam's colleagues puts it: "You know how hard it is to make fifteen grand a month *outside*." (Bhagat 2007: 232, emphasis added) This attitude mirrors one of Jonathan Murphy's interviewees who works at a call centre and says that "[m]ost Indians only earn maybe 10,000 to 12,000 rupees, and I make 15,000 to 17,000" (Murphy 2011: 425). This shows that Shyam and his co-workers earn a lot of money – "several times more than traditional middle class employees such as government primary school teachers" (ibid.: 420). They represent a new form of middle class and they have 'new' middle class aspirations – such as owning their own home or business. And the characters work in a sector that pays well so that the achievement of their dreams is highly possible. But these issues are only touched upon in passing, with Vroom the only one wanting India to stand up for itself and facing the 'capitalist' West, even devoting his life to this aim.

With regard to the romance plot, Shyam is in love with Priyanka, whom he has known for four years and with whom he went out some months before the novel

---

18 As stated above, the clients' intelligence is ridiculed frequently. Thus, the call centre agents' special skill with regard to contact with customers is the patience they have to exercise when they answer a call.

starts. His plan is to re-propose to her once he has risen in the company but with Bakshi in place and his own submissive behaviour this is not going to happen. Priyanka, who had agreed to an arranged marriage shortly before the story of the novel begins, eventually tells Shyam that she broke off the engagement to the other man – ironically, he is an Indian IT worker living in America – and would like to marry him. In order to break the news to Shyam, she reverts to a comparison by rather obviously likening Shyam to India:

> 'Shyam, you know how Vroom said just because India is poor it doesn't mean you stop loving it? [... W]e love India because it's ours. But do you know the other reason why we don't stop loving it?'
> 'Why?'
> 'Because it isn't completely India's fault that we are behind. Yes, some of our past leaders could have done things differently, but now we have the potential and we know it. [...] I thought, this is the same as my Shyam, who may not be successful now, but it doesn't mean he doesn't have the potential, and it sure as hell doesn't mean I've stopped loving him.' (Bhagat 2007: 297-298)

One could go even further and regard the whole novel as an allegory, with Bakshi representing the obnoxious and imperial West, the call centre standing in for India and Shyam for the Indian population that could do so much better if it just learned to realise its potential[19]. Here, Bhagat blurs the generally laddish attitude with an early-Millennial India: both need to believe in themselves and poise themselves in order to achieve greatness[20] – and it can be argued that this novel wants its readers to recognise and explore their potential (for India), too.

At one point during the novel, the whole team skives and goes to a lounge bar to have a drink and talk about Bakshi's revelation that they are going to be 'right-sized'. On the way back from the bar, they have an accident and cannot call for help as there is no reception. Suddenly, God phones[21] and is willing to rescue them when

19 Vroom would be a revolutionary leader and guide in the spirit of Mohandas 'Mahatma' Gandhi.

20 At the 60th anniversary of India's independence, the *Lead India* campaign was initiated which features a poem comparing the two Indias they felt were struggling with each other – one trying to rise, the other holding it down (cf. *The Times of Money* 2007).

21 This device is literally a *deus ex machina* solution and even Chetan Bhagat from the frame narration doubts the probability of the presumed 'true tale'. But the woman telling the tale to fictionalised Bhagat says "[j]ust like life[:] Rational or not, life is better with God in it." (Bhagat 2007: 314)

they tell Him what they really want from life and what it would take to achieve this goal. For the first time, Shyam is able to express his wish to stand up for himself and man up for Priyanka in the latter's presence (cf. ibid.: 256). God agrees to help the helpless call centre agents but advises Shyam – and the others, as they are present – to realise the four ingredients of success: a medium amount of intelligence, a bit of imagination, self-confidence and experiencing failure so as to find out that one does not need to be afraid (cf. ibid.: 257-259). After the rescue, Shyam sheds his laddish and underachieving identity and regains his self-confidence. He stands up for himself and gets back together with Priyanka. However, they do not marry directly, granting her the chance to finish her university degree to become a nursery teacher. Shyam is not afraid of losing her or of failing in his business – he now knows that he has made it once already and he can do it again. Although the call centre open-plan office is the only one in which a bond between the workers is successfully created, it remains a restrictive place. Shyam needs to leave it to fulfil his aspirations to become his own boss and it is no coincidence that Priyanka leaves with him so that she can follow her dream, too. Their similar attitude towards the open-plan office shows their spatial compatibility.

Minal Sharma, the protagonist of Swati Kaushal's *Piece of Cake*, is an associate product manager at the Indian food company International Food (IF). The novel deals with Minal's new assignment to the cake division within the company and her struggles with superiors, a rival company and her transferral due to a scandal. The romantic plotline, however, is not the primary focus as is usually the case with chicklit but rather cleverly intertwined with the workplace plot. Thus, it does not come as a surprise when the novel ends not with an acquired boyfriend, but only a very slight hint that Minal might date one of her colleagues in the near future.

Directly at the beginning of the story, Minal is shocked that her mother wants to set her up with men by putting an advert in the matrimonial pages of a Delhi newspaper (more on arranged marriages follows): "I guess [mother]'s never completely recovered from the blow of my choosing an MBA over a Masters in Human Services, or a multinational company over her numerous pickling and spinning societies." (Kaushal 2004: 5) Minal is very self-confident when it comes to her job, truly enjoys it and, as her boss Vik puts it, she is "enthusiastic, [has] got a good grasp of the business and [is] not afraid to stand up for [her] convictions." (Ibid.: 28-29) Kaushal never lets the reader doubt Minal's ardour for her profession: she comes across as very determined and resourceful with regard to her job. Her goal of getting to the top is connected to an enclosed office which functions as the typical marker of hierarchy and status:

Vik's office is the stuff my dreams are made of. Thick pile carpeting, wood on the floor and walls, leather on the chairs. A towering map of India, three easy chairs around a small coffee table and, straight up, a mahogany and glass case full of IF packs from around the world, a vase full of fresh flowers and a wide desk that gleamed with dignity and was polished twice daily.

Maybe, someday, I'd be arranging my family pictures in a discreet corner of that desk, putting my feet up to watch the sun set. (Kaushal 2004: 28)

This office clearly marks its occupant as one who has 'made it'. The office, which has enough floor space to house a workstation and a social space (three easy chairs and a coffee table), is fitted with expensive materials which convey the image of wealth and power. Additionally, the desk is polished multiple times a day, a sign of Vik's professional function of hosting – explaining also the social space – and that the desk as centrepiece is less of a workstation than a marker. The desk and its perfect surface are noticed by visitors to the office and it suggests that the desk has been installed to impress due to the materials used to build the workstation. If one assumes that executives are used to their contacts having large offices, it is the furniture and tiling that stand out and set the proprietor apart from others, just as the size of the office is to impress and maybe even intimidate Vik's guests. The office also features a geopolitical dimension: the map shows the direct link of the company to the country they work in and provide goods for. The case of various international samples of the company shows the interconnectedness of the multinational business. At one point in the novel, Vik is going to attend a conference in the United States of America connoting again his function as one of the figureheads of the company. Minal dreams of occupying such an enclosed office one day and it is telling that she intends to arrange family photos on her desk, something which is not referenced on Vik's desk and thus can be taken as being absent. Just like in *Ethan Grout*, the workstation adorned with signifiers of a private life aims to combine the two worlds which are otherwise separate. Minal deems herself capable of managing both a private family life and a career in a multinational company. Putting up the pictures in a discreet corner of the desk means that she wants the photos to herself and not to display a happy family to visitors.

At one point in the story, Minal even gets her own enclosed office but has to realise that it is not what it promised to be. Due to a misunderstanding regarding a heart-shaped cake[22], she is demoted and a new position is assigned to her. But instead of working more freely or creatively, the enclosed office comes with

22 The heart-shaped cake can be regarded as a metaphor and it foreshadows Minal's life. When the concept for the cake is stolen and Minal has to focus on another product instead, she is able to pursue her own ideas and is eventually more successful this way. However, it shows that she has to forsake romance (the heart-shaped cake) to advance her career.

restrictions and has Minal "plummet[…] to the very depths of mindlessness." (Ibid.: 223) She is now responsible for checking petty expense vouchers and equipping her staff with promotional material. She used to take assignments and other work home with her (cf. ibid.: 212-214) and thus enlarge the workspace far beyond the walls of her workplace, but now her joy to work has evaporated as she is suffocating under the weight of bureaucracy as signified by lists: "I am chief custodian of the great cabinet that contains file upon file of exhaustive lists of distributors and redistributors, of bakers, chemists and grocers, […]. They may just as well have called me 'Keeper of the Lists'; I even have a list of Lists." (Ibid.: 223) She can no longer identify with her work, hence her musings about a new name, and the enclosed office, just as with the English and Australian characters, imprisons her. However, at one point she has an idea regarding promoting the product assigned to her and it is this idea which has her break free of the imprisonment of her office. The idea is the key to unlock the door to her office from the inside and, just like Richard Derrington stripping (*Zigzag Street*), Minal frees herself from her lists to pursue her idea. Leaving the enclosed office is the only option to rediscover her sense of self and what she initially wanted from life – namely to make it in the corporate world – and not to stagnate. However, as getting to the top is indeed connected to an enclosed office, Minal will have to make sacrifices at some point. At the end of the novel this is already foreshadowed when she complains that, because of the idea that freed her from her prison-office, her workload and stress has increased and that she has not "slept in weeks [and does not know] if [she]'ll make it through alive." (Ibid.: 357) The enclosed office and the accolades it signifies are too irresistible to stay away for too long and despite her complaint, Minal is happy.

With regard to her private life, two male distractor characters almost ruin this dream of 'making it': her new superior Rana, with whom she has had a feud since school, and her fiancé Sunil, whom she has also known since her childhood. It appears that her childhood is haunting her although she thought she left it behind when she moved away from home. But the novel never stoops so low as to suggest that Minal cannot make it in the corporate world because she is a woman, which distinguishes her significantly from Lexi Smart (*Remember Me?*). Professionally, she is without fault and it is never referred to that her sex might be a reason to dismiss her or any idea of hers, therefore dismissing possible misogynist claims. The case is slightly different with Sunil, though, as he wants *his* wife to see to *his* home and *his* personal well-being. Yet, although one can see misogynist traces in Sunil's attitude, he never infects other characters or indeed the plot to be as prejudiced towards female professionals as he is.

When Minal is assigned to the cake division she finds out that her boss is going to be Rana with whom she shares a mutual dislike. Being her direct superior, his office is a clear marker of territory and he uses it to put Minal in her place: when she comes to talk to Rana, "[h]e waited till [Minal] took five steps in, and then pretended to just notice [her]." (Kaushal 2004: 58) Rana deliberately has Minal feel inferior to him by behaving as if he had better things to do than to engage with his visitor the moment she enters. Even after acknowledging her presence he still lets her wait for over a minute, thus clearly establishing his workspace as being more important than his workforce as represented by Minal. He is, however, put in his place by Vik's secretary – a friend of Minal's – when he tries to get her to make coffee for him and his 'guest' and thus tries to take over part of Vik's workspace, his territory. But the secretary tells him to call the cafeteria himself. Rana tries to enhance his power by occupying Vik's territory in front of Minal but this attempt is thwarted by Vik's secretary, who functions as a prosthetic enlargement both of her boss and his territory: she guards the space against hostile takeovers. Minal is used to Rana's obnoxious behaviour from their school days. To her, Rana is a *babu*, such as the boss in *One Night at the Call Centre*: Rana uses 'big words' saying very little and demands surveys which, in Minal's opinion, amount to nothing but the very obvious facts they already know (cf. ibid.: 74). Whereas Minal deems Rana inefficient, he is quite adept at covering up this absence of new information with a mesmerising presentation which has Vik believe that Rana has indeed gathered new insights (cf. ibid.: 94-99). Rana's professional quality lies in the fact that he can display the image of a clever person doing his job, despite not knowing or saying anything of value. In Minal's opinion, Rana can do nothing correctly and that it should be her occupying his position and consequently the office.

Eventually, as the plot continues, she is able to push through a suggestion of creating a new cake. Rana is not convinced that this will work but it is in a meeting with the company's production team that he shows that he is not the clueless *babu* Minal paints him as: without her interfering he tries to convince the production team to give Minal's idea of the heart-shaped cake a chance. This scene does not fit into the general characterisation of Rana as given by first-person narrator Minal and grants Rana a new layer, namely that of the indeed effective worker: he might have been prickly when it came to engaging with Minal but, on the one hand, he is new to the company and used to work in a consultant firm, thus an entirely different workspace, and on the other hand, Minal did not make it particularly easy for Rana by being very biased and by behaving slightly disrespectfully towards him. Whereas she regarded each of his moves and comments as intended to lash out at her, this might have been the case with Rana, too, so that it translated into a self-fulfilling prophecy with regard to their professional collaboration. This can also be seen in the last encounter with Rana when Minal tries to convince Vik of a new idea of hers. Rana has found out that she is planning something whilst being in her new office after she has been transferred and has gotten hold of the presentation she intends to show Vik. Minal is devastated as she thinks Rana will now either claim the idea as his or convince Vik to dismiss it. But the opposite happens: Rana likes the idea and even puts money originally meant for another project of his behind Minal's idea (cf. ibid.: 345-348). He still does not particularly like Minal or her behaviour but he is not trying to manipulate her career or ideas the way she thought he would.

Whereas Rana is solely connected to her professional sphere, her fiancé Sunil tries to divorce the professional from the private sphere – which Minal does not intend to do, hence the family pictures at her dream workstation. In fact, he constantly tries to discourage her from working altogether because, after their wedding, he can provide for her. He is even telling his bosses and colleagues about 'her' plans of quitting her job, because her hours clash with his – without consulting with her (ibid.: 237). Sunil is characterised through two features which are directly related to his attitude towards work: as he is a gifted cancer surgeon, he is quite arrogant and obnoxious when it comes to other professions, especially Minal's, and, moreover, he is willing to compromise and adjust his 'convictions' according to what people with the potential to further his career say.

Sunil 'appears' at a very crucial time because Minal just found out that Ali, the neighbour she is dating, is five years her junior (see chapter 6). Minal feels pressured by society – represented by her mother and other married women – to tie the knot and Sunil indeed appears to be perfect: he is slightly older than her, has a promising career, wants to settle down, takes her to expensive restaurants and is fair-skinned[23]. But the perfect picture is soon tainted as he tries to take control of her life. Not only does he constantly belittle her work as not being on par with his – "Who's [sic] life did *you* save?" (ibid.: 350, original emphasis) – he expects Minal to subordinate her work (ethics) to his demands. When Minal, after she has regained confidence in her work, has her sales team come in on a Sunday to receive extra training, Sunil gets really angry as she does not accompany him to a lunch with a potential benefactor and accuses her of letting him down (cf. ibid.: 271-274). He expects Minal to make time for him and to adjust her life to his job, but he is only prepared to adjust *his* convictions to humour influential people, to which

23 Although never explicitly mentioned, this is an important topic in Indian society: the desire to be as fair-skinned as possible (cf. Singh 2013). Minal's other suitor and neighbour Ali's dark skin is repeatedly connoted with a carnal sexiness and lust, whereas Sunil as the fair-skinned doctor represents distinguished and well-to-do society. The obsession of many Indians with fair skin is also referenced in *Trust Me*, when Bollywood actor Rahul claims that he likes his tanned complexion but as he plays the hero he "has to encapsulate people's aspirations." (Rajashree 2006: 180-181) This topic can be regarded as a postcolonial leftover and as it is never critically addressed in the novels, it can be taken as to signify a deeply-rooted issue in India.

Minal as future wife does not belong: on one of their first dates, he refuses to drink alcohol but when a pushy boss of his wants him to drink champagne he immediately does so. Although Minal is rather superficial when it comes to the reasons why her neighbour cannot be a potential husband, she however never compromises her ideals. She lets herself be persuaded if the arguments are sound – for example readjusting her opinion about Rana – but she will always make up her own mind. This bears a strong connection to her work as she is committed to her job and does not put her workers on hold for a simple lunch which is repaid by the workers' newly-fuelled enthusiasm for their sales manager Minal.

What makes Minal break off the engagement in the end is when she finds out about Sunil's betrayal: in order to get in his boss's good books, Sunil has given his boss's son the advertisement and ideas for the heart-shaped cake Minal has worked on so hard[24]. To him, this betrayal does not mean anything as he does not care about her job (cf. Kaushal 2004: 273): "I work too you know[. ...] And I'm a *doctor*, not some salesgirl pretending the world depends on me." (Ibid.: 353, original emphasis) These two sentences sum up Sunil very well – his aloof self-perception, his ignorant behaviour, his hierarchical and conservative thinking. He deliberately destroys Minal's workspace so that she cannot work properly. It is this betrayal of her work that is the last straw because, so far, she was able to overlook or excuse all the comments and snide remarks. Therefore, there is no spatial compatibility as he does not even grant Minal her own space: whereas she is prepared to create a heterotopic life (the family pictures on her imagined, perfect desk), he wants her to dedicate her life and space to him. Sunil does not want her to have a life of her own, her life and thus spaces have to accommodate his persona: he wants her to move in with him, he wants her to accompany him to every event and wait for him. With Sunil, Minal might have family pictures but definitely not a desk to put them up on, proving Kerstin Fest correct as she suggested that a woman's professional success is only possible at the cost of a family life. Yet Minal is happy despite not having a partner at the end, which is in stark contrast to the English chicklit characters, who might have achieved professional success on their own but cannot enjoy it without a man at their side.

Harsh Snehanshu's 2013 novel *Because Shit Happened* depicts the trials and tribulations of Amol Sabharwal, who starts his own internet start-up company. What makes this novel interesting is the constant mirroring of business matters in

---

24 The man Sunil gave Minal's ideas and advertisement to belongs to a rival food company which introduces the heart-shaped cake to the market slightly earlier than International Food, as all the work has been done already. This scandal results in the demotion of Minal's to the promotional team, which is the company's equivalent of exile.

Amol's relationships, especially with regard to his on/off-girlfriend Priya and Shikha, a girl with whom Amol has a (business) affair.

Amol is a student at Delhi's renowned Indian Institute of Technology (IIT) as well as a published and successful author of a ladlit novel. Directly at the beginning he has the idea to create a website on which people can document and archive ideas for witty one-liners (cf. Snehanshu 2013: 6-7). In order to make money from this website he comes up with ideas but needs external help with both the distribution of marketing commodities and the creation of the website. Like all the other students at IIT, Amol lives in a hostel belonging to the IIT's campus, a situation similar to that of the protagonists in Bhagat's *Five Point Someone*. The hostel becomes a beehive-like location behind whose doors students reside that can bring their unique talents to Amol's venture. The hostel is structured like a very large cloud working space: the various inhabitants can be 'sourced' to get their input or technological expertise. Moreover, the hostel is also structured hierarchically:

> I was entering the room of one of the best coders in my hostel. [...] His words used to hold such authority over my batchmates that if anyone affirmed that Sarthak had said something, it was considered an irrefutable fact. I chose him first, not because I saw a technological partner in him, but to get connected to someone he recommended. (Ibid.: 30)

The hostel is composed of batches, which are the various students of one year. It is a rhizomatic construction in that it houses the various talents at IIT. Additionally, the senior students at the hostel, as well as at IIT in general, can function as advisors to junior batches and attach respectability to the newer students. This is the function that Amol wants to employ for his venture. What the spatial structure of the hostel depicts on a micro level, the novel shows on a meso or even macro level later on when Amol has a senior advisor or guide to help him in his entrepreneurial venture: "I was your senior, from the same alma mater, and I felt it to be my responsibility to guide you with pros and cons about pitching for investment this season." (Snehanshu Ibid.: 251) This senior alumnus of IIT is angry with Amol for not having consulted him before Amol and his business partner went forth with a particular marketing strategy and it shows that this system is considered to be rather strict in terms of importance. The connection via IIT is regarded as essential for junior alumni of IIT are supposed to pay heed to their seniors and it discloses the rigid (spatial) structures of hierarchy.

After having established his company and having found members to help him running his website, Amol and his business partner relocate to their own abode. Just like before at the hostel, the living space becomes an office space which Amol himself terms "office-cum-home" (ibid.: 184). This move and the subsequent blurring of spaces is crucial in the problems that will ensue eventually: Amol considers his company his 'baby' (cf. Snehanshu 2013: 294) and by establishing a heterotopia that encapsulates both his home and his office, his attitude towards his 'baby' overshadows his personal feelings towards his human partners. By being constantly in his workspace, Amol has problems distinguishing between time spent at his workstation and leisure time. Having become a teleworker, Amol needs to be reminded by his business partner and house-mate that there are "strict office hours where we will have to report to each other at 8 am sharp and work till 6 pm in the evening, with a one-hour break in the afternoon i.e. minimum 9 hours of work daily." (Ibid.: 231) As the office-cum-home is the core locality of Amol, namely the space in which almost all of his life is happening, stricter rules have to be applied in order to be able to work efficiently. Before this reprimand, Amol just worked as he saw fit. However, Amol has dedicated most of his time to his venture and by incorporating his romantic relationships into his workspace, he actually spent more time contributing to the website than the nine hours his business partner asked of him.

From the beginning of the novel, Amol is in a relationship with Priya. She has always supported him and rarely asked for anything in return. What is more, he uses her as a 'punching ball', transferring all his aggression amassed in the workplace onto their relationship[25]: "I hate you, Amol. You have used me for over a year. Whenever you need me, you call me; and whenever I need you, you are never there." (Ibid.: 140) Amol takes Priya for granted and only calls her when he needs comforting or someone to verbally abuse when he encounters problems with his website. Their relationship used to be one of playful banter once but since Amol has started his venture, Priya has become a diversion. As she only functions as 'punching ball' she is not of direct use to his website and therefore he confesses at one point that he "came face to face with the reality of [their relationship]. My work held priority" (ibid.: 176). Their relationship even turns rather mean-spirited when Amol decides to hurt her: he makes Priya feel bad and cry because he feels that she did not support her boyfriend properly (cf. ibid.: 142).

---

25 *Because Shit Happened* features a main protagonist who is rather unlikeable. Compared to other ladlit protagonists, his character traits deteriorate instead of changing for the better. Whereas Rob Fleming (*High Fidelity*) and Govind Patel (*The 3 Mistakes of My Life*) are equally despicable in the beginning, they see their errors, change their behaviour and are rewarded for their changes of character with a relationship in the end. Amol, however, is not able to improve and consequently will be single by the end of the novel. In a way, he can be compared to Gopal Mishra (*Revolution 2020*), who is the antagonist in Bhagat's 2011 novel. Yet *Revolution 2020* cannot be considered a ladlit novel because the protagonist does not display any laddish characters, which Amol in *Because Shit Happens* does.

That their relationship could have deteriorated so far can be attributed to Amol's urge to boast and his need to be admired. He justifies this character trait of his by claiming that it is normal for "IITs [to boast] about big placements and even bigger pay packages [because boasting] is considered a *status symbol*[26]." (Ibid.: 80, emphasis added) Whereas Priya was his reason to boast among his single batchmates before their graduation, when the time comes for the IIT alumni to be hired by prestigious companies, she loses her function as status symbol. She cannot compete with a good placement and a big pay package but would have only been considered an accessory to a professionally successful boyfriend. The fact that she has lost her qualities to be some*thing* to boast about, Amol's abuses become more frequent. There is no space for her in his life as she has lost any function eventually: Priya cannot be included successfully in Amol's workspace. Their on/off-relationship mirrors the fate of his company and it suggests that the 'baby' – his company – has to 'die' just like his relationship dies inevitably. When Priya leaves him for the last time, Amol's website operator leaves on the grounds that he does not feel appreciated and when Amol's business partner seizes the position of CEO and takes away Amol's 'baby', he feels lonely without Priya. The novel is consequent in its connection of events which happen on a personal level with those that take place in Amol's workplace. *Because Shit Happened* suggests that blurring the boundaries between the home and the workspace will have (disastrous) effects on a non-spatial level as well.

Moreover, there is another female character that Amol abuses for his own means: instead of entering a reciprocal relationship with a designer named Shikha, Amol exploits her for his website. Shikha has been oppressed by her ex-boyfriend, who assaulted her and blackmailed her into having sex with him (cf. ibid.: 145), and although Amol knows of this, he still tricks Shikha into designing his website by pretending to be her boyfriend: he, too, blackmails Shikha into actions she is not comfortable with. It is no coincidence that Amol's despicable behaviour is played out in his office-cum-home, as he can pretend to incorporate Shikha in his private life (the home) but at the same time uses her to further his company (the workspace). He justifies his behaviour (to the novel's readers) as follows: "You may think that I was shrewd, but it's a trait that I was proud of. Every bootstrapped entrepreneur is on the lookout for opportunities to get quality work for free. There is nothing wrong with that." (Ibid.: 158) Although Shikha tries to separate the two spheres of work and private life, she cannot succeed as Amol has never been earnest about the relationship. For him, the spheres were blurred from the moment he moved into his office-cum-home and, if put on the spot, he will choose his

26 In none of the other novels featuring the IIT is such behavior detectable, thus questioning Amol's 'justifcation' of boasting.

website over his girlfriends anytime, hence the prime position of 'office' before 'home' in his designation of his abode.

The novel shows the length towards which a person will go to become successful in the current economic climate. It is constantly hinted at that only a professionally successful person is a valuable individual (cf. Snehanshu 2013: 95). This attitude is punished by having Amol abandon both his 'baby' and his office-cum-home in the end. He has to witness that Priya becomes happy in another relationship and he realises that he needs to separate the spheres if he is to be successful on both levels in the future. Amol seems to have learned a spatial process from the failure that was the office-cum-home, namely that one should be careful not to blur the boundaries between the anchor-points that are so important in a person's life.

Two characters who do not have an office in the sense as elaborated on above are Aisha Bhatia (*Almost Single*) and Parvati 'Paro' Chandramukhi (*Trust Me*). They work in a hotel and on a Bollywood film set, respectively. Apart from having to deal with *babu*-like bosses[27] too, they have to negotiate their lives in their respective workplaces as to carve out individual workspaces.

With regard to the former, Aisha might not have an enclosed or an open-plan office, but she does have a workstation in the form of a luxurious hotel's reception desk from which she performs her job as guest relations manager. Additionally, the whole hotel can be regarded as her workspace as she has to perform various tasks which range from checking on housekeeping, attending to and waiting on VIP guests and overseeing weddings at the hotel's premises, which is a "little nugget in the midst of a very polluted New Delhi." (Kala 2009: 15) Just like Shyam, Aisha has to assume a different, professional identity to mask her more comfortable, private self: she has to wear a traditional sari, which is not Aisha's favourite garment – as it makes all efforts of improving her body futile (cf. ibid.: 191), and has to be on stand-by for guests (cf. ibid.: 72)

Through her work, she also meets her perfect partner: Karan Verma, who is a guest at her hotel. When she loses a slip of paper on one of her early-morning routes, it flies into the private garden terrace of Karan's. Here, Aisha is presented with a dilemma. On the one hand, the whole hotel is her workspace but on the other hand the space her paper has flown into is currently occupied by Karan. For the duration of his stay, the room is under Karan's control and despite the fact that his dominion is just an illusion (see chapter 4), Aisha has to obey his privilege to the space. On the spur of the moment, she decides to climb quickly into the garden to retrieve the paper before he finds it and to maintain the illusion of the room's impenetrability. But she encounters Karan, who is standing in his garden – "stark

27 Not only are the women's bosses' arrogant, they are also quite lecherous.

naked. I stare right back at him, gawk actually, and am about to express outrage at his audacity when I realize that I am the offender. This is his space and I am the intruder." (Ibid.: 27) This incident already foreshadows their many interactions in which the professional and the personal space or sphere come into contact. Especially of the first instance, gawking at naked Karan, one can say that it is happening in a heterotopia as two spaces overlap in which both have their own agenda and which – at this point – do not gel.

Their whole courtship is characterised by the two spheres overlapping and by the question who is in charge of the various spaces. When Karan asks Aisha to help him find a flat, for he has just returned from abroad, she agrees although she wonders why she should "help a guest who pays three hundred and fifty dollars a night to find alternative accommodation?" (Ibid.: 100) Here, she has to venture outside her actual workplace but still considers it to be part of her work as she answers the just quoted question with a "Duty calls." (Ibid.) She assumes the identity of a female guide, not yet girlfriend, who helps a guest with a request. After they have found suitable accommodation, Karan asks Aisha to his housewarming party. She assumes he invites her as a guest but again has to realise that she is to help preparing the party. Their spaces do overlap but Aisha is not able to shed the professional layer which constantly subdues her private longing to be installed in this space as Karan's girlfriend. Although she does try her best to shed her professional identity as the ever-helpful guest relations manager and be single and alluring Aisha, Karan does not call on her when his requests are not in some way work-related, hence the helping with the housewarming. The way she presents herself as being constantly available, Aisha cannot penetrate his sphere but will always intersect it with her professionalism. The heterotopia presents itself here as a barrier which obstructs the couple's chance of being together.

Being very disappointed, Aisha starts drinking at the party and is too drunk in the end to go home. Karan lets her sleep in his bed while he takes the couch and this is the first time that she is able to shed her perfection as guest relations manager, which was an obstruction before. Eventually, Karan sees the Aisha behind her professional veneer and they start dating. However, the heterotopia remains, for he asks her to oversee a wedding of a business partner of his and to put his mother up in her hotel. The latter action is the more important one as Aisha thinks Karan believes that she is still in love with her ex-boyfriend[28] and she now tries to show him how much she cares for him by being very attentive to his mother. In order to accomplish this task, Aisha again retreats behind her professional veneer and has to re-animate the professional sphere, which she thought she could leave behind now.

28 Her ex-boyfriend is the groom at the wedding Karan asks Aisha to oversee, which both did not know beforehand.

The return to the workspace can be seen when she wonders how she should address his mother: "I have to decide whether to call her 'Aunty' or 'Mrs. Verma.' She is a guest at my hotel, but she is also Karan's mom. Will 'Aunty' be too familiar? No. What would be familiar is 'Mummyji.'" (Kala 2009: 242) Especially as Karan's mother is at *her* hotel it becomes a question in what sphere she is to approach her as the mother is clearly in Aisha's professional sphere but at the same time Aisha tries to establish a personal, private connection which extends to Karan's private sphere. In the end, it is Karan's mother who approaches Aisha and thanks her for being so attentive and kind – Aisha had her collected from the airport and put her into a nice room. The bridge between the professional and the private sphere is established – though not really by Aisha.

This paves the way for Karan to try to express his feelings for Aisha but he only manages to offend her by reading a matrimonial advertisement to her which has been put in the papers by Aisha's mother. Furious, she leaves him and realises only very late that she misses him so much that she cannot be without him. While he is on a business trip in Mumbai, Aisha calls at his hotel and through a trick gets into his hotel room but when the door opens, "[i]t isn't Karan but some strange man" while she is naked (ibid.: 270). In a reversal of the first meeting of Aisha and Karan's, she has been in the wrong room which has been booked for Karan's boss. This reversal is twofold if considered spatially: firstly, she has now penetrated Karan's professional sphere whereas previously he has always penetrated hers by using her professionalism to achieve a goal of his – finding a flat, the housewarming party, the wedding and putting up his mother. Secondly, the hotel business is her work sphere so now Karan – and his boss – are intruding into her space and seeing her naked, which is a direct reference to their first encounter. As it is not his but his boss's space, Karan cannot claim this space as he was able to when Aisha burst into the garden of his hotel room. Aisha, after a moment of shock, takes control – which she was only able to do so before when it was work related – and tells Karan that she wants them to be together but not as a married couple: "I'm okay with being the oldest bride in India just as long as when I do get to be a bride it is to the right man." (Ibid.: 272) Karan accepts this and acknowledges that they are now on an equal level in which they can construct their life and spaces together as nobody is superior anymore. Through the reversal of spheres the spatial compatibility, which was misunderstood beforehand, becomes apparent and the couple can realise their coupledom.

For *Trust Me*'s narrator Parvati Chandramukhi the road to bliss is somewhat thornier: her boyfriend has cheated on her and left her pregnant, she thus had an abortion and, on top of that, her boss at the advertising company where works tries to rape her and she is now without a job. Her next job, however, is with a Bollywood movie production and she is in charge of costumes and continuity. That she has no previous experience with both these jobs does not matter to her new boss, the director of the movie, as "[e]verybody does everything here." (Rajashree 2006: 24) Additionally, she has a workspace assigned to her – the Costume Room, which is introduced to her as 'her kingdom' (cf. ibid.: 39): "It was a funny thing, the way it had become 'my' Costume Room in the one month that I'd been working there." (Ibid.: 69) She has two dress-men at her disposal, meaning that she holds some power over her own workspace within the workplace of the Bollywood set. Yet, and this connects her to Aisha's office-less workspace, she spends more time on set and not in her realm of power. Outside her Costume Room – to which everybody has access, thus diminishing her power to a nominal one – she is under the jurisdiction of the director of the movie and has to go wherever and do whatever he wants. Throughout the novel she is more often depicted as obeying orders from the director or the assistant director than commanding her own staff.

Although the novel presents its heroine as strong and inured, the workspaces Parvati encounters present an altogether misogynist picture. Parvati has a rather untypical life of suffering when it comes to chicklit heroines: having been 'dumped' by her 'boyfriend' after he forced her to have an abortion, she finds out that he was at least two-timing her. Being vulnerable, she talks to their boss who seizes the opportunity to almost rape her:

> Suddenly he leaned over and kissed me on the lips. I was too surprised and too drunk to react immediately, and before I knew what was happening, he was pushing his fat, pudgy hands down my kurta, sticking his tongue into my mouth. I tried to push him away, but he was too strong. (Rajashree 2006.: 13)

Parvati leaves the company in which both her boss and her cheating ex-boyfriend work. Although her friends try to persuade her to sue for sexual harassment, she declines as she does not see the point in waiting for a court to sentence her former boss or trusting the system (cf. ibid.: 17).

At her new workplace, Parvati finds new love very quickly, this time in the shape of aspiring Bollywood actor Rahul Kapoor. Although Parvati is reluctant at first to admit her feelings, they start dating and due to her trust issues – hence the novel's title – their courtship is anything but easy. Their major argument is about the infamous casting couch, which influences the Bollywood workspace and its occupants in more than one way.

The issue regarding the casting couch starts with the unknown actress Mrignayani, who has her first starring role in the Bollywood film: she is allowed to wear whatever she wants – both traditional saris and modern miniskirts, because, as one colleague tells Parvati, "[s]he looks good in both get-ups" (ibid.: 41). The actress is objectified because her only function is that of being admired. Yet, the character also exemplifies a hierarchical system in the Bollywood work sphere: the novel implies that, in order to get the job, many aspiring young actresses – and actors – have to sleep with the producers of the movie they want to be in. Mrignayani tells Parvati of an actress who had to sleep with everybody, even the ones who are not directly connected to her job (cf. Rajashree 2006: 71). The actress becomes a (rape) victim of both the men and the system. The most shocking fact, however, is when the same male colleague, who comments on Mrignayani's dresses, states without remorse: "The unit which fucks together, sticks together" (ibid.). This statement justifies female exploitation for it reduces the woman in question to a common property to be used as seen fit. The workspace is exposed as highly abusive, which reflects a bleak truth in India, in which – at the time of writing this book – stories of multiple, sometimes even lethal, gang rapes are surfacing frequently[29] and yet they are "depressingly common" (*The Economist* 2013). In the novel, 'sexual favours' are accepted as part of the work environment and in the beginning, even though Parvati is uncomfortable with it, she makes fun of the males and their double standard of sleeping around but demanding a virgin bride (cf. Rajashree 2006: 73).

The situation becomes unbearable for Parvati when the director, who sleeps with Mrignayani, tries to 'pimp' his star out to the distributor as a way of securing a deal, which the actress vociferously refuses. The connection to Parvati, Rahul and their workspace comes in Rahul's acceptance of the fact that this is common practice in Bollywood:

> 'The distributor must have talked it over with the producer and Jumboji [the director; C.L.]. The market's down, so whatever this distributor asks for, they'll give,' Rahul explained. 'Two months ago, even Mrignayani would have gone quietly, but now she feels she doesn't belong to that category any more. Actually, I think Jumboji's been getting mad at the way she's throwing her weight around after she started sleeping with Mehboob Khan [the film's major star; C.L.]. This was the last straw. It's more of a prestige issue for him than anything else.' (Ibid.: 135)

Whereas Parvati is truly appalled by 'the common practice', Rahul merely looks the other way as he admits a little later:

---

29 One crime that shocked the world was a gang rape of a 23-year-old by (at least) six men on a bus in Delhi. The woman died from the injuries shortly after the incident in December 2012. This is however not the first incident: India has the second-highest number of rapes in the world (cf. *India Tribune* 2012) with Delhi 'leading' with 585 reported cases alone (ibid.), which is higher than most of the other cities combined (cf. Biswas 2013). Yet, as this is just the official crimes, the actual number of rapes which were not reported is probably much higher.

Our set doesn't turn into a whorehouse just because they've got three whores here today. Or even because they've been using the casting couch for casting the female artistes[. ...] I don't approve of Jumboji's arrangement for the AC van[30], but that has nothing to do with the actor-director relationship we share. [He continues that] you don't just have to be nice, you have to lick their boots if you want to get anything from them. (Ibid.: 205-206; 208)

Parvati cannot accept this behaviour as she thinks that Rahul actively participates in these practices too – by not saying anything. Parvati struggles to accept the structures which govern the workspace of Bollywood productions. It appears that the aforementioned exploitation of females is a common practice as Jumbo and Rahul have worked on other films before and their behaviour and reactions suggest that they are used to it. Additionally, many of the practices described in the making of the Bollywood film are known to be standard (cf. Dudrah 2006: 51-53), heightening the 'realism' of the story. The Bollywood production is a clearly masculine territory in which males dominate the females, for even Mrignayani, who refuses to oblige to Jumbo's wish for her to sleep with the distributor, can only do so – temporarily – because she is sleeping with the film's male major movie star. Once that is over, as happens in the novel, she will again attach herself to Jumbo and presumably fulfil his wishes to keep her prestigious status.

Parvati realises that she cannot work in this environment and quits directly after the movie has wrapped shooting, although she could have continued to work on the film in editing. The main reason for quitting, however, is that the movie puts a strain on her relationship to Rahul. As she cannot accept that female exploitation is the norm on Bollywood sets, she takes her anger out on Rahul and wants him to confront Jumbo. She thus grants her boyfriend the power to be heard and to change something as she will only be regarded as a woman who did not know better (cf. Rajashree 2006: 57). The workspace becomes a problem for the two as Parvati cannot trust Rahul not to succumb to the male-dominated system of exploitation which this workspace promotes. As the novel makes strong points as to the problems females have to deal with on a rather regular basis in India, the final resolution is somewhat disappointing: following a typical case of chicklit misunderstandings – Parvati thinks Rahul is cheating on her with a dancer[31] – they address her trust issues which result from her ex-boyfriend, who was indeed cheating on her, and the problems are resolved rather quickly. The problems with

30 The director hired three prostitutes for a party and every male could go and 'visit' them in their abode for the night, the AC van.

31 In an ironic twist, this is the hapless actress Mrignayani was talking about who was forced to accommodate every male's wishes on her last Bollywood film in order to star in the movie.

the workspaces, however, remain but are not talked about anymore. The novel suggests that there are problems but, as they cannot be changed, they should be ignored and only then can a happy ending come about. The workspace as troubling or endangering the relationship is acknowledged but never resolved as the novel and Parvati choose to ignore it in order to enjoy the happy ending. Ultimately, she has 'learned' from Rahul to look the other way and her resolve is that as she cannot stand the misogyny of the Bollywood film, she will look for work in advertising again – which, with regard to the beginning, is equally male-oriented.

All of the characters have found their respective perfect partners whilst being at work and thus the novels depict a form of romance which can result in what Patricia Uberoi calls "love marriage" (2009: 24). In India, "romantic love is a conspicuous motif in the popular mass media [like chick- and ladlit], and young people frequently express a preference for 'love marriage' in the course of attitudinal surveys.[32]" (Ibid.) She continues to explain that this preference is even said to be welcomed as a 'love marriage' does not require a dowry. But, as she has to concede, "the institution of arranged marriage has proved surprisingly robust, continuing to account for the vast majority (an estimated 90 per cent) of marriages in all communities, and this is by no means restricted to the 'traditional' sector of rural society.[33]" (Ibid.) Indian society still works under the assumption that an arranged marriage is a favourable practice. This structure of arranged marriage permeates all scales from the individual's home (micro) to the community (meso) to the whole country (macro). It also interlinks the structure of arranged marriages with the agents, who try to enforce this structure – the parent generation. Nearly all protagonists have to fight their mothers[34] who are trying to set them up to meet potential spouses: either via a matrimonial adverts in the local newspaper or by

32 Uberoi herself admits that "[f]igures are hard to come by, and [that] attitudinal surveys are not necessarily a good guide to actual behaviour." (2009: 43, footnote) However, the sources she cites present a trend in attitudes which cannot be dismissed.

33 As chick- and ladlit are strongly connected to young urban professionals, a rural example is missing. But it can be assumed that it would very likely feature a 'love marriage' as well in order to display the rural as not being in the shadow of its 'cooler', more 'sophisticated' urban sibling.

34 In Harsh Snehanshu's Kanav and Tanya trilogy, Tanya's mother is an important distractor and plot device because she does not allow her daughter to meet any men. When she finds out that Tanya is seeing Kanav and has kissed him (cf. Snehanshu 2012a: 187-192), she sends her daughter to America to live with her uncle. The representatives of the spatial structures that govern parts of India deem it their task to keep their offspring under control.

arranging 'meetings' with the offspring of friends or distant relatives, which can be regarded as a step from the micro to the meso level – so as to increase the pool of potential suitors. The parental characters do not think that the protagonists of the various chick- and ladlit novels are going to find a suitable partner as they are indeed spending too much time in their respective workspaces. Moreover, the first meetings between potential spouses bear a resemblance to the brokering of business deals and the matrimonial adverts reduce their 'candidates' to products the parents offer. In the following, these two practices – arranging marriages and placing matrimonial adverts – will be looked at in Indian chick- and ladlit.

Both Krish (*2 States*) and Aisha's friend Misha (*Almost Single*) are set up – without their knowledge or consent – with potential partners by their respective families. Whereas the former's meeting is not going the way the protagonist's mother wants it to go, the latter's patriarch[35] is more successful with his scheme. Their 'interviews' are going to be interspersed with Kanav's marital interview in *She Is Single I'm Taken We're Committed...*, which he scheduled himself. In all three situations, marriage becomes part of a business transaction or 'joint venture' and the homes (Krish and Kanav) and hotel lobby (Misha) become spaces of business in which deals are being brokered.

When Krish is back home after he completed his courses at IIMA – and has met the girl of his dreams, Ananya – his mother coaxes him into accompanying her to a friend of hers, Pammi. From the moment Krish and his mother have entered the home of Pammi, the latter is constantly referring to the wealth she is surrounded with and which will be 'part of the bride'. She never refers to it as a dowry, but it has the same qualities – to convince the suitor of the bride's financial potential. Aware of this practice, which appears to be a structure in the Punjabi community, Krish's mother repeatedly echoes the details to her son so that he might see how desirable Pammi's daughter is. Pammi can thus be rather choosy and Krish's mother is alternatingly trying to humour her or highlighting Krish's advantages. According to Krish, it is "almost courteous among Punjabis [to which both families belong; C.L.] to encourage someone who is flaunting his wealth to brag some more." (Bhagat 2011b: 61) It seems to be the norm to ask for prices and receive an answer – albeit a probably rounded-up figure – as a later incident at a Punjabi wedding proves[36]. When the eligible daughter finally arrives, for she does not

35 This is the only male relative who interferes in the singles' lives. However, he is rather indirect and not as pushy as the other examples who happen to be exclusively female.

36 A Punjabi wedding of one of Krish's cousins is nearly cancelled because the bride's father gives the bridegroom's parents the wrong – read: less expensive – kind of car: "But it was a Hyundai Santro. [Hyundai] Accent costs five lakh, Santro only three

participate from the beginning in order to guarantee an entrance which has to be noted, the two mothers try to encourage a conversation between the two. However, it becomes clear rather quickly that Krish and Pammi's daughter have next to nothing in common.

When they are 'allowed' to continue getting to know each other in private at a coffee place the daughter lets on that she knows that Krish is in love with Ananya and that she does not mind. They agree that they are no match and when the daughter asks him what she should tell her mother, he answers: "Say I am a geek, boring, lecherous, whatever" to which her reply is that her mother "doesn't understand all that" (Baghat 2011b: 67). In the eyes of the mother – and very likely Krish's mother as well – there is no reason why incompatibility on an intellectual level or with regard to the lifestyles should prevent the union of their children. It is only when Krish says that he intends to quit his lucrative job with an international bank that the mother is desisting from marriage because she does not comprehend why someone would voluntarily forsake wealth and the connected prestige. The business transaction between Krish's mother and Pammi has failed and Krish objects to be drawn into the merger of the two families. His refusal to be part of the Punjabi (socio-spatial) structure shows that he cannot remain in the bubble the various families have created to accumulate their own wealth or prestige. This is not to say that this system is wrong but it shows that 'love marriages' are indeed considered in India.

In *She Is Single I'm Taken and We're Committed...* there is another 'meeting' that appears like a business interview because it is directly compared to one: "I was

lakh." (Bhagat 2011b: 209) This is in tune with a general trend in India in which, due to globalisation and increasing consumerism, the "custom of dowry has increased among all groups in India – Hindu, Muslim, and Christian." (Bala, qtd. in Purkayastha et al. 2003: 518) In their "Study of Gender in India", Purkayastha et al. have found that, "[i]n addition to cash and jewelry, the groom's family demands cars, scooters, TVs, and refrigerators. Brides who fail to bring in an adequate dowry face intense verbal and physical abuse, sometimes leading to death." (2003: 518) Yet, the All India Democratic Women's Association warns: "dowry is not a problem that concerns women alone; it afflicts the whole society. The struggle against dowry is a struggle for gender equality and social justice; it is a struggle against the base consumerist values created by the liberalisation policies of the ruling classes; and it is also a struggle against the debased, obscurantist ideologies of the divisive and communal forces." (Moghe and Dhawale 2003: 1) In the novels, however, this is hardly ever touched upon: it is either totally absent from the narratives or, in the case of the aforementioned Punjabi wedding, the problem is solved very quickly and never spoken of again.

wrong about no more interviews. This was going to be the major one. I couldn't even imagine failing in it." (Snehanshu 2012b: 172) Although the story depicts a love relationship, it still needs parental validation before it can proceed to the next level, the marital stage. For all the progress that the novel implies is happening in India – even depicting 'relaxed' parents, it ultimately opts for a traditional route. The couple even agrees to "[n]o kissing, [n]o hugging. No touching" until they are married (ibid.: 200). Snehanshu's conclusion to his Kanav and Tanya trilogy shies away from describing a completely modern India. The mother of the bride-to-be wants her daughter's future husband to earn more than his spouse and is of the opinion that he must hold a profitable and respectable job in order to be eligible for her daughter. The question of marriage is therefore still closely linked to a business transaction. Moreover, the novels *Ouch! That 'Hearts'..* and *She Is Single* depict protagonist Kanav as a prolific writer, who chronicles his relationship to Tanya in his best-selling novels. He has turned his love into a business opportunity before the mother did so. When Kanav is asked by his future mother-in-law what his plans for his career are, he answers that he sees himself as "a celebrated writer" (ibid.: 176), fusing the notions of love and profession. Kanav and Tanya's love might be based on romantic feelings but Kanav exploits it to his own advantage just the same. Regarding it from a positive point of view, he has found a way to sustain his life through his love to Tanya, but looking at it more critically, he is not as romantic because he ponders new ways to get money out of his relationship: "why not keep our readers attached to us as we grow old. I'm planning to launch Kanav-Tanya conversations as cartoon strips in newspapers." (Ibid.: 205; cf. Snehanshu 2012a: 166-173)

A somewhat different approach is fashioned in *Almost Single*: here, Aisha's friend Misha is set up by her family's patriarch without her knowing about it. The patriarch has Misha take a distant cousin who lives in Canada but is currently in India out for a meal. This thwarts her actual plans of going to a speed-dating event and she decides that she just wants to get the night over with as quickly and uneventfully as possible. Although Aisha even voices the idea of this being a set-up, Misha dismisses this on the ground of her 'date' being "a complete nerd" (Kala 2009: 258) for she used to know him when he was younger. When an attractive and apparently successful man awaits Misha, she instantaneously revises her image of him and embraces his "Bollywood-style extravaganzas" to leave with him the next day to meet his family: "They chatted all night long and decided that this was 'it'. Just like that, friendship blossomed into love […] and a quickie roka[37] has been

37 A *roka* is the first step in a Punjabi wedding ceremony which corresponds to the Western engagement party: the families meet, presents are exchanged and a date for the official wedding is set.

arranged" (Kala 2009: 261). Here, the business transaction is not as visible as it is in *2 States*, but when Misha obeys her family's patriarch and meets her cousin in a hotel lobby, it resembles the entertainment program for an important business client.

Looking at it critically, the patriarch could be sure that his plan was going to work due to two reasons: firstly, from the beginning of the novel, it is "Misha's one and only ambition [...] to net the perfect NRI – non-resident Indian" (ibid.: 5). She even dates a man whom she finds unattractive because he ticks off (seemingly) the correct box. Therefore, the fact that her distant cousin is both handsome and an NRI have greatly helped in this scheme. Secondly, it is known to her family that she moved to New Delhi to meet an NRI and they probably know about Misha's many attempts, which also prompts Aisha to 'call the spade a spade': this marriage is founded on the same principles as an arranged marriage because the spouses-to-be do not know each other properly – they announce their engagement after four days – and thus it can be regarded as the outcome of the scheme of Misha's family's patriarch. However, it is pretended that it was *only love* that led Misha and her fiancé to announce their plans to marry, but the above-mentioned facts point in the direction of Misha seizing a man who meets all her requirements: Misha herself is under the strong impression that her and her cousin's friendship has become love. But there was no friendship to begin with: she has known her future husband when both were very young and she had not seen him since. So, describing falling in love as the last step of a process is an exaggeration. The way Misha talks about her fiancé might be very romantic but, given her previous business-like attitude towards marriage, it is unlikely she has had such a drastic change of heart all of a sudden. Especially as she only moved to the city to 'bag' an NRI – moving closer to the workspace in order to work more efficiently. Not willing to admit that she might be more traditional than she lets on, Misha rather believes in this being love and destiny rather than planning on the family's side. By juxtaposing Misha's rushed wedding with Aisha's plan to wait and to get to know Karan better before tying the knot, *Almost Single* presents the two ways – arranging a marriage and the love relationship – which might lead to a love marriage (Uberoi 2009: 24). However, Kala's novel does make the case for being sure of one's love before marrying by having the novel's main protagonist wait and not a minor character. Furthermore, it is the only Indian novel considered in my corpus in which both a divorce occurs and a married woman praises Aisha for not having married too early: "Aisha, it's good you've waited. You have a job, a life, friends, an identity... [...] you will never be lonely." (Kala 2009: 267) Whereas the reader does not know whether the divorced woman or the unhappy wife have (had) their marriages arranged, the novel takes a clear stand in that it favours Aisha's way of dealing with a marriage, namely to sound out one's partner. Taken together with Minal's experience with almost-husband Sunil in *Piece of Cake*, Indian chicklit novels present their readers with two different possible outcomes of married life – divorce and unhappiness – that are not the stereotypical 'happily ever after' if the partners are not on the same page before getting married. Additionally, *Almost Single* does not present the divorce as socially shunned: the divorced woman is shown as independent and happy when she can start over again. However, Kala's idea is slightly tainted by the fact that the divorcee does so in another country (cf. ibid.: 262). Although *Almost Single* portrays very modern Indian women, it appears that India as a society might still have some way to go.

A little while later, Misha and tells Aisha that she wants to take their relationship to the next level:

Misha calls me […] and voices her steely determination. "I'm going to sleep with him." […]
"Do you think he expects you to be a virgin?" I ask, finally getting to the point.
"I guess not. We haven't talked about it."
"Are you going to?"
"No, it's not important, I'm sure he's not [a virgin]." […]
[Aisha thinks about Misha's call:] Sexual compatibility is important, but is it sufficient? These days, it's like the last bastion to be conquered before one travels down the aisle. A betrothal is a visa to a preconjugal tryst and most people are keen to make the trip, which makes me wonder how many virgins there are in the world.
Anyhow, the question itself seems outdated (ibid.: 263-264).

In India, the idea of marrying a virgin stems from "the ideology of *kanyadana*, the purest of gifts" (Uberoi 2009: 25): the bride's virginity. Again, the idea of 'gift', of giving one's untouched body to one's husband, promotes the notion of a business transaction. Misha is again presenting a picture of a modern Indian woman as she does not want to marry a man she is not sexually compatible with. Yet two points are important here: if one is cynical, one might say that, after having had sex, Misha is 'second hand' – should she choose not to marry her fiancé after all. She will not be able to grant another man *kanyadana* and will be 'second hand' on the marriage market (like a divorced woman). Secondly, as she has already tricked herself into believing that their love has blossomed from friendship, it is very likely that Misha will also convince herself that her husband-to-be is sexually compatible with her – after all, she has no comparable experiences. The reader never gets to find out how their first sexual encounter went as the novel never re-visits Misha. But it can be assumed that she will continue with the marriage as her fiancé is all she ever wanted – good-looking and an NRI – she will not let come anything in the way of her merger.

Parents setting up their offspring is just one tactic; the other, which is also employed in many of the novels, is putting a personal advertisement in the marital section of the local newspaper. Compared to lonely hearts adverts, the Indian variety is always foregoing the steps of a relationship but has a wedding as the imminent goal. The adverts can be put in a newspaper (e.g. *Piece of Cake*) or even posted online (e.g. *Almost Single*). What is common in all cases is the fact that the advertisement is manipulated to present the best possible image. While sometimes it is done to single out potential suitors and to keep away others – "[h]ike up your annual income by a couple of lakhs, it'll keep the broke types away" (Kala 2009: 4) – in other cases it deliberately neglects certain facts in favour of others: "Sixty words of specious shorthand, and not one mention of any key attributes (sunny personality […]) or even of stuff like strong leadership potential […] or 'highly creative and innovative in approach' […]? What we had instead was ancestry, height, make, colour, date of manufacture." (Kaushal 2004: 2-3) This does not only apply to the females: whereas one of the respondents to Minal's advertisement fails to mention that he has a girlfriend already, Priyanka's male suitor (*One Night at the Call Centre*) had "been against tempering with the picture [which was sent to Priyanka as the only visual available; C.L.] but had to agree when his mother insisted." (Bhagat 2007: 292) These stories have in common, then, that they are selling a product, but not a human being. Before a meeting with a suitor who answered her mother's newspaper advert of her daughter, Minal ignored the fact that her mother offered her like one of her daughter's products, which is again referencing the heart-shaped cake. Yet, when she is treated like a 'thing' on their date[38], she feels no longer like an individual.

Doing business in India is not solely reserved for actual workplaces or work-spaces where one can make money; it also applies to attracting the right spouse – representing the right family – and thus increasing one's profile. Treating their offspring like a product that needs to be marketed, the Indian mothers presented in the novels offer their children to the most suitable consumer. But the novels show that this practice is to be associated with an older generation which generally does not reside in metropolises but is located either in smaller cities or even rural areas. Chick- and ladlit show that modern urban singles tend to find their perfect partners when they pursue their respective careers, showing again the connection between workspaces and love.

Characters like Krish (*2 States*) or Minal (*Piece of Cake*) do not want to be locked in careers their parents deem appropriate but make up their own minds about

38 Minal finds out that her suitor has actually a score sheet with the categories 'beauty', 'family', 'hostess skills', 'values' and 'personality', ranking her in exactly this order, and she instantly dismisses him (Kaushal 2004: 84).

their professions. Consequently, they are rewarded by this liberating move with their respective perfect partners, even if they have to wait a bit longer like Minal. The same goes for the other characters, too: only when they master their work-spaces or excel in their professions, they will find love. Indian chick- and ladlit present a difference here to English and Australian novels. Although in these books, as the analyses have shown, a successful career is followed by a rewarding romance just the same, the Indian varieties depict their protagonists as being happy without being attached to a perfect partner. Of course they are usually going to be enveloped in a favourable union by the end of the novel, but characters like Minal, Misha (*Almost Single*) and Shyam (*One Night at the Call Centre*) show that happiness can be achieved when romance and professional success remain divorced, it is the personal attitude that matters. Moreover, *Almost Single* shows that Indian (chicklit) novels can actually function as a mirror image of society by presenting various models of unions: the love relationship and the arranged marriage but also the failed and the unhappy marriage. The current position as one of the world's leading global players is reflected in the novels and so is the change of attitudes that appears to take place in Indian society. By advertising the novels as Indian varieties of Western bestsellers – such as acknowledging the sisterhood to *Bridget Jones's Diary* and locating Chetan Bhagat within a ladlit context – the novels are put into the global context as well. In creating national varieties of chick- and ladlit, the authors are able to write back at the former colonial master England. Furthermore, publishing them in English allows for a global readership. It might be regarded as neo-colonial grovelling on part of the authors or publishing houses as well as a very positive image of the power of chick- and ladlit, but these novels might help to bring about a change for their readership. They can result in a change on a larger spatial scale, instead of only in modern(ised) metropolises, and liberate India from the notion that they are merely the world's sweatshop – to put it in Chetan Bhagat's words as put forward in *One Night at the Call Centre* (cf. 2007: 232) – but indeed an important global force.

AFTER WORK

The workspace is an important anchor-place for human beings as it is part of their daily lives and all of the characters presented above meet their partners through work, either by coming to a new workplace and meeting them there or by getting to know them through a work-related matter. This might also be the reason why Will Freeman eventually realises he should find a job, albeit one which not exactly 'pays money':

> [Will knew] he had a lot to offer. Great sex, a lot of ego massage, temporary parenthood without tears and a guilt-free parting – what more could a man want? Single mothers – bright, attractive, available women, thousands of them, all over London – were the best invention Will had ever heard of. His *career* as a serial nice guy had begun. (Hornby 1998: 32, emphasis added)

And so Will becomes a comforter for single mothers: being a temporary partner to them and becoming a short-term father to their kids, getting sex and the feeling of belonging in return. His primary workspace becomes the venue of SPAT – Single Parents Alone Together – where he can 'acquire' new females to 'do business' with. As they only meet every fortnight, Will needs to be more adaptable as to his workspace, and he considers his service not to be tied to a workplace like an office but more flexible and personalised, as he accompanies the women to picnics for example. This will then account for a secondary, more different workspace: he is not bound to a workstation or enclosed office but he can turn spaces he is in into work(able) places.

This chapter explored the various implications that offices can hold for their occupants. What transpired from the analyses is that workspaces are intricately entwined with the workers' identities and the emotions that connect the workers to their workplaces. After all, the workspace is a locale that is heavily dependent on centrality, in that it supports the performance of the human (within a work-related context) and creates a place-person bond. Depending on how much time and energy one invests in one's workspace, it can even be elevated to a crucial component of one's locality as that is the space in which most of one's life is spent and which presents a network of social relations. Looking back at all the examples laid out in this chapter, it becomes apparent that most characters do indeed have a problem with their workspaces as it does not enable centrality, let alone locality: they struggle to find their place within a territory that is striated by the managers or corporate structures. Ethan (*Ethan Grout*), Ash (*Taking Off*) and Shyam (*One Night at the Call Centre*) face difficulties when they work in an open-plan office just as much as Bridget (*Bridget Jones's Diary*), Becky (*Confessions of a Shopaholic*) and Emma (*Can You Keep a Secret?*). The characters have to negotiate the workspace in order to find their place within this pre-striated space. The open-plan office is characterised by its repetitive work which turns the workers into Taylorist cogs within the larger machinery of the workplace for they have hardly any agency. This non-agency is expressed on a spatial level as well as the example of *Ethan Grout* has shown: workers are not meant to feel at home, they are there to *function*.

In this respect, the analyses have proven that there is indeed not that much of a difference between the open-plan office, which is to create equality between workers, and the enclosed or private office, which is supposedly signifying seniority, superiority or exclusivity, for Jon (*Bachelor Kisses*), Lexi (*Remember Me?*) Richard (*Zigzag Street*) and Minal (*Piece of Cake*) struggle to create a sense of place, too. The occupants of these workspaces are regarded above the average worker and when Lexi became the 'Cobra', she was promoted away from her open-plan workstation into her own enclosed office. Yet, the notion of the enclosed office as a prison is not as black and white as it might seem. Out of the four characters that occupy such an enclosed workspace, only two will leave it permanently because their ventures failed: Lexi's department is closed and Jon has to give up his research. The other two characters leave their enclosed offices eventually and are not depicted in them any longer, but it cannot be ruled out that they will return to them – the prestige that is connected to them is too tempting.

That the workspace-prison does not need to come in the form of an office can be seen in the example of Nick Hornby's *High Fidelity*. In this novel, Rob Fleming has his own record shop. However, the little shop becomes just as restrictive as the enclosed office or indeed the open-plan office as both of these spaces are connected to stagnation. Rob compares his life at the record shop to that of a Pompeian victim of Mount Vesuvius: "I'm stuck in this pose, this shop-managing pose, for ever" (Hornby 2010: 19). His confession how he became the owner of Championship Vinyl is tinted with regret and, surprisingly for a lad, honest awareness – especially with regard to the reasons: "Here's how not to plan a career: a) split up with girlfriend; b) junk college; c) go to work in record shop; d) stay in record shop for rest of life." (Ibid.: 19) However, he finds it too difficult to break out of his felix rigor mortis. Therefore, the record shop becomes his most important territory, his life space. But when his last relationship ends, Rob projects all his anger and frustration onto his workplace, which, incidentally, he created – on purpose as well as by neglect. The record shop has become a prison of his own making and through his stagnation he has lost his girlfriend. He confesses that the shop is the spatial manifestation of his stagnation, his laddish Neverland, just like Richard's (*Zigzag Street*) and Jon's (*Bachelor Kisses*) enclosed offices: "I know I'm going to have to do something about the shop – let it go, burn it down, whatever – and find myself a career." (Ibid.: 221) The record shop is not connected to actually having a career which testifies to its resemblance to the open-plan office. As a workspace, the record shop can be located between the open-plan office and the enclosed office: it shares the quality of being a dead-end with the open-plan workspace, the illusion of superiority with the enclosed office (after all, Rob owns the shop) and it is linked to both offices by the stagnation that characterises these spaces. Incidentally, it is his ex-girlfriend who helps him with his dilemma and enables him to pursue a second career as DJ (cf. ibid.: 245). This is actually an exception for it does link laddish Rob to the heroines of chicklit who need their partner to enable them to feel truly happy by way of the stereotypical resolution of the felix rigor mortis.

Happiness is an important motivation in work-related chick- and ladlit novels. Incidentally, it is strongly connected to identity and thus to the transformation from a space into a place. The idea of this transformation means that one is able to striate a previously blank or neutral space. The notion of having created a place means that one was able to infuse the space with markers of identity or to have the place reflect the person. In the workspace-related chick- and ladlit novels, most characters struggle to appropriate their workplaces, which must be regarded as the space. Emma (*Can You Keep a Secret?*) is constantly passed over by her boss and colleagues and thus fails to make her mark within her company. The same can be said for *Taking Off*'s Ash, whose identity is stripped from him and is replaced by the name of a magazine. None of their workplaces support their identities and it is this lack that turns the open-plan office into a smooth space, impossible to striate or to personalise into a place. As the offices frustrate most attempts at turning the space into a place and the workplace into a personalised workspace, the characters' identities are kept in check. However, one's identity is important in meeting the perfect partner for it presupposes spatial compatibility: if a character cannot develop properly – and this includes the transformation and re-appropriation of space – then they cannot display their identity and thus ideas about space, the foundation for spatial compatibility. Being constantly restricted, the characters opt for the leaving of the spaces and it is only then that they can find or properly get to know their perfect partners. It appears that the office cannot be successfully mastered, which is the reason for the characters' defeat and withdrawal. This seems to be the easiest way out as the characters do not try to overcome the obstacle but instead ignore them, like Bridget Jones does for example. However, it is at least some form of coping and not giving in to stagnation.

Moreover, the workplace has misogynist tendencies. Almost all female characters in this chapter achieve some form of promotion or professional success, but they tend to feel entirely happy only once they are able to share it with their perfect partner. Furthermore, this partner is sometimes the reason for the success of the heroine as in *Bridget Jones's Diary*. In *Trust Me*, the problems that led to the heroine abandoning the unstriatable and clearly misogynist space are even ignored at the end, lest they endanger the protagonists' love life. It is a conspicuous trait that almost all women can achieve success but not one of the women is promoted into an enclosed office to signify her promotion spatially. In *Piece of Cake* the otherwise desirable enclosed office is even used as a form of punishment. When Minal is taken off her original assignment due to a misunderstanding, she gets 'imprisoned' in an enclosed office that signifies that, in her new undesirable job, she is now responsible for an undesirable part of India – a fact that is smugly commented upon by her rival Rana (Kaushal 2004: 327). It gives her a first impression of what a promotion into a real enclosed office is like, because solitary confinement cannot be shared with a partner, which is the reason why all the other characters – both male and female – leave these spaces behind. Yet Minal wants to succeed in her job and that includes an enclosed office. That her way is not going to be easy has been shown in her undesirable office as well as in the relationship to her sneaky fiancé, who almost destroys her career. This aspect of one-dimensional femininity has not been discussed by Fest, who writes that chicklit heroines have to decide what to give up – either their career or their love life. Minal tried to have both, but when her conservative fiancé obstructs her career Minal feels betrayed and choses her profession over the man's ideas of traditional femininity: their spatial incompatibility is therefore more than proven, as she prefers an office and he wants her to prefer the home. The fact that Minal does not compromise and chooses her career over a (loveless) marriage proves Fest correct. But Minal is very happy with her decision and although it does not include the stereotypical union, concluding the narrative with a happy heroine is the norm in chicklit. Minal is the only character that is able to create a sense of locality at her workspace, even though this is due to her long working hours. Moreover, her decision proves that Indian chicklit novels are much more progressive than their English and Australian counterparts, in which the heroine might achieve professional success but cannot enjoy it because she would have preferred a boyfriend instead of a promotion.

Fest has written about the fact that women have to give up their femininity to be successful in their professional careers and this has been found to be correct with regard to offices. Most chicklit heroines do regard femininity as a distinct part of their identity and when offices force the women to choose between a career and their femininity, they ask the heroines to give up their identity and thus their claim to striate their workspaces. Offices in chick- and ladlit are generally unsupportive of their occupants' identity, which results in the fact that none of the characters can really identify with their professions, as they are either reduced to nameless cogs or solitary beings. Chetan Bhagat addresses the questions of identity in his novel *One Night at the Call Centre*. Here, the office is shown not to distinguish between male or female workers but between American and Indian characters who participate in a business transaction (money for advice via the telephone). Bhagat uses one of the minor characters to state that a workspace must be supportive and respectful of their workers' identity and, for example, not push them to change their names just because some clients cannot pronounce or even remember their interlocutors' names. The criticism Bhagat voices with regard to American callers' neo-colonial arrogance and presumptuousness, Indigenous writer Anita Heiss remarks in her Australian chicklit novels. She creates heroines who are all proud Aboriginal women and who, in their professional functions, address these post- and neo-colonial issues: Alice Aigner (*Not Meeting Mr Right*), head of the history department at a private Catholic school for girls, is invited to a function to celebrate a historian's long service to the community. She is appalled by the (conscious) lack of knowledge and disrespect of some of the male guests concerning her heritage and thus also her profession when they pretentiously say that "here at the Eastern Suburbs Local History Association [they] recognise Australian history, Aboriginal history and prehistory" (Heiss 2007: 281). Alice is furious: "What Aboriginal history? Everything that happened post-invasion is *Australian* history. Aboriginal people didn't dispossess themselves, they didn't poison their own watering holes or place themselves on government-run reserves and church-run missions. The colonisers and settlers – the so-called *Australians* – did that. That's *Australian* history." (Ibid.: 281-282, original emphasis) Alice's identification with her heritage has led her to take up a job in which her identity takes centre stage. She knows about the historical and historic events which led to her and the country's present state and as a history teacher she can give this knowledge to future generations and raise their awareness for the history of their birthplace. Just like Alice, the heroines in Heiss's other novels are equally argumentative when they encounter racially-insensitive people. It has to be noted, though, that they are fairly sensitive as to this subject and as all of them hold jobs which deal to a large extent with the (historical) visibility of their Indigenous culture, the opportunities are many. With regard to their partners, they will end up with men that are either equally of an Indigenous heritage or accept their girlfriends' vocation to their work. Alice does not have an office which might restrict her and although Heiss's other characters do occupy such workspaces, they are seldom seen in them as they refuse to be restricted by them.

Here, chick- and ladlit disclose their relevance and because these novels are marketed as light-hearted entertainment (see chapter 2), they are able to reach a large audience. In order to remain relevant as well as up-to-date the novels take up recent developments. With regard to workspaces, this can be seen best in *I've Got Your Number*. In Sophie Kinsella's 2012 novel, Poppy Wyatt finds a mobile phone after having lost hers. Immediately after her recovery of the phone, Sam Roxton calls it because he thinks his assistant will answer it, oblivious to the fact that she has quit her job and disposed of the mobile. He does not even ask Poppy but demands that she helps with a problem of his which she does because he threatens to take the mobile away from her[39] (cf. Kinsella 2012: 26-32). They work out a deal: Poppy gets to keep the mobile put promises to forward any emails the mobile may receive and she has to update Sam with regard to his meetings and appointments. Poppy, a physiotherapist by trade, assumes the position of Sam's personal assistant – without any previous work experience or qualifications. However, these

39 Due to a series of misunderstandings, Poppy needs Sam's mobile phone because she has lost her engagement ring – and her own mobile phone – and she gave everyone 'her' new number to call should they find her ring.

are hardly necessary as the novel proves because all she needs is the mobile phone, which becomes the connecting device both to Sam and to a world of commerce and business decisions which was previously closed off to Poppy. The novel presents the mobile phone as a mobile workstation from which Poppy is able to support her temporary boss Sam. It is important to note that the mobile phone allows Poppy to maintain both her individual identity and to enable her to take on a different professional one at the same time. As the mobile receives texts and emails at any given time, the mobile phone signifies a constant workspace and this has Poppy forwarding and sometimes even answering Sam's correspondence at night or whilst being out with friends. However, the mobile phone as workstation also highlights a negative aspect of the workspace-without-workplace: having no office to go to and consequentially *leave* at the end of a workday, the identity of the worker might eventually fuse with one's after-work identity. This gets even more pronounced when Poppy and Sam start to fall in love with each other. As their only connection is via said mobile and both (initially) regard the other only as the necessity to get what they want in a business transaction, the phone also influences the romantic lives of the protagonists and turns their love into a feature of their workspaces.

The phone becomes a meta-workspace which blurs the boundaries between the level of work-related matters – Poppy may keep the phone if she 'works' for Sam – and the level of personal interaction – the two talk on the phone after work hours or text each other. The work phone becomes a substitute for Sam, just as Poppy had become a substitute worker for Sam through the phone. Therefore, when their business deal is finished, she gets to keep the phone. It has been transformed from a meta-workspace into an emotional connection. In *I've Got Your Number*, the phone is a signifier for a workspace which is not tied to a static location, one which has a fixed address such as Sam's company's building. In the end, Will Freeman might be on to something after all: one needs to find a workspace one is comfortable with, no matter whether it entails a workplace or not, and as the example of Poppy has shown the workspace might turn into a space of love.

A Metropolitan Pleasure Hunt

What a feeling. Excitement, expectation, apprehension, tension.
BEN MALBON *CLUBBING*

COMING OUT TO PLAY

Forms of leisure can be observed in all societies from all ages, even if these forms differed from what is considered 'leisure' today: in prehistoric times, "[h]unting and gathering were the primary activities and provided resources to maintain life. There was little 'free time' as we it know it today. [...] Once prehistoric people could create tools and were able to store information in a larger brain, more free time became available." (Genoe, Kennedy and Singleton 2013: 22) This free time was spent by engaging in rituals and ceremonies (cf. ibid., Kraus 1978: 127). Moreover, it is believed that in primitive societies, "[p]opular juvenile or adult games are often vestiges of warfare – [today] practiced as a form of sport. Occasionally play activities depict historical events, transportation practices, or the use of household or farming implements." (Kraus 1978: 127) Here, already a connection to cultural geography can be seen as these territorial practices enable the spatial actors to learn processes that will form their attitudes and further develop their perception.

With the evolution of communities and societies, "playlike activities were also a means to relax, to recover, and replenish strength after work" (ibid.). Ancient civilisations engaged in recreational activities such as sports (Greeks) or watching spectacles at the Coliseum (Romans), but also bullfighting (Egypt) and gardening (Babylon) were considered leisure activities (cf. Kraus 1978: 130-137, Genoe, Kennedy and Singleton 2013: 22-25). During the rise of the Catholic Church, following the fall of the Roman Empire, a different opinion about leisure emerged: "Having suffered under the brutal persecutions of the Romans, the early Christians condemned all that their pagan oppressors had stood for – especially their hedonistic way of life." (Kraus 1978: 137) As leisure is the antithesis to work, Christians strongly believed in the "concept that 'idleness is the great enemy of the soul' […], and doing nothing was thought to be evil." (Genoe, Kennedy and Singleton 2013: 25) But even in medieval times, playful activities were undertaken, such as hunting and gambling, singing and dancing (cf. Kraus 1978: 138-139): "As life in the Middle Ages became somewhat easier, a number of pastimes emerged. Many modern sports were developed at this time in rudimentary form." (Ibid.: 140)

In the Renaissance, this divide between the development of leisure activities and games and the Puritans' rejection of the same grew bigger (cf. ibid.: 142, Genoe, Kennedy and Singleton 2013: 25-26). The diversification of leisure continues and in the nineteenth century, due to the Industrial Revolution, the working people in Western civilisations needed forms of compensation for their strenuous work (cf. Kraus 1978: 158-160).

> Particularly in larger cities, new forms of commercial amusement sprang up or expanded during the nineteenth century. The theater, in its various forms, was more popular than ever. Dime museums, dance halls, shooting galleries, bowling alleys, billiard parlors, beer gardens, and saloons provided a new world of entertainment for pay. (Ibid.: 165)

Although Kraus describes the development in the United States of America, he acknowledges that this "trend towards increased recreation was not unique to the United States." (Ibid.) In industrialised countries, "concern about the uses of leisure began to arise – less in terms of the sinfulness of play than the broader question of the potential role of leisure in modern society." (Ibid.: 166) People no longer wanted to work but enjoy their time off their workspaces as well (cf. Rojek 1995: 43). Today, following a turbulent twentieth century, in which two world wars happened and the advent of the internet and increasing globalisation had people, communities and countries 'move' closer together, "leisure is […] deemed vital for the maintenance of a reasonable quality of life" (Hookway and Davidson, qtd. in Walmsley and Lewis 1993: 203).

The development of leisure in other countries has followed a similar path. In non-Western countries, activities undertaken in one's pastime have been impacted by the notion of social structures, religion and work. In India, the various faiths and castes have influenced the notion of leisure. With regard to the topic of this chapter, in specific regions of the subcontinent, certain forms of leisure activities – which might also be practised as professions – are dominant: for example, classical music, dance and art as well as folk forms like wall painting, iconoclastic sculpturing and scroll painting (cf. Bhattacharya 2006: 77). Through a system of governmental patronage, "activities that were not considered leisure activities but ways of life and livelihood have been transformed into leisure activities for the modern amorphous mass." (Ibid.: 77-78) What is more, due to the many Indian festivals, fairs and holidays, Indian men and women of all ages can engage in a multitude of leisure activities that are connected to these times and dates, especially in more rural areas (cf. ibid.: 82, 84-87): "Fairs spawn a carnivalesque ambience in which there is a happy blend of commerce and merriment." (Ibid.: 87) Among Indians a form of leisure tourism has developed with (modern) pilgrim travelling to holy sites to engage in festivals: "Tourism as a leisure activity has gained popularity and this has been helped by the existing railway network, airlines and the hotel and hospitality industry." (Ibid.: 86) Of course, there are differences with regard to castes and the wealth of certain people or communities and Bhattacharya observes that, for example, "most sports are beyond the means of the many." (Ibid.) However, in India – just as in any other country – people have found a way to indulge in leisure activities: "Leisure in India reflects the dynamics of class and economics of its people, further defined by geographical location, education and the tradition in which they have been socialized." (Ibid.: 87-88) Around the world, leisure can be seen to be a very geographical practice.

Leisure itself "encompasses activities in which individuals may indulge of their own free will either to rest, amuse themselves, to add to their knowledge and improve their skills disinterestedly and to increase their voluntary participation in the life of the community after discharging their professional, family, and social duties." (Walmsley and Lewis 1993: 201) Moreover, leisure "can refer to any of all of the following: unobligated time, state of being, and consumption patterns. One widely accepted element of leisure is that it is not work but rather an antidote to a person's working life[1]." (O'Sullivan 2013: 4; cf. Pronovost 1998: 8) However, leisure is not simply time to be idle:

> Leisure is more than play. It is a discrete period set aside for play, a systematized way in which time is divided. It is the counterpart to work. As such, it emerges into the consciousness and daily routine as a consequence of the transition from the home-centred workplace to the workplace – the factory, the office – outside the family and the household. (Gusfield 1991: 404)

A similar argument is made by Chris Rojek, a prominent scholar of leisure studies, who writes that "leisure cultures typically focus upon *surplus*; that is, leisure forms and practice are organized around surplus time and wealth, every individual and group is located in a context of scarcity." (2010: 19, original emphasis) He furthermore emphasises that "[l]eisure is not just a matter of form and practice. It is a question of how form and practice is *represented* in relation to power." (Ibid.: 19,

1 "Even in Sanskrit […], leisure is signified by entertainment and relaxation. The Sanskrit word for leisure is *vinoda*, synonymous with pleasure, entertainment, enjoyment, and so on." (Bhattacharya 2006: 80)

original emphasis) As leisure is usually identified to be comprised of the unique features of being "liberated, disinterested, hedonistic and personal" (Pronovost 1998: 5, 9), it puts the activities of leisure in stark opposition to time spent at workplaces. There, workers have to fulfil tasks (usually) set by others, whereas they are free to explore their own preferences during their own time. The activities exercised then can have the traits of "freedom, personal satisfaction, play [or] creativity" (ibid.) – but the list is not exhausted.

David Crouch writes in his article on the "Geographies of Leisure" that "[l]eisure happens, is produced and consumed, in spaces." (2006: 127) He continues to explain that "[t]hese spaces may be material, and relate to concrete locations. Yet the spaces, and therefore geographies, of leisure may be metaphorical, even imaginative." (Ibid.) Crouch's idea reflects that all forms of spaces, both material and immaterial, support the activities of leisure. Although his argument appears too all-encompassing, it reflects an important notion of spaces of leisure, namely that they can be engaged in as an everyday activity without investing a lot of money or time:

> A more personal, and shared, symbolic geography is produced from places where people make leisure. The symbolic geography of this activity consists of parks, everyday streets, clubs and bars, walks in fields and woods as well as the commercialised sites of consumer leisure […]. This means that leisure geography is 'all around us', in familiar places and 'down the road'. This is an everyday geography of leisure. (Crouch 2004: 272)

He explicitly refers to "the new commercialisation of leisure [as] a route to a new lifestyle, a promotion of 'product' directed at both young and old." (Ibid: 268) People are "[i]nvesting in new clothes, cars, kinds of food, visiting new places, taking a longer holiday and taking up a new pastime provide a new style that offer the prospect of real change in one's life." (Ibid.) Crouch concludes that "[l]eisure plays a very central part in this, and has become a major object of contemporary lifestylisation, making oneself anew, 'freshening one's image', gaining status among one's peers, gaining 'street cred'" (ibid.: 268-269).

These leisure practices can be found prominently in the novels belonging to the genres of chick- and ladlit. Therefore, this chapter investigates the spatial practices which are most prominent in these genres: the leisure activities of shopping, going to clubs and parties and going out for drinks and meals. These three main practices of leisure activities are examined with regard to their qualities to finding a love match. In the following, this chapter looks at depictions of these practices, which are closely linked to space but also to the establishment of an appealing persona the opposite sex might (hopefully) find endearing. All the following activities are connected to economics for, "[a]t the extreme, people 'buy' [or, less biased, consume] leisure rather than 'make it' amongst themselves." (Ibid.: 269) Which is not to say that there are no alternative forms, as the example of the roof-top party in *Almost Single* proves. Yet the notion of consumption is a strong one in all of the following three building blocks of this chapter: shopping, clubbing or partying and going to restaurants, bars or pubs. All these practices account for what Phil Hubbard calls "the 'vitality and viability' of the city centre" (2007: 118) and in consumption the metropolitan seekers of love and relationships are united: for they want to be consumed by love, passion and a partner and in order to achieve that they consume themselves in the spaces of leisure (cf. Bauman, qtd. in Hubbard 2007: 124). The novels themselves are products which are (mostly) consumed during their readers' leisure time, too. They thus mirror the idea of sellable and consumable lifestyles, as expressed in the possibility of readers recognising themselves – "This is me!" – and aspiring to a similar life(style). The "transformation of people […] into modern consumers in a global market-place may well have been the greatest social change since industrialization." (Langman 1992: 41)

GOING SHOPPING

The character of Rebecca 'Becky' Bloomwood (*Shopaholic* series) is the first name when it comes to the joys of shopping (cf. Van Slooten 2006). Indeed, Becky can hardly walk past a shop which presents her with the chance to indulge in her favourite pastime: "suddenly my eyes focus and snap to attention, and my heart stops. In the window of Denny and George is a discreet sign. It's dark green with cream lettering, and it says: SALE." (Kinsella 2007: 13) Becky is a character for whom conceptual artist Barbara Kruger seems to have created the witty slogan "I shop therefore I am", establishing a close connection between the act of consumption and the shopper's sense of self. This motto has been integrated so much into Becky's being that she considers how to buy goods wherever she is, turning every space into a potential marketplace. In the following, the connection between the act of shopping or consumption and spaces will be explained and investigated further. This chapter considers acts of consumption for the creation of an identity as well as the connection to both spaces and the search for the perfect partner. Especially Pierre Bourdieu's concept of habitus is used and the importance of the cultural as well as economic capital explored. Referring back to these ideas, the function of commodities to construct an identity is analysed in chick- and ladlit novels. Here, the appeal to the other sex via products and spaces of consumption is in the focus and leads to the analysis of Anita Heiss's novel *Paris Dreaming*. In this book the ethnic qualities of both the protagonist's identity and the commodities she promotes are sounded out and they will be juxtaposed with another ethnic minor character.

In their book *Shopping, Place and Identity* Daniel Miller et al. define "contemporary consumption [as] a social process that goes well beyond the isolated act of purchase into cycles of use and re-use as the meaning of goods is transformed through their incorporation into people's daily lives." (1999: ix; cf. Jackson and Holbrook 1995: 1914, Reimer and Leslie 2004: 188) They continue to remark "that shopping is an investment in social relationships, [...] as much as it is an economic activity devoted to the acquisition of particular commodities" (Miller et al. 1999: x) which echoes the idea of "shopping for goods [as] a social activity built around social exchange as well as simple commodity exchange" (Shields 1992a: 102). Similarly, consumers can be defined as beings that are "constituted as autonomous, self-regulating and self-actualizing individual [spatial] actors, seeking to maximize their 'quality of life' – in other words, to optimize the worth of their existence to themselves – by assembling a lifestyle, or lifestyles, through personalized acts of choice in the market place." (du Gay 1996: 77) It is especially these commodified and emphasised lifestyles of the characters with which they hope to attract their respective perfect partners.

Consumption and the construction of identity, as in the example of Kruger's witticism, are crucial concepts in cultural studies. In the 'circuit of culture', Paul du Gay connects the two concepts as important processes in the production of meaning (1997: 3). The objects which the various characters procure are represented in a specific way (another part of the circuit of culture), and play "a crucial role in fixing the meaning and image"; not only of the product itself but they "establish[...] an *identification* between object and [its] *consumers*." (Ibid.: 4-5, original emphasis) Therefore, the products which can be bought at different places show that, considering the Actor-Network-Theory (ANT), they become agents themselves in the construction and maintaining of identities, localities and spatial practices. Not only the person who buys is important but the inanimate object, the commodity, must be regarded on the same meaningful level as the human actor with the same space-determining qualities: "for many geographers, the great appeal of ANT lies in its capacity to provide more sophisticated explanations of the emergence and consolidation of social structures, including the ways such structures impact or transform 'local' interactions" (Duff 2014: 49-50). In the introductory quote, the sign proclaiming the sale becomes a teaser for the 'joys' which await Becky inside the store, granting it both agency as pull-factor as well as creating a layer of reduced-price shopping on top of the otherwise pricy shopping experience. Whereas the Denny and George store is usually a territory Becky is unable to afford shopping at – something she is painfully aware of (cf. Kinsella 2007: 13) – the sign turns the shop into an accessible space which can be now mastered by Becky's money and from which Becky can buy a new part to construct her identity with: "Everyone I know in the entire world aspires to owning a Denny and George scarf." (Ibid.) She finally can become part of a group of people the usual prices have previously prevented her from joining and she can realise her "hedonistic view of life, [which is] based on materialist possessions" (Montoro 2007: 69)[2].

Becky can be considered a contemporary Little Red Riding Hood, with the wolf being the alluring shopping opportunities. Moreover, in contrast to the girl in the fairy tale, who is eaten alive by the wolf and, in the Grimms' version, learns her lesson not to stray from the path, Becky appears unable to understand not to give in to temptation: "There is a drama of attractions and interests, desires and choices, in which minds are forever seeking and forever failing to capture the object that will satisfy their longing once and for all." (Bowlby 1993: 115) The shopaholic cannot but listen to the siren song of her addiction, always lying to herself by proclaiming that this object is the last she buys on a whim because "[t]he new Rebecca has more self-control than [the old Rebecca, who was always giving in]" (Kinsella 2007: 308). Becky's intentions are good but longing and presumed gratification almost always get the better of her. Geographically, being 'abstinent' in terms of shopping is going to be hard for Becky for she cannot escape the ever-present shopping opportunities which surround her, especially as she lives in a metropolis. The process she fails to learn in her territory is that of moderation and buying out of necessity, not for pleasure. This process is played out in space as she has to master the art of not diverting from her path and become a consumer: she must learn to refuse the "seduction by the commodity calculus" (Miller et al. 1999: 8). The only way she is able to escape the constant temptation of sales and this-season's-must-haves is by staying with her parents in a smaller village, which does not offer the opportunities to go shopping. This is more of an easy way out than Becky dealing with her addiction and the accompanying debts as it does not mean a change of her behaviour but stalling it temporarily. Becky is aware of the spatiality of her weak spot and by relocating she thinks that she can minimise the seductive power of shopping[3]. It is conspicuous that Becky refrains from buying 'outside' of shops most of the time. She appears to need the instant gratification from exchanging

---

2 Just like the Denny and George scarf in Becky's first outing, it is a Vera Wang dress in the second novel of the Shopaholic series: "And I just stared at myself, mesmerized. Entranced by what I could look like, by the person I could be. There was no question. I had to have it." (Kinsella 2004: 251; cf. Van Slooten 2006: 229). In the third novel, Kinsella even surpasses herself when Becky moves from dress to a whole New York-socialite-wedding extravaganza (cf. Van Slooten 2006: 233-234): she is under the impression that her identity is dependent on specific commodities.

3 Here are connections to the escapist behaviour with regard to dealing with problematic workspaces. Chick- and ladlit do not want to confront problems, they rather escape and ignore them.

money for goods and immediately possessing the commodities. Buying online, for example, would defer this gratification as it divorces the act of paying from that of receiving the commodity.

When it comes to shopping as a form of consumption, it is both a stereotype and a prejudice that women are more likely to do and to enjoy it. Yet, "the vast majority of the world's shoppers have been women" (Reekie 1993: xi) and this does not cease to hold true:

> Women are becoming more important in the global marketplace not just as workers, but also as consumers, entrepreneurs, managers and investors. Women have traditionally done most of the household shopping, but now *they have more money of their own to spend.* Surveys suggest that women make perhaps 80% of consumers' buying decisions—from health care and homes to furniture and food. (*The Economist* 2006, emphasis added)

The fact that there is even a term for this phenomenon – "Womenomics" (ibid.) – points towards the somewhat essentialist notion of females as consumers (cf. Rojek 1995: 31-33). Of course, the claim that women are "becoming more important" is masking the insight that women have never been unimportant as consumers. In many chicklit novels, the goods the women buy are mostly related to establishing a sense of self with regard to their femininity. But the phrase that "they have more money of their own to spend" (ibid.) is rather interesting: it emphasises the independence of women from men as breadwinners. As established in the previous chapter, all the female characters in chicklit work and although they do want to find their perfect partner, they are just as determined to be successful in the corporate world. Both Becky and Sabrina Falks (*The Wedding Planner*) marry millionaires but they are not depending on them for financial support, since they both earn their own money. Especially the example of *The Wedding Planner* traces the success story of a young woman who comes from a working-class or lower middle-class background. Since her absent father and her depressed mother could not provide for the family, Sabrina went on to earn the necessary money. Due to her iron will, Sabrina has managed to become a successful actor and although she is about to marry an equally successful businessman, she does not spend any money apart from that which she earns herself (cf. La'Brooy 2010: 269). Yet, Sabrina Falks is one of the few examples of those who have managed to rise economically on their own. Most of the other female and male characters in chick- and ladlit come from a comfortable middle-class background or caste[4]. They never really had to worry about money. Even if some of the ladlit characters display 'slacker' qualities which

4 For information on the relationship between class, consumption and geography, Mark Jayne's *Cities and Consumption* is recommended (2006).

reflect their meagre income, by the end of the novel they will have a job which enables them to live comfortably again.

Moreover, Rebecca's shopping also has a representative function, as do Bridget Jones's acts of consumption and those of Will (*About a Boy*). All of the characters establish a sense of self via the products they consume which points to what Pierre Bourdieu termed *habitus*[5], which is comprised of "acquired modes of thought, actions, orientations, dispositions that are unthinking (habits)" (Pini and Previte 2013: 257). Comparing processes of a specific social stratum to games, Bourdieu establishes that "one is born into the game, with the game", knowledgeable of the game's 'language' "in the form of grammar, rules and exercises"[6] (Bourdieu 1990: 67). Bourdieu complements this idea by stating that the games take place in a field, which is "an arbitrary social construct, an artefact whose arbitrariness and artificiality are underlined by everything that defines its autonomy – explicit and specific rules, strictly delimited and extra-ordinary time and space." (Ibid.) By being part of a specific social stratum, certain behaviour and thus 'taste' is learned, which creates a habitus: "It can be thought of as the mediating mechanism between the objectivity of social reality and the subjectivity of personal experience." (Chatterton and Hollands 2003: 80) Yet the element of origin has to be attenuated by acknowledging that it is founded "not [on] natural but *social* aptitude" (Wacquant 2011: 318, original emphasis) and that it includes principles of *sociation* and *individuation*. The former refers to "our categories of judgement and action, coming from society, [which] are shared by all those who were subjected to similar social conditions and conditionings", and the latter highlights the individual "by having a unique trajectory and location in the world" (ibid.: 319). It is a form of conflict between the attitudes towards processes and objects of the one (individuation) and the many (sociation). With regard to cultural geography, the tension mirrors the single actor and the spatial structure, which has developed through long social processes.

Due to the fact that one is integrated into structures of habitus very early on, the "unthought presuppositions that the game produces and endlessly reproduces" (Bourdieu 1990: 67) most often escape the actor because "practices can circulate and reproduce culture without their meanings passing through discourse or consciousness." (Fiske 1992: 159)

---

5 The term "habitus" originates from Aristotle but has been made prominent by Bourdieu (cf. Wacquant 2011: 317).

6 Although human beings can become 'fluent' in their habitus, it does not "suggest that we are determined by habitus. Rather, Bourdieu and his proponents argue, while habitus governs and shapes our practices it also has generative and dynamic capacities" (Pini and Previte 2013: 257).

> Between learning through sheer familiarization, in which the learner insensibly and unconsciously acquires the principles of an 'art' and an art of living, including those that are not known to the producer of the practices or artefacts that are imitated [...], every society provides structural exercises which tend to transmit a particular form of practical mastery. (Bourdieu 1990: 74-75)

This will result in "cultural capital" (ibid.: 124-125, Bourdieu 1978: 834) through which the social stratum, class or group defines itself – by setting itself apart or by including previously unobtainable cultural capital: "Everywhere [the redistribution of practices (or lack thereof) is] observed, these consecration cycles perform the fundamental operation of social alchemy, the transformation of arbitrary relations into legitimate relations, *de facto* differences into officially recognized distinctions." (Bourdieu 1990: 125) To paraphrase Bourdieu: shopping, "like any other practice, is an object of struggles between [...] the social [strata[7]]" and has its "origin [in] the system of tastes and preferences that is a [stratum's] habitus" (1978: 826, 834). Additionally, it displays a strong notion of sociation. Becky knows that introducing a Denny and George scarf into her couture means that she will be acknowledged by the cognoscenti and thus taken to be a member of this social group, a process that can be considered as sociation via conspicuous consumption that locates her among the many. She is constantly "refashioning her identity by means of her label-driven purchases." (Van Slooten 2006: 219)

But without money to buy commodities or afford a certain lifestyle, the cultural capital, which might also be called "consumer 'taste'" (Jackson 1999: 29), cannot be enjoyed fully, thus economic capital is needed (cf. Bourdieu 1978: 834). To characters in chick- and ladlit, shopping seems to come easy for they have almost without exception well-paying jobs. Even those without a profession or even previous work experience manage to obtain a job, like Miriam Falks in *The Wedding Planner* or Dec McPherson in *Street Furniture*. The characters do not have to worry about occupation and therefore, money is hardly an obstacle. They become yuppies – young urban professionals – who are "part agent, part victim [and who have] a lifestyle ruthlessly dedicated to consuming" (Mort 1989: 160). This suggests that "[p]ossession becomes psychologically conflated with being" (Rojek 2010: 80). Thus, Becky's behaviour is never chastised in the novels and although she is highly indebted, she always manages to find a way out of financially precarious situations rather easily: "Throughout the series, [...] Becky never *really* suffers privation because of her spending habits. Instead, her problems almost miraculously disappear, suggesting to readers that there are no real consequences to Becky's behavior

7 Bourdieu himself speaks of classes, but the argument is just as valid if one transfers his logic from a higher level to that of meso or even micro level.

and providing readers a 'safe' consumerist fantasy world" (Van Slooten 2006: 219, original emphasis).

Additionally, "[t]here is a continual smudging of personas and lifestyles, *depending where we are* (at work, on the high street) and the spaces we are moving between." (Mort 1989: 169, emphasis added) This indicates that no matter the location, the identities of an individual are multiple but the individual will always consider consumption. It comes therefore as no surprise that Becky meets her perfect partner, entrepreneur and millionaire Luke Brandon, whilst trying to find money to buy the expensive Denny and George scarf, and she has no qualms lying to Luke to embezzle money from him. Jessica Lyn Van Slooten suggests that Becky buys commodities which "are consumed quickly and temporarily replace the emotional need for a boyfriend." (2006: 222) However, this holds only partially true: she does indeed consume items whilst being single, sometimes fantasising that she will be more alluring for men with her latest commodity, yet she does not stop when she is in a relationship. Therefore the act of shopping or consumption does not compensate for the lack of love in her life – it *is* the love of her life. At the end of the second instalment of the *Shopaholic* series, Becky leaves Luke following a misunderstanding and establishes herself as a personal shopper in New York's famous department store Barneys. When Luke comes to her repentantly, he 'disguises' himself as a customer and congratulates Becky on her vocation: "'You look as though you're flourishing.' He looks around with a little smile. 'This environment suits you. Which I suppose comes as no great surprise...'" (Kinsella 2004: 383) Luke's observation corresponds to the notion that "shopping is not just about purchasing goods; goods must be understood as symbolic containing imagistic and lifestyle associations which relate to both *desire* and assumed, or anticipatory, *status*." (Featherstone 1998: 917, emphasis added) Becky's desire to shop is now merged with status, however not through the result, the purchases, but through the practice as such, the shopping.

Her new profession is the apogee of the construction of her identity for now she is recognised not as the woman who is constantly in debt but as the one who can put (other people's) money to good use, making the novels "a consumerist fantasy world in which reality never fully intrudes." (Van Slooten 2006: 237) It has to be acknowledged that the gratification she gets from shopping is merely the seconds when she stands at the till and buys something. The moment she arrives at home, most of the items are no longer rendered valuable by her as she does not use or wear most of them. Rebecca cannot even remember buying certain items at times, which suggests that "her shopping behaviors mimic that of a bulimic; she binges and purges regularly, buying ridiculous amounts of clothing, feeling guilty about her purchases, and then vowing vehemently to reduce." (Smith 2008: 22-23; cf. Van Slooten 2006: 223) It becomes clear that "[t]he actual products are not as important as the fantasies that revolve around the products" (Van Slooten 2006: 222), and these fantasies translate mostly into accumulating cultural capital. Thus, Becky has inevitably found a profession in which "the distinction between work and leisure is blurred" (Walmsley and Lewis 1993: 202; cf. Mort 1989: 171). She gets paid for what she would have done anyway, namely shop. For Becky, shopping is not "a leisure pursuit involving a choice of consumer 'lifestyles'", it emphasises "consumption as work, accomplished by skilled social actors with finite resources." (Peter Jackson 2004: 173) Becky never had the economic capital to shop without accumulating debts but now she has found a space in which she can still achieve the gratification that the spending of money has bought her previously. In her new job, she can spend *other people's money* on clothes and therefore does not have to clutter (to borrow Will Freeman's phrase) her own place with commodities, which were only ever the result of her shopping, never the reason. She has turned the department store in which she works into a hybrid space that functions both as a space of consumption and of work, but in a way different from other sales clerks. She can accommodate her producer and consumer self at the same time and same space. On a private level, her method does not even change for although she still holds the job at Barneys in the third instalment, she quite frankly admits that she is "all for sharing money. In fact, hand on heart, [she] *love*[*s*] sharing Luke's money." (Kinsella 2002: 30, original emphasis) Luke, who will become her husband later on, is reduced to be the money to Becky's notorious shopper. It is important to note that although he tries to reprimand her, he never actually does anything about her obsessive shopping or the abusive 'sharing' of his money. With regard to the aforementioned fantasy world, it is striking that Becky has found both the perfect job and husband to live her life undisturbed and is likely to shop till she drops.

Whereas Becky first and foremost shops to gratify herself and meets her Mr Right Luke through shopping by chance, other chick- and ladlit protagonists are more offensive. Through consumption they create an identity with which they hope to attract their perfect partners. The next examples will further elaborate on Bourdieu's ideas and prove their significance for chick- and ladlit. Spaces of consumption like shops are considered as well as the places in which the 'bought' identity can be displayed.

Bridget Jones's skills in the kitchen are infamous because she is barely able to produce anything edible in this space. This, however, has not prevented her from buying numerous tools which now adorn her kitchen but are not used. Focusing merely on her New Year's Resolutions, Bridget's futile consumption becomes apparent: "I WILL NOT [w]aste money on: pasta-makers, ice-cream machines or other culinary devices which [I] will never use; [I will not s]pend more than [I] earn." (Fielding 1998: 1) The tools she lists are not standard equipment in a kitchen, which makes them noteworthy: although these commodities show that she spent too much money on them, the fact that she did not have to think about spending the money, shows that she must have a sufficient salary, a fact which is supported by her living in gentrified Notting Hill. The New Year's Resolutions prove that in this example the economic capital is part of the cultural capital because Bridget wants to pass herself off as a person who actually makes her own pasta and ice-cream. The two machines are to signify to visitors of her flat that she is a culinary connoisseur, a scheme which can only impress the uninitiated. The kitchen commodities – and consequentially her (shopping) behaviour – are conspicuous in this respect and are meant to establish her as a "brilliant cook" (ibid.: 82): "What becomes important to Bridget is not the final cooking act but the love and admiration [of a man] that she imagines will accompany that act." (Smith 2008: 113) Bridget envies her married friend Magda, whose house and the commodities displayed in it "symbolize those sentiments that Bridget associates with married life – order, security, and everlasting love." (Ibid.)

But her commodified identity is not only restricted to the kitchen. Additional to her unused kitchen tools she buys "exotic underwear" and books she does not read (Fielding 1998: 1). Through these items she tries to enhance her sexual and intellectual allure. The living room with the books, the bedroom in which she can present her lingerie and the kitchen with the luxury tools are to round off the image she wants to create of herself but they only help to disguise the 'real' Bridget. It is therefore no surprise that her commodity-enhanced identity only attracts the wrong man, namely the one who is after fun: Daniel Cleaver. This distractor character is contrasted with Bridget's perfect partner, Mark Darcy, whom she has known since her early childhood when she did not need masks of culinary sophistication and bodily improvement. Later, Mark will say that he deems her natural compared to other women. However, he is apparently only able to tell the *very* manipulated female body, which he describes as "lacquered" (ibid.: 237), from the 'normally' farmed female body such as Bridget's. Incidentally, it is this "lacquered" body which Bridget herself considers perfect and aspires to (cf. ibid.: 177-178). The novel never questions the 'need' of female characters to manipulate their appearance to appeal to the other sex: Mark Darcy is supposed to be more likeable because of his love for 'natural' Bridget but at the same time the heroine never stops in her endeavours to manipulate herself. Even after Mark's comment, Bridget continues to consume commodities to enhance her chances to attract her perfect partner. She does so because she is advised by magazines like *Cosmopolitan* and her friends, who are equally influenced by these publications, that men will only consider beautified or manipulated women as partners. It is a form of sociation that has proven to be successful because of its hegemonic qualities: as many sources, which are arguably referencing themselves like a *perpetuum mobile*, claim to know how to attract the perfect partner they have become part of Bourdieu's game. These sources have become very adept at including agents in their structure of sociation: Bridget is probably aware of the fact that men like Mark are so used to hyper-enhanced women, whom he terms "lacquered", that they do not want to see a really 'natural' or pre-harvested woman.

In a similar vein, *About a Boy*'s Will Freeman is equally not above buying products to manipulate other people's perception of him so that they interpellate him into the role of 'father' for example. Yet, he is helping young Marcus too, with his knowledge of cultural capital (and his own significant economic capital) to achieve an upgrading of the lonely boy's status. Very early on, Will wants to establish himself as a single father so as to date single mothers. In order to be believable he creates Ned, his 'son', who is always conveniently absent. The void Ned perpetually leaves behind has then to be filled by a signifier of Ned's existence: Will goes out and buys a car seat because "he felt he should at least make some concession to Ned's reality."[8] (Hornby 1998: 85) Going even one step further, he litters the brand-new car seat with biscuits and crisps as to add more realism to the idea of Ned. Will feels comfortable that he can convincingly tread on single-parent territory now, as he can produce a signifier for Ned and thus consequentially his fatherhood. The fact that the seat is conspicuously 'safe' (cf. ibid.) even accredits him 'premium' fatherhood status, upping his cultural capital to the heights of one who knows how to protect his offspring with the best appliances. Will can be (wrongly) identified by other parents as a father since the untidy car seat turns his sports car into a family vehicle. Being very conscious about keeping his home-as-bubble clutter-free (see chapter 4), he only uses his car to signify his fatherhood and when Marcus unexpectedly comes to his flat, the boy draws the correct conclusions: "You haven't got a kid, have you? […] You've got one bedroom, you've got no children's toys in the bathroom, there are no toys in [the living room]… You haven't even got any photos of him." (Ibid.: 99-100) Will's reluctance to clutter his personal space exposes him as not being a father at all and the consumption of 'fatherhood' fails. He does not have the cultural capital to successfully signify fatherhood and therefore his individuation discloses this lack. Had he been more thorough with his personal space he might have managed to convince others of his status but as he cannot bring himself to introduce other human beings permanently into his place (yet) his clutter-free flat unravels his constructed identity. Moreover, and in connection to previous

8 Will has a problem with the name of the shop in which he buys the commodities of fatherhood: "'That's sexist, you know,' he said to the assistant smugly. 'Sorry?' 'Mothercare. What about the fathers?'" (Hornby 1998: 85) Although he cannot claim the identity of 'father' he does still feel that he is not represented by the shop's name. The fact that he is supposedly not the first to remark on this fact shows that the shop refuses to acknowledge their male clientele.

analyses, Will is shown as not being ready yet for family as his single household signifies. Only when the absence of Ned is covered by surrogate son Marcus does Will warm to the idea of family and consequently meets Rachel, his perfect partner.

Although Will does know now that solitary signifiers – such as a car seat to pretend to be a father – do not necessarily work, he clings to this method with regard to constructing an identity via consumption. Just as he has created a veneer of fatherhood to mask his true identity, he tells Marcus that "[y]ou can be as weird as you want on the inside. Just do something about the outside" (ibid.: 118) when the boy confesses that he is too visible and thus the victim of bullying. Will suggests that Marcus disguises himself in order to fit in with the other kids. At first Marcus is not convinced because his mother taught him that when people have not got a mind of their own they are merely sheep (cf. ibid.: 119): he advocates individuation over sociation. In Will's book, however, sociation is a good thing because it means that one is accepted by the 'flock'. This idea is reflected on a spatial level too: when they go shopping for shoes – again, Will deems one item enough as a signifier for a new identity. "The trainer shop was huge and crowded, and the lighting made all the customers look ill; everyone had a green tinge, regardless of their original colour." (Ibid.: 118) Just as Will tries to 'help' Marcus to blend in so as to forego further bullying, the shop creates a homogenous human environment of its customers. The green tinge of the shop's lighting reduces the individual so that only cultural capital – knowing what shoes to wear and that they are available at this high street shop – and economic capital – the shoes are not cheap – matter. The customers of the shop are therefore united and equalised in their habitus. The shop is a perfect example of the commodified enhancement of the self. It shows that Will might have failed in his attempt at buying 'fatherhood', but is otherwise very knowledgeable in how to blend in by using spaces of consumption to this means.

But even for Will, cultural capital does not come naturally: Will has to constantly consume external sources to redeem the façade of sophistication and hipness. In that respect he is no different from Bridget Jones as both consult magazines to construct their identity against the magazines' suggestions. Both characters need external sources to navigate the meta-space that is attractiveness for others, in this case Marcus: "Will bought a *Time Out* [to] make it clear to Marcus that he was not dealing with your average, desperately unhip thirty-six-year-old here." (Ibid.: 82) This example shows that cultural capital is not a static or transhistorical quality, as it needs constant updating or re-affirmation by investing (financially) in one's 'identity'. And even then Will is not safe from (shop) mirrors revealing the truth: "Will caught sight of the pair of them in a mirror, and was shocked to see that they could easily pass for father and son; he had *somehow imagined himself* as Marcus's elder brother, but the reflection threw age and youth in sharp relief" (ibid.: 118-119, emphasis added). The spatial environment of the trendy trainer shop represented by the mirror betrays Will's hipper-than-thou persona as being so shallow that it does not hold up against the merest of scrutinies. The shop's mirror discloses Will's true identity – the single man who has aged more than he would have thought. It appears that cultural and economic capital can only temporarily mask one's identity, hence Will's constant alertness to the newest trends.

Melanie La'Brooy's *The Wish List* is also rather interesting when it comes to consumption. The novel mainly focuses on Lucinda 'Lucy' Millbanke, a struggling actress. Although portrayed as a hopeless romantic by both her friends and the figural narrator, she sleeps with her on/off-boyfriend when she is in fact seeing someone else, throwing her devotion to romance in question[9]. She admits to her mistake and breaks up with the man she has cheated on. However, she has already bought her ex-boyfriend his birthday present: Vikram Seth's novel *A Suitable Boy*.

Talking about the novel with her friend Meg, Lucy reasons that the novel was not the best present to begin with: "The title is loaded with symbolism. And it's too big." (La'Brooy 2005: 72) Lucy thinks that the book's title could have given her now-ex-boyfriend a wrong impression as to what she wanted to imply. However, what this symbolism is supposed to be, Lucy never discloses. Additionally, she appears to have no idea what the novel is actually about, as she swiftly changes the subject from the title to the size of the novel. The fact that it chronicles the lives and relationships of four large families against the backdrop of an arranged marriage in post-1947 India (cf. Kasbekar 2006: 91, 102) seems to have been irrelevant to Lucy selecting it. Seth's novel is indeed a large book, having more than a thousand pages, but Lucy's reasons for buying it were as follows:

> Well, firstly, it was as though I was testing him to see whether he had the staying power to make it through something *serious*. And secondly, you always want to know what someone thinks of a present you give them. So it was pretty presumptuous to assume that I was still going to be around in three and a half years when he finished reading it. (La'Brooy 2005: 72, emphasis added)

It transpires that the idea behind the book was neither the pleasure of reading it, nor the appeal of the story but rather an elaborate scheme to prompt the longevity of their relationship. The book is reduced to a simple test of whether the relationship would mean enough to the man so that he would read the novel to show his appreciation for Lucy as the giver of the present. She equates the seriousness of the book with their relationship, yet at the same time her reasoning implies a hierarchical structure because only *he* has to read the novel, not her. It is therefore no surprise

9 Her devotion, however, is only – if ever – questioned extradiegetically, never by the characters in the novel.

that *she* ends the relationship. Apart from the fact that she lacks the stamina and attention span to follow a story like Seth's, it also suggests that, to Lucy, love is measurable through commodities. Additionally, it betrays Lucy as being a shallow person as she does not care whether the story of the novel would be of interest to somebody – only the equalisation of length and seriousness as a test is important. She thus empties Seth's book of its qualities of being a marker of cultural capital. She could have considered a man's literary preferences but is only interested in his 'stamina'.

Lucy's superficiality is equally evident when she asks her friend Meg to accompany her to the store to return the book. She correctly identifies Meg as the more able person to deal with as rational a matter as refunding, giving Lucy the opportunity to scout the space of the bookstore for men – and not books. Thinking only about appearances, Lucy wants to present herself as intellectual as possible and wears glasses and an outfit to the store which Meg describes as "librarian" (ibid.: 74). The fact that Lucy can hardly see anything with her glasses does not matter as it is in tune with her idea that appearances are more important than content. The irony of the idiom 'Don't judge a book by its cover' is lost on everyone around her except rationally-thinking Meg (ibid.: 84).

At the store, Lucy picks up a book, and she 'reads' it in such a way that it displays the book's title to passers-by while she scans the area for men. What she is actually holding in her hands is for the benefit of others and only in a consecutive step for herself[10]. She tries to attach cultural capital to her self in the bookstore while at the same time being ignorant about the books' contents. Lucy's spatial practice of scouting for men turns the bookstore into a place which is not characterised by its products but by its consumers. Ironically, she still wants to take a literary commodity home from the shop but Lucy wants it to be a literate man – having proven that she does not like reading herself. This notion adds another layer to the store for the duration of Lucy's stay, namely that of the hunting ground. With regard to Foucault's heterotopia, the bookstore becomes a temporary utopia as Lucy takes it to be the perfect place to hunt for literary men. Lucy uses the book she holds up conspicuously to attach a specific agency to her person where there was previously only the 'idea of agency'. The 'idea of agency' means a person coming into a store intends to buy something or at least has some incentive as to the products the shop sells. The book construes identity *on* Lucy and now she can be

10 This practice is also adopted by Bridget Jones: she has "waste[d] money on: […] books by unreadable literary authors to put impressively on shelves." (Fielding 1998: 2) That she works for a book company is a particularly ironic statement as to her unliterariness. This, again, echoes *Ethan Grout* as most of the employees of The Book Place are as averse to reading as Lucy.

considered to have agency: "a person-object relation is regulated [through cultural or biographical forces] which in turn gives rise to identities, understanding and everyday practices." (Lunt and Livingstone 1992: 85) Not being a reader, she becomes an 'erudite' woman through seizing the book. The commodity she holds up for others to acknowledge justifies her presence in the location, thus gaining direct agency. Through this action, she is able to striate a space which otherwise is smooth to her due to her ignorance. Before taking up the book, she had been unable to generate any place-specific agency: as Lucy does not want to read anything, even less buy a book to read it, her identity is not compatible with the general outset of the store. The book, then, can attach agency to her as (pretending to) reading it gives her a reason to be at the bookstore, it alters her direct place within the space of the bookstore as well as initiating a transformation of Lucy's identity (cf. Belliger and Krieger 2006: 34), again testifying to the existence of the heterotopia. It might be a passive object but in combination with Lucy, the book becomes an active agent as it transforms 'fake librarian' Lucy into a reader. The book's 'natural habitat' is the bookstore or the book lover's shelf, thus by 'using' it within the spatial context of the bookstore Lucy becomes 'naturalised' and appears to have a reason to be there. However, when she is at home, any book will lose its original agency and becomes merely a souvenir of her pretentiousness and lack of interest and stamina as she hardly ever touches any of her books again (cf. La'Brooy 2005: 73). And the fact that all her friends know of her lack of interest in books condemns the purchased goods to useless dust collectors, which fail to impress anyone outside the realm of the bookstore.

Her friend Meg does not understand why Lucy would sacrifice her integrity to herself in order to impress somebody Lucy is very unlikely ever to see again. The fact that Meg is not reliant on objects to be able to striate the bookstore or, more precisely, be regarded as a customer, puts her in opposition to Lucy. Indeed, it is exactly this spatial quality of Meg's, namely not to construct appearances and fake identities, that enables her to return the book because "[s]ales assistants always hate [Lucy] and they always bend over backwards to help [Meg]." (Ibid.: 71) Meg is actually successful because she does not fabricate stories to justify her actions, which is very much lost on Lucy. The latter thinks that one can only be successful in transactions – such as the returning of a purchased product – if one goes by the "unwritten laws of conduct regarding retail exchange and returns [...] all women were born" with: "Lying about your reasons for returning something was not just common practice it was bloody well *expected*." (Ibid.: 75-76, original emphasis) This attitude which is expressed attaches an essentialist as well as escapist quality to Lucy[11]: not only does she deem it an innate trait of women to basically lie to achieve anything they want in a transaction, she also romanticises it as she seems to like the idea to invent stories about the reasons for the return and, at the same time, herself. Yet, her fabrications and angst to be put on the spot hardly lead to success, whereas Meg's direct approach achieves results.

When Lucy eventually sees a handsome young man in the bookstore, she wants him to come to her instead of approaching him directly. Although the bookstore as a commercial place does not grant any of the two more power in terms of spatiality, Lucy withdraws into the passive role, which she deems more appealing. Meg assumed correctly that Lucy enjoys looking for bachelors at the bookstore because she "fantasise[s] that every male who walks in is a poet who is going to make [Lucy] his muse" (ibid.: 72-73). It is ironic, then, that the man Lucy becomes smitten with is an Italian named Byron, who has a lock of stray hair – evoking images of Romantic poet Lord George Byron. As Lucy is only passive, Meg becomes active and arranges for the two to meet. This questions both Lucy's idea of the agency of women and shows that even men are not always as active as Lucy fantasises. However, Lucy's problem is that she is prone to "chasing after some guy that [she has] decided is [her] perfect man on the basis of a book he mentioned reading three years ago." (Ibid.: 335) Lucy bases her compatibility with men on commodities, which – as the novel exemplifies – does not work, and this leads – in the case of Byron – to a total misapprehension with regard to his character. Just like the books at the bookstore, she cannot read him properly and thus gets more drama and romance than she bargained for (cf. ibid.: 107). It transpires very quickly that Byron is as concerned with appearances as Lucy is, which leads to many misunderstandings and eventually the break-up of the two. They appear to be very compatible but the novel proves that abusing a space and its commodities in the way Lucy does at the bookstore is going to be punished.

The example of *About a Boy* proves that ladlit is not devoid of shopping experiences. Attributed predominantly to the burgeoning diversity of masculine identities, it is especially the New Man who has made territories of consumption his own (cf. Miller et al. 1999: 13, Benwell 2003: 18, Ochsner 2009: 23-25). That consumption can go wrong with regard to identities is apparent in Duffy's near-traumatic IKEA episode in *Mr Commitment*. Benjamin Duffy has commitment issues but when his girlfriend Mel presents him with the choice either to marry her or being left by her,

11 This essentialist idea is mirrored in Lucy's idea of novels, because in her opinion chicklit is for women, sci-fi for men: "We [women] end up feeling superior to men because of our greater emotional development and men end up feeling superior to aliens because they don't have to fulfil exhausting destinies and can spell their own names…" (La'Brooy 2005: 81).

he is so scared of the latter that he agrees to the former and accompanies her to IKEA to buy a wardrobe. The store presents two structures, both of which Duffy fails to fully appreciate: "I didn't understand the concept of shopping for home furnishings at all. To me a chair was a chair. [...] But to Mel these things took on a mysterious significance which I couldn't begin to comprehend." (Gayle 2000: 93) Duffy's concept of 'furniture' is oppositional to Mel's as to her the home should represent its dweller, whereas he deems the pieces of furniture mere commodities without any signification attached. The store therefore presents the overlaying structure of turning a space into a place, which clearly favours Mel's approach to shopping for furniture. The second structure is connected to the shoppers themselves as "teeming multitudes of Proper Couples had felt the mysterious urge to come here." (Ibid.) Shopping at IKEA or for furniture becomes a spatial process which signifies coupledom. The cultural capital of the store is therefore more important than the commodities themselves. The fact that, in both statements, Duffy uses the adjective "mysterious" points towards his incomprehensibility of both structures which permeate their shopping experience and which will ultimately lead to the break-up of Duffy and Mel. Duffy enters IKEA under the wrong impression that he just has to be there in order to appease Mel and to prove that he wants to marry her. Mel, on the other hand, overcompensates for Duffy's inability to commit to a wardrobe beyond the description of "nice" and selects a wardrobe that, in Duffy's words, "would've looked fine" in her bedroom, but in his bedroom "it would've looked crap" (ibid.: 95). This shows that the act of consumption has strong repercussions on their life together as only Mel is wholeheartedly 'into' the shared accommodation which is the first step to marriage.

Mel's home represents married life and her wish for it, whereas Duffy's home signifies a life together but not in terms of dwelling, which doubles for married life. The wardrobe, then, becomes the container for both the wish to push the agenda of marriage (Mel) and the reluctance to acknowledge it as the next step (Duffy). To Mel, the wardrobe becomes an object of safety, of "reassurance" (ibid.: 97): if Duffy can finally see the beauty of the wardrobe and find that it goes well with his home she would have a sign of his will to commit. It is no coincidence that Mel wants to move in with Duffy, not the other way around, because installing the wardrobe in his laddish space means that he is forced to give up his previous unaspiring lifestyle and fully acknowledge Mel's presence in his life and lifespace, it is a form of 'romantic hostile takeover'.

When Duffy makes a comment about their previous failure at assembling an IKEA chest of drawers, Mel realises the different stages they are both at and retires to a display of a dining room and they sit at opposite ends of a table. They occupy a fake home just as Mel's dream of living together evaporates. They both come to the conclusion that they have tricked themselves into believing that Duffy can commit to 'them', and that Mel has ignored this truth. The display they are having the argument in is symptomatic of their relationship status: it looks good from the outside but it is a static space as the dining room leads nowhere and is thus uninhabitable. Mel and Duffy cannot remain at this stage in their relationship for the rest of their lives and they both know it. But while Mel wants to take the next step, convinced that Duffy will see the benefits of commitment, her boyfriend is scared that this might lead to the realisation that their living together – and consequently marriage – is just as unendurable as the IKEA display. As an ironic comment, the display doubles as a theatre stage because their argument becomes a show to passers-by, who stop and watch their relationship come apart: Duffy becomes "the recipient of an increasing number of sympathetic glances from the men and condemnatory glances from the women, as if Mel and I were the sex war writ large." (Ibid.) Because IKEA is a store for blissful "Proper Couples" to display their union and unity, a meltdown of the façade of this status becomes a spectacle. The fact that the two sexes watching the scene respond very differently suggests that they recognise Duffy's and Mel's dilemma, that they have experienced what Duffy and Mel are going through. But as this is a store which is founded on the structure of happy couples, such behaviour is intolerable and it comes as no surprise that Mel and Duffy leave the display (the image of their happy relationship) and the store (the epitome of happy coupledom) separately (cf. ibid.: 100). The cultural capital which is attached to IKEA commodities forces a sense of sociation on the consumer and in a consecutive step creates a striated space: only "Proper Couple" customers will be able to purchase goods at IKEA. Everyone else is chastised and this echoes Lucy's experience at the bookstore. Spaces of consumption prove to have a strong agency, which is powered by a consensus manifested in sociation.

Following the break-up, Duffy intends to compensate for the loss of Mel by buying a pair of speakers. At this store, he quickly realises that the other shoppers are young men just like him who equally should not spend that amount of money on speakers but on "food, light or shelter" (ibid.: 110). While IKEA clearly caters to happy couples, the electronics shop "employed people who thought like me to sell to people like me. […] It was like being seduced by the most beautiful woman in the world" (ibid.). But, and this distinguishes Duffy from Becky, who tends to give in to these sirens of consumption, he manages to use the shop to his advantage: Duffy has the assistant play the song that he would have wanted to have played at his wedding and whilst standing in a sound-proof chamber he listens to "Three Times a Lady" on full blast (ibid.: 112). When he finally buys the equipment, it is less because he is convinced by the shop assistant but rather because his purchase signifies oppositional attitudes: on the one hand, it is the laddish idea of spending money on commodities one does not necessarily need. On the other hand, the purchase fills the void Mel's disappearance has left and which he already tried to fill temporarily by listening to "Three Times a Lady" on a similar hi-fi set. Just like Mel at IKEA, he tries to convince himself that purchasing the equipment will make him happy and it is going to cover up his doubt and sadness concerning the break-up. It comes as no surprise that the feeling of wellbeing he has attributed to the equipment fades within minutes of leaving the store (cf. Gayle 2000: 112). With the help of the shop he has managed to lie to himself that the high-tech equipment can substitute Mel, and in that respect the shop has been successful with the capitalist ideology to marry desire with commodity: Duffy resorts to a commodity to signify his (lost) love, because "love [is] the condition of a happiness that cannot be bought[. It is] the one remaining object of desire that cannot be sure of purchasing fulfilment." (Belsey 1994: 72) As he could not 'buy' Mel (the wardrobe) when they were at IKEA, because he acted against the structure of the store, he now has to fall back on commodities which only indirectly refer to love: the hi-fi set that plays the record he wanted to have listened to on his wedding day. The speakers create a utopian dreamscape in which Duffy hears the sound meant for a specific place-bound activity – a church wedding.

At the end of the novel Duffy realises that he indeed wants to marry Mel – and this time his heart is in it too. Therefore he purchases a commodity to signify this change of heart: an IKEA wardrobe. He tries to assemble it in Mel's flat so as to show her that he truly will commit to them. Here, three strands with regard to significations are combined spatially: firstly, the wardrobe is from IKEA and thus signifies Duffy's wish to be once again part of the community of "Proper Couples". That IKEA merely represents a staged form of happiness does not seem to bother him any longer. Secondly, he tries to assemble the wardrobe at Mel's flat, which means that he accepts her way of being together, by moving in together and getting married. His flat, which signifies laddish underachievingness, must not taint the wardrobe as a substitute engagement ring. Lastly, he never manages to assemble the wardrobe completely before Mel returns home (cf. Gayle 2000: 295-296). Duffy explains to her that "The wardrobe *should've been* yours on that day we argued in IKEA, so I give it to you now." (Ibid.: 300, original emphasis) It represents only his half of the relationship, as he cannot erect the wardrobe on his own, he needs a helping hand to make it work. Duffy mentioned in IKEA that they had failed to construct a chest of drawers before, which means that they were not ready, he was not ready, to enter the life of a happy couple who shop at IKEA and only now are they able to assemble the parts into a fully functioning piece of fu(rni)ture. Additionally, Mel tells him that she loves Duffy *because* he hates shopping in IKEA, which suggests that she does not want him to merely pretend to be part of a "Proper Couple". However, the fact that he is able to procure the wardrobe from the store shows that he has been successfully integrated into the sociation the store signifies. Duffy might hate IKEA but he has become one of the shoppers and thus has lost his principle of individuation in the process. Moreover, he appears to accept the fact that Mel is right, which is the reason he erects the wardrobe in *her* flat. Instead of finding a middle way with Mel, Duffy chooses the easiest way and appeases Mel by showing her that she was right to propose a shared flat and eventually married life. It seems as if Duffy is still only thinking in binary oppositions. When he tried to combine them it did not work, as can be seen during the shopping experience with Mel at IKEA. Therefore, Duffy's only development is the acceptance of choosing either his flat and way of life, which means being a laddish single, or Mel and her flat, which signifies coupledom. Although Duffy has chosen Mel's space and life-style, it must be questioned if this can be called a grown-up learning outcome.

That shopping can actually support one's identity (construction) quite well can be seen in two examples from chicklit. Here, the two heroines are aware of the consumer(ist) power they hold and present. First, there is once more Rebecca "Becky" Bloomwood. In *Shopaholic Takes Manhattan*, Becky has accompanied boyfriend Luke to New York because they are thinking about re-locating there. In order to decide whether Becky would like to really live there, she starts to explore the city. Yet, she is not just a tourist, but what Urry and Larsson term a *post-tourist*. This term encompasses three aspects: firstly, post-tourists do not have to leave their homes anymore to travel or see other things. TV, pictures and the internet have made it possible to experience all things foreign and exotic by pressing buttons and keys or looking through books. This can be seen in Becky's notion of feeling at home in New York before even being on American ground – she considers her multimedia diet enough to be a New Yorker[12]. Secondly, "[t]he post-tourist is freed from the constraints of 'high culture' on the one hand, and the untrammelled pursuit of the 'pleasure principle' on the other." (Urry and Larsson 2011: 113-114) Lastly, but in Urry and Larsson's eyes most importantly, post-tourists are aware of their status as tourists. They know that entering an old and historic building does not make them re-live the experience of former times and people. Becky incorporates these last two aspects in just a few steps – literally: Luke has to leave Becky alone quite often, and one morning he suggests she should go on a guided walking tour through New York to get to know the city better and to establish a sense of place and possibly a cognitive map. Donning her high heels, which the tour guide[13] and

12 Becky has the impression that she will come to a familiar environment. She even discloses that she feels "an affinity towards it" (Kinsella 24: 137), which does not makes her an insider in all things New York, but neither a complete stranger (albeit a very one-sided and media-deluded fan of the city).

13 The tour guide is a controlled navigational device (cf. Golledge 1999), but Becky quickly decides that he is not helping her creating a valuable (cognitive) map of New York and abandons the tour guide.

the other members of the group deem highly impractical for a three-hour-tour, she gets distracted many times when they walk down East 57th street towards Fifth Avenue. But the objects of desire and consequentially her gaze are not tourist attractions the guide points out but shops. She cannot understand "why everybody else in the group is following [the guide] happily, not even glancing at the amazing sights around them. [...] What is *wrong* with these people? Are they complete philistines?" (Kinsella 2004: 169-170, original emphasis) Her decidedly different outlook on 'touristy' sights culminates when the group comes to a halt and the tour guide explains that they are standing in front of a historic building of worship. But whereas the tour guide is talking about St. Patrick's Cathedral, Becky is admiring Saks Fifth Avenue right next to it. To her, there might be cultural value attached to the cathedral as she sheepishly admits, but Saks as a signifier of consumption and popular culture is more noteworthy in her book. She ponders on that, telling herself that she

> should take in some culture and come back to Saks later.
> But then – how is that going to help me get to know whether I want to live in New York or not? Looking around some old cathedral?
> Put it like this – how many millions of cathedrals do we have in England? And how many branches of Saks Fifth Avenue? (Ibid.: 172)

This is in tune with post-tourism as it refuses to adhere to limits and thus hierarchical structures telling people what is more gaze-worthy. To Becky, who has to decide whether she wants to live in New York permanently, shopping centres are more important than cathedrals. Although she calls the other tour members "philistines" because of their non-appreciation of places of consumption worship, she is aware that she is the odd woman out as tourists are supposed to look at historical and historic sites, not Saks. To her, one cathedral is like the next, and indeed the American variety is no different from the British in her opinion, but shops show a country's 'true' cultural value. The irony that many shops of one chain look rather identical is lost on Becky. But as she is not explicitly marked as believing in any faith but shopping, she deems the visit of the cathedral futile. Furthermore, her description of the interior of Saks Fifth Avenue echoes the description of the cathedral by the tour guide. Thus, she can appreciate structures and design, but it is the function of the building that matters. In her eyes, the cathedral is merely a building that ceased to be of use many years ago, but as she is addicted to shopping, these shrines of consumption are of far greater importance to her – they are the landmarks that will matter in her cognitive map of New York.

This is also further explored when her guilty conscience eventually takes hold of her and she wants to visit the Guggenheim museum. However, she ends up in the museum *shop*, which is nowhere near the actual museum, and can combine the felt need to visit an important New York landmark and indulge in her passion for shopping at the same time. She buys a book of pictures by Picasso, "[b]ecause the thing is, do you actually need to see a piece of art in the flesh to appreciate it? Of course you don't." (Ibid.: 210) Her post-tourist stance to pictures and images is clear here: she reasons that she will learn much more from the book which holds many pieces of information on the various pictures than by just looking at the real ones in the museum, for the picture itself does not change. After all, there is a copy of the original in her book, only the size might be different. This form is probably even more honest than having been to a real museum and having looked at the paintings, because many tourists simply go the Guggenheim museum because it is something that one does when in New York. It is Urry and Larsson's idea of tourists that they might visit places because of the simple exoticism of the place in which the object can be gazed at[14] (cf. Urry and Larsson 2011: 13).

The second example is concerned with a specific aspect of the identity as commodity, namely the ethnicity of the protagonists in Australian chicklit novel *Paris Dreaming*. Libby Cutmore is not only an avid shopper but she also sells something very important which has strong bearings on her usage and consequentially production of space: her Aboriginality (see chapter 4). Consumption means displaying both one's cultural as well as economic capital, and so it becomes personal advertising for the people themselves – as the examples of Bridget Jones, Will Freeman and Lucy Millbank have shown. Libby, who works at the National Aboriginal Gallery (NAG) in Canberra, wants to present her culture and history to other people, so they will "understand [...] who [they] are as a people, the First Peoples." (Heiss 2011: 35) Libby even comments on the importance and increased interest in her field of expertise:

> It was amazing how my 'public interest' workload had increased since Kevin Rudd delivered the national Apology to the Stolen Generation on February 13, 2008. That symbolic gesture in the Australian parliament somehow opened the pathway for increased communication between Black and white Australians. It was as if Rudd had endorsed a greater interest in Aboriginal art and culture or so it seemed from my desk anyway. (Ibid.: 49)

---

14 This is also mirrored in Bridget's problem with London: "Realize [...] that whatever I am doing I really think I ought to be doing something else. It comes from the [...] feeling [...] which periodically makes you think that just because you live in central London you should be out at the RSC/Albert Hall/Tower of London/Royal Academy/Madame Tussauds, instead of hanging around in bars *enjoying yourself*." (Fielding 1998: 149-50, emphasis added) In her eyes, enjoying oneself and seeing sights are not compatible.

Through Libby, her (Indigenous) boss at the NAG wants to establish a closer (business) relationship with international education and scientific centres (Heiss 2011: 70-75; cf. Heiss 2010: 55-58). It becomes already apparent that both women's objective is to present their culture in other cultural contexts and to build up new connections so as to create an Indigenous network. The spatial dimension is important when they have to negotiate previously (white) striated territories in order to offer their products and ultimately their identity 'for sale'. And the means for them to do so is Aboriginal art.

In *Paris Dreaming*, the reader is presented with exhibitions and pieces of art through the admiring eyes of Libby:

> I felt a special surge of pride and inspiration as I read a quote in the book by artist Gulumbu Yunupingu whose work *Garak, the universe* was a massive ceiling installation [at the Musée du Quai Branly] that allowed the millions of visitors to the musée to enter the artist's own universe over time. Yunupingu said of her contribution, "This is my gift to you, to the French people, and to the people of the world, this is my heart." (Heiss 2011: 35)

This actual piece of art by Yunupingu, *Garak, the universe*, is made visible and approachable to the world in the French museum, which has been a project by former French president Jacques Chirac and was opened in 2006. In terms of space, one artist, Judy Watson, remarked that "it is as if the artists 'are swallowing the building. We are looking out on the street, we are everywhere.'" (Qtd. in Button 2006) Here, a double form of consumption takes place: in the words of Watson, the Indigenous artists are consuming the museum, yet not in a destructive way, in fact the opposite – for, now, the public can consume the art and through the art the culture and (hi)story[15] of Indigenous peoples from South America, Africa, Asia and Oceania (cf. Musée du Quai Branly n.d.). The Indigenous artists claim the museum space and re-appropriate it to have their (hi)stories consumed by exhibition visitors of all ethnicities, thus giving whilst consuming. They are not purposefully trying to appeal to visitors in the same way Bridget Jones or Will Freeman attempt to manipulate their identity to attract others. However, it is the job of curators such as Libby to do so and to devise accompanying texts, promotional material or other means to 'seduce' the public to consume the artists. At the museum as a space of consumption, "ethnicity [is] given the characteristics of marketable attributes in the market place." (Anthias 2001: 386) While Bridget and Will offered themselves for consumption, Libby does so indirectly as she first and foremost offers other artists. But

15 It goes without saying that this wording does not favour one gender over the other and is respectful of both the historical and historic roots of the peoples as well as their mythological and traditional oral and written traditions.

as they share the same Indigenous background, it can be suggested that she presents herself to visitors of her exhibition via her identity, which is influenced very strongly by her Aboriginal heritage. This is also a connection to the artists, who claim the same influence. Therefore, the museum becomes not only a showroom for the great artists but their Indigenous curator Libby just as much.

The Musée du Quai Branly (MQB), as perceived by Libby, is presented as modern and technologically advanced – it has video screens and exhibitions texts and plaques in Braille (cf. Heiss 2011: 142-143). Libby compares the French with the Australian museum and reflects that she

> liked the peacefulness of the MQB. The NAG had more energy and was more brightly lit throughout, but the musée was enjoyable in a different way. It was almost sombre. […] The space was contemporary, although it held materials, artefacts, objects and artwork that belonged to land and times far more traditional and ancient. (Ibid.: 142)

Just like her 'home' institution, Libby is presented as energetic and 'shining', and she stands out through this energy and her attitude. At the same time, she presents this hybrid identity of being both a descendant of a long-lived tradition and the present[16]. Thus, by way of the pieces of exhibition (like *Garak, the universe*) and museums dedicated to Indigenous cultures, Libby as representative of a specific culture can be consumed and she does her best to present her/self in the most favourable light: "I looked around the space [of the musée] and started planning where my own pieces would be hung: […] where Emily McDaniel's soundscape *would best work*, and where the mannequin with Michael McDaniel's possum-skin cloak *would have the greatest impact*." (Ibid.: 144, emphasis added) Libby can be regarded as even higher on a representative level as the artists themselves: she is entrusted with the task of re-presenting the artists – in the sense of presenting again *and* standing in for (*OED*: "represent")[17] – who themselves represent their

---

16 With regard to her identity, at times Libby and her Indigenous friends ponder the question of it: "Lauren and I often discussed the issue of Black woman on Black woman criticism, confused that we were supposed to get educated and get good jobs and have decent, healthy lifestyles only to be condemned by some for selling out when we did. We were apparently 'living like whitefellas'." (Heiss 2011: 43)

17 According to the *OED*, to represent can also mean "to give back", which in the context of Aboriginal cultures has a somewhat bitter connotation with the colonisers taking the land of the Indigenous cultures from them. Also, "giving back" can refer to the act of being grateful for something and thus showing this by actions or words, which – again – is an uneasy definition in the colonial and exploitative relationship between Aborigines and (white) colonisers, such as the French once were, too.

Indigenous culture and history, just like Libby. Therefore, she becomes both the mediator and the most important part of the exhibition as well as of the space of the NAG. Libby creates a (second) museum space (at the MQB) to offer the artists' and pieces of art's identities for consumption. However, only people with sufficient economic capital are granted access to the Aboriginal heritage and space. Although this might suggest a rather far-fetched argumentation as the entrance fee is not extraordinarily high – it appears that the tickets are not as expensive as the entrance to the Louvre, for example – the novel does present characters in its human environment who could not afford to visit the Musée: a homeless man, who is referred to as gypsy, and a Roma woman called Sorina, who sells bags she makes herself on the streets (cf. Heiss 2011: 154, 160-163). By giving her a name and becoming a minor character in the novel, the previous member of the human environment gains more importance.

Sorina functions as a companion piece and foil to Libby: they are similar in the way the Aboriginal woman describes the Roma by positively assessing Sorina's multi-ethnicity and work-ethic, which does apply to Libby as well. Both women operate their transactions – money for identity – in the public sphere, Sorina mostly on the street and Libby in public institutions. But Sorina has to use 'temping work' or more often employ illegal means to sell her crafts and to (economically) survive. By external force(s) she must remain a nomad in the sense of Deleuze and Guattari because her space is rather smooth as the French authorities do not want her to 'stick' – she has "a permit to work. [But n]o-one is safe anymore" (ibid.: 161). This is opposed to Libby, who is almost always welcomed with open arms.

Libby compares her social position to that of Sorina. The Aborigine woman is under the impression that they are both occupying minority positions in political spaces. Although they come from different ethnic backgrounds, they share "solidary bonds relating to origin or cultural difference" (Anthias 2001: 376) and are therefore foreign to the French space to which they have come to work. But whereas Libby is correct in assuming a marginalised position similar to Sorina's, she is wrong in so far as she does not take their divergent economic capitals into consideration: Sorina has no economic power, which makes her vulnerable to the French xenophobia (Heiss 2011: 145). Libby, however, does not need to be afraid as she has the economic capital to be a respected consumer instead of only a producer like Sorina with her bags and jewellery. To put it crudely: Libby can buy and thus help the French economy, Sorina can only produce but can hardly support herself financially and is therefore just "one of the Roma gypsies [the French] are tossing out of France" (ibid.: 163).

At one point, Libby decides to help Sorina to establish herself as a designer. But the phrases Libby uses have a bleak connotation: she figures Sorina will be more successful with "more promotion and perhaps a proper place to sell", and when

Sorina confesses to not even owning her own sewing machine, Libby dismisses these worries quickly: "What if I got you your own machine and your own materials, do you think you could *make more bags, even on order?*" (Ibid.: 189, emphasis added) Libby becomes a benefactor but she does so because she wants to buy Sorina's products – and so do her equally fashionable friends with high economic capital. It is only logical that a patronising demeanour must be attributed to her. Moreover, the place Sorina will work from is a designer's "Parisian facilities [which she put] at the disposal of several artists from the *banlieues* [...]. She is a fabulous patron for emerging designers." (Ibid.: 191) The designer is a true patron as she does not expect any form of commodity for her services – contrary to Libby. The fact that the facilities are described as being on the "outskirts" where "'people of colour', often disenfranchised" live (ibid.: 190) puts Sorina in the same marginalised position as the mostly black French population in the banlieues. This puts Libby, who lives in rue Saint-Blaise in the middle of the city, in the position of the powerful and hierarchically superior: firstly, *she* can make Sorina successful, secondly, it is *Libby*, who wants to establish Sorina as a designer and, thirdly, it is again *her*, who can claim rights to Sorina indirectly, as everyone inquires after Sorina *through* Libby. Although Sorina must have lived in Paris much longer than Libby, it is the latter who can successfully striate the foreign territory, which attributes colonising qualities to her. With Libby's help Sorina is (temporarily) able to turn smooth, closed-off Paris into an "econotope", which is defined as the meeting place in which "the interdependence between [the] access to space on the one hand and access to money and (purchasing) power on the other" are negotiated (Rostek 2013: 58). Sorina, as an Eastern European immigrant, is "pushed to the country's geographic [the banlieues], economic [she does not find a permanent occupation], and social margins [she is deemed as a 'threat' to Frenchness[18]]" (Rostek 2013: 58). It is therefore not surprising that Sorina is not able to establish a romantic relationship in the course of the novel as she neither commands a space like Libby does, nor is she as economically powerful as the Aboriginal woman. Recurring back to Bourdieu, John Fiske defines habitat – a form of the territory – thus:

> A habitat is a social environment in which we live: it is a product of both its position in the social space and of the practices of the social beings who inhabit it. The social space is, for Bourdieu, a multidimensional map of the social order in which the main axes are economic capital, cultural capital, education, class, and historical trajectories; in it, the material, the symbolic, and the historical are not separate categories but interactive lines of force whose

18 This notion of immigrants as threat to a nation's identity is uttered in connection with Muslims, but Sorina occupies the same marginalised position (cf. Heiss 2011: 144-145).

operations structure the macro-social order, the practices of those who inhabit different positions and moments of it, and their cultural tastes, ways of thinking, of "dispositions." (Fiske 1992: 155)

There is a distinct difference between the social environments the two women live in and instead of being a permeable heterotopia, *Paris Dreaming* constructs two different spaces that overlap at times but are not compatible. The novel suggests that the Eastern-European ethnicity is not as valuable or alluring as Libby's Aboriginality: whereas Libby is granted museum space to exhibit herself via other Indigenous artists, Sorina's goods are eventually sought after (however, by other women of a non-white background and through Libby as a mediator) but they are not connected to her heritage as often or clearly as Libby is to her exhibits. This shows that cultural capital is indeed an important marker for and of commodities. Moreover, the novel exemplifies the process of sociation by highlighting Aboriginal culture as worthy of museum space because the society deems it so, but Sorina as Eastern European is not considered exotic enough by general consensus or cultural tastes: the novel depicts the xenophobic climate of France but instead of strengthening the marginalised women equally, it elevates Libby over Sorina by the means of spaces assigned to them.

The analysis of Libby in terms of consumption shows that the spaces she uses to offer commodities – art and herself – differ greatly from Sorina's, although both, as suggested in the novel, start from a minority position, therefore showing that their habitats differ greatly although Libby makes the reader believe it to be not so. Libby can command spaces to sell and purchase objects and identities and the goods Sorina makes help to attribute even more 'minority credibility' to Libby: Sorina's products become "the fashionable political statement", but only on Libby (Heiss 2011: 245). Therefore, Libby becomes attractive to high-power men, such as "the first secretary at the Australian embassy, [...] a Blackfella." (Ibid.: 217) The secretary has realised Libby's potential both as product and as vendor, and when her assignment with the Musée ends, he recruits her to develop Indigenous arts and culture in Western Europe, with the embassy as operating basis. Libby accepts the offer and they will establish a romance, too. However, she has to work *for him*, she cannot dominate him like she could Sorina. Their spatial compatibility is achieved on the level of being able to turn previously striated spaces – 'white' France – into a place in which Indigenous culture and arts have staying power. On this level the secretary and Libby are equal, but on the level of work they will never be, but as Libby is only a product which sells (literally) she could not be happier. The novel never criticises the essentialist stereotype that men are (economically) more powerful with Libby happily submitting to the secretary's power: "Women are less likely to gain positions of high economic value because they are women. This is true of women from all social class backgrounds and relates to the system of gender hierarchies in direct relationship with material inequality." (Abbot, qtd. in Anthias 2001: 383) The narrative smoothly disguises the lack of economic value by attributing economic capital to Libby and by positioning her as the guardian angel of Sorina. The women are only able to offer their cultural capital to be consumed, turning themselves into products. In the novel, Paris has become one large store and ethnicity is a fashionable commodity.

This subchapter has shown that spaces of consumption such as the trainer shop (*About a Boy*), the book store (*The Wish List*) or IKEA (*Mr Commitment*) have their own agency. Shaped by their customers' habitus, they have become influential spatial agents, which support a striating structure. Trying to go against this structure by behaving non-compliantly with regard to consumer identities – Will is not Marcus's cooler older brother but a father figure, Lucy must not judge a book or a person by its cover or their appearance and Duffy cannot buy a wardrobe if he is not part of a "Proper Couple" – the stores refuse to bestow the desired identities on the consumers. Moreover, this consensus also influences ethnicity as depicted in *Paris Dreaming*: whereas Libby's Aboriginality is considered valuable and is put in museums to be marvelled at, Sorina's Eastern-Europeanness is regarded as a threat to the Frenchness exhibited in the novel. Spaces are very much intertwined with the habitus of the sociation they can be found in.

GOING CLUBBING AND TO PARTIES

In the introduction to *Lifestyle Shopping*, Rob Shields remarks of the quality of leisure spaces that the "performances of leisure sites include spatial practices of displacement and travel to liminal zones, thresholds of controlled and legitimated breaks from the routines of everyday, proper behaviour" (1992: 7). Although he is generally concerned with the practice of shopping as consumption, Shields's observation is just as valid for the spatial practices of clubbing and partying. These activities take place in "leisure spaces [which] are controlled *limen*: [...] they are truly a threshold, but leisure spaces are an adjunct to everyday life – not fully differentiated, not fully liminal[19]" (ibid.: 8). It is exactly this closeness to the

19 Although Shields calls leisure spaces "not fully liminal", the only proof of this can be the temporal limitation, which makes clubs (and parties) a fleeting, never entirely stable space: clubs have to close at some point and thus the(ir) spaces dissolve. However, for the time being – and also on a regular daily, weekly or even irregular basis – the club will open once more, presenting a *fully-realised space* again. This allows for regarding clubs and parties as liminal spaces.

everyday which positions leisure spaces as mediators of the common and the extraordinary: "As spaces commonly associated with fun, enjoyment and leisure, they are frequently described as an other reality or an 'otherworldly environment' (Thornton 1995: 21) whose absorbing atmosphere facilitates the distantiation from routines of everyday life; paradoxically, whilst reproducing routines quite similar to everyday contexts." (Rief 2009: 4) Spaces of leisure are integrated into the locales of the everyday but because of their playfulness, they attain a quality of spatial otherness: "Clubbing spaces and experiences are inscribed with images of transgression, freedom and liberation." (Ibid.)

This triad can be attributed to the spatial surface of clubs. The territory of the everyday is characterised by activities which do not favour playfulness, because they function according to fixed sets of rules (spatial structures) like for example a company's guidelines regulating hours of work. Outside this territory of the everyday are "zones of quests and searches for alternative social arrangements and new social statuses for individuals" (Shields 1992: 8), such as the desert, the wilderness, the forest or the sea (cf. ibid.), which in Deleuze and Guattari's *A Thousand Plateaus* are smooth spaces (see chapter 3). In spaces outside the everyday territory, agents do not need to pay heed to the structures of the striated territory but can experiment with their identities as well as their relationships with both other people and space. Within the striated territory, due to the rules made to favour and further productivity and seriousness, structures dominate the social interaction and forbid deviant behaviour, which has the potential to threaten the philistine order by flaunting it. On the other side of the border, the limen, spaces are located which are unruly and uncontrollable because of their smoothness. It is here that excessive behaviour and playfulness can roam free. By positioning the practice of going out to enjoy company and possible dancing as a night-time activity,

> the night-time is a liminal time in which the world of work is seen to lose its hold[20]. A time for and of transgression, a time for spending, a time for trying to be something the daytime may not let you be, a time for meeting people you shouldn't, for doing things your parents told you not to [...]. [Lovatt concludes that] this invitation to transgression, marginal in the Fordist city of work[,] is now central to contemporary consumerism. (Lovatt 1996: 162)

This is in accordance with Paul Chatterton and Robert Hollands, who call the "varied nightlife activities in licensed premises such as bars, pubs, nightclubs and

20 "For some, 'going out' in the city at night induces anxiety-like symptoms and uncertainty, and is something they prefer not to" writes Phil Hubbard (2007: 120) of the 'good city citizens' who surrender their space to the night-time dwellers such as youths (cf. Sparks, Girling and Loader 2001: 891-894).

music venues, as well as the streets and spaces in-between" nightscapes (2003: 4). Of course, the term includes many different practices and activities but what they have in common is that "[n]ightlife is simultaneously conflictual and transgressive, at the same time as being segregated, commodified and sanitised. It has emotional (enhanced through alcohol, drugs, dance, sex, encounter) and rational elements (planning, surveillance and policing), which are not always easy to understand and reconcile." (Ibid.) It demarcates nightscapes such as the club or the party as a liminal space in which binary or oppositional forces are at work as well as constantly at loggerheads: in a club the consumption of alcohol at the bar is part of the concept. Drunken clubbers, however, pose a safety risk and a nuisance to other (more sober) guests and therefore are likely to be evicted by the club's staff.

The location of the club in a liminal space makes use of its in-between state. This space is "betwixt and between the positions assigned and arrayed by law, custom, conventions, and ceremonial." (Turner 2008: 95) In liminal spaces there is the possibility "of homogeneity and comradeship", "of a generalized social bond", which results in community (ibid.: 96). Moreover, "the liminal process creates a safe *game-space* for the putting-into-play of values or behaviors inimical to a given power structure." (Gilead 1986: 184, emphasis added) The liminal space offers a haven to those who want to try out ideas, attitudes and identities, it can "provide a speaking position for those moving within in-between or marginal spaces to live out [...] more radical, open and hybrid identities" which ultimately aligns the liminal with the carnivalesque (Smith 2007: 138). However, the psychological energy thus created "eventually [feeds] back into the [structured, non-liminal] system. Social rules, categories, classes, and institutions are strengthened by enacting a fantasy of their weakness." (Gilead 1986: 184) What is more, the freedom to try out ideas, attitudes and identities is inevitably only a disguise as the structure of contemporary territories of leisure marks them as striated[21]. The liminal is merely a threshold, it is not yet the counterpoint to the centre, and it is not too far away from the normative majority either: when spatial agents have 'played' for a certain amount of time, they will be tame again and their energy will have been restored so that they become productive rule-abiding citizens once more. In order to return easily and frequently, the liminal spaces must not be too far away from the centre: the ecstatic crowd of clubbers may let go of their restraints at night but, like Cinderella at the ball, they

21 An example would be a festival which is supposed to tolerate all forms of celebration but there will be wardens and security and, usually, there is also a mutually-agreed upon 'contract' between the guests and the organisers as well as among the guests themselves to behave according to this contract. The contract, then, represents a form of (spatial) structure (cf. Mitchell 2000: 163).

need to return home and change their glad rags for their working attire the next morning.

The liminal space is the perfect stage for a carnival or carnivalesque behaviour. Mikhail Bakhtin derives his idea of the carnivalesque from medieval and Renaissance "carnival folk culture, the culture of the marketplace" (1994: 197) and locates it firmly in the realm away from authorities like the Catholic Church: "Carnival is not a spectacle seen by the people, they live in it, and everyone participates because its very idea embraces all the people." (Ibid.: 198) The carnivalesque "inverts hierarchies (however temporarily)" (Roberts, qtd. in Morris 1994: 250) and "always simultaneously ridicules and celebrates, crowns and decrowns, elevates and debases." (Morris 1994: 21; cf. Bakhtin 1994: 199, Bakhtin 1994a: 223) Through its most prominent forms, the grotesque and the exaggeration (cf. Bakhtin 1994: 205), the carnivalesque "marked the suspension of all hierarchical rank, privileges, norms and prohibitions." (Ibid.: 199) It is "an atmosphere of freedom, frankness, and familiarity." (Bakhtin 1994a: 223) Moreover, the carnivalesque is "a powerful set of tools for subordinated culture that constantly undermine[s] the presumptions of elite culture. The inversion of symbolic domains of 'high' and 'low', for instance, pokes fun at the establishment and irritates the agents of dominant culture." (Cresswell 1996: 78) Therefore, the carnivalesque, the grotesque and the exaggerated have been displaced "to the margins of the geographical and social order", the liminal space (Mitchell 2000: 163). It has to be acknowledged, though, that the carnivalesque has been appropriated by the dominant force, by legalising carnivals, creating inner-city spaces for festivals and clubs and – most importantly – commercialising the qualities of the carnival. People still might feel that they escape the centre by engaging in carnivalesque practices, but all the joy and excess cannot mask the conservative forces the carnival once set out to ridicule.

One can still detect carnivalesque traits in "[p]op festivals and raves [which] signify a new *temporary* rural geography of leisure. Here warehouses and large barns *outside* the city or large fields and *abandoned* aerodromes have spawned a nationwide diary of music festivals: Phoenix, Glastonbury, Reading, Chelmsford and Leeds V98" (Crouch 2004: 265, emphasis added). The highlighted characteristics of the description emphasise the liminality of the music festivals with regard to their carnivalesque behaviour while at the same time appeasing the public that these spaces of leisure are not going to be there for long periods of time and definitely not in their direct line of sight. Instead of disturbing the normative centre (for a limited time span), the carnivalesque becomes obedient to the rules that envelop the carnival, even in its liminal position. This is so because the law-abiding public does not want to see the human "body's momentary release from its social definition and control, and from the tyranny of the subject who normally inhabits it, [which] is a moment of carnivalesque freedom" (Fiske 2011: 67). The habitus of the celebrating few thus needs to be contained in a location to which temporarily the status of carnivalesque freedom is granted and whose spatial liminality shields the habitus of the majority, the hegemony, from the excess and possible spectacle.

Spectacles always aim "to produce excessive reactions [...] and at [their] most effective [they touch] highly sensitive spots in the changing nature of the human psyche by dealing directly with extremities of power" (Kershaw 2003: 592). The spectacle is a means to attract attention and to create a form of visibility even if "it had no immediate audience or happened only in the imaginary" (ibid.), linking it to the moral panic. As later examples in this subchapter will testify, it is easy to turn something into a spectacle: "The social is the audience, and the crime is the drama – the *spectacle* of deviance is thus the assurance of its own operational activity. [...] In this respect, there is an important link between deviance and its social effectivity; and the linchpin is the spectacle." (Acland 1995: 34, original emphasis) It can be said that this quality of the spectacle is a "key paradox [for] it deals with the human in inhumane ways." (Kershaw 2003: 594) However, the spectacle can also be employed by the non-normative agent to attract attention to an issue of their choice and this practice is often used by activists, protesters or artists. For both agents, normative and non-normative, the spatial dimension of the spectacle is the same: it needs a stage on which it can be performed (cf. ibid.: 601, 603). Therefore, a spectacle can be staged in the liminal space of the club and the agent can decide how far they want to take the spectacle. The club is a safe game-space because it is regulated by its policing force (the normative agents of dominant culture). It has become a regulated carnival which consequently keeps the spectacle in check.

It has to be acknowledged, though, that I distinguish between the practices of clubbing and partying, respectively between clubs and parties. Although Phil Jackson argues that "[a]ll the social interactions found in clubs can be found within common notions of what makes a good party: a welcoming friendly environment, a loosening up of social boundaries, [...] laughter, smiles, flirtation, communication and inclusivity" (2004: 88), there is actually a difference. Whereas both operate in a space that is claimed by a group of people, the human environment is stronger in its anonymity with regard to clubbing than it is with partying, a fact which will be important for the following analysis. "Clubbing is an overwhelmingly urban form of leisure and is now a major cultural industry" as Ben Malbon writes in his seminal study, fittingly entitled *Clubbing* (1999: 6). The fact that clubbing is a means to make money already hints at the economic quality clubbing has in contrast to partying, which can be achieved by a group of friends and which does not need to become a commercial enterprise. Obviously, this could actually happen and at this point the border to clubbing blurs. It also goes to show that the carnivalesque is not as strong in a club context as it can be in a party context, for the commercialisation of the former has harnessed the potential for exaggeration and the grotesque and turned it into a means to make money. The club still encompasses the idea of the party – the "party is the heart of clubbing" (Phil Jackson 2004: 88) – but the enveloping commercial frame stifles the potential for excess and aligns the club towards the centre rather than the truly unruly.

A defining feature of "[c]lubbing is [that it is] heavily dependent on musical forms (mediated through technology) and the ability of music to transform (and 'create' certain types of) space." (Malbon 1998: 271) It is no coincidence that clubbing can be subcategorised due to the many styles of music played at the venues – among others hip hop, rave or alternative music as well as an eclectic mix – but also due to the people it targets (cf. Malbon 1999: 7). Malbon even argues that "it is the ability of music (and sound more generally) to create an atmosphere (an emotionally charged space) which is of crucial importance, for it is largely this atmosphere that the clubbers consume." (Malbon 1998: 271) With regard to partying – on which a decisive study has not been conducted yet – it can be assumed that the motivation or pull factor 'music' can be downgraded if not neglected entirely. Both practices, clubbing and partying, share, however, "more traditional reasons such as letting go, *courtship* or seeking casual sex" (Chatterton and Hollands 2003: 69, emphasis added) and it is especially the romantic aspect which is of importance here. Partying usually entails a group of people who gather at a location in order to have a good time. While 'having a good time' is a motivation for clubbers too, as can be deduced from the factors socialising and atmosphere, the playful feeling of party guests can be achieved without the input of music or a specific locale in the form of a commercial venue.

I argue that the *sociality* of partying is stronger than that of clubbing because of the closeness of the partying crowd and the unanchored location of the party location[22]. Developed by Michel Maffesoli, sociality is defined as

> 'the play-form of socialization[23]'. In the framework of the aesthetic paradigm […], the play aspect is not bothered by finality, utility, practicality or what we might call 'realities', but rather it is what stylizes existence and brings out its essential characteristic. Thus, [Maffesoli believes] that the being-together is a basic given. (1996: 81)

22 The partying crowd is closer through its familiarity with the other guests. The unanchored quality is due to the fleetingness of the location as a party can be held anywhere but a club needs a specific address, a fixed location.

23 Many critics attest a strong connection of Bourdieu's concept of habitus to the practice of clubbing, such as Thornton (1995), Chatterton and Hollands (2003) and Phil Jackson (2004). However, this idea is not pursued in this particular subchapter.

Maffesoli's aspects of utility and practicality hint at commercialisation which is inherent in enterprises such as running a club. Sociality is characterised as "the *glutinum mundi* and connecting tissues of everyday interaction and cooperation" (Shields 1992a: 106) and it is "the basic everyday ways in which people relate to one another and maintain an atmosphere of normality, even in the midst of antagonisms based on gender, race, class or other social fractures" (Glennie and Thrift 1996: 225). Malbon then writes that "[t]he practices which comprise sociality consist of ways of dressing, spoken and unspoken languages, traditions and customs, myths and folklore, and the sharing of styles, knowledge and passion." (1999: 25) The closeness of partying as opposed to clubbing is visible in the "tactile or proximate forms of communality" (ibid.: 26). At parties, the guests are more likely to become friendly with one another and get to know more of the other guests than a clubber has the potential to in a club. Moreover, the fact that one speaks of clubbers at a club, but guests at a party hints at the closer affiliation of the human environment to the fixed location of the club, whereas the guests at a party merely need an invitation to gain entrance to the fleeting locale at which the party is (temporarily) held. Clubs via their management, reflected in their door policy, but also their target crowd can – but need not – be very selective as to their audience "according to sexuality, age and location" as well as "types or strands, such as mainstream, gay, student, S&M, indie, 'local'" (ibid.: 32; cf. 7) and of course the music they play. The social system which is at work at a club "allows the integration of members while ensuring that they all share the minimum of the same values." (Pronovost 1998: 17) The minimum of values is the appreciation of the music, the location or the crowd. Party guests do not tend to fall back on music, for there might be none, or they have no or entirely equal influence on it and the location can be rather unstable or spontaneously created. But party guests share the same values, which can be traced back to their sociality.

Lastly, one additional marker of studies on night-time behaviour has to be acknowledged, namely the clubbers' ages. Many studies have concurred that it is usually a younger demographic which enjoys and regularly goes clubbing (cf. Thornton 1995, Malbon 1999: 9, Chatterton and Hollands 2003): clubbing is "an integral part of many young people's consumption lives [and] encompasses a complex array of youth cultural styles, experiences, identities and spaces" (Chatterton and Hollands 2003: 68). As the characters in the novels are almost exclusively in their late twenties, early thirties, they present an age group which is on the brink of leaving this particular space of leisure behind for other, more 'respected' (and seemingly age-appropriate) spaces, like the bar or pub – which is the focus of the next subchapter. Additionally, the aspect of romance plays an important role here, as the characters deem the spaces of clubbing and partying their last chance before they are confining themselves to the home – the quintessential space of coupledom.

In the following, various forms of clubbing and partying will be discussed and analysed with regard to their romantic-spatial potential. Although the clubbing experience differs from that of a party, all spaces of leisure to be discussed expose the spaces as being able to form, affirm or challenge identities, both as motif and motive. The clubbing and partying experiences are characterised by their liminal quality of the spectacle as much as by the presence of a policing force, which punishes behaviour, considered (by them) even *too* deviant for these kinds of spaces. The examples display the (social) behaviour in commercial clubs (*Mr Commitment*, *Two to Go* and *Almost Single*) as well as in liminal spaces, which become the stage for parties and spectacles (*Almost Single*, *The Wish List* and *Piece of Cake*). The last example, *Bridget Jones's Diary*, shows what happens when the carnivalesque is included in a space belonging to the everyday, the space of the normative majority. All clubbing and partying experiences have a strong connection to romance but, in most cases, not in a good way.

After Ben Duffy has been broken up with by his girlfriend Mel, the future *Mr Commitment* intends to take his mind off the break-up and to go clubbing with his mates Dan and Charlie (cf. Gayle 2000: 147). Before even setting out to the club, both the intentions and reservations are made clear by the characters: for one night Duffy wants to forget that his girlfriend has left him, Dan wants to forget that the only woman he has ever loved is marrying someone else and Charlie that he is about to become a father. Ironically, Charlie feels too young to be a dad, but too old to go 'clubbing':

> 'I'm not going to a nightclub!' […]
> 'Nightclub?' goaded Dan. 'Have you just beamed in from 1962, Grandad? "Nightclubs", as you so quaintly call them, lost their "not daylight" prefix a long time ago. You need to get out more.'
> 'All right, then,' said Charlie, 'I am not going …' he faltered as if the word alone was making him feel nauseous … 'clubbing.' He paused to see what effect it'd had on him. 'I can't believe you made me say that. […]' (ibid.: 146-147).

He attributes the practice of clubbing clearly to a younger demographic than the one he deems himself belonging to. However, Charlie is only six years Duffy's and Dan's senior, but to him this is enough. It appears that he regards his days of being part of a liminal space and creator of spectacle as being over. His notion of youth being a marker of clubbing is not coincidental as it is usually deemed to take place in "a variety of youth cultural spaces" (Chatterton and Hollands 2003: 1). Finding clubs and therefore spaces of leisure which are 'hip' – a practice called "cool hunting" (Klein 2000: 80) – means that "young professionals go in search of the latest cool, chic, fashionable bar or club, leaving yesterday's stylish haunt in their wake. Indeed, much of the new nightlife economy is all about being 'cool'." (Chatterton and Hollands 2003: 3) The marker of age appears to be rather important to Charlie as a younger clubbing crowd would marginalise him as older in his opinion, even in a carnivalesque, presumably open-minded space. Eventually, Charlie agrees and, due to the good mood of the three friends, they even invite obnoxious, soon-to-be-married Greg to accompany them.

Deciding on a venue for the big night out follows the consideration about where it would be easiest to 'pull':

> The club, just off Leicester Square, was called in predictably kitsch fashion 'Boogie Nights'. The decision to go Seventies had been unanimous. We'd briefly considered trying to get into one of the capital's trendier clubs, but the feeling amongst the super studs of seduction (i.e. [Duffy] and Dan) was that the women in clubs like those tended to be of the choosier variety. So, for a night of guaranteed good times with the kind of girls whose expectations were as low as our own, the Seventies night was ideal. (Gayle 2000: 151)

The artificial Seventies present a safe space in which they might be able to relive their former (glorious) clubbing experiences and do not have to compete with adolescent or twenty-something males for the attention of willing female clubbers. The premise of the club itself hints at a form of the grotesque as it 're-constructs' the Seventies for a twenty-first century audience. Before the group even enters the club, the incentive for the night is made clear: although it was meant to make them forget their problems for the night, the two singles in the group want to meet women. But the way it is narrated by Duffy suggests that they do not intend to find a new girlfriend but rather a woman to spend the night with. This incentive shows that for singles, clubs present a space to get to know other people. The liminality of nightscapes such as the club means that through the carnivalesque behaviour, which furthers the loosening of everyday attitudes and boundaries, it is considered easier to meet somebody. Moreover, under the cover of liminality, the chance to engage in exaggerated behaviour like one-night-stands is regarded as higher.

By midnight, however, the friends find themselves discouraged and disgruntled on a sofa, looking on as Greg dances with a girl because he is "the only one to have spoken to a member of the opposite sex all evening." (Ibid.: 153) Not only is the sofa a traditionally domestic piece of furniture and signifies placidity, it is also a spatial testament to the men's failed attempt to make the place their own: they failed to establish a form of dominion by talking to or dancing with a woman. The playful sociality proved to be too elusive and the men are out of their depth. Duffy has no idea how to 'pull' which is "supposed to be like riding a bike – something you never forget – but somehow [he]'d managed it." (Gayle 2000: 154) When an attractive girl comes up to him and pulls him (literally) off the couch and onto the dance floor he gives in. The idea of 'super studs being in charge and active' might be ridiculed here as at least Duffy does not come across as a suave ladies' man during the course of the novel, but it also establishes the truth about clubs being an equalising space in which everyone has the chance to make the first move. However, this has to be taken with a grain of salt: when the men entered the club a drunken woman pinched Charlie and the girl 'pulling' Duffy wears a wig. Both events prove that the exaggerated behaviour of the club encourages the clubbers to engage with the opposite sex. Especially because of the alcohol and the wig the women are able to flaunt archaic gender roles of the passive female[24], for they cannot be held accountable the next day (alcohol as de-inhibitor) or relax into anonymity (by taking off the wig). With regard to alcohol as a means to loosen one's inhibitions, scholars have found that only 21.3% of British women use alcohol for that reason (cf. Jayne, Valentine and Holloway 2011: 63-65). Yet, the notion of what happens at the Seventies club suggests that the loosening of inhibitions cannot be disregarded. The club presents itself as a liminal space which operates outside prudish rules and, in contrast to a party, here it is predictably harder to find someone if they do not want to be found as there is no inherent connection to the other clubbers.

However, the night does not end as Duffy might envision it when the girl takes him to the dance floor. Not only is he slightly irritated when he realises that the girl is adamant on not letting him go and patronises him, he also feels guilty because the girl is not Mel, his ex-girlfriend (cf. Gayle 2000: 155). Duffy is not entirely sure what to do as his feelings for Mel inhibit him in a way that cannot be mended by either an attractive woman or alcohol. But the ultimate problem is the girl's age for she is really just that, a girl aged sixteen. The club's spatial quality of presenting an open space to anybody who wants to celebrate to the offered music and who passes the door can become a trap: the only reason why the men have gone to the club was the presumed easy access to women, as Duffy confesses he does not even like the music. But as actors they fail to penetrate the space of the club, which leaves them as bench-warmers on the side line, represented here by the sofa. Additionally, the anonymity of the club and the de-inhibiting qualities of alcohol result in the

---

24 This is clearly an essentialist stereotype, which, however, can be found in various magazines for both men and women. The stereotype of the active male and passive female is even addressed in the novel, when the girl puts herself in charge and tells Duffy what she wants: "Surely things haven't changed this much since I last went out on the pull? […] Surely I was the hunter and she the hunted?" (Gayle 2000: 156)

dilemma that Duffy is 'pulled' by a minor and Greg cheats on his fiancée by kissing the woman he is dancing with.

This is also the moment when the club's staff intervenes and discloses their presence as a regulating force. The moment these two transgressions are made visible – Dan hits Greg and creates a spectacle, the girl admits to her age – the perpetrators of transgression are evicted and the grotesque element is eliminated. This shows that the unruliness of clubs is but a mirage and the presence of the policing force more pronounced than the clubbers might be aware of. As a place of possible romance – or at least one-night-stands – the Seventies club proves to be total disaster. Just like the Seventies, it appears that the men's time of going to clubs is over. They can no longer relate to the spatial structures of the club and are even shocked by the possibilities the liminality of the space presents, namely cheating on partners and kissing minors. Duffy and his friends realise that they would rather spend their time in relationships and domestic spaces, hence their seizing of the couch, rather than engaging in clubbing experiences.

Clubs appear to be spaces of embarrassment for males: in Nick Earl's *Two to Go*, for one night, Philip Harris works on ship which houses a club. That night, he deems himself lucky as he kisses a girl. The problem is that when she is willing to go further than just kissing, he prematurely ejaculates. And his humiliation is far from over, because his boss-for-the-night catches him 'in a state'. He is fired that very moment and the girl mocks him by calling him 'Speedy' in front of her girlfriends: "I groan, she keeps laughing." (Earls 2003: 131) Philip behaves grotesquely by turning his body into an unruly spectacle when he cannot perform the sex act satisfactorily (for the girl). Moreover, he transgressed another boundary as he works at the club and is not supposed to engage with the customers on a sexual level.

Now, the clubbing experience of *Almost Single*'s Aisha Bhatia is considered[25]. Her friend Anushka gets invited to stylish parties on a regular basis and usually asks Aisha and Misha to accompany her. This time however, before even getting to the space of leisure, Anushka faces the dilemma that her ex-husband will also be there and she "can't bear to be around him at a social do." (Kala 2009: 46) She is afraid that the club's size does not grant her enough space so as to not meet her ex. Thus, when she arrives at the club and is informed that her ex is indeed present, she seizes the club's heterotopic potential and establishes a place within the club's space as

25 Asha Kasbekar writes that discotheques are not as popular in India as in Western countries which she attributes to "[t]he absence of a western-style club culture and draconian curfews for noise pollution" as well as to "the Indian preference for singing along with Indian film songs and remixes rather than listening or dancing to trance music" (2006: 282). But due to Western influences the Indian night-time industry in bigger cities such as Mumbai and Delhi is undergoing changes.

the ex is "at the bar, on the other side" (Kala 2009: 49): Anushka claims a seating arrangement at some other part of the club as hers, seizing temporary sovereignty.

As the night progresses and drinks are consumed in vast numbers, Anushka expands her territory to the dance floor: "She is on the dance floor, clearly high as a kite, in one of those sandwich dances, making a complete *spectacle* of herself. You know, the kind that's also termed a 'threesome on the dance floor.' The two guys are obviously enjoying themselves." (Ibid.: 53, emphasis added) The spectacle Anushka creates is three-fold: firstly, Anushka is not wearing traditional Indian clothes like a sari or salwar kameez, which signifiy "Indian's puritan identification of 'vernacular' and 'decent'" (Saldanha 2002: 343), but "a gold off-the-shoulder top, coupled with a formfitting pair of black trousers." (Kala 2009: 47) Her attire is "an eroticization of the youthful body and a challenge to traditional authority." (Saldanha 2002: 343) Anushka presents her body in a very eroticized way as to signal her unmarried status for a married Indian woman is rather unlikely to be this revealing with her clothing. This is the second issue she flaunts with her spectacle – she is a divorcee and sandwiched between two men, for everyone to see. The dancing she indulges in can be seen as an act of resistance against social 'norms' of prudery or "as an embodied statement by the clubber that they will not be dragged down by the pressures of work, the speed and isolation of the city, the chilly interpersonal relations one finds in many of the city's social spaces." (Malbon 1998: 271) Anushka, by being part of the sandwich on the dance floor, refuses to be "dragged down" by the fact that she is now a divorcee and makes her resistance and joie de vivre visible by taking two men to share her personal space on the dance floor. Alcohol as an de-inhibitor – just like in *Mr Commitment* – might have played a role in her not caring about social norms and traditions, but it is the club in whose safe liminality she is able to live out this lifestyle: "clubbing usually assumes positive notions of transgression into liminal states, in which 'other' modes of being, acting and living can be explored." (Rief 2009: 5) It is furthermore interesting that she will leave the club with her ex-husband. But, as Aisha will find out the next day, Anushka only went home with her ex to have break-up sex with him, to achieve closure (cf. Kala 2009: 57). The club's experience has enabled her to reclaim her life by concluding the relationship she had had with the man. Now, she is truly free of him and does not even need to care about his presence anymore – she no longer feels the need to establish a liminal space *within* a liminal space to be spatially separated from her ex. Anushka has achieved full closure and thus can reclaim any space, both of the everyday and of leisure, as being open to her. The last instance is that Anushka does not behave according to her age – she is a thirty-something – but behaves like youth run wild: she consumes alcohol, has a 'dance floor threesome' and takes a man with her for a one-night-stand. Anushka – and for that matter all the other clubbers – is one of the "creative agents of change" who "fully acknowledge [their perpetual] in-betweenness": "Theirs is an identity existing *in* the dialectics between impact of the West and Indian tradition, a dialectic not subsuming into a synthesis but into something intrinsically *different*" (Saldanha 2002: 345-346, original emphasis).

Almost Single depicts its characters as being constantly aware of and torn between the traditional Indian way and Westernised identities. The in-betweenness of their identity is mirrored just as it is played out in the liminality of the club in the form of the spectacle: the clubbers, entirely consisting of well-off and at least middle-class young urban professionals, celebrate themselves and the release from out-lived, archaic traditions which are still prevailing in India (cf. ibid.: 345):

As one of these spaces of identification, with its rituals and customs, its intensive sociality, its overwhelmingly sensuous and emotional ethos, its re-citing and re-fusing of musical histories, boundaries and cultures and its seeming dislocation from the binds of a life which appears increasingly uncertain, *the club situation offers clubbers opportunities to inscribe their own creativities upon a shared space, to create a space of their own making* of which they are also customers. (Malbon 1998: 280, emphasis added)

The club presents a space in which the clubbers can feel part of the global scape of youthful Singletons, and in which the local and traditional ways of their families cannot reach them – which is mostly exemplified in Aisha's mother calling her daughter on her mobile phone: she tries to keep tabs on her daughter from afar, from the rural, traditional India. But Aisha can ignore the call or keep it short, for the metropolis grants her the possibilities of a modern life, of modern India, and the club becomes a space in which to explore this further – without fearing any consequences.

Karan, Aisha's perfect partner, is also present at the club. He is introduced to Aisha although they have met before: he is a guest at Aisha's workplace, the hotel. Meeting him now outside the restricting realm of her workspace, Aisha is able to engage in the playfulness of the club. They are no longer separated by their daytime identities as guest and employee of the hotel, respectively, but are equals in the liminal space of the club. The club becomes an auspicious place in which the two can engage with each other and Karan even asks her to dance with him (cf. Kala 2009: 52). This is preceded and followed by playful banter which serves to familiarise one with the other. The conversation before the dancing features multiple sexual innuendos which mirror Anushka's dance routine on a linguistic level. Aisha's comments:

Frankly, I am shocked that I dared to say anything at all. But then I am not at work and I can't be accused of fraternizing with the guests. Giving my hair a toss and adding that extra swing to my hips, I saunter off, reveling in *the freedom of being all woman.* No demure seedha pallav sari to hold back the sex appeal tonight. (Kala 2009: 52, emphasis added)

As is the case with Anushka, the club empowers and frees the women of their traditional position and enables them to be "all woman" as opposed to "demure". The fact that Aisha turns the noun 'woman' into an adjective speaks volumes of her perception of selfhood and identity. Thus, she is able to mock Karan when he comes to ask her to dance with him: "What? Are we at a debutante ball or something? It's trance music in a lounge bar, darling[26]. Just close your eyes and move." (Ibid.) She demonstrates her superior hierarchical position by being in the know about the structure which governs the club – here, how to dance to the music played. The fact that Karan is not discouraged from then asking her to close her eyes and move *with him* shows that he is accepting of the fact that she holds power. But as with any other space of leisure, they have to leave inevitably and it is then that they have to occupy their former positions as guest and guest relations manager, leaving the open and unruly space of the club behind.

Almost Single juxtaposes the club as a space of leisure with the rooftop of Aisha's friend Misha's house, which functions as another temporary liminal locale. Misha hosts a *havan* 'party' during which a (symbolic) sacrifice is burned to purge the guests and to appease and strengthen one's karma. Directly from the outset, the religious connotations of the *havan* are omitted by eclipsing the traditional background in the form of the (almost exclusively Brahmin) teacher, the *pandit*: "you don't need a pandit, you only need to know how to start a fire." (Ibid.: 78) This attitude discloses Misha's real reason to host the *havan*: firstly, to get together with friends and to have a good time and, secondly, Misha wants to exonerate her (and her friends') bad dating experiences in order to be free for their perfect partners, which is probably not the intended reason for the spiritual ceremony. Susan Smith, following Mikhail Bakhtin, distinguishes between ritual ceremonies which "are serious, formalized, official occasions designed to be observed rather than engaged with" and the carnival, "an all-embracing public *spectacle* based on laughter, consecrated by tradition and performed by the people." (2007: 133-134, emphasis added) Misha and her friends have thus re-appropriated the ceremony and by re-designing it to cater for their needs have turned it into a carnivalesque spectacle. Although Smith already concedes that "most festive forms fall somewhere between [these two] ideal types" (ibid.: 135), it is noteworthy that Misha's version of the *havan* only shares the basic idea of burning a token to purge oneself, creating a new more personal 'ritual', which is infused with markers of 'party'. Thus, at the *havan*

26 The fact that they are listening to trance music is an indication of the Westernised practice of clubbing (cf. Kasbekar 2006: 282).

'party' a major difference to the club as space of leisure becomes evident: Misha's guests are all good friends with the host as well as with one another, exemplifying a party's heightened factor of sociality. The space they choose for the *havan*, the roof top, is not exclusively Misha's but it is not as heterotopic as the club, in which all clubbers produce a small-scale territory within the liminality of the club. When the friends are having the *havan*, they take over the space of the roof, albeit temporarily. They are able to do so because there is nobody else on the roof who contests their space – yet.

In commercial spaces of leisure there is always a policing force, usually in the form of agents directly associated with the management of the space. At the residential building, on the top of which the *havan* is held, the policing entity is a neighbour of Misha's whose "life's ambition [it is] to get Misha evicted." (Kala 2009: 79) The female neighbour is of the impression that Misha is not *bhadralok*, which is a Bengali word denoting upper castes or at least a person of impeccable manners (cf. ibid.). Misha – and her guests – do not restrict themselves to being demure (house)wives and live their lives according to their modern-Indian ideas – they, thus present a new notion of Indian "middle-classness" (Dawson Varughese 2013: 47). The club has the advantage of being a place shielded off from people who do not agree with the lifestyle of the clubbers. The roof top, then, although it is a liminal space, is hardly invisible. Ironically, the characters' lives are influenced greatly by the traditional notion of finding their perfect partners and becoming installed in a loving relationship – which is the ideal life's station of a *bhadralok* as well. It does not take long for the neighbour to see the group of friends, who are not behaving well-manneredly, and she calls the fire brigade. The fire on top of the roof signals to her the debauchery and slackness of a generation, "the *ashleel* (vulgar) youth of today." (Kala 2009: 84) The fact that the neighbour employs many Indian terms for the (in her opinion) debased 'youths' shows that she herself represents the traditional India, the one she deems "decent" (ibid.) The party becomes the spatial manifestation of the liberal, cosmopolitan and Westernised younger generations, an alternative space characterised by being experimental, local, informal, alternative/resistant and criminalised (cf. Chatterton and Hollands 2003: 5-6): "Additionally, the development of a prolonged 'post-adolescent' phase and rapidly changing labour market transitions has meant that young people are continuing to engage in youth cultural activity for much longer periods of time." (Ibid.: 68) No longer content with going out to shut-off spaces such as clubs, Misha and her friends may have created the visibility 'subconsciously-on-purpose' as they could have known that the neighbour's attention was bound to be attracted and they could have hosted the *havan* somewhere else, where they could not be disturbed.

The neighbour can be regarded as the personification of the moral panic, a form of the spectacle: "A moral panic may be defined as an episode […] of exaggerated or misdirected public concern, anxiety, fear, or anger over a perceived threat to social order." (Krinsky 2013: 1; cf. Jayne, Valentine and Holloway 2011: 20-28) Compared to Anushka creating a spectacle on the dance floor, there is a striking difference here: the spectacle is created *on* the group by somebody else and it is not contained in an enclosed space such as the club. It appears that once the spectacle is no longer spatially controlled, the person creating the spectacular event is not the one who is at the centre of the same and when the spectacle is not limited to a particular space, it becomes negatively connoted. The neighbour is able to use the moral panic because she involves other people by attaching the label "*ashleel*" to the group of friends and alarms the fire brigade. Whereas Anushka created a spectacle that shocked Aisha, it was not negatively connoted. Aisha merely had not seen her recently heart-broken friend engage in a sandwich on a dance floor and have a one-night-stand with her ex-husband. The neighbour, however, explicitly wants to create a negative spectacle in order to get rid of the liminal element that she deems threatening to her *bhadralok* sensibility. Instead of being only liminal, which means that there is still a connection to the centre, she wants to demonise the friends and thus push them further away from the centre to a completely marginalised position.

With regard to the actual practice of the *havan*, two things must be considered. To begin with, the fact that none of the guests is able to light the requisite fire points towards their inexperience to carry out traditions properly, they have to find a watchman to light it for them. It is debatable here if it also hints at a gender bias that women are unable to work with fire as it is 'dangerous', rendering them 'incapable'. What weakens the idea of the 'useless' female is the fact that they try first to do it themselves but they happily admit to themselves that they cannot light anything but cigarettes (cf. Kala 2009: 78). Moreover, they know how to solve the problem and, as far as problem-solving goes, this is just as valuable as if they had been able to light the fire themselves. The second aspect which is important is that the party guests get very drunk up on the roof. They enjoy the fact that they can get themselves inebriated outside the walls of their own flats, challenging the *bhadralok* notion of demureness. The religious aspect of the *havan* is re-appropriated due to their increasingly drunken state when they start to play Truth or Dare and all of the guests confess that they had affairs with an ex-boyfriend of Aisha's. The guests make the religious practice their own by re-fashioning it as a children's game, which, however, brings the same result of exonerating oneself of previous misdeeds with regard to men. Therefore, not having a spiritual leader present has all the guests on the same level hierarchically speaking, and none of them is above the other. This egalitarian system is also part of the playful liminality the party presents.

Yet, whereas they are equal in their own company, they still have to beware of the policing force, and before the neighbour can gain access to the roof top and discover the crossing of the borders of the spiritual, decent and moderate, they douse the fire and get rid of the alcohol (cf. ibid.: 82). There is also a reference to turning off music, which is not mentioned before as being turned on, and it can be assumed that the music is probably not of the spiritual, decent or moderate variety either. The lacuna which is created by mentioning the music only in connection to turning it off means that, for a party, the music is of lesser importance than at a club, where it is vital.

The party proves to be a very fleeting spatial concept indeed, with only one person holding the power to dissolve it whereas it took five to establish it. The club proves to be more resistant to external forces by boasting a fixed and shielded-off locale, but the fact that it is rather easy to establish a liminal space in the form of a party at any given time without much preparation proves that it is a space the characters can create in order to live out their identities and desires. The practice of the party can be considered a form of resistance:

> The practices of youth cultures can be as much about *expression* as about resistance; as much about *belonging* as excluding; as much about temporarily *forgetting* who you are as about consolidating an identity; as much about gaining *strength* to go on as about showing defiance in the face of subordination; and as much about *blurring* boundaries between people and cultures as affirming or reinforcing those boundaries. (Malbon 1999: 19, original emphasis)

Although not being young anymore, the behaviour of the party guests suggests a strong affiliation to youth cultures, which is visible in them drunkenly playing childish games. The binaries Malbon enumerates fit the group rather nicely and the practice of partying presents the perfect opportunity to revel in the bordering of space but also of identities (carefree youth as opposed to working adults) by showing that traditions are not forgotten but need to be re-appropriated in order to maintain their meaning and use in modern (Indian) times. The neighbour plays an important part in the construction of the liminal: although she spoils the *havan* eventually, she also ensures that the excess is not gaining the upper hand. She (rudely) guides the party people back from their liminality to the centre lest they go astray and cannot find back to a society of which they are a productive and important part – both as workers as well as (future) partners. Although it is not her incentive – she wants Misha to get evicted from her building – her creation of the moral panic reminds the friends that they must only inhabit liminal spaces temporarily.

In *The Wish List* a similar party is depicted which features many elements of the carnivalesque and in which the aspect of sociality becomes a spectacle. The novel is mostly about Lucinda 'Lucy' Millbanke, but she is seldom depicted without her friends. The particular night which is of interest here sees one of the men, Lucy's love interest Tom, going out with his mates with whom he also plays football. The girls feel left out as they spend almost every evening together and they talk about Tom's mates: "They all have ridiculous nicknames like Bazza or Wazza or Ferret. And they spend the whole night getting drunk and throwing beer at each other and reminiscing about bucks' night where they all got drunk and threw beer at each other." (La'Brooy 2005: 172) The carnivalesque element becomes already apparent in the names the men give themselves. These nicknames are different, if not deviant, from their Christian names, which are connoting their 'normal' life. When the women eventually 'crash' Tom's party, Meg, who is a solicitor, calls Bazza by his 'real' name Bartholomew, as she knows him due to his previous unsociable (carnivalesque) conduct when he was caught with a prostitute (cf. ibid.: 174). Bazza tries to save face in front of his mates and tells her that his name is Barry and thus tries to establish a persona that is neither Bartholomew, his philistine identity, nor Bazza, his carnivalesque persona in which he can flaunt society's rules. 'Barry' is fashioned as the mediator between the every-day 'Bartholomew' and the deviant 'Bazza'. The 'Barry' identity becomes a liminal identity, a threshold which holds the promise of becoming a spectacle as 'Bazza', but always maintaining the possibility of returning to 'Bartholomew' in case he needs to present a norm-conforming person(ality). The bar in which the men meet is therefore a space of possibilities: by turning it into a fully liminal space in which carnivalesque behaviour is possible, Barry can turn into Bazza. But even if the bar remains just a space in which the mates have a few beers, Barry is not required to embody his professional day-time identity Bartholomew. Tom, then, is rather afraid of Meg's behaviour and wants her to stop 'deflating' the identity of Barry – but he is unable to become a respectable policing force for he is a part of the location and group that are constitutive of the carnivalesque. For the remaining evening, Tom will try to limit the damage that is created by having his two circles of very different friends meet: the bar becomes a heterotopia, and the moment the two spheres of friendship gel is Tom's worst nightmare, because if the women take on his mates' behaviour, the carnivalesque loses it temporality due to women's constant presence in Tom's life. Equally, this means that when his mates lose their deviant, hyper-masculine attitude, meeting them can no longer function as the counterweight to the otherwise very feminine friends he usually socialises with.

Tom is reduced to uselessness and forced passivity because the bar is not his space to command: "it [is] a pub after all. It's not as though [the women] crashed a private party." (Ibid.: 186) He has to look on as his female friends get as drunk as his male friends and it is the infusion of alcohol that actually works as the lubricant that has the two spheres intertwine. But as the others "descended cheerfully into messy inebriation, [...] fear had rendered Tom completely sober." (Ibid.: 176) The liminality of the pub as party location is heavily dependent on the de-inhibiting qualities of beer and spirits, and because Tom does no longer participate in the practice of drinking, he becomes an outsider and 'Other' at the liminal party location. The pub is fashioned as a male space, with the men being able to live out their carnivalesque personas and desires, as expressed in the sneer by one of the women that they only get drunk to brag about having gotten drunk before. With the women now becoming masculine in that respect by getting very much drunk themselves, they take over the male practice of bragging, and because Tom is the only sober person, he becomes feminised in this process:

"I'm going to help now," Lucy whispered. She turned to Wazza. "Tom has a very large vocabulary you know," she said, stumbling slightly over the pronunciation of 'vocabulary'.
"Eh? What is that then?" asked Wazza, his brow furrowed.
"Vocabulary," Tom explained briefly. "It's Latin for penis."
A leery smile cracked open Wazza's face. "You dirty dog," he said fondly.
"I helped, didn't I, Tom?" asked Lucy [...]
"No you didn't." [...]
"Well if your 'cabulary won't impress them, what will?" slurred Lucy.
"Will you say that I slept with you and Chloe at the same time?" Tom asked hopefully.
Lucy's brow creased. "Why would I say that?"
"Because that would confirm what he's already told them," said Meg. "Bartholomew told me."
"Bazza," said Tom through gritted teeth. "His name is Bazza." (Ibid.: 177-178)

The women ruin his 'Tommo' identity in front of his mates simply by behaving non-conformingly themselves: by belittling Tom or by refusing to use the carnivalesque names. The only way Tom can maintain his hyper-masculine identity in the liminal space is by attributing a spectacular quality to his identity, hence his idea to lie about the threesome. Without the women present in this space, he could have maintained the idea of him being a ladies' man, but now, the presence of the females diminishes him and he even has to beg the women to repair his image in his stead.

At the same time, he tries to protect the women from the men by telling the latter that they "can't perve on them" and they "shouldn't be objectifying [the women]." (Ibid.: 179) But by being so overtly protective of his female friends, he patronises them by deeming himself the only one responsible – and sober – enough to know what is good for them. He tries to save the girls from embarrassing themselves with drunken behaviour or by having a one-night-stand with his "footy blokes": "If you go home with one of [the footy blokes] you'd instantly regret it but you'd still end up being talked about for the rest of the year." (Ibid.: 180) The women, however, do not see that as problem: for them, the party is a liminal space too, which means that they are allowed to cross the boundaries of decency and socially approved behaviour and create a spectacle for the night. Tom is not used to seeing his female friends engaging in this kind of behaviour. Usually, he is the one who brings the stereotypically male qualities of not caring, not being romantic and not getting too attached into his circle of female friends. Now, he has to realise that the liminality of the party exposes the presumed respectability of the females as normative veneers and the women tap into their inner careless and casual-sex loving selves, fuelled by the presence of alcohol and equally willing men. It is not that they invent a new side to them, but the carnivalesque quality of the party does not chastise them for 'deviant' behaviour. The inadequate policing force Tom, trying to represent the society outside the liminality of the party, is ridiculed and dismissed as being too prudish, rendering him once again useless:

"Are you drinking *mineral water*?" [Meg asks Tom.]
Bazza moved his chair back a foot or so in case Tom was contagious.
"Look, considering that I've been running around after you lot [the women; C.L.] all night I'm surprised I've had time to drink anything," Tom flared.
"We never asked you to run around after us. Have a drink and stop being such a misery guts." (La'Brooy 2005: 183, original emphasis)

The females have become even more powerful than the present males, Tom's mates: on the one hand, Tom only cares about the 'well-being' of the women and thwarts the men's attempts to flirt with and bed the women, and on the other hand he is constantly put down by the women in front of his mates. This party presents a variety in which the women infiltrate the space the men had established at the pub and take it over. Although the pub is a public space, which Lucy also acknowledges, the party they crash had tendencies to be private. It consisted of a closed group of people who have a strong personal connection – previous adventures and football – and it is no coincidence that none of the other patrons of the pub join their conversations. It is only when the women arrive that the rather close-knit structure of the place within the heterotopia of the pub is compromised and rearranged in order to accommodate the women and turn Tom into an outsider in the same instance. The women's takeover of the pub is in stark opposition to essentialist notions of female pub-goers: "the pub is a male environment where girls may go with their boyfriend [sic] but do not feel confident to go on their own or even in a group of girls" (Lee, qtd. in Chatterton and Hollands 2003: 149). The males' territory is compromised – and so is their assumed dominance – and the rest of the novel does not grant Tom another outing with his mates because the boys' night out has turned into a total nightmare for Tom.

The following example presents another pub party. In *Piece of Cake*, Minal Sharma is invited by her neighbour Ali, who is a hip radio disc jockey, to "this party [...], one of those usual radio affairs. It'll be loud and noisy and terribly boring. Come with me?" (Kaushal 2004: 108) However, in contrast to *The Wish List*, the chicklit heroine does not feel at home at the party because she cannot get into the spirit of the carnivalesque.

The location the party is held at mirrors the fact that the night is not going to progress as Minal has hoped, because

> [i]t seemed to be some kind of pub; small and undistinguished, save for the small blue neon sign above heavy dark doors. Hard to make out anything in the dark and the building ended abruptly in a dense patch of trees. [...] I could distinguish a few blue shapes and silhouettes as we neared the entrance, then someone opened the door and a momentary splash of bright light from within illuminated the tangle of motorcycles around which they stood. Up close I could see that there was a fair crowd. Largely male, though with some it was hard to tell. Some had long hair, some were smoking and some were pierced in surprising places, but for the most part they were just lounging about with harmless swaggers and loud opinions, like guys without dates at college rock shows. (Ibid.: 113-114)

Already from the outside, Minal feels like the odd woman out; this is clearly not her 'scene' as she tells Ali: "Quite a young crowd!" (Kaushal 2004: 114) It is especially the long hair which is another indicator how the evening is going to end. On the way to the location Ali has told her that he used to have long hair, which is therefore linked to "wild parties [and] experimenting" (ibid.: 111). The long hair is the bodily marker for a crowd of people who are not yet ready for a relationship potentially resulting in getting married and settling down. The club reflects this idea spatially: the building is rather shady and ends "abruptly" in the woods. This suggests that the men frequenting the club have no clear idea where they want to go in life, they lack direction and sight ("Hard to make out anything in the dark") – at least this is what Minal thinks. The building ending in the woods hints at the fact that one could get lost in the dark if one had no idea where to go, another indicator as to the directionless youth to which Minal does not want to belong.

Minal eventually finds out that Ali is twenty-four to her twenty-nine, leaves the pub immediately and refuses to speak to him for quite a while. The unease she has felt even before entering the location has now been manifested in his age and Minal cannot but break up with him. From now on, her whole argumentation why she broke up with Ali is based on the fact that he is five years her junior:

> "Ali, I'm twenty-nine!"
> "You told me that already."

"You have to understand; you're way too young for me."
"I don't feel too young right now."
"I don't mean right now. I mean later. For ever. I mean for a relationship that's good for a lifetime. […] Ali, you can't put attraction above everything else! *There are a lot of things that matter; career, marriage, long-term-plans.* You won't understand; you're still a kid." (Kaushal 2004.: 164-165, emphasis added)

The triad Minal seeks in a partner is what she thinks the men standing in front of the pub must lack: no career but college, no marriage because no dates, no long-term plans because everything is rather in the dark. The light that illuminates the men in front of the pub can be interpreted as a foreshadowing of Minal's visit to the location because it is here that she will find out about Ali's age and jumps to the conclusions about his state of mind with regard to marriage. Minal assumes the position of the regulating force in this leisure space: instead of thinking only of the moment because all carnivalesque experiences and spaces are temporary, her thoughts are directed towards the time *after* the party. She does not want a younger man, she needs someone who is presentable as her husband because the social pressure on her increases with age, hence her phrase "I want to get married, I *need* to get married." (Ibid.: 165, original emphasis; cf. ibid. 129) Ali as a (toy) boy is not considered appropriate in normative spaces, whereas the age difference is very unlikely to have posed to be a problem at the space. After all, Ali has invited her to the liminal experience and thus he represents the attitude of the party guests. The fact that he is fine to engage with an older woman in the space suggests that the space and the crowd within the same are just as okay with it.

When Minal and Ali finally enter the pub, the feeling that this is not exactly the night Minal has hoped for does not subside. Her description of the party connotes bacchanalian mayhem: the place is

packed, smoky, and roof-rattling loud. […] Men with glazed eyes pressed in multiple layers around bar stools, trying to attract the attention of the harassed bartender, while women congregated like satellites around them. TV screens […] played multiple channels; a montage of soundless cricket, MTV and what looked like some teen horror movie in split screen. (Ibid.: 114)

Whereas the men outside were mostly without girlfriends or female company, inside the women behave like satellites orbiting around the men, their earth. The image this transports is that of female dependency. The men, however, do not orientate themselves towards the females but the bartender, who can supply them with drinks. This constellation will be repeated later by Minal and her fiancé Sunil: he expects Minal to give up her job and to be there for him alone (satellite) while he charms and smarms over his bosses to further his career (drinks from the bartender) (see chapter 5). Minal finds the behaviour of the pub's patrons strange and when Sunil tries to introduce the same male-oriented organisation of a relationship into their 'romance' later, Minal does not comply. It can be traced back to the feelings of alienation she has experienced at the party and she is not willing to feel this strange her whole (married) life instead of on temporally-restricted occasions. The TV screens at the bar reflect Minal's experience of the party: she feels like an outsider, an 'Other', who can only look on to the whole 'tableau': a performance which is staged regularly but in which Minal is not able to participate. The TV shows three different formats, none of which is particularly endearing to her and both the split screen and the sound turned to mute renders the whole viewing experience dissatisfying. It is a club decidedly directed at youth to which Minal does not count herself.

While being at the pub, Minal gets to talk to two kinds of people, who make her feel both irritated and uncomfortable: one is a middle-aged 'voice artist', who is trying to seduce Minal and is less than subtle about it, and the other kind is comprised of Ali's co-workers. All of these people behave in a way that suggests that the location and the crowd are the 'toast of town', and Minal 'others' herself by asking a transpiring man why he is wearing a leather jacket inside the hot pub and by commenting negatively on the loud music. Whereas the voice artist's approach merely shows that Ali leaves her alone long enough to become the target of a womaniser, the group of co-workers exemplifies the superficiality of the radio station's staff. They are very concerned with being not only up-to-date but up-to-the-moment. They flaunt their pop-culture knowledge every chance they get. This marks them as indeed superficial and at the same time it shuts Minal out from their group of radio people because she has not "been to a disco for almost a year", which has her interlocutor gaping at her for a moment (ibid.: 120).

The experience at the pub clearly positions Minal on the margins of the people there: she is not part of the radio-funky group, and from her behaviour one can deduce that she does not want to be either. There is no sociality involved here and the location becomes a hostile environment. The fact that Minal has not set foot in a club in almost a year hints at topo-aversion of youthful spaces, not as strong as topophobia but clearly not topophilia. It represents a life(style) Minal does not think she can happily claim any longer, being almost thirty years old. The location is fashioned as a space of superficial youth flaunting their aloofness, which is the reason why Minal – after finding out about Ali's age – escapes from the place: her Cinderella does not leave a glass slipper and is reluctant to ever visit the ball again.

The last example is taken from *Bridget Jones's Diary*, and presents yet another variety of the party, namely the dinner party. Although Bridget attends numerous parties or functions (a book launch, her own birthday party, Mark Darcy's celebration of his parents' wedding anniversary), it is this one party which stands out: the Smug Marrieds dinner. It is characterised by its guests creating the Singleton as spectacle within the 'normative' space of married people. In a second step, the analysis of the Smug Marrieds dinner will be compared to a dinner within the Singleton sphere to show that they indeed share specific traits and that a transgression between the spaces is punished.

Bridget's feelings towards the Smug Marrieds dinner already foreshadow what is going to happen: "Such occasions always reduce my ego to [the] size of [a] snail" (Fielding 1998: 39). The difference to the other parties in this chapter is that here, the party is not held at a liminal space but at the centre of the non-carnivalesque, a married couples' home: almost all guests are married and are far from any liminality that has characterised the previous parties and clubs. By being the only female single at the dinner table, Bridget is swiftly 'othered' by the married guests, and they 'reason' that it must be indeed Bridget's fault that she is single. The men who talk down to her put the pressure solely on *her* and stress that, surely, she cannot want to be one of the "single girls over thirty. Fine physical specimens. Can't get a chap." (Ibid.: 41) These opinions cast the woman as the active part that has to search for a man to marry as well as the reason that a union is yet to be achieved because she has not tried hard enough in her endeavours. The other single present at the dinner party is male, but he is never included in the ridicule by the Smug Marrieds. There seems to be a strict division between the 'othered' single female and the (socially) invisible male single.

The Smug Marrieds fashion Bridget as a spectacle: not only is she the centre of attention as well as the topic of their conversations, by talking about her and down to her, the Smug Marrieds re-affirm their function as policing force. They consider it their duty to 'normal' society, to which they consider themselves to belong, to 'give' Bridget good advice and more incentive (by showing her marital bliss) so that she will be able to form a union. Moreover, as Bridget is the only female single guest, the Smug Marrieds are safe from any repercussions as she is in *their* territory: they consider themselves to be in the position to say to Bridget what they want. The Singleton is no position of power in the space of the everyday. The practice employed by the Smug Marrieds is similar to that of the neighbour in *Almost Single*: by taking the spectacle out of the liminal space, it becomes a moral panic and because nobody defends Bridget the novel suggests that the centre, the normative couples, are afraid of the Singleton which then results in a form of the moral panic.

In *Bridget Jones's Dairy*, the carnivalesque is abused because as it usually ridicules the ruling authorities through exaggeration and the grotesque the Smug Marrieds re-appropriate the liminal means and apply them to the single female: they exaggerate Bridget's inability to find a husband and thus render her person grotesque – for there *must* be a reason why she is not married yet despite being 'physically fine'. Bridget herself assumes that Smug Marrieds create such a carnivalesque spectacle on her because singles are not like them in their unruly (sexual) behaviour (cf. ibid.: 40). Smug Marrieds even appear to be afraid to go back to the position of being single as Magda's visit to Bridget's Singleton space shows when she found out her husband has had an affair (see chapter 4) – it is the core of their (moral) panic. Therefore, the only way forward is to demonise the Singleton status and thus to affirm their own married position. That the Smug Marrieds are able to treat Bridget in this fashion can be attributed to a problem of the carnivalesque itself, because it "often demonized the weaker, not the stronger groups." (Rief 2009: 9; cf. Stallybrass and White 1986: 19) The space of the dinner party becomes a stage, a freak show, and Bridget is the main attraction. By venturing into the heart of socially established 'normality', she is no longer protected by her friends or her own leisure space (of bars). Staging such a dinner at home grants the hosts more power than their guests and it is conspicuous that the hosts of this dinner do not help Bridget but remain silent and watch as the other Smug Marrieds deflate Bridget, which in itself seems to be the entertainment program accompanying the food.

Some eight months later, Bridget hosts a dinner party herself. The major difference is that none of the guests is married and most are single, and the location of this dinner is in Bridget's realm, her Singleton space. However, a spectacle is created again by Bridget as she is unable to present her guests with a "proper" meal but serves almost inedible food (cf. Fielding 1998: 271). Although this mishap is expected of Bridget and is not commented upon negatively by her guests, it exposes an important trait of the dinner party: only smugly married people are successful at it. At Magda's dinner everything went fine and the fact that Bridget tries to copy the dinner party in her Singleton space but fails shows that this practice of the party is not meant to be engaged in by non-married people. Singletons can only be successful at parties if they embrace the liminality of their spaces as well as of their identities. Yet when they try to take on practices not meant to be performed in their territory, a spectacle will be created and it attaches the carnivalesque to the dinner, in this case the grotesque food (cf. ibid.). At the Smug Marrieds' dinner, the married guests produce the carnivalesque by inviting Bridget and by insulting her in the manner of a freak show, it is a fully controlled activity. At her own party, Bridget is helpless in the face of the culinary disaster despite all her efforts and expenses and she has no choice but to offer the grotesque meal to her friends so that they become witnesses to her failure. One can even suggest that by eating the grotesque food, they become grotesque themselves.

Furthermore, the dinner party betrays Bridget's reason for giving it in the first place: she wants to be part of the realm of the Smug Marrieds. Inviting her perfect partner Mark Darcy to this event was meant to display her qualities as hostess, homemaker and potential Smug Married. Her invitation to Mark suggests that Bridget does not want to be a single any longer and wants to move away from her Singleton space. This affirms the taunts of the Smug Marrieds about her not having tried hard enough in the past. The dinner was a first foray into the territory of coupledom but it has proven to be harder to achieve than Bridget thought possible. It is somewhat telling that Mark and her friends help to save the dinner so that they can at least consume some food: it shows that the Singleton (dinner) space has a similar close-knit community like the Smug Marrieds. The practice of the adult dinner itself, however, shows that it is not meant to be performed by Singletons.

The practices of clubbing and partying are part of a liminal experience. The spaces of leisure that the characters engage in invite carnivalesque behaviour such as the consumption of alcohol as de-inhibitor and the adoption of (grotesque) identities. Especially the latter is depicted in the novels *The Wish List* with the 'mates' assuming laddish identities to break free from their everyday or philistine personas and in *Almost Single*, the characters are allowed to flaunt social norms by engaging in behaviour which is 'unruly': the characters create spectacles. However, especially men seem to be uneasy when their temporary break-out of social norms is called attention to and when they see women not behaving in a way that they are used to. The novels pretend to depict carnivalesque behaviour but ultimately enforce essentialist notions of how the respective sexes should behave. But *Piece of Cake* has shown that women can be as uncomfortable with the freedom liminal spaces of leisure present as men. It appears that all of the characters are aware that the practices of clubbing and partying are limited to a specific time and place: when the time of the party or at the club is over they have to leave the space, which dissolves, and return to their everyday lives. Yet, this is exactly what they want: the characters of Duffy in *Mr Commitment*, Minal in *Piece of Cake* and Bridget in *Bridget Jones's Diary* crave to be part of the normative centre. Their stay at liminal places fortifies the characters' longing for coupledom, which is the quintessential concept of the centre in chick- and ladlit. Being in liminal spaces becomes a form of epiphany that they want to belong, and because the spaces are only temporary the chick- and ladlit protagonists can search for a way into the normative centre very soon. They are helped in their endeavour to be part of a couple and thus the centre by the various policing forces: these can come in the form of the club's staff (*Mr Commitment, Two to Go*) or philistine characters (*The Wish List, Almost Single, Bridget Jones's Diary*) but also in the form of the protagonists themselves, who realise that they do not want to be in a liminal space but in a domestic one with a partner that is like them (*Piece of Cake, Mr Commitment*). Thus, when the policing forces of the various spaces interfere or the liminality of the place dissolves, the heroines and heroes of chick- and ladlit, respectively, are more than willing to return to their everyday lives and their search for their perfect partners.

GOING FOR DINNER AND DRINKS

This last subchapter will now focus on another space of leisure and considers "[b]ars, pubs, taverns, lounges, whatever the name[27]" (Chrzan 2013: x). They share some traits with spaces of consumption as well as clubbing and partying spaces, as the analyses will testify to: bars, cafés and restaurants are not only places for the consumption of food and beverages, nor are they only spaces just outside the realm of the everyday – in these particular geographies "people gather […] to talk, to relax, to make new friends and *find lovers*." (Ibid., emphasis added) That these ideas about restaurants, bars and cafés are very optimistic can be deduced from the analyses of various chick- and ladlit novels. Following a brief introduction into the history of bars or cafés and their function as third places, this subchapter will consider how these spaces of leisure help, further or even prevent (romantic) relationships in chick- and ladlit.

It has been noted that "the best way to find out about a […] community is to understand how people use bars." (Ibid.) Having established how closely-linked communities and the genres of chick- and ladlit are (see chapter 4), bars are some of most frequented spaces of leisure for young urban professionals: they go there for a quick drink after work, to relax during their free time or to spend the night there in the company of their friends. The pub, bar or café can be turned into a dislocated living room, or living room-away-from-home, in which the patrons feel 'at home'. Scholarly texts "discuss pubs as social centres for communities" with food and beverages "as social glue" (Bell and Valentine 2006: 15; cf. Forster and Möhring 2009: 2). This practice suggests that there is an important connection between the consumption of food and sociality, which is mostly played out in social settings such as the pub, the café or the bar: "Bars enhance communities by providing a place where people can gather informally, share news, make plans and create new alliances." (Chrzan 2013: x)

---

27 I will not adhere to a strict distinction between the various forms of bars, pubs or taverns, but will regard them on an equal level. However, it should be noted that there are distinctions between the pub, the inn, the alehouse, the gin palace or the tavern with regard to the clientele they serve. For an introduction to the history of the predecessors of the 'modern' pub, see Smith (1983): 367-369, Earnshaw (2000): 5-14, Brandwood, Davison and Slaughter (2005): 1-25, Jennings (2007).

This is not a new development as people have used bars as a (spatial) node in their territory before: during the Industrial Revolution, for example, pubs were a "centre for conviviality, political discussion, and [through] the rituals of drinking [...] men affirmed in shared communion a collective identity." (Adler 1991: 391; cf. Jennings 2007: 14-16, 109, Chrzan 2013: 4, 45) Until the 1950s, pubs were principally a male-dominated sphere which meant "no women, no children and no meals just working men who enjoyed a pint." (Delplanque 2009) However, critics have found that "women were also in pubs, and in greater numbers than is sometimes believed." (Jennings 2007: 112) Nowadays, people can enjoy a family outing to pubs and even have a Sunday roast there if they want. It is no longer solely the working man's home-away-from-home, where they are in the company of 'mates'.

But the heightened sociality of especially the pub as a space of leisure was not regarded entirely positive. After all, if people spend most of their day at work and go to the pub directly afterwards, they are hardly at their anchor-point of the first order, their home. However, some critics, such as James Kneale dismiss the claim of "pub and home as rivals", stating that in the Victorian age "these [places] were not strictly separate spheres" (2001: 45). They fashion the pub as "an oasis. It offers warmth, friendship, jokes, gossip, food, pint-pot philosophy and a pleasant release from the daily grind [...]: a home from home available to everyone." (Earnshaw 2000: 1) As Jennings himself terms the pub "an extremely heterogeneous institution" (2007: 15), this book does not settle for pubs only and thus excluding other forms of social hubs in which the sociality, consumption of drinks and food, as well as the possibility of meeting that 'special someone' are on the menu. The notions of pub, bar or restaurant shall be subsumed under one category as they function on the same spatial level of the institution and structure. The spaces of leisure might differ in appearance but they share similar features. Eating and drinking places are "[a]t once open and secluded, significantly *located in between* public and private space" (Forster and Möhring 2009: 2, emphasis added). And this points in the direction of spaces of leisure such as bars or cafés as living rooms-away-from-home.

Historically, the pub was not the only space dedicated to creating sociality (cf. Chatterton and Hollands 2003: 180, Brandwood, Davison and Slaughter 2005: 65), with the coffee-houses in the later seventeenth century also being associated with "social activity, [...] lively discussion, the dissemination of news and ideas[...]. Coffee-houses were meeting places for both business and pleasure: though exclusively male, they were otherwise egalitarian and sometimes described as 'the penny universities'." (Burnett 2004: 4) Just as the pub has now become a destination for the whole family, the "coffee-house was [...] another strand in the development of both the modern café and the restaurant" (ibid.: 5).

In India, places to consume drinks – both alcoholic and non-alcoholic – have undergone a transformation which is most prominent following independence from

Great Britain in 1947: with regard to alcoholic drinks, the state prohibited the selling of them for reasons both religious – Hindus and Muslims do not favour the inebriation alcohol can achieve – and reverential – Gandhi was strongly opposed to alcohol "because he saw it as a direct road to ruin for millions of poor workers in cities and the villages" (Kasbekar 2006: 281). Heightened consumerism as well as the end of censorious decades are regarded as the main reasons why alcohol has escaped its stigma: "The loosening of restrictions on alcohol in most states has led to a burst of investments in bars in the major towns and cities. At first, many of these bars tried to go for volume and were open to all and sundry. Now many have increasingly turned their attention to specific segments of society." (Ibid.) Especially the many metropolitan dwellers have money and time to spend and thus spaces of leisure flourish, which has even led to the phenomenon that bars and cafés are 'attached' to hotels or jewellery shops (cf. ibid.: 283).

What connects the development of Indian to British or Australian spaces of leisure, is that they represent a third anchor-point, next to the home and the workplace, which points towards a concept by Ray Oldenburg, the third place: "The third place is a generic designation for a great variety of public places that host the regular, voluntary, informal, and happily anticipated gatherings of individuals beyond the realms of home and work." (Oldenburg 1989: 16) To be even more specific, it is "a neutral space that is neither home (first place) nor work (second place) and where the rules and hierarchies governing those locations are mediated by communal norms negotiated by local agents." (Chrzan 2013: 46) It is a place "in which people relax in good company and do so on a regular basis" (Oldenburg 2001: 2). Oldenburg's concept mirrors Homi Bhabha's *Third Space* (1994), but third places are less liminal than third spaces: bars, pubs or restaurants are located nearer to the centre and even though liminal qualities have been attributed to third places (cf. Chrzan 2013: 98), they cannot be located too far away from the centre. Their decidedly commercial 'nature' and the fact that they are open both during the day and at night construct them as less liminal than clubs, which are (traditionally) part of the night-time economy and are not always open every day of the week. Moreover, there is no door policy involved which opens third places to (almost) everybody. To Oldenburg, adjectives such as "warm" and "friendly" make all the difference (Oldenburg 2001: 3, 4; cf. Chrzan 2013: 45). The first example is going to further the understanding of Oldenburg's concept: In *Bridget Jones's Diary* the protagonists claim bars as their living room-away-from-home and thus appropriate the third place into a more homely territory. Following this introduction, the remaining chapter will be concerned with the advantages and liabilities bars, pubs and restaurants pose for romances and love.

"State of emergency. Jude just rang up from her portable phone in flood of tears [...]. Her boyfriend, [...], had chucked her for asking him if he wanted to come on holiday with her. […] I immediately called Sharon and an emergency summit has been scheduled for 6.30 in Café Rouge." (Fielding 1998: 19) The bar in which the women convene becomes a place of consolation and (female) Singleton bonding: opposed to the space of Smug Marrieds dinner party, the bar becomes a stronghold of singles in the public sphere. Here, they are able to talk about their problems which are usually men-related, echoing Oldenburg's idea that third places are first and foremost about conversation (cf. 1989: 26-32). The friends comment on each other's various troubles they have faced during the day, opening up the dichotomy between the laborious and strenuous day and the relaxing and friendship-related night. Sharon, after hearing Jude's problems, launches into an attack on the slyness of men but it is exactly then that the living room-away-from-home's privacy becomes brittle: Bridget and Jude try to shut their friend up because "there is nothing so unattractive to a man as strident feminism." (Fielding 1998: 20) In chapter 4, the living room-away-from-home was defined as granting the urban family identity, stimulation and security, the latter expressed in the quality of the urban family members being able to say what is on their minds. However, there is one exception: as long as the topics talked about only concern the present urban family they will say anything, but the moment the other patrons of the heterotopic bar could be (romantically) affected this invisible barrier becomes too fragile: to the women in *Bridget Jones's Diary*, the bar is still a space in which they might meet an eligible bachelor and by being associated with ranting Sharon, they deem their chances decreasing. The fact that Jude is still mourning her ex-boyfriend and Bridget is pining for her boss does not to matter here – both are single in the public opinion as they do not have a partner and thus the bar can be a potential meeting place. Interestingly enough, the bar appears to take on the qualities of Speaker's Corner for Sharon as she is usually ranting in spaces of leisure about the shortcomings of men with regard to relationships (cf. ibid.: 68-69, 77). Sharon's rants draw attention to the women which they usually would have not attracted for they participated in the unspoken law of not paying any attention to one's fellow citizens (cf. Hubbard 2007: 123-124). Bridget and Jude become uneasy for they do not want to be associated with feminist ideas which might get stuck to them in an unbecoming way since they frequent the bar very often.

It is at bars like Café Rouge and especially in this company that the women are able to flaunt 'societal rules' and be unruly. But, as Bridget's mother warns: "There's nothing worse than a woman drunk, darling" (Fielding 1998: 47) – echoing eighteenth- and nineteenth-century claims that "[t]he wider issue of women drinking was always a cause of concern, as they were seen as the mothers of the nation's future workers and soldiers." (Jennings 2007: 112) Letting go of problems and feeling comfortable or *gezellig*, which indicates "a cozy, friendly, open atmosphere that creates a sense of belonging and connection to other people" (Chrzan

2013: 45), this feeling is only ever realised when in the company of friends. Bridget does not drink overtly much when she goes out with Daniel or Mark. Her behaviour shows that drinking, "more than most other leisure activities, derives its meaning from its *social context and setting*." (Barrows and Room 1991: 7, emphasis added) Moreover, "[t]he essentially social nature of drinking is indicated by the fact that solitary drinking is commonly considered to be a problematic symptom [and that the] timing, frequency, and, above all, *company of drinkers* can tell us a great deal about sociability and shared values." (Ibid., emphasis added) The consumption of alcohol is strictly reserved for a *gezellig* atmosphere with friends, although the amount of entries of Bridget's which are related to her alcohol intake suggests that she does drink on her own too. But it is the social component and the *gezelligheid* or sociability of the location which equipoises the close-to-alcoholism intake[28] and the normal spatial practice of drinking when out with friends. Alcohol functions as a bond between the friends, they use it as a lubricant for their thoughts, desires and anxieties – not that they would need much prompting with regard to drinking alcoholic beverages – as well as a major component on which their friendship is founded (cf. Fielding 1998: 90, 106-107) Bridget is even considered boring by her friends when she is vice-free, i.e. not drinking. Thus, when she manages to control her alcohol intake in the company of male suitors, she attaches another layer to the already heterotopic bar, a space for dates. Bridget wants to present herself as a suitable, well-behaved woman to the men and therefore pays heed to her mother's warning.

Drinking outside the home, which is sociable as opposed to sad when it is done at home without company, can be traced back to the eighteenth century: consuming gin and frequenting locations to consume it was "especially popular with single, working women, enjoying the benefits of rising real wages in the capital, the cheapness of the dram itself and the relative freedom of the metropolis over the rural areas from which many of them had come." (Jennings 2007: 112-113; cf. Warner and Ivis 2000) Today, in the company of men, there is too much at stake, hence Bridget and Jude's attempts at silencing ranting Sharon: single women may drink (too much) when amongst themselves, but when there is the possibility of a relationship, the spatial practice of the relaxing consumption of alcohol, which is strongly connected to bars and pubs, must be abandoned in order to appear "poised and cool [and] confident" (Fielding 1998: 2-3). This is supported by Bridget herself, "[f]eeling v. pleased with self [as well as] empowered" (ibid.: 77), when she is still with her friends, but once home regrets being single and wishes to be in a relation-

28 Bridget's alcohol intake is generally slightly above the 'normal' amount of alcohol the NHS suggests for females (cf. drinkaware.co.uk 2015) and she is likely to drink at any given day of the week.

ship (Fielding 1998: 77). The third place Café Rouge becomes a sphere for a proud and independent single female, whereas the home, the first place, is that of coupledom, and a boyfriend's absence turns it into a space of the unhappy and lonely single female. It is no coincidence that the wish for a boyfriend will win over the (presumed) independent and 'proud' Singleton identity: Bridget can get drunk merrily with her friends, but wants to return to a loving boyfriend any time. Moreover, the fact that the home is the most important anchor-point in one's life (see chapter 4) signifies that the identities assumed in other spaces – especially time-limited spaces of leisure – are not as definitive or even lasting as the characters try to make others and themselves believe.

Spaces of leisure such as the pub or the restaurant become places which are constitutive of a collective. The characters in *Bridget Jones's Diary* create a new term for their status: they are not singles – for that is rather pathetic in their eyes – but Singletons, a new form of singles in a metropolitan setting at the end of the twentieth century and beginning of the twenty-first. The Singleton identity is not only contrasted with the 'pathetic' singles but also with the Smug Marrieds – as the dinner with them has shown. In *Bridget Jones's Diary*, the Singleton identity is under constant threat from all sides, especially the media, creating a moral panic about the problems of people choosing to live as singles (cf. Klinenberg 2012). But creating a new term for their status and attaching a form of pride to it, which is abandoned at the next possible opportunity, it characterises the Singleton identity as a form of hypocrisy: the Singletons are only outwardly happy and independent, but really crave to be part of the normative centre of society by being in a stable relationship. They even go so far as to create a substitute family, the urban family, to compensate for the lack of a biological family of their own (see chapter 4).

After this introduction and quick revision of the connection between singles and bars as living rooms-away-from-home, the next examples depict the bar as a meeting place for perfect partners. Four novels display such a feature, but only in *Avoiding Mr Right*, *Five Point Someone* and *About a Boy* is the romance actually started. The fourth novel, *Dinner for Two*, depicts the re-establishing of a connection after the ladlit protagonist and his wife have split up due to a misunderstanding. However, the successful result of their visits to spaces of leisure can be attributed to the neutrality and thus possibilities of these spaces.

In *Avoiding Mr Right*, chicklit heroine Peta Tully has relocated to Melbourne to pursue her career in the Indigenous Arts. One night, the job finds her attending an eco-poetry slam. The slam is staged in a Melbourne pub, which is located in a hotel. Many clubs and pubs are located in hotels in Australia, converting previous structures and adding new layers to the already rather heterotopic hotels. Therefore, it is not surprising that the people present at the pub are a mixed group of poets, who dress without exception in black only, the attendants of the slam and the normal pub crowd whose "local hotel" it is (Heiss 2008: 121). When Peta goes to the bar to get some drinks, a man promptly flirts with her. The suitor, Mike, does so quite unabashedly and Peta is torn between finding his one-liners annoying and being flattered by his incessant adulation.

Due to the openness of the hotel as a space, she becomes available to people. She decides to meet law enforcer Mike again under the pretext of 'educating' Mike and to heighten his sensitivity towards the issues of Aboriginal peoples, as she considers the police enemies of Aboriginal causes. The neutrality of spaces of leisure (cf. Earnshaw 2000: 1) grants spatial agents to use bars, restaurants or cafés for various purposes: not only is Peta able to have drinks with her friends like the women in *Bridget Jones's Diary*, she can also use these spaces to engage with similar-minded people at the slam or to use the spaces as a form of school in which an extracurricular lesson can be taught.

The pub or restaurant can be regarded as the starting point for processes which are not only spatial but also ideological. Shortly before her job in Melbourne is finished, she meets Mike again for dinner – but cannot go through with it. Just as she has sensitised policeman Mike to Aboriginal issues, so has he helped her to overcome her prejudices regarding the police. Their exchange of ideas has brought about a change in Peta and she realises that she has developed feelings for Mike. The spaces of leisure have ceased to be neutral for the sole reason that Mike is in them. His presence overshadows the neutrality – Peta cannot be 'just friends' with him any longer. He has taken over and relocated the space closer to her heart, meaning that she cannot pretend that their meetings will end soon and that she can live as if nothing ever happened the next day. Spaces of leisure, such as the pub or the restaurant, are spaces in which to start relationships when one is unsure where it might take one. The moment one's feelings become more serious, the agent has to abolish the spaces' neutrality or ambiguity: Peta realises that Mike is not an affectionate puppy following her every whim – whom she can command to read novels or force to reconsider his ideas – but that Mike has penetrated the liminal space in the direction of her heart and (be)longing. Peta did not take into consideration that a space of leisure permits the exchange of ideas in both directions and by frequently engaging with Mike in these spaces she had to be influenced, too. Had they conducted their 'lessons' in her home, for example, Peta would have been in a superior position and would have been more likely to have fended off Mike's influence. It has to be said, though, that she does not change her attitude towards the police in general but only towards Mike personally.

Considering that Peta's actual boyfriend is geographically on the periphery – in Sydney to her being in Melbourne – the distance to the boyfriend is juxtaposed with the proximity of Mike. Peta has felt that her boyfriend does no longer fit into the life she wants for herself before she left for Melbourne and the spatial distance that she created puts the boyfriend and the occasional visits the two pay to each other in a marginal position which is fading into oblivion. Through his sheer persistence and willingness to change, the cop has managed to leave his previously distant position and becomes her new partner. In the novel's epilogue Peta reflects on the fact that her now ex-boyfriend always had a very locational quality by being 'there' or not, whereas Mike manages to bridge the actual geographical location by appealing to her mind and heart. Their love story shows that spatial compatibility can also be found on a meta-level, by *being there* not only geographically, which will inevitably affect the decisions on the actual spatial level.

The next example shows that bars, cafés and restaurants can be used as neutral contact zones when one's relationship is in danger. Whereas Peta used the neutrality to further her agenda, Hari Kumar and his girlfriend Neha (*Five Point Someone*) use a leisure space to escape the (spatial) domination of Neha's father. She is the daughter of one of Hari's professors at college (IIT) and meeting her is a delicate affair, which is even likened to the plot of a Bollywood movie: "The girl's father damn near killed the boy who flirted with his hot daughter, but ultimately the hero's love and lust prevailed." (Bhagat 2008: 37) As they all live on campus and Neha's father is a prominent figure on the same, she suggests a place outside the realm and power of her father, an ice-cream parlour. The parlour becomes a neutral space, as the two are forbidden to meet – or date – anywhere else, which even leads to them arriving and leaving separately so as not arouse any suspicion[29] (cf. ibid.: 43). Whereas Neha is wary and guarded outside the leisure space, "inside the [...] ice-cream parlour she was a different person." (Ibid.) She is characterised as being rather traditional, which is evident both in her behaviour in the public sphere and her traditional attire, but the ice-cream parlour frees her from the oppressive power of her father, who striates every other space in which the two can come into contact with each other. Hierarchically, Hari and Neha are not on the same level as her father, who represents a meso-level hybrid of agent (as the person), institution (as professor at the IIT) and structure (as the head of a traditional Indian family). The restricted access to Neha makes her even more attractive to Hari, who spends all of his other time with his two best male friends.

29 A similar 'secret' meeting is employed in *Oops! 'I' Fell in Love!* by protagonist Kanav and his perfect partner Tanya: "Kashmere Gate [a train station in New Delhi; C.L.] was chosen primarily due to two reasons. First, it was quite distant from Tanya's home so we could avoid rendezvous with anyone familiar, plus there was a McDonalds in the station premises." (Snehanshu 2012: 131) Two people meeting for a romantic tryst in India appears to arouse suspicion by the policing forces. In this case both Tanya's and Kanav's families and friends and the general Indian public, who seems to be suspicious of public displays of love.

But getting to know Neha, he wants to see her more and be closer to her, which is why he starts to reduce the safety radius Neha has carefully established. With every new step during their romance, Hari gets closer to her spatially and through his actions, he also gets closer to her heart – because, although she is shocked when he takes the initiative to get closer, she almost always encourages him to be more assertive: "And next time, don't be this shy IIT boy" (ibid.: 47). But for over a year, Hari does not escape the status and marginalised position of being a friend: "First, I was just a friend. Then I was a good friend, then a friend who was special, then really-really good and special or some crap. […] Her dad made her promise that she would never have a boyfriend, and she wanted to keep it." (Ibid.: 85-86) He realises he has to leave the zone which Neha has established with him at the border to her father's territory and Hari thus chooses a specific space to break down her barrier of reluctance and commitment, the roof of one of the buildings of the IIT (cf. ibid.: 106). The roof top has the qualities of being "so near […], yet so far" (ibid.: 111): it is both located within her father's realm of power (so near), but above his line of sight or conjecture (so far). Hari's next coup will then be to come to her house in the middle of the night to be the first to wish her a happy birthday, for which he will receive his first kiss (cf. ibid.: 131). The development of their relationship, which will lead to them being together openly – even in front of her father, had to start at a neutral space and the café is a very good place: it sponsors anonymity as many people will patronise it and it provides a cover story (just meeting a friend to have an ice cream) and it can be turned into a locale to establish the only possible meeting place for the two lovers.

Just as in *Avoiding Mr Right*, however, the spaces of leisure are only very temporal and have to be left at some point. This is also the moment where *Five Point Someone*'s love story becomes tainted: Hari is constantly driven by sexual urges, especially as he frequently gazes at Neha's body and mouth. He wishes she was more like one of the Bollywood heroines, who are "eager to please" (ibid.: 37). When she finally gives in to Hari on her birthday, he comments on this development as follows: "Maybe it was the flower [he gave her as present], or just the whole excitement of breaking in, or maybe even that *she had finally grown up*." (Ibid., emphasis added) The first two reasons, Hari suggests, are connected to Hari himself and his ideas to seduce her (flowers and being the first to congratulate her), the last, however, points towards her transformation from girl to woman – she turns nineteen – and that she is now ready to choose a partner. Hari likes Neha's respectable appearance but increasingly wishes she would shed her "goody-goody prof's daughter" image (cf. ibid.: 114). The neutral space of the ice-cream parlour therefore not only presents a safe space from the eyes of Neha's strict father but it also provides safety from the hands and libido of the young men the IIT is full of.

Before *About a Boy*'s Will Freeman finds a new hunting ground in the 'help' group of Single Parents Alone Together, he meets Angie, a single mother, at a café. Thinking it is the same woman he overheard inquiring after a record at his 'local' record shop, he uses this information as an entrée into a conversation with her. However, she appears not to know what he is talking about: "She looked at him, smiled nervously and glanced across at the waiter, probably calculating how long it would take for the waiter to hurl himself across the room and wrestle Will to the floor." (Hornby 1998: 26) Just like in *Avoiding Mr Right*, the café they are in functions as a neutral space in which the approach from a stranger might not be uncommon, but it also has the benefit of being too public for anything harmful to happen. Angie can be assured of a policing force in the shape of the waiter and because she and Will do not know each other, the conversation can be terminated without any real harm done: "They returned to their newspapers, but [Angie] kept breaking into a smile and looking across at him." (Ibid.)

Establishing a territory is achieved by erecting a newspaper front to hide behind, but gazes and looks as well as smiles serve to establish bridges between the patrons of the café, and Will realises that Angie's smiles and looks do not chastise him for having approached her. On the contrary, they have piqued her interest. Because Will has already made a first advance into a conversation, Angie now is able to use the same topic to return to the conversation and it can be regarded as an 'admission ticket': no matter how random or preposterous the entrée, it has created a common feature between two strangers as they can now talk about the record shop, the record she has never bought and the conversational starter in general. Will "had never before attempted to start a relationship cold in this way, but by the time they had finished their second cappuccino he had a phone number and a date for dinner." (Ibid.) Initiating a conversation is important but then it is up to affection and attraction how the conversation continues. Will Freeman could be one amongst many but his unusual start – by asking about a record Angie never bought – establishes him as more interesting than other potential interlocutors, who might have tried to start a conversation with Angie on more obvious topics. What *About a Boy* testifies to is a sense of subdued spectacle: the spaces of leisure – bars, cafés as well as the clubs or parties – invite carnivalesque behaviour which is not 'everyday'. Only here can people approach others and do not have to fear excruciating consequences. Even if Angie had never spoken to Will again, it would have only meant a slight chink in his confidence's armour. Additionally, as Will has never used such a direct approach before, his behaviour can be put down to the open structure of the café in which the two are located. Being engrossed in their respective papers, they establish separate realms, micro territories, within the larger space of the café but these are very permeable. The waiter functions as constant traveller between the various realms and proves that these realms are not strongholds like one's home. Thus, realising that an external force can come into the direct vicinity of the person one wants to talk to can lead to another person gathering their courage and make a foray into this person's realm in order to start a conversation and a possible relationship. Although this meeting bears resemblances to Will's first meeting with Rachel (see chapter 4), the latter has occurred in a private home. This immediately changes the parameters from playfulness (space of leisure) to potential for a shared future (home).

However, the perviousness of the realms established in public spaces of leisure can also be used to break off a relationship as one is less likely to 'make a scene in public': Angie breaks up with Will after six weeks of coupledom. The space they occupy at that moment, a table at a restaurant Angie chose as location, is as fleeting as at any other time, meaning that it will not burden the participants of the break-up by leaving a stain on their home or other, more important places. They do not establish an enduring territory at the restaurant and have to confront it all the time because the restaurant is not an emotionally charged landmark. Additionally, the public space in which they are located at this particular point suggests that neither of the two has the advantage over the space – not like being in somebody's home and having 'home advantage'. Spaces of leisure, as has been proven before, have a liminal quality and this feature lends itself well to actions one does not particularly want to extend over a longer period of time. The neutrality of the place the break-up is staged in is hardly compromised. Just like at any other event, it will regain its glossy surface once the (ex-)couple in question has left the premises.

Even for a recently separated couple like Dave Harding and his wife Izzy (*Dinner for Two*) the incorruptibility of the neutral spaces of leisure holds: when Dave and Izzy split up, because he has kept his juvenile daughter Nicola a secret from her, they keep meeting for dinner "once a week to talk about what [they are] going to do." (Gayle 2002: 336) Starting with the name of the various restaurants and the day of the week, the narrative organises the conversations into starter, main course and dessert. As their relationship is no longer characterised by a shared household, Dave and Izzy update each other in neutral spaces, which they cannot personalise permanently as they did with their flat. It is conspicuous that they do not patronise the same restaurant twice, it seems as if they want to prevent any anchoring from happening. In the first three weeks they cannot even bring themselves to order dessert, which changes in the last, fourth week: "For the first time we have dessert and share a *crème brûlée* and I feel suddenly that there is renewed hope between us." (Ibid.: 348) The act of sharing the dessert signifies the couple's rekindled familiarity – "food and drink [are used] as metaphors for the character of a relationship" (Farb and Armelagos 1980: 103) – and it is no coincidence that Dave becomes hopeful. Additionally, the *crème brûlée* has special properties which cannot be neglected here. In order to consume this sweet dessert, one needs to break and penetrate the flambéed surface. Dave and Izzy have to work hard and, most importantly, together to become a functional couple again and in order to achieve this they have to get to the bottom of their problem, which is the illegitimate daughter Dave has. Previously, Izzy refused to be told about Dave's daughter and did not want Dave to see Nicola either. Coincidentally, Dave also meets Nicola in public spaces to get to know her[30], thus doubling the approach to the two most cherished women in his life. In the third week, Izzy finally opens up and asks Dave about her, even wants to see a picture of Nicola, which lays the foundation for the sharing of the dessert in the final fourth week. The story ends with Izzy arranging to meet Dave again for another fifth dinner at a restaurant – but this time she has invited his daughter too:

> "I decided it was time," says Izzy, looking into my eyes, "for all this to stop. I was tired of feeling angry, tired of feeling sorry for myself, tired of missing you. And I wanted to meet Nicola. So I called her last week [...]. And that went so well I asked her to join us for dinner tonight – and she said yes, and then we both kind of came up with the idea of meeting early without you so we could have another little chat on our own without you getting in the way." [...] Izzy kisses me again and then we sit down at our table, the waiter brings over the menus, opens a bottle of wine and together we begin our very first dinner for three. (Gayle 2002: 363-364)

Izzy called Nicola after she and Dave had shared the *crème brûlée*, which brought down the reservations she had with regard to a family Dave has outside wedlock. Sharing a meal together signifies the beginning of a new chapter in their lives, which are no longer characterised by dinners for two: it becomes the first meal they will have as a family, albeit a blended one because Nicola still has a mother. Yet, it shows that the neutrality of the space of leisure of the restaurant can present a safe space in which problems can be solved, no matter how long it takes, and it helps to unite families and rekindle love relationships[31]. Yet, the fact that the blended family meets in a temporary space of leisure shows that Nicola is not fully accepted into the marriage of Dave and Izzy. It might still take a while before she is invited into their home and truly into their lives.

30 Nicola was conceived during a holiday fling. Dave never knew he had a daughter until the girl contacted him.

31 A similar notion of the dinner as constitutive moment for family can be found in *Ethan Grout* and *The True Story of Butterfish*. In the latter, the main protagonist and his estranged brother bond over the course of many meals that are first consumed in the public sphere and finally in the brother's home – from bistros to home-cooked food.

The last group of experiences in bars is characterised by problems that can ensue in spaces of leisure. These problems can vary and they exemplify that a relationship cannot succeed if one does not act according to the (normative) standards of chick- and ladlit. In *Brand New Friend*, Rob goes on a bloke-date, which incidentally is quite successful. But, because it depicts a homoerotic 'romance', his 'relationship' with another man is not pursued as it goes against the notion of the heterosexual couple that must be at the centre of chick- and ladlit. Similarly, if one 'cheats' during dates and tries to rekindle a love which is no longer existing, the endeavour must fail inevitably as Lara in *Twenties Girl* has to realise. The last example, a bar in *My Legendary Girlfriend*, even prevents its protagonist Will from starting a relationship. Not having overcome his feelings for his ex-girlfriend, the loneliness of his home is transported to his visit to a pub and prevents him both from making it his local and from establishing interpersonal relationships in this space.

Rob Brooks (*Brand New Friend*) is feeling rather lonely, despite the fact that he has a girlfriend. For her and their relationship he relocated to Manchester, leaving all his London mates behind. Back in London, he had a local at which he and his mates met regularly (cf. Gayle 2005: 9-12). It was the quintessential third place, in which Rob felt happy, safe and welcome. In Manchester, on the other hand, he has not found a mate with whom he can establish another local or indeed third place. But Rob has a plan how to establish contact at a pub: although he gave up smoking years ago, he now puts a cigarette "to his lips and bravely scanned the bar. This is it, he thought, *my way in*. A cigarette and nothing to light it with." (Ibid.: 75, emphasis added) Rob is intent on using what is known as "friendship homophily" (cf. Kobus 2003: 41-42) because by using smoking as his entry into a friendship, he is able to establish a connection without much effort or interaction – smoking is a visible sign and in this case doubles as a marker of similarity as well as a conversation starter. Sociologists have found "that individuals who are similar to each other are most likely to choose each other as mates and are most likely to be successful in the relationships." (Kerckhoff and Davis 1962: 295-296) Although this is mainly applied to monogamous romantic relationships, the idea can be employed in finding a friend just as well: Rob speculates on the sociability of smokers, and that they are more likely to engage in a conversation – especially as he has a veritable reason to talk to them as he needs a lighter – and the openness of the pub suggests a high success rate. His idea of the consensus value is very much linked to spatial compatibility as smokers forming a community in public spaces[32] functions according to

32 With the advent of anti-smoking laws, the community of the smokers is even more visible outside pubs and bars as they are united by their 'Otherness' of being smokers.

the same principles as lasting love relationships. And it is exactly this idea, linking the forming of friendships and love relationships, which has Rob stumble and abort his attempt.

Because his plan actually works: he spots a man who – just like Rob – is sitting alone, drinks a pint, reads a book and "[a]ll in all, [...] looks like [Rob's] type of guy." (Gayle 2005: 80) As with the cigarette, the reading and casual attire speak to Rob and this is when he feels he is already crossing a border from a potential friendship into something entirely different: Rob becomes uneasy because he approaches the man in a similar vein as he would a potential love interest, as, for example, Mike did with Peta in *Avoiding Mr Right*. Rob does indeed ask the man for a light, but the situation becomes homoerotic when the man confesses he does not have a lighter, but offers Rob to light his cigarette with the end of the man's. This method of lighting a cigarette can be read in a way that strongly suggests two phallic symbols touching each other's tips and Rob chastises himself thus: "Come on, idiot! Say something! Anything! Don't just stand there staring like you're in love with him." (Ibid.: 81) The man is apparently not interested in a conversation as he returns to his book when Rob is lighting his cigarette, deeming the situation normal – after all he suggested the method of lighting Rob's cigarette this way – and by returning to his book he is on the safe side with regard to the homoeroticism of the situation. Ironically, Rob seems to have anticipated his unease before even setting out, for he created a playlist on his iPod, entitled "How Gay Is This?" (Ibid.). The actual realisation that the situation can indeed be construed as (at least) ambiguous, however, still takes him by surprise.

Later in the novel, Rob actually encounters the same 'problem' again, when he accepts his girlfriend's idea of going on a "bloke-date" (ibid.: 189). Rob's girlfriend has posted an advert in the local newspaper and three men have answered it. Dismissing the first two as unsuitable – Rob has attempted to meet them at a bar but felt even more uneasy than in the situation with the man with the cigarette, which is chronologically later than the first two "bloke-dates" – he accepts the third man's proposal to meet at a bar for a pint. Rob meets Andy and they get along quite well:

> he'd felt so relaxed with Andy that for a few moments he had forgotten he wasn't talking to his London friends. But Andy wasn't an old friend he had known for over ten years: they had met through an advert and until an hour and a half ago had been complete strangers. (Ibid.: 192)

The two men share the common feature of feeling 'mate-lonely' and this has paved the way for them to enter a situation which could be read in many ways, including those Rob has been uneasy with when he approached the 'cigarette man'.

Rob and Andy talk freely and extensively about subjects like music, movies, football or even Luton, but when the evening draws to a close, neither man wants to go and leave the pub

> because they didn't want to break the spell. They knew that once outside the restaurant [to which they have relocated after the pub] everything would go weird. [...] What was more, things might be worse now: at the beginning of the evening they hadn't known each other and therefore couldn't like or dislike each other. Now they weren't strangers: they were two guys who liked each other – with added tension. [...] If Andy *had* been a girl and this *had* been a date Rob knew exactly what he would have done next – he would have tried to have kissed her. [...] But Andy was a bloke. And despite Rob's gay-o-meter being in the red all evening, neither of them were that way inclined. So the big question in his mind was: How do two heterosexual men make the first step towards friendship? (Ibid: 194-195, original emphasis)

The pub and later the restaurant function on the same level, catenated by the animated conversation between Rob and Andy, namely of being a safe space for the two to get to know each other. The spaces of leisure present themselves as locales in which the two men can talk freely and achieve (spatial) compatibility. With the 'cigarette man', two features had doomed the operation from the outset: first of all, Rob felt highly uneasy when approaching a man. Contrary to the essentialist stereotype of men wanting to be the hunters in relationships, they are just as vulnerable as women when it comes to matters of the heart. When meeting Andy, Rob calms himself by telling himself "that he wasn't meeting Andy for himself but for Ashley and [he] felt better." (Ibid.: 189) He goes on a "bloke-date" to please his girlfriend, which has the added benefit of strengthening his heterosexual identity. Secondly, the 'cigarette man' appeared not to be interested in having a conversation with Rob as he merely extended his cigarette for Rob to light his own with but immediately resorted to reading his book, establishing a solitary territory within the space of the pub.

Andy, on the other hand, *wants* to meet Rob. This diffuses the awkwardness of the situation as Rob was on his own wanting to engage the 'cigarette man' in a conversation, whereas Andy even takes "the lead in their conversational début." (Ibid.: 191) Being constantly aware of the homoeroticism of the situation – two men engaging intimately over drinks and dinner – Rob is nevertheless happy with the situation because he feels a connection to Andy. Under the cover of leisure spaces, they can engage in a "bloke-date" that appears to have no visible markers to distinguish it from a romantic date. Thus, when the date comes to a close, Rob only knows how he would have ended the situation if Andy had been a woman. Proving that the whole situation is indeed as close to a date as possible, the rules how to end an evening like this with *another man* escape Rob.

Suddenly, Rob saw that he and Andy had been doomed before they met because men in their thirties *did not* make friends like this. [...] There was no talk of seeing each other again, of calling or exchanging emails, just a brief but firm handshake, a warm smile and a sort of half-nod in acknowledgement that, great as the evening had been, they weren't going to see each other again. (Gayle 2005: 195-196, original emphasis)

The space of leisure presents Rob with the possibility of being somebody different for one night – Rob going on a date with another man and feeling good about it, even pondering (albeit rather briefly and hypothetically) to kiss him[33]. But as the night has to end, so must the liminal quality of a homoerotic date for heterosexual males dissipate. Rob and Andy have searched for comfort in the presence of another male, and within the space of the pub and restaurant as well as under the comforting cloak of night, the two men have found the perfect relationship[34]. The fact that they never repeat their "bloke-date" is telling, for a second date would have steered them firmly in a romantic and thus homoerotic direction. By leaving it at one (bloke-) date, they can always claim (carnivalesque) immunity concerning the intention of their nightly experience. A repetition of the date could have been construed as intent and no longer as just 'blokey'.

Turning from the good date that must never be repeated to the relationship that must not be rekindled, Lara Lington still pines for her ex-boyfriend Josh, who ended their relationship two months before the events of Sophie Kinsella's 'ghost story' *Twenties Girl* set in. Due to a supernatural twist of the story, Lara can see the ghost of her recently deceased great-aunt Sadie, who possesses the gift of making

33 Ladlit positions their protagonists as strictly heterosexual even though moments of homoeroticism do occur. In *Taking Off*, Ash is kissed by a gay man and he is "a little freaked out that [he is] not really freaked out." (Howard 2008: 164) It is the first kiss by another human being in a long time and he reasons that he quite likes the fact that somebody is willing to kiss him and deems it a good sign for future encounters with women.

34 Regarding the three perfect relationships of Rob, they can be categorised thus: Andy is only a one-night-stand, his girlfriend Ashley is the one to stay and whom Rob will marry and have at least one child with, but there is also Jo, the female mate, who functions as a combination of Andy and Ashley. Jo will become the little sister Rob never had and who, when she develops feelings for Rob, will inevitably be substituted by Ashley and Rob's daughter. The daughter and Jo function on the same level because Rob wants to protect both and his love is freed from any erotic imperatives. That Jo does not feel the same way is punished by the novel because she has to leave Rob.

people do her bidding. It is through Sadie that Lara sees a chance of getting Josh back. The ensuing 'second' relationship between Lara and Josh is depicted via three dates, two of which are at the restaurant they used to go named Bistro Martin. To Lara, Bistro Martin is anything but a neutral place, it is connected strongly to nostalgia, making the place a container for memories of happier times now gone by. Contrary to the home, which can also display qualities of previous lives which influence or even infiltrate the present (see chapter 4), the bar as a space of leisure is not under the home dweller's jurisdiction and thus the memories need to be constantly rejuvenated by going there. This is the reason why Lara is furious with Josh – and to an extent also with the fleetingness and smoothness of the Bistro – when he does not take Lara on a date there but another woman:

> I still can't believe Josh is taking this girl to Bistro Martin. How can he? It's *our* place. We had our first date there, for God's sake. He's totally betraying all our memories. It's as if our whole relationship is an Etch-a-Sketch and he's deliberately shaking it clean and drawing a new picture, and forgetting about the old, much better and more interesting picture which used to be there. (Kinsella 2010: 146, original emphasis)

Lara decides to go to the Bistro and spy on Josh and the woman he has a date with. When they arrive she is livid when she realises his attire: "How can he be doing this? Does he have no heart? He's wearing *my* shirt in *our* place." (Ibid.: 149, original emphasis) She is clearly possessive of both Josh and the place, thus intertwining the two entities by catenating them through Lara and Josh's shared past[35]. That this connecting device, their past, does no longer hold is irrelevant to her. In Lara's opinion, the past is still present, expressed in the ghostly form of memories, which only signify history[36]. She claims Josh and the bar by referring to bygone events (their first date) and previous actions (Lara giving Josh the shirt). It is never clear whether Josh attached as much meaning to Bistro Martin (or the shirt)

35 This is reminiscent of Will Self's idea as depicted in his short fiction "Big Dome" (see chapter 3): a city is composed of the memories of previous actions or emotions and occasionally, one cannot but realise that former ideas about a place have (been) significantly changed. This is a striking example of a synchronic heterotopia, in which many notions about the same place are in conflict at the same time, as well as a diachronic heterotopia: it used to be Lara and Josh's 'place' but now – as it has always been actually – it is more neutral and enables Josh to bring a new woman here.

36 The whole plot is an elaborate allegory of the (literally) haunting past, with the story of Sadie's ghost doubling Lara's romantic past as well as another minor plot including an old painting.

as Lara does, but it is apparent that to him the restaurant is as smooth and thus neutral a place as any other café or bar he could have had his date in. Yet, Lara cannot accept this forward-oriented approach to life and interferes in Josh's date by using Sadie's power to make Josh confess why he ended their relationship. The outcome of this is twofold: on the one hand, Josh's date leaves Josh and the restaurant because he appears "obsessed" with his ex-girlfriend (Kinsella 2010: 155), which is both untrue and more applicable to Lara, and, on the other hand, Lara uses this intelligence to re-model herself and to ask Josh on a date with her 'new' self.

This second date is not staged at Bistro Martin, but Lara deliberately 'chances' upon Josh in front of his company's building and they go to a pub under the (false) premise that it is just a quick drink. The pub functions as the setting for a repeat of a first date. Lara "agree[s] with everything he says, and the time just whizzes by" and she concludes that "[w]e look like a happy couple. I know, because I keep checking out our reflection in the mirror." (Ibid.: 232) The idea of the mirror is quite striking here, as it attaches an unreal quality to the 'date': it is a retake of the original first date, mirroring it but being not the real thing at the same time. It is only a *reflection* of a happy couple, not an *actual* happy couple. This is further stressed when Lara needs to call upon Sadie to 'convince' Josh that he is still in love with Lara. The novel's heroine has become so obsessed with being with Josh that she fails to see that their time has clearly ended. Lara wants to prove to her friends and family that she and Josh are meant to be together, presenting the image of a happy couple – her true feelings, or indeed any of his, are rendered irrelevant by her (cf. ibid.: 312). This is also the reason why they did not go to Bistro Martin for their second 'first' date: the Bistro is solely for the happy times or memories, and the pub presents an unscheduled lapse in their biography. The moment Lara, with Sadie's help, has changed Josh's mind – literally – they have their next date at Bistro Martin again, because now they can continue as if they had never split up. The neutrality of the pub poses a mirror image of the restaurant: not quite the real thing, but close enough in its properties.

In order to take their 'relationship' up again, they meet at Bistro Martin, which has the added benefit, Lara reasons, of exorcising all memories of the date with the other woman. In an ironic twist, Lara will exorcise Josh not only of the other woman but of herself too, as well as annihilate her own obsession that she and Josh are meant to be together. Lara realises that their love is over and that no place can save their relationship. Tellingly, they never even make it to ordering any food, which can be considered as a negative companion piece to the *crème brûlée* in *Dinner for Two*. She realises that "this is all a mistake" and points at the table (ibid.: 319). The table stands metonymically for both the whole Bistro and their relationship: Lara realises that she tries to resurrect something dead, which is impossible – even Sadie's ghost will eventually disappear. Lara has to acknowledge that both she and Josh had to change so much in order to make the relationship work that none of their original features and character traits remained. Lara comes to terms with the reality that Josh – and consequentially a re-animated Bistro Martin as a signifier of their 'love' – is but a fantasy. Spaces of leisure are fleeting and once gone it is hard to re-establish them, which – it appears – will always come at a price, namely of changing the parameters that originally made the place so special. By attaching a whole emotional construct like a love relationship to a space of leisure such as a bar or restaurant is impossible, its neutrality does not support this weight. Bars and restaurants can only present a starting or meeting point but never a territory in which to establish constant dominion. Although urban families can erect a living room-away-from-home, it is still a fragile construct and not fit for romantic dependability. Spaces of leisure are spaces with many possibilities – yet only for a limited time.

The last example explores a ladlit character's failed attempt to striate a pub in order to make it a third place and thus to establish a relationship of any kind with the human environment within the (leisure) space. In *My Legendary Girlfriend*, Will Kelly feels very lonely at home and decides that he needs "to go out to the pub where [he] can mix with real people" (Gayle 1999: 207). He discovered a suitable pub only the other day "while trying to find out how many off-licences in the area sold Marlboro Lights" (ibid.: 208). Will's practice of wayfinding has actually shown him the possibilities his direct neighbourhood has to offer. At home, there are only memories of his ex-girlfriend, which haunt and taunt him, but at the pub, he reasons, he must be very likely to find a connection to others which might exorcise his life from the demons of the past.

Just as he recently relocated from another town to London, so did workers move from all places to big cities during the Industrial Revolution. Feeling dislocated, the new metropolitan citizens frequented pubs because "the community of the tavern [or pub or bar] offered to the urban migrant a haven in an otherwise anonymous urban environment" (Adler 1991: 391), a "social centre" (Burnett 2004: 37). Will mirrors this practice and thinks that the benefits of the community-creating pub must still work more than a century later. And as Will has no actual living room, the pub can become the space his flat lacks, by outsourcing the living room to "a centre of warmth, light and sociability for the urban poor, [...] a magnet for the disoriented newcomer and disgruntled regular alike[37]." (Bailey 1978: 10; cf. Earnshaw 2000: 1) At least this is what Will has in mind when he sets out to patronise a pub called 'the Angel'.

37 Bailey actually writes on the connection between Victorian culture and the public house, yet what he establishes still holds true today.

But even before he enters the pub, doubts start to appear that he might be considered a 'loser': "I'd never felt the need to go to a pub on my own before. There had always been someone to go for a drink with" (Gayle 1999: 208). Moreover, Will wonders what to do – once inside and without any friend to keep him company – and decides to go with 'second-hand experiences' from (American) movies, expecting a flirty chat with the barmaid and an "allotted quota of wanton women." (Ibid.) That this expectation is misguided dawns on him very quickly as the barmaid does not engage in flirty talk, or any other personal kind of conversation. The character of the barmaid is reduced to her mere function, establishing her as part of the human environment and highlighting Will's alienation as he does not get close to anybody at the pub. His confessional, internal monologue depicts the barmaid in two rather contrasting ways. In her first incarnation, she is elevated to a saviour of his bleak existence – "I want to be served by her, I decided. *I need to be served by her*." (Ibid.: 209, emphasis added) The barmaid is not even his type as he confesses when he first sees her (cf. ibid.), but as she is the first woman he actually encounters in the flesh in London, she becomes an easy target for all the emotions he previously had to project on incorporeal presences such as his ex-girlfriend, about whom he constantly reminisces, and his 'girlfriend', with whom he only ever talked on the phone. The second version of the barmaid is constructed shortly before Will leaves the pub: "I made ready to leave, casting a last glance in Archway Kim Wilde's direction that said: 'This is your last chance, babe. I'm walking out that door now and I ain't ever coming back." (Ibid.: 215) Will re-constructs her as inferior by making himself overtly desirable. Through his earlier encounter with her, he is aware that she is unlikely to give him the light of day. He saves his ego through elevating himself because the phrasing of Will's suggests that she could have counted herself lucky to have him. Additionally, his wording is reminiscent of the stereotype of the solitary, manly cowboy in American western movies, who is passing through many towns but does not settle down. Via movies, Will creates a "[milieu] of escape, fantasy, and distraction" (Harvey 1992: 302) as he is unsure how to act in such a novel situation without the help of faux 'second-hand experiences'. That he connects the American cowboy in a saloon to his visit to an English pub is telling insofar as it means that Will is entirely out of his depth. Having no experiences of his own to tap into, he takes the manipulated images of the American West and applies them to Archway. It is not surprising that the visit to the pub must fail if it is overshadowed by such images. The pub, with its supposedly open spatial structure, meaning that everyone has an equal chance of making it one's local and engage with other patrons, could have been a good starting point for Will to practise his social or flirting skills on a woman who (stereotypically) should be used to engaging with strangers, but, as with everything else, Will is more talking than acting.

The barmaid's rejection already foreshadows what is to happen to Will during his entire stay at the Angel (before he leaves, never to come back): he is the odd man out, and the much-touted "community" of the pub is but a concept.

I looked for a seat well away from the bar because I was scared I might 'say' something in a casual glance, offensive enough to get my head kicked in. I ended up sitting next to the fruit machine and the door to the Ladies'. I settled myself down and searched for my fags and then sighed as I realised I'd forgotten them. I stared at my solitary pint, the head of which was already beginning to go flat. For the first time in over a year I felt like crying. [...]
The table in front of me was bare. No cigarette butts, empty glasses or crisp packets. It would be obvious to everyone in the pub that I was here *Alone*. I didn't even have the energy to go into the pretence of being early for a date. It was written all over my face anyway: 'It's my birthday tomorrow. I have no friends. I hate my job. I can't get over my ex-girlfriend. *Shun me. For I am a latter-day leper*. (Gayle 1999: 211-212, emphasis added)

To Will, this pub experience is the lowest point in his life (cf. ibid.: 212). The most disappointing and frustrating part of his visit to the pub appears to be the fact that he is there on his own, emphasised by the capitalised "Alone". He associates the solitary visitor to a pub with a "latter-day leper", which is not helped by the fact that the barmaid only engages with him on the most basic level – asking him what kind of drink he wants. Being alone at a pub is quite contrary to the jolly companionship of the local and it suggests that the positive connotations have a mythical quality to them: an impoverished version of actual history, a tamed richness, a loss of historical reality in favour of a 'natural' image (cf. Barthes 1999: 56, 58). It seems to be fairly obvious that not every visit to a pub will result in joviality and the feeling of community, yet the myth of this stereotype prevails. It is even furthered by Oldenburg, who claims that the bar or pub as third place is "the people's own remedy for stress, loneliness and alienation [..., a] shelter against the raindrops of life's tedium and [...] a breather on the sidelines of the rat race" (1989: 20-21), perhaps a bit too enthusiastically and naively.

Having been hypertrophied so extensively, even – or especially – by (American) movies, the bar acquires the quality of being *too much* about community: Will feels that without a companion, he becomes an outsider in the pub which was supposed to shelter him from the cruel anonymity of the metropolis and the community readily dwelling in the pub was to enfold him in their comfortable and comforting collective: "The temper and tenor of the third place is upbeat; it is cheerful. The purpose is to enjoy the company of one's fellow being and to delight in the novelty of their character – not to wallow in pity over misfortunes." (Oldenburg 1989: 26) Oldenburg later admits that those "[s]eeking to gain respite from loneliness or boredom [... only] manage [...] to intensify those feelings by their inability to get anything going with another. They are doomed, almost always, for if silence is not immediately broken by strangers, it is rarely broken at all." (1989.: 34) Oldenburg's third place appears to rely heavily on the newcomer's stamina and their gaining trust of the regulars (cf. ibid.: 35). However, it might equally own much to happenstance.

Realising that his loneliness is not going to dissipate, Will feels close to crying but deems it inappropriate or unmanly, and he withdraws to the restrooms "to get away from humanity for a while." (Gayle 1999: 215) When he returns he intends to go and a couple already hovers nearby to occupy his table. The advent of the couple suggests two interpretations: first, despite the fact that the pub appears to be filling up, Will is still as lonely as he is in his flat. This means that the depressing notion of his home is also transferable to his dislocated living room-away-from-home: any space Will occupies is turned into a saturnine place, be it at home, at work or in spaces of leisure. The pub becomes another indication of his rigor mortis, which is felix only insofar as he loves to wallow in self-pity. Secondly, Will leaves his table to a couple, which points towards the fact that coupledom trumps the lonely male, who stereotypically is supposed to be more at home at pubs than the couple should be. Supposing that it is a heterosexual couple, it shows that the pub becomes a space for couples who have already found their 'significant other' and even in the case the couple should consist only of two friends, it still means that there is a sense of belonging[38] which is diametrically opposed to Will's feelings. Failing both to feel at home and to engage in flirty chatting with the barmaid, Will has no choice but to leave the pub. The lonely male is defeated, yet his return to his lonely flat means only a change of address, but not of his sense of place – for his home is just as lonely and depressing as his visit to his 'local'.

COMING BACK

The protagonists of lad- and chicklit are constantly on the lookout for love, and spaces of leisure provide them with environments in which they can pursue their search. Activities of leisure are regarded as "a legitimate and progressive feature of civilized social life." (Rojek 1995: 39) By locating the search for the perfect partner in spaces of leisure, the desire to be part of a couple becomes a property of "civilized social life" and thus of the normative centre. This practice of finding the perfect partner is an anchoring device that ensures that even if people engage in carnivalesque behaviour or visit liminal spaces, they will always return to the centre

38 There is even the possibility that the two people are always sitting at that table because it is their living room-away-from-home's table.

for it is there only that the couple is able to thrive as many examples in this chapter have shown.

Moreover, the spaces of leisure analysed displayed a strong connection to essentialist notions about spaces, gender and behaviour, suggesting that possible deviant behaviour does not lead to the desired outcome of coupledom. Chick- and ladlit novels are part of the dominant culture, they hardly ever challenge ideas and attitudes, most obviously played out in the depiction of coupledom as the ultimate goal. As this is the basis for all the characters' actions, coupledom is at the core of the various experiences the heroines and heroes of chick- and ladlit make in spaces of leisure. This is most visible in the traits of identity (shopping), spectacle (clubbing/partying) and neutrality (going out for drinks or food). These three traits are always connected to an essentialist understanding of society. Therefore, the two genres are employing spatial practices in leisure spaces in a very similar way. That way it can be ensured that female and male characters will return to the centre after they have spent a limited amount of time in the playful spaces of leisure.

With regard to the first trait, the behaviour of the various characters show that spaces of leisure become stages to perform a new identity at, like the father (*About a Boy*), the rich fashionista (*Shopaholic*), the book lover (*The Wish List*) or the committed fiancé *(Mr Commitment*). However, while the spaces allow for the creation and usage of these new identities, they are never enduring. In all of these cases the characters are found out and even punished for their transgressions. Considering the idea that "certain forms of identity […] are appropriate in leisure time and leisure space while others are not" (ibid.), spaces of consumption actually prove that this is not entirely correct. Whereas the transgression of certain identities are forbidden in leisure spaces such as the club or bar, for example drunkenly causing trouble, shops and stores appear to be more open towards the identities of their consumers. Nonetheless, there is the possibility of punishment but this is only applicable when one leaves the leisure space and re-enters the normative space outside. The liminal quality of these spaces only allows the adoption of new identities for a limited time, namely the duration of the stay at the shop. The moment the characters try to outstay their presence in the created persona *outside* the realm of the leisure space, they will be found out and penalised: Will is no longer allowed at Single Parents Alone Together (*About a Boy*), Lucy's boyfriend turns out to be a burden (*The Wish List*) and Duffy enters IKEA as an engaged man and leaves a single (*Mr Commitment*). The only character to escape this punishment is Becky Bloomwood: although being publicly humiliated when she has to confess to being highly indebted on a TV show whilst being the show's financial advisor at the same time, she nevertheless gets to keep a fraction of her fashionable identity, which is most important to her – the shopper. But even here, it has to be taken with a grain of salt for she has to leave the show and will only find fulfilment in America, not in her native England. That only Becky is allowed to keep her identity can be explained by the fact that the other characters' 'identities' were too far away from their core identity: Will *is not* a father, Lucy is *cannot handle* being surpassed with regard to flamboyancy and Duffy simply *is not ready* to marry his girlfriend. Becky is thus similar to Libby Cutmore (*Paris Dreaming*): Libby has turned her Aboriginality into the most important feature of her identity and therefore she is able to display her overtly ethnic qualities outside the spaces of consumption, making her a product wherever she is. It appears that especially chicklit heroines are prone to having been subjected to spaces of consumption for such a long time – and also through agents of consumption, such as their friends and magazines – that they are hardly able to return to their 'natural' selves anymore. *Bridget Jones's Diary* has exemplified that the heroine attracts the wrong man if she tries to be somebody entirely different. But she does not stop beautifying or 'harvesting' her body once she gets together with her perfect partner. Chick- and ladlit protagonists use spaces of consumption in a similar fashion and are punished if they perform their identities outside the borders of these spaces. But whereas the men's laddishness is ultimately abolished because it does not fit the norms of the centre, it is expected of females to present a beautiful persona, not entirely natural, but not overtly 'lacquered' either, for that would turn their body into a spectacle.

The prominent feature in clubbing and partying experiences *is* the spectacle, the second trait. Only the partners who see beyond the spectacle – in itself another time-limited practice – will remain with the protagonists. Assuming the attribute of the non-conformist clubber or party guest, the characters attach youth to them; a practice which is deemed transgressive by the policing forces. Thus, they set out to detect such deviant behaviours, be they a disregard for traditional values like *bhadralok* behaviour (*Almost Single*) or sexually or romantically diverging performances – cheating on one's fiancée (*Mr Commitment*), ejaculating prematurely (*Two to Go*), being too young (*Piece of Cake*) or behaving gender-inversely (*The Wish List*): the policing forces will see to it that the transgressors do not remain in a liminal position for a longer time. Especially the Smug Marrieds' dinner (*Bridget Jones's Dairy*) stands out here, because the previously positively-connoted spectacle of being a Singleton is questioned and marginalised. The Singletons, who through the term itself distance themselves from couples and singles alike, are made aware of their status as not being part of the norm and the positive quality of being a Singleton is ridiculed for they want to become part of a couple themselves. Within the Singleton community they can convince one another that being a Singleton is preferable to the other two statuses but, secretly, they pine for their single(ton) days to be over – and because being a Singleton is a liminal spectacle, they can rest assured: it will end inevitably. The essentialist notion presented here is the normative status of the couple. Protagonists of chick- and ladlit strive to be included in the centre – the territory of the couples. Realising their marginalised position by being turned into a spectacle by the policing force, they come to terms with the fact that they cannot remain in a playful or carnivalesque space forever. Once the time in their respective leisure spaces is over, they try to approach the centre and thus coupledom reverently. It is noteworthy that they sometimes even acknowledge their deviant behaviour and have to extract themselves from the spaces of leisure, like Minal (*Piece of Cake*) or Duffy (*Mr Commitment*): they find out that liminal spaces of parties or clubs, respectively, do not present them with their perfect partners and they swiftly leave the leisure spaces.

As the last trait, the idea of neutrality shall be looked at. Pubs, bars, cafés and restaurants are places in which community is supported and which can double as a dislocated living room. Already a specific direction is visible with both qualities – home to a community and the living room-away-from-home: they present the chick- and ladlit characters with a space in which they can build a family, yet only an urban one. These particular spaces of leisure are very open locales for they allow their patrons to experience neutrality, which means that no hierarchical structure is detectable. Of course, these spaces are not smooth for they are policed by representatives of the owner, such as waiters. But it is conspicuous that here, in contrast to the other two spaces of leisure, relationships can be started as *Avoiding Mr Right* and *About a Boy* have shown, but it requires the willingness of more than one person involved as the protagonist in *My Legendary Girlfriend* has to find out. The bar or café can present a neutral and safe haven, not only from the taunting Smug Marrieds (*Bridget Jones's Diary*) but also the watchful eyes of parental figures (*Five Point Someone*). As with the other spaces, a stay at these spaces is limited and at some point the characters have to relocate to either another temporary location or their other anchor-points. However, not only the time spent at bars, restaurants and cafés is limited, the spaces' neutrality is questioned when behaviour is flaunted. More than the other two spaces, spaces of drinking and eating construct rather strict gender roles, which refers back to the above-mentioned quote about permissible and forbidden identities: the bars are too open to display non-conformist behaviour such as "strident feminism" (*Bridget Jones's Diary*) and one cannot engage in homoerotic behaviour more than once before one's sexual orientation is doubted (*Brand New Friend*). Only gender-normative behaviour as displayed in the examples named above will result in a relationship. Furthermore, the neutrality of bars and restaurants can turn these spaces into smooth ones. Each visit can pose a new start if the characters themselves cannot bring enough 'connection' to turn the space into a familiar structure. In *Twenties Girl*, the protagonist's relationship with her boyfriend has ended and trying to rekindle it merely through space fails. But that this quality can also be a blessing is exemplified in *Dinner for Two*: Dave Harding and his estranged wife meet in restaurants and because of the neutrality of these leisure spaces they are able to overcome their marital problems. It can be summarised that bars, restaurant, pubs and cafés are similar because of the neutrality of these locales: they are equally as open as they are smooth to all the patrons.

It is this last feature, the neutrality and equality of a space of leisure, which points towards the grander scheme of spatial compatibility: feeling that they can actually engage in, through and with the space at eye level, the characters find out whether their interlocutor can be the one to share one's life with. Yet, this shared life will be played out primarily in the home, the space of coupledom to which the chick- and ladlit protagonists have to relocate eventually. After all, spaces of leisure have a temporal limit. Characters can compare their attitudes and match them up against other people, regarding the compatibility of their habitus and find out if they want to continue engaging with their interlocutors in a more private surrounding. The spaces of leisure are testing grounds to see how the characters' love interests will behave in public and in the company of others or whether the potential partners are able to see through their disguises the characters developed due to 'pressure' to become commodities in capitalist societies. The idea to buy something on a whim is chastised because – paraphrasing the famous adage – they have not tested well enough before joining forever. *Almost Single* can be cited as an example when Aisha tests on the dance floor how modern her love interest Karan is. The fact that he passes the test makes her confident that he will also be willing to go out for an indefinite time so as to 'be sure' before they tie the knot and not marry instantly like her best friend Misha.

The mentality of today's single culture resembles that of a window-shopper – looking at what is 'out there', trying (on) new identities 'for size' (as the partner of somebody) and leaving the space if it should (not) satisfy their needs[39]. Characters in chick- and ladlit venture out to spaces of leisure to find new partners and attitudes but they will always come back to the centre, for there the couple must be.

39 Eva Illouz has published on this subject in her book *Consuming the Romantic Utopia*. Additionally, there is even an online dating site called "Shop a Man" in which women can put men in their shopping carts with the men becoming passive goods, ready for consumption.

Placing the Happily Ever After

So this is love, so this is what makes life divine.
DISNEY'S *CINDERELLA*

Love is everywhere. A quick glance at any music chart of any country reveals that there are numerous love songs in the top twenty: songs about lost love, about unrequited love, about perfect love and about everlasting love. Cinemas show movies and television sets broadcast TV shows, telenovelas and daily soaps that include a romance plotline at some point. Many writers have written about love and quite successfully so, their titles spanning almost all genres – from thrillers to science fiction, from drama to poetry. Across all these different media, the most successful products revolve around love.

Love is everywhere and it has been turned into a multi-billion pound business: "Single people in Britain spend more than 3 billion pounds a year in their search for a partner, a new study has found." (*Indian Express* 2012) Of course, this business is not only exclusive to Britain and its former colonies, where love has become an equally large business opportunity like for example in Australia (cf. *Business Lounge* 2014) and India, but "the whole idea of marriage and relationships [is] going through a revolution, and Indians, like their counterparts in the Western world, [are] looking to date a potential partner before making a decision about marriage." (Rajan 2012) With the advent of new technologies, the search for love has entered new spaces: one can search for love online or use location-based dating apps for smart phones. One does not need to leave it to chance to become part of a couple or to partake of romance(s).

Love is everywhere and it is indeed every*where*. Not only in its various forms (movies, novels, music) and through the various media (from books to the internet), but love can always be found on a geographical level. This book set out to show the spatial dimensions and qualities of English, Australian and Indian chick- and ladlit. By looking at the home, the workplace as well as spaces of leisure, it proved that love is very spatial and that chicklit heroines do not act differently from ladlit protagonists when it comes to finding their perfect partners. What is more, they all need to find a person with whom they are spatially compatible, otherwise their love is not going to last. The various heroines and heroes can find love in all places – and indeed they do so, too. They fall in love with people they sit next to during a dinner, they meet at their workstations or they talk to because they need help with wayfinding.

In the following the results and findings from the previous chapters will be once more taken up and will be applied to the two novels presented in the introduction: *Bridget Jones: Mad about The Boy* and *Turning Forty*, being the latest instalments in their respective series. It will be shown that, despite slightly transgressing the boundaries of stereotypical chick- and ladlit, these two novels incorporate the various notions analysed in the previous chapters. In a final step, a more critical approach to the cultural politics of the two genres themselves will be undertaken.

While love and relationships have positive features, at the same time, it becomes a form of pressure to be part of a couple, since not being in a relationship means one is not being 'whole'. "Love is [...] endlessly pursued and ceaselessly suspected. [...] Sought after as the ultimate good, feared as constraint, doubted as an illusion, [... love] cannot speak, and yet it seems that it never ceases to speak in late twentieth-century Western culture." (Belsey 1994: 74) Not being part of a couple is turned into a discouraging spectacle. The chapter on spaces of leisure has proven that singles have to defend their non-relationship status against the (only sometimes subtle) accusations of the non-singles or, in *Bridget Jones's Diary*'s coinage, Smug Marrieds. The latter functions as a policing force vehemently guarding their realm, the centre of society. They want singles to come to their side and no longer 'play' at the margins. Chick- and ladlit protagonists, however, do not want to resist – they desperately and dearly *want* to be part of the Smug Marrieds' realm: in *Bridget Jones: Mad about The Boy* and *Turning Forty*, the two protagonists Bridget Jones and Matthew 'Matt' Beckford, respectively, affirm this notion.

The widow and the divorcé have lost the person they loved but do not want to remain single any longer. At the beginning of the respective stories, they are occupying a new marginalised position for they are singles but have been married once. Thus they are closer to the centre than 'real' singles but through their respective losses have deteriorated from the (smugly) married core of society. While Bridget resumes dating five years after Mark's death, divorced Matt quickly returns home to his parents and looks up his old girlfriend Ginny, who has broken his heart in the prequel *Turning Thirty*. The reactions of the characters' surroundings are quite telling because Matt's mother starts crying on the revelation of her son's divorce, confessing that "I just worry, that's all. All your dad and I ever wanted was for [...] you to be happy and when things like this happen *it feels like we've failed*." (Gayle 2013: 46, emphasis added) The happiness of Matt's mother depends on her son being installed in the centre of society by means of his marriage, and the removal from the same by divorce is regarded as a (personal) failure of hers. A similar attitude is displayed in Fielding's novel when Bridget's mother tries to set her daughter up with a fellow resident of her retirement home: "we really should get you together with Kenneth Garside! He's on his own. You're on your own" (2013: 183). The sole fact that one is single appears to suffice to trigger matchmaking. Both mothers create a spectacle on the singles and Bridget's mother as well Matt himself try to get rid of the (social) stigma of solitariness by attaching her daughter and himself, respectively, to the next available person – literally. Neither of these 'couples' (Bridget and Kenneth, Matt and Ginny) will form a union, because there is no spatial compatibility involved: the retirement home in which Kenneth lives and Bridget's family home are two different constructions that are not compatible[1] and in Matt's ex-girlfriend's home another man is already installed. The four personal spaces of the characters do not imply any similarities nor qualities that can be matched – the retirement home (Kenneth) with the family home (Bridget) and the parents' home (Matt) with the non-single home (Ginny).

Love has come to signify the most important goal in a person's life and thus it is everywhere – it infiltrates every space and can be at any place. The previous paragraph has already hinted at the spatial compatibility that needs to exist between the partners of a perfect couple. The home is the most important place in which this notion needs to be fulfilled as it is the primary anchor-point and it marks the centre of a person's territory. It is a space of locality. The characters' homes presented in the novels are charged with meaning: Bridget's life is presented seldom outside her abode and Matt has problems with the three homes he inhabits in *Turning Forty*.

Shortly after Mark's death, Bridget and her two kids moved out of the mansion in Holland Park and now call a terraced house in Chalk Farm their own (cf. ibid.: 7), as she could not bear living in *their* home anymore. Yet Bridget feels incarcerated in her new house. The problem is that Bridget, despite being a fifty-something now, has not matured but merely gotten older, because she behaves as childishly as her kids (cf. ibid.: 181). When her twenty-nine-year-old boyfriend Roxter comes to stay at her place, she tries to "de-child" her abode (ibid.: 192) but gives up soon because it is too much effort: after all, everything she does is actually 'childing' the home as she striates the place with her childishness anew every time. This means that her home is constantly a childish place and all three 'children' contribute to the overall messiness of their abode. However, Bridget might have given up on 'de-childing' her home, but she will keep Roxster away from her offspring in her bed-

1 The novel suggests that Bridget's mother and Kenneth Garside will eventually form a couple (cf. Fielding 2013: 340). Here, the spatial compatibility of the home is more of a match than in the other pairing.

room (cf. Fielding 2013: 18). This can be regarded as carefulness in order not to demand too much of her kids, but as Bridget is very childish, it suggests that she wants to keep her toy (boy) to herself instead of sharing it/him with the other kids. As can be seen in her futile attempts to keep her home in order, Bridget cannot manage her home – despite having a full-time nanny and a cleaning lady. She is constantly overwhelmed with housework and is as useless a homemaker as in the first novel.

However, what she excels in is turning her home into a meeting place, a sanctuary: it becomes the first address when her unmarried friends experience problems with their boyfriends. Again, this usage of her home has two sides. On the one hand, Bridget's home offers security and stimulation for her friends leave her home elevated after arriving in a depressed mood. But on the other hand, the aspect of identity shows that her home is connoted with relationship failure: Bridget is unable to keep a man and neither can her nanny, who comes to *Bridget's* home when her boyfriend left her, nor her friends. In the end, Bridget will move out of this home, mirrored by her break-up with toy boy Roxster, and moves in with an organised, military-trained divorced father of two into his country house, which echoes the wedding-cake mansion of Mark Darcy in the first *Bridget Jones* novel. Throughout *Bridget Jones: Mad about The Boy*, Bridget's new man takes care of her numerous times as she has a penchant for getting herself into impossible situations and by moving into his home, she is closer to him and thus easier to control. Bridget states at the end that "now I have not two children but four" (ibid.: 386); however, her new partner has five – Bridget included.

The homes of Matt Beckford display a similar idea, proving that chick- and ladlit do indeed employ geographies in a very similar fashion: following his divorce, he moves out of his London house and back in with his parents. As they will move house a few months after that, he moves in with his (then) girlfriend only to eventually buy his parental home to live there. Already his constant moving implies that Matt has not established a space of centrality that supports his everyday life. Starting with the first home, the London abode is hardly described, except for one feature – a garden shed:

> a real man only buys a shed when he has to take stock of his life, has surveyed all that he has achieved and is one hundred […] per cent satisfied with the results. […] I had a great job as head of development for a financial software company; owned a huge four-bedroom house in Blackheath […]; and in Lauren, my wife of six years, I had not only the longest-standing relationship of my adult life but easily the best-looking partner of anyone I knew. […] Can I have my shed now? I think I bloody well can! (Gayle 2013: 11-12)

The shed signifies everything Matt appears to have achieved and when his job and his wife are lost, so will he lose his home and the shed: the striating of his life space that the shed was to represent turns out to be a masked smoothness. He should have been more attentive to his wife becoming a stranger to him and his job being a serious threat to his health as it results in anxiety attacks. Additionally, it is quite telling that when Matt asks his estranged wife whether he could sleep in the shed during their separation she denies his request, signifying that he has lost control over his home-ly space and is forced to give up the source of identity, security and stimulation and move back in with his parents.

The return to his parents, the second in ten years (cf. Gayle 2001: 31-32), is as stressful as his first *home*coming: his parents are not happy with their eldest son to live at home without a job and any aspiration to change his problems. The parental home becomes a place of failure and regression instead of progress. Although Matt thought he had shed his Peter Pan-attitude, he is forced back into the same by 'reclaiming' the room of his youth and he promptly tries to rekindle the relationship with Ginny. He embraces the nostalgia of a past, carefree (laddish) life which is spatially represented by living in his old room. But Ginny is going out with his best friend, who tries to talk some sense into Matt: "We're not kids anymore, Matt, you can't claim first dibs on Ginny […]. We're adults and it's about time you realised that." (Gayle 2013: 149) That Matt has not learned any (spatial) processes becomes clear when he gets together with a twenty-three-year-old woman.

It appears that, despite their age, both Matt and Bridget try to re-create their youth with younger partners. But while Bridget never visited Roxter's shared abode because she would feel too old, Matt even moves in with the young woman. Her flat presents a form of escapism as it is the only abode he can afford without re-entering the workforce, which he is terrified of (cf. ibid.: 250). It does not take long before this relationship fails – mainly because he keeps secrets from the woman – and he is out on the street again. But now that his London home is sold, he comes into money. However, instead of buying a new home for a fresh start, he buys his parents' old home: "At forty you realise you've spent half your life trying to leave home and the other half trying to find somewhere to belong." (Ibid.: 385-386) Although he eventually belongs and feels at home in the place of his childhood, in terms of space, this does not mean progress; on the contrary, he severely regressed from having had it all – as represented by the shed – to being where he started about twenty years ago. It does not come as a surprise that he ends his narrative as a single man, as he has not learned any spatial processes and is romantically punished.

The home is a place in which romances can flourish and which mirrors the protagonists. Moreover, it is the locale in which spatial compatibility can be observed and realised. But the two characters cannot realise spatial compatibility with anybody in their homes. Therefore, Bridget moves out of her child-ish home into the grown-up place of her new partner and Matt regresses further into his parents' former home and disables himself of realising spatial compatibility with anybody except his past self.

Having no luck with their homes, the workspaces of the two protagonists are equally stifling: both Bridget and Matt have problems in their jobs and need to let go of their workspaces. In the case of the chicklit heroine, Bridget has two 'jobs' – that of a mother and being a screenwriter, which are both performed in the domestic sphere. Just as with the previous two *Bridget Jones* novels, Bridget is easily distracted and does not really care for either job. Therefore, she hires a nanny to take care of her children and is oftentimes stressed when her nanny's private engagements prevent the help from doing school runs and thus keep Bridget from 'enjoying' her 'family' life. Her second 'serious' job is writing a modern adaptation of *Hedda Gabler* – in itself an ironic comment on Bridget's dissatisfactory marital situation as she feels just as imprisoned as Ibsen's heroine. When her agent is able to place her script with a production company, Bridget does not follow the meetings with the producers but instead constantly checks her mobile phone for messages (cf. Fielding 2013: 208-209, 237-239) and is ultimately fired from the job. At the end of the novel, Bridget appears not to hold any kind of profession, but is content with being part of a couple again. Bridget leaving the workspace becomes paramount in finding her perfect partner.

Matt's professional life is equally ill-fated: two years after starting in his "great job", he starts to get "chronic stomach pains" (Gayle 2013: 23) and ultimately leaves his position. He had become a cog in a machine, being pushed to the limit by being constantly sent out to clients all around the world. Although he does not experience the restrictions of the enclosed office or the anonymity of the open-plan office, *Turning Forty* exemplifies that (chick- and) ladlit characters cannot continue working in professions they are not content with. It is also the workspace that discloses that he does not share a spatial compatibility with his then-wife for she suggests that Matt tries to find a similar job to the one that "broke" him (cf. ibid.: 34). His ex-wife cannot understand why he does not continue to earn good money, displaying a different outlook on choosing a career. It is no coincidence that her job is that of a strategic analyst, specialising in accounting, favouring numbers over people. Matt has developed a form of topophobia which is strongly connected to workspaces that do not care for the human side of work, echoing the Taylorist workspaces of open-plan offices. Eventually, Matt will find work in a charity shop, where he will meet his twenty-three-year-old girlfriend. As with his home, this workspace is dedicated to second-hand commodities, already invested with meaning by their previous owners, and it mirrors the Peter Pan-attitude of the resurrected life of his youth.

Both Bridget and Matt have an uneasy relationship with workspaces: although they are going to be happy in their final positions – Bridget as a wife and Matt as the manager of a Cancer Research shop – they first have to leave their previous positions behind. Matt could not have been happy in the relationship with the young woman as he destroys her trust in him when he secretly meets Ginny, which duplicates his nostalgic position at the shop. Hence, the workplace becomes a threat to romance in many novels and the latest additions to the chick- and ladlit canon are no exception.

The spaces of leisure the two protagonists come into contact with are characterised by their notion of the spectacle. They have qualities of the liminal as they are temporal but are ultimately informed by the idea of being spaces of youthfulness. As Bridget and Matt are no longer thirty-somethings, they attach carnivalesque qualities to themselves, which will become clear by looking at how and where the characters go out.

Bridget is invited to her new best friend's birthday party. Directly from the start, it is made clear that this party has a grotesque quality to it: "Darling, I just want to let you know that it's my sixtieth on the 24th of May. I'm not SAYING it's my sixtieth, obviously." (Fielding 2013: 1) Instead of owning up to the fact that the characters in *Bridget Jones: Mad about The Boy* are no longer 'spring chickens', the age is masqueraded, setting the tone for the ensuing party early on. Incidentally, it is also Roxter's thirtieth birthday but he happily accompanies Bridget. The two birthdays are contrasted by the ages of the characters and just as the host is unwilling to disclose her age, so does Bridget by attaching the youthful qualities of Roxter to herself. After Roxter rescues the host's dog from the swimming pool, he climbs out of the pool and the water drips of his topless ripped physique. The scene not only echoes the famous re-emerging of Mr Darcy in the BBC version of *Pride and Prejudice* Bridget loves so much (cf. Fielding 1998: 246-249, Fielding 2004a: 170-178), it also rewards her the envy of every person at the party (cf. Fielding 2013: 246-249). The Smug Marrieds present at the event first taunt Bridget as she appears to have come alone – just like Bridget's mother, they are under the impression that a single woman, regardless of her widowhood, is incomplete without a man at her side – but are flabbergasted when they realise that not only is her boyfriend Roxster present and sexy, he is also visibly younger than Bridget. Therefore, Bridget becomes a spectacle despite freeing herself from the initial stigma of singledom that used to be the reason for being regarded as grotesque. The space of the party becomes a heterotopia for it merges the spaces of the Smug Marrieds with that of those people that attach youth to themselves by means of toy boys[2]. However, the

2 Bridget is not alone as also the host and Tom, her gay best friend, are in relationships with younger men.

party has to end at some point and this is when Roxster confesses "I heart you. I've never said this to a woman before. *I wish I had a time machine*. I heart you." (Fielding 2013: 250, emphasis added) The fact that Roxster is well aware of the age difference between himself and Bridget is now drawn into the open, despite Bridget's efforts to avoid appearing old. Moreover, it is the beginning of the end of their relationship and suggests that the whole relationship was played out in a liminal space that extended its time far beyond the usual liminality of leisure spaces: Bridget was allowed to feel young again once more but ultimately she has to realise that this state is not an eternal one. Just like clubbers and party guests inevitably have to leave the club or party and return to their identities of respectable members of society, so does Bridget have to let go of young Roxster. This is even supported by the fact that it takes less than a fortnight until her husband-to-be kisses her for the first time and therefore restores (social) order: Bridget is rewarded for leaving the liminal space for a man her own age.

A similar situation is presented in Mike Gayle's novel. After having found out that Ginny is going out with his best friend, Matt agrees to spend an evening with three of his former class mates. All of the men are in good shape as Matt enviously observes and all of them are either divorced or separated (cf. Gayle 2013: 158). The evening is a stereotypical laddish outing, "involving the consumption of a ridiculous amount of alcohol at a phenomenal pace and conversations that rarely leave the realms of football, high-performance cars and which of the many attractive women in the bar [the three men] would or wouldn't 'do'" (ibid.: 158-159). They even assume carnivalesque personas for the night and bestow one on Matt as well – 'Boffin' (cf. ibid.: 160). The men's laddish behaviour despite their age can be regarded as the reason why all of their relationships failed, as none has progressed from his Peter Pan-self. However, Matt is surprised that the men are successful in attracting young women at the bar: the laddish personas become a spectacle that – for the duration of the night – holds up and enables the men to satisfy their basic desires of sexual encounters. But Matt feels uneasy in their company, not realising that he, too, acts not according to his age, and seizes the first opportunity to leave.

By accident he meets former rock legend Gerry, a musician Matt idolised in his youth (again an indication of Matt's clinging to the past), becomes friends with him and spends many nights with Gerry and his young girlfriend. Not only might Gerry as a role model have inspired Matt to engage in a relationship with a twenty-something, he is in awe that Gerry is in charge of the Cancer Research shop Matt will later manage himself. But just as Bridget's relationship to Roxster has to end, Matt has to realise at some point that Gerry engages in spaces of leisure each night with his young 'girlfriend' only to return to his wife and two kids in his family home at the end of the night (cf. ibid.: 327-330, 363-364): contrary to Matt's perception, being in a space of leisure, in a liminal space, cannot be a perpetual state.

The youthfulness which is attached to spaces of leisure in chick- and ladlit novels becomes a refuge for some characters; other characters realise that this is not what they want and quickly withdraw from such leisure spaces. These are spatial processes that have to be learned in order to become a perfect partner and to move towards the centre of society. By artificially prolonging the experience in these spaces, the spatial agents disturb the order of the carnivalesque, for it is no longer independent practice but very much kept in check by the authorities. Bridget might enjoy the envy from her Smug Married friends, and Matt might revel in the company of his childhood idol, but at some point they have to realise that the club's lights have been switched on and that they have overstayed their welcome.

The two novels featuring Bridget and Matt, respectively, are good examples to prove the spatial qualities of chick- and ladlit. Looking at these popular genres from a (cultural) geographical point of view helps to explain the notions of love and relationships. Not only have the succinct analyses proven cultural geography as a perfect and valuable approach, they have also shown that the respective characters behave very similarly if not uniformly. Bridget and Matt make use of locations and spaces in an equal fashion, but the reason that only Bridget is able form (another) lasting relationship can be found in Matt's Peter Pan attitude: he refuses to acknowledge the fact that he is no longer in his twenties as his best friend points out. Loving a younger partner is a 'valid' option but chick- and ladlit novels show that the spaces of youth are not those of thirty-somethings or people older than that. It is a conspicuous trait of chick- and ladlit novels that characters who are perfect partners will use spaces similarly, hinting at spatial compatibility and spaces of youth are not those of Bridget's and Matt's anymore. The various novels discussed in this book show that disregarding or rejecting spatial rules is not considered appropriate behaviour and will result in the harshest form of punishment the two genres have to offer: singledom.

Looking at the two chick- and ladlit novels, it is noticeable that the characters are not stereotypical protagonists as they have grown too old to be considered 'true' heroines and heroes of these genres. In one of the few scholarly articles which bring a comparative approach to chick- and ladlit, it is observed that "as the original chicklit writers grow up, meet partners, have babies and experience the working motherhood dilemmas of their own, the lead characters are going to become more interesting, more complex and more enthralling." (Dique, qtd. in Cockin 2007: 110) Of course, this argument can be extended to ladlit as well. However, despite the age difference to other characters analysed here, Bridget and Matt do behave conspicuously similarly to stereotypical chick- and ladlit protagonists. Bridget has children and Matt wishes he were a father (cf. Gayle 2013: 75), but one can conclude that neither *Bridget Jones: Mad about The Boy* nor *Turning Forty* can be considered mum- or dadlit[3], nor are the novels more complex than other books in my corpus. Fielding and Gayle have experimented with the genres' boundaries but have not taken their novels entirely to another genre. However, the books show that the boundaries have become more fluid and, just as some of the discussed novels conclude with a happy, yet single main protagonist, in the future chick- and ladlit novels might also change the rather static formula. Already, the latest novels depict their characters taking to new technologies to meet partners: Bridget meets Roxster through Twitter and her best friend Jude is obsessed with online dating sites, while Matt uses Facebook to find out about Ginny's relationship status. The actual geographical spaces might be turned into cyberspaces in the near future as real-life dating has taken to the cyber sphere as well.

Of the fifty novels analysed, only seven do not close with a union, but still with a happy ending – therefore there is an 86% chance that a protagonist will not be single when the novel ends. Despite not everyone finding their perfect partner, it is conspicuous that almost everyone will be happy at the end (the only exception is *Ouch! That 'Hearts'* – but as it is the middle part of a trilogy, even here the protagonist is eventually granted his happily ever after). The characters have dated different people and finally realise that even heartbreak is not the end and that they can be happy the way they are: they have undergone a development at end of which the protagonists are more refined and happy with themselves.

Moreover, of the seven novels only one chicklit heroine remains single and six ladlit protagonists have not formed a lasting relationship. Compared to the many singles who might be reading these novels, this is quite an astonishing quota. It can be suggested that chick- and ladlit novels are part of the romance industry, catering to the needs of twenty- to thirty-somethings who feel that the novels depict their metropolitan lives and lifestyles: chick- and ladlit enforce and legitimise the search for love as being omnipresent. The novels can be considered to be part of the larger idea that love is one of the only grand narratives that provide an anchor in the turbulent, globalised twenty-first century: "A good relationship acts as a buffer against stress, depression and the general toughness and challenges of life"

3 A more fitting example of dadlit is Nick Earls's novel *Perfect Skin*, which revisits Dr Jon Marshall from *Bachelor Kisses*: "Dadlit flourished as a genre in the dying years of the last century. The formula was simple: take one small family unit a hopeless but lovable pair of males (usually father and preadolescent son) plus a beautiful and adored mother figure and contrive the sudden removal of the female by divorce, mental illness, or, ideally, tragic early death. Then examine the consequences as the blokes, soon submerged beneath the domestic detritus of dirty washing and takeaway containers, muddle through the trauma, bonding as they go." (Paling 2007) *Perfect Skin* does indeed include most of these motifs.

(Mansfield, qtd. in Rice 2003; cf. Little 2013). In order not to lose this buffer or anchor, people get married, thus encasing their love in "a legal framework. It's a way of saying that the relationship is bigger than the people in it. Wills, inheritance, rights of property, pensions, separation, children and access to them are all affected by marriage." (Rice 2003) Legalising one's love is a step towards security[4].

What is even more, being in a relationship has been slowly yet steadily turned into a form of consumption and thus echoes claims that a neoliberal ideology "seem[s] to have sedimented into the western imaginary and become embedded in popular 'common sense'." (Hall, Massey and Rustin 2013a: 17) Desiring a relationship is 'common sense', because who wants to be single after all? Therefore an "anything goes" attitude is adopted (cf. ibid.: 18) and "'[t]he market' has become the model of social relations, exchange value the only value." (Ibid.: 9) In the novels, this is visible in the commodification of the characters: not only do the protagonists enhance themselves to be more attractive (as a product) for potential partners, they also adapt a neoliberal mentality when it comes to the choice of partners, as perfectly exhibited in Will Freeman (*About a Boy*), who considers his 'relationships' with single mothers a transaction – they get comfort and a father for their children, and he receives grateful sex partners (see chapter 5): he therefore becomes a serial dater. The female heroines in Anita Heiss's novels *Manhattan Dreaming* and *Paris Dreaming* act according to the credo that their partner must 'fit' to them, meaning that he must understand their Indigenous background effortlessly, which is why they eventually choose Native American and Aboriginal partners, respectively – their partners' ethnic backgrounds becoming their major selling point. The protagonist as consumer/product is eventually carried to an extreme in *Can You Keep a Secret?*: here, the founder of a company for lifestyle products uses the novel's heroine – his girlfriend at that time – as a guinea pig because he deems her the quintessential everywoman and the embodiment of his target group. He thus fuses the notions of love and entrepreneurship without any qualms or problems. What is more, he is even applauded for it by the other characters and despite the fact that the heroine feels betrayed she is quick to forgive her clever perfect partner and a happy ending can ensue.

The commodification of partners, by now a 'standard' as the existence of countless dating websites strongly suggests, is due to the fact that in a neoliberal society its members are constructed as "entrepreneurial identities" (Hall, Massey and Rustin 2013a: 19). As all singles want to be part of the hegemony as represented by the couples at the centre of society, they need a partner, who becomes an entry ticket to this space. By being able to elicit a "This is Me!" response from the

4 In past ages, marriage was used to secure alliances and heirs, being a "purely economic institution" (Rice 2003).

novels' readers, they are invited to identify not only with the characters but their practices alike. Furthermore, it is no coincidence that all main protagonists stem from a comfortable (lower) middle-class, and are likely to have enjoyed a good education. It can be suggested that the readers, like the novels' characters, are not part of the margin: although the single characters deem themselves marginalised, they are actually complaining about not belonging to the direct centre, giving the impression of school kids lamenting their exclusion from the cool in-group. The protagonists forget that the spaces they inhabit are already comfortable and crisis-resistant and that they are just a partner away from the centre: almost all characters depicted in the novels, certainly the main protagonists, are not struggling economically and their spaces, jobs and attitudes betray a clear hegemonic ideology. Even Heiss's Aboriginal characters, who continuously draw attention to the problems of their peoples, are well-off, live in splendid abodes and only sporadically come into contact with truly marginalised characters such as the Roma woman in *Paris Dreaming*. They are Indigenous women, whose ancestors have surely suffered under colonial rule, but the heroines of chicklit now have to turn around in order to face the genuine 'othered' characters (cf. Hall, Massey and Rustin 2013a: 17), for they have left this identity behind and are no longer located at the periphery but help to keep the (white) hegemonic ideology in its (central) place by being part of it. At the same time that chick- and ladlit novels legitimise (white) middle-class values and aspirations to pursue love they, if read by members of the working or lower classes, function as an escapist fantasy: as the novels have a high rate of 'happily ever afters', they inspire readers who cannot directly identify with the protagonists to aspire to the characters' lifestyles as these also include the sought-after commodity of the perfect partner. Especially chicklit can be regarded as a modern fairy tale (cf. Isbister 2009), suggesting to young women that if they cannot have a prince, they at least can get the human rights lawyer (*Bridget Jones's Diary*), the secretary of culture (*Paris Dreaming*) or even a multi-millionaire (*Can You Keep a Secret?*). With these men at their side, readers would be able to secure a place in higher classes – just like their literary role models.

There are hints at a darker reality in some of the novels and they are usually related to workspaces, such as the misogynist Bollywood production in *Trust Me* or the burnout of Matt in *Turning Forty* for example, but they are shrugged off quickly. Massey writes that "[w]ork is usually, and certainly should be, not a liability and a sacrifice, but a central source of meaning and fulfilment in human lives." (2013: 11; cf. Hall and O'Shea 2013: 6) Some of the characters might feel like machines in their workspaces, but they will come out on top at the end, because they have simply chosen to abandon the calamitous workspace. Instead of changing the working conditions, they leave one workspace for another and they can usually find a new profession without any significant problems. Chick- and ladlit are all about glossy surfaces, nothing is to obfuscate the happy/romantic atmosphere of the novels. This is especially visible in *The Fix*, as it is the main protagonist's job as a spin doctor to gloss over problems perpetually and to ensure good press for his law firm employers. Despite realising that he was hired to mask a fraud, the protagonist never actually lets his employers down and follows his assignment through. The perpetrator of the fraud will be punished in the end, but only in private – lest the potential spectacle disturbs the general order to happiness (of the law firm): "Neoliberalism has as one of its basic presuppositions the idea that the human world is composed essentially of individuals, who should as far as possible be free to make their own choices and to advance their own interests, in pursuit of whatever they may deem their happiness to be." (Rustin 2013: 1) In chick- and ladlit, this pursuit of happiness is clearly the forming of a happy couple and nothing must stand in its way. As neoliberalism is only concerned with the individual but not with an equality of all social strata (cf. Hall, Massey and Rustin 2013: 9-10), the characters in chick- and ladlit are rewarded for focusing on themselves: within the formula, the various protagonists must only try to achieve personal happiness, which traditionally lies in the arms of a partner of the opposite sex – everything else will fall into place afterwards. It is interesting to note that a totally self-centred character, such as Matt Beckford, is ultimately punished for his attitude. It appears that a visible departure from society cannot be tolerated for it exposes the faux-happiness of the 'we're all in this together'-mantra as ultimately hollow (cf. ibid.: 16). Protagonists, who only think of themselves but buy into the general narrative of love being the ultimate goal, are (naturally) rewarded.

In this, the novels fulfil also the function of a pacifier, soothing the reader by incessantly and conspicuously reinforcing the notion that love is possible and that it is out there (somewhere). Readers of these works of fiction can indulge in a world in which the forming of a romantic union has an 86% success rate, whereas in their own reality "romance can no longer be equated with permanence" (Bauman 1998: 25). They have to content themselves with a love story that is fragmented and with each new novel another piece is added to the big picture, which, alas, is never fully realised – and never can be: readers are presented with spaces and places in which characters have found, find and will find their perfect partners, hoping maybe that the same is going to happen to them. Many of the results of a geographical analysis of chick- and ladlit are indeed applicable in everyday life, too, because, for example, a couple must realise its spatial compatibility; otherwise it is going to face problems fairly soon. Furthermore, women and men might appear to be from different planets – referencing one of Bridget Jones's self-help books – but they will eventually and inevitably have to agree on a space in which to pursue their love. The novels indoctrinate their readers with the 'common sense' knowledge that there is a perfect partner out there for everyone and this notion could be criticised relentlessly. However, chick- and ladlit also literarily represent one of the most deeply-rooted desires – be it innate or socially implanted – namely to find somebody to be with. Contemporary readers feel entitled to a perfect partner as all other claims have recently fallen flat in the years of the twenty-first century because of economic crises (cf. Little 2013: 1-2). Chick- and ladlit are successful genres, because a quick (fictional) reassurance that love is possible can be bought at a small price. Many writers contribute to the steadily growing canon world-wide, hinting at a global phenomenon as well as the immortal belief and hope that there is a place in somebody's heart for everyone.

Bibliography

Acland, Charles R. (1995). Youth, Murder, Spectacle. The Cultural Politics of "Youth in Crisis". Boulder, Oxford: Westview Press.

Adler, Marianna (1991). "From Symbolic Exchange to Commodity Consumption: Anthropological Notes on Drinking as a Symbolic Practice." In Susanna Barrows and Robin Room, eds. *Drinking. Behavior and Belief in Modern History*. Berkeley, Los Angeles, Oxford: University of California Press. 376-398.

Ahmed, Sara (1999). "Home and Away. Narratives of Migration and Estrangement." *International Journal of Cultural Studies*, vol. 2: 3. 329-347.

Aitken, Stuart C. and Gill Valentine, eds. (2006). *Approaches to Human Geography*. Los Angeles, London: SAGE Publications.

Aitken, Stuart C. and Gill Valentine (2006a). "Ways of Knowing and Ways of Doing Geographic Research". In Aitken and Valentine (2006). 1-12.

Allen, Gary L. (1999). "Spatial Abilities, Cognitive Maps, and Wayfinding: Bases for Individual Differences in Spatial Cognition and Behavior". In Reginald G. Golledge, ed. *Wayfinding Behavior. Cognitive Mapping and Other Spatial Processes*. London, Baltimore: The John Hopkins University Press. 46-98.

Anderson, Benedict ([1983] 2006). *Imagined Communities. Reflections on the Origin and Spread of Nationalism*. Revised Edition. London: Verso.

Anderson, Earl R. and Gianfrancesco Zanetti (2000). "Comparative Semantic Approaches to the Idea of a Literary Canon." *Journal of Aestheticism and Art Criticism*, vol. 58: 4. 341-360.

Anderson, Jon (2010). *Understanding Cultural Geography. Places and Traces*. London, New York: Routledge.

Anderson, Rachel (1974). *The Purple Heart Throbs: The Sub-Literature of Love*. London et al.: Hodder and Stoughton.

Anthias, Floya (2001). "The Material and the Symbolic in Theorizing Social Stratification: Issues of Gender, Ethnicity and Class." *British Journal of Sociology*, vol. 52: 3. 367-390.

Archibald, Diana C. (2002). *Domesticity, Imperialism, and Emigration in the Victorian Novel*. Columbia: University of Missouri Press.

Aronoff, Stan and Audrey Kaplan (1995). *Total Workplace Performance. Rethinking the Office Environment*. Ottawa: WDL Publications.

Arthur, Paul and Romedi Passini (1992). *Wayfinding. People, Signs, and Architecture*. Oakville, Ontario: McGraw-Hill Ryerson Ltd.

Auchmuty, Rosemary (1999). "Foreword." In jay Dixon. *The Romance Fiction of Mils & Boon 1909 – 1990s*. London, Philadelphia: UCL Press Ltd. ix-xii.

Augé, Marc ([1995] 2008). *Non-Places*. Transl. John Howe. London, New York: Verso.

Austen, Jane ([1813] 1967). *Pride and Prejudice*. London, Glasgow: Collins.

Bachmann-Medick, Doris ([2006] 2007). *Cultural Turns. Neuorientierungen in den Kulturwissenschaften*. Reinbeck bei Hamburg: Rowohlt.

Bailey, Peter (1978). *Leisure and Class in Victorian England: Rational Recreation and the Contest for Control 1830-1885*. Henley-on-Thames: Routledge & Kegan Paul.

Bakhtin, Mikhail ([1965] 1994). "From M. M. Bakhtin, *Rabelais and His World*, 1965." Transl. Helene Iswolsky. In Morris (1994). 195-206.

--- ([1965] 1994a). "From M. M. Bakhtin, *Rabelais and His World*, 1965." Transl. Helene Iswolsky. In Morris (1994). 207-226.

Baldry, Chris and Alison Barnes (2012). "The Open-Plan Academy: Space, Control and the Undermining of Professional Identity." *Work, Employment & Society*, vol. 26: 2. 228-245.

Bardo, John W. and John J. Hartman (1982). *Urban Sociology. A Systematic Introduction*. Wichita: F.E. Peacock Publishers Inc.

Barrie, James Matthew ([1902/1911] 2004). *Peter Pan: Peter and Wendy* and *Peter Pan in Kensington Gardens*. London et al.: Penguin Classics.

Barron, Colin, ed. (2003). "A Strong Distinction Between Humans and Non-Humans Is No Longer Required for Research Purposes: A Debate Between Bruno Latour and Steve Fuller." *History of the Human Sciences*, vol. 16: 2. 77-99.

Barrows, Susanna and Robin Room (1991). "Introduction." In Barrows and Room, eds. *Drinking. Behavior and Belief in Modern History*. Berkeley: University of California Press. 1-25.

Barthes, Roland ([1970] 1974). *S/Z. An Essay*. Transl. Richard Miller. New York: Hill and Wang.

--- ([1973] 1999). "Myth Today." In Jessica Evans and Stuart Hall, eds. *Visual Culture: The Reader*. London: Sage. 51-58.

Bassett, Jonathan F. (2006). "An Experimental Test of the Discontinuity Hypothesis: Examining the Effects of Mortality Salience on Nostalgia." *Journal of Articles in Support of the Null Hypothesis*, vol. 4: 1. 1-7.

Baudrillard, Jean ([1981] 2001). "From The Precession of Simulacra." In Vincent Leitch, ed. *Norton Anthology of Theory and Criticism*. New York: Norton. 1732-1741.

Bauer, Wilhelm et al. (2012). *Arbeitswelten 4.0. Wie wir morgen arbeiten und leben/Working Environments 4.0. How We Will Work and Live Tomorrow.* Dieter Spath, ed. Stuttgart: Fraunhofer Verlag.

Bauman, Zygmunt (1998). "From Pilgrim to Tourist – or a Short History of Identity." In Stuart Hall and Paul du Gay, eds. *Questions of Cultural Identity.* London: Sage. 18-36.

Beeton, Isabella Mary ([1861] 2012). "Arrangement and Economy of the Kitchen." In Chiara Briganti and Kathy Mezei, eds. *The Domestic Space Reader.* Toronto: University of Toronto Press. 230-232.

Bell, David and Gill Valentine ([1997] 2006). *Consuming Geographies: We Are Where We Eat.* London, Abingdon, New York: Routledge.

Belliger, Andréa and David J. Krieger (2006). "Einführung in die Akteur-Netzwerk-Theorie." In Belliger and Krieger, eds. *ANThology. Ein einführendes Handbuch zur Akteur-Netzwerk-Theorie.* Bielefeld: Transcript. 13-50.

Belsey, Catherine (1994). *Desire. Love Stories in Western Culture.* Oxford, Cambridge: Blackwell.

Bentham, Jeremy ([1787] 1995). *The Panopticon Writings.* Miran Božovič, ed. London, New York: Verso.

Benwell, Bethan (2003). "Introduction: Masculinity and Men's Lifestyle Magazines." In Benwell, ed. *Masculinity and Men's Lifestyle Magazines.* Oxford: Blackwell Publishing Ltd. 6-29.

Beynon, John (2002). *Masculinities and Culture.* Milton Keynes: Open University Press.

Bhabha, Homi (1994). *The Location of Culture.* Abingdon, New York: Routledge.

Bhagat, Chetan ([2004] 2008). *Five Point Someone. What* Not *to Do at IIT.* New Delhi: Rupa & Co.

--- ([2005] 2007). *One Night at the Call Centre.* London: Black Swan.

--- ([2008] 2011a). *The 3 Mistakes of My Life. A Story About Business, Cricket and Religion.* New Delhi: Rupa & Co.

--- ([2009] 2011b). *2 States. The Story of My Marriage.* New Delhi: Rupa & Co.

--- (2011c). *Revolution 2020. Love. Corruption. Ambition.* New Delhi: Rupa & Co.

Bhattacharya, Kumkum (2006). "Non-Western Traditions: Leisure in India." In Chris Rojek, Susan M. Shaw and Anthony J. Veal, eds. *A Handbook of Leisure Studies.* Basingstoke, New York: Palgrave Macmillan. 75-89.

Bible ([1611] n.d.). *The Holy Bible. Containing the Old and New Testament. Authorised King James Version.* Boston: The Christian Science Publishing Society.

Biswas, Soutik (2013). "When Can We Expect Change in Delhi's Rape Statistics?" *BBC.co.uk.* www.bbc.co.uk/news/world-asia-india-22901918 (27.09.2015).

Black, Max (1954). *Problems of Analysis. Philosophical Essays.* London: Routledge & Kegan Paul.

--- ([1972] 1992). "How Do Pictures Represent?" In E.H. Gombrich, Julian Hochberg and Max Black, eds. *art, perception, and reality*. Baltimore, London: The John Hopkins University Press. 95-130.

Blunt, Alison and Robyn Dowling (2006). *Home*. London, New York: Routledge.

Bly, Mary (2005). "A Fine Romance." *The New York Times*, 12 February. www.nytimes.com/2005/02/12/opinion/12bly.html?_r=0 (29.09.2015).

Bosco, Fernando (2006). "Actor-Network-Theory, Networks, and Relational Approaches in Human Geography." In Aitken and Valentine (2006). 136-146.

Bourdieu, Pierre (1978). "Sport and Social Class." *Social Science Information*, vol. 17. 819-840.

--- ([1980] 1990). *The Logic of Practice*. Transl. Richard Nice. Stanford: Stanford University Press.

Bowermaster, Jon (1989). "10 Pictures That Changed America." *American Photographer*, vol. 12: 1. 30-36, 46-47.

Bowlby, Rachel (1993). *Shopping with Freud*. London, New York: Routledge.

Boym, Svetlana (2001). *The Future of Nostalgia*. New York: Basic Books.

Brandwood, Geoff, Andrew P. Davison and Michael Slaughter ([2004] 2005). *Licensed to Sell. The History and Heritage of the Public House*. London: English Heritage.

Brill, Michael et al. (1984/1985). *Using Office Design to Increase Productivity*. 2 vols. Buffalo: Workplace Design and Productivity Inc.

Brooker, Joseph (2006). "The Middle Years of Martin Amis." In Philip Tew and Rod Mengham, eds. *British Fiction Today*. London: Continuum. 3-14.

Brookfield, Harold (1969). "On the Environment as Perceived." *Progress in Geography*, vol. 1. 51-80.

Bryson, Bill (2010). *At Home. A Short History of Private Life*. London et al.: Doubleday

Burnett, John (2004). *England Eats Out: A Social History of Eating Out in England from 1830 to the Present*. Harlow et al.: Pearson Longman.

Business Lounge (2014). "Infographic: Valentines Day: The Business of Love." 5 February. http://businesslounge.net.au/2014/02/infographic-valentines-day-the-business-of-love/ (27.09.2015).

BusinessDictionary "Taylorism" (n.d.). www.businessdictionary.com/definition/Taylorism (27.09.2015).

Button, James (2006). "Paris Infused with Indigenous Spirit." *The Age*, 20 June. www.theage.com.au/news/national/paris-infused-with-indigenous-pirit/2006/06/19/1150701485063.html (27.09.2015).

CABE (Commission for Architecture and the Built Environment) and Llewelyn Davies Yeang (2005). *Better Places to Work*. London: Thomas Telford Publishing.

Carsten, Janet and Stephen Hugh-Jones (1995). "Introduction: About the House – Lévi-Strauss and Beyond." In Carsten and Hugh-Jones, eds. *About the House –*

Lévi-Strauss and Beyond. Cambridge, New York, Melbourne: Cambridge University Press. 1-46.

Chatterton, Paul and Robert Hollands (2003). *Urban Nightscapes. Youth Cultures, Pleasure Spaces and Corporate Power*. New York, Abingdon: Routledge.

Chrzan, Janet (2013). *Alcohol: Social Drinking in Cultural Context*. New York, Abingdon, London: Routledge.

Cieraad, Irene, ed. (1999). *At home: An Anthropology of Domestic Space*. New York: Syracuse University Press.

Cieraad, Irene (2002). "'Out of My Kitchen!' Architecture, Gender and Domestic Efficiency." *Journal of Architecture*, vol. 7: 3. 263-279.

Cockin, Katharine (2007). "Chicks and Lads in Contemporary Fiction." In Steven Barfield et al., eds. *Teaching Contemporary Fiction*. Heidelberg: Universitatsverlag. 107-123.

Colgan, Jenny (2001), "We Know the Difference Between Foie Gras and Hula Hoops, Beryl, But Sometimes, We Just Want Hula Hoops." *The Guardian*, 24 August. www.guardian.co.uk/books/2001/aug/24/fiction.features11 (27.09. 2015).

Cooke, Philip (1989). "Locality, Economic Restructuring and World Development". In Cooke, ed. *Localities: The Changing Face of Urban Britain*. London: Unwin Hyman. 1-44.

Couclelis, Helen et al. (1987). "Exploring the Anchor-Point Hypothesis of Spatial Cognition." *Journal of Environmental Psychology*, vol. 7. 99-122.

Crang, Mike (1998). *Cultural Geography*. London, New York: Routledge.

Cresswell, Tim (1996). *In Place / Out of Place: Geography, Ideology and Transgression*. Minneapolis: University of Minnesota Press.

Crouch, David ([1982] 2004). "Leisure and Consumption." In Vince Gardiner and Hugh Matthews, eds. *The Changing Geography of the United Kingdom*. Third edition. London, New York: Routledge. 261-275.

--- (2006). "Geographies of Leisure." In Chris Rojek, Susan M. Shaw and A.J. Veal, eds. *A Handbook of Leisure Studies*. Basingstoke, New York: Palgrave Macmillan. 125-139.

Curry, Michael (1996). "On Space and Spatial Practice in Contemporary Geography." In Carville Earle, Kent Mathewson, Martin S. Kenzer, eds. *Concepts in Human Geography*. Lanham: Rowman and Littlefield. 3-32.

Dhar, Subir (2013). "Inspiring India. The Fiction of Chetan Bhagat and the Discourse of Motivation." In Krishna Sen and Rituparna Roy, eds. *Writing India Anew. Indian English Fiction 2000-2010*. Amsterdam: Amsterdam University Press. 161-170.

Daniels, Stephen and Simon Rycroft (1993). "Mapping the Modern City: Alan Sillitoe's Nottingham Novels." *Transactions of the Institute of British Geographers*, vol. 18: 4. 460-480.

Davidson, Colin (1995). "Preface." In Fischer (1997). v-vii.

Davidson, Tonya K. (2011). "Nostalgia and Postmemories of a Lost Place: Actualizing 'My Virtual Homeland'." In Davidson, Park and Shields (2011). 43-55.

Davidson, Tonya K., Ondine Park and Rob Shields, eds. (2011). *Ecologies of Affect. Placing Nostalgia, Desire, and Hope*. Waterloo (Ontario): Wilfried Laurier University Press.

Davis, Fred (1977). "Nostalgia, Identity and the Current Nostalgia Wave." *The Journal of Popular Culture*, vol. 11: 2. 414-424.

Davis, Matthew C., Desmond J. Leach and Chris W. Clegg (2011). "The Physical Environment of the Office: Contemporary and Emerging Issues." *International Review of Industrial and Organizational Psychology*, vol. 26. 193-237.

Dawson Varughese, Emma (2013). *Reading New India. Post-Millennial Indian Fiction in English*. London, New York: Bloomsbury.

--- (2015). The Post-Millennial Indian Woman on the Book Covers of Kala's *Almost Single* (2007) and Gokhale's *Priya in Incredible Indyaa* (2011)." In Lisa Lau and E. Dawson Varughese. *Indian Writing in English and Issues of Visual Representation. Judging More Than a Book by Its Cover*. 91-123.

Day, Elizabeth and Tasmina Perry (2011). "Should We Mourn the End of Chick-Lit?" *The Guardian*, 2 October. www.theguardian.com/commentisfree/2011/oct/02/death-of-chick-lit-debate (27.09.2015).

de Certeau, Michel ([1984] 2011). *The Practice of Everyday Life*. Transl. Steven Rendall. Berkeley, Los Angeles: University of California Press.

Deane, Neil and Elke Schuch (2010). "*Merseypride* or, the Importance of Geography in the Construction of Home and Belonging." In Klaus Stierstorfer, ed. *Constructions of Home. Interdisciplinary Studies in Architecture, Law, and Literature*. New York: AMS Press, Inc. 83-99.

Dear, Michael J. and Steven Flusty (2002). "Introduction: How to Map a Radical Break". In Dear and Flusty, eds. *The Spaces of Postmodernity. Readings in Human Geography*. Oxford: Blackwell Publishers. 1-12.

Deleuze, Gilles and Félix Guattari (1987). *A Thousand Plateaus*. Transl. Brian Massumi. Minneapolis: University of Minnesota Press.

Deleyto, Celestino (2009). *The Secret Life of Romantic Comedy*. Manchester: Manchester University Press.

Delplanque, Paul (2009). "Pub Grub… A History." 21 August. http://rememberwhen.gazettelive.co.uk/2009/08/pub-grub.html (24.03.14).

Dixon, jay (1999). *The Romance Fiction of Mills & Boon 1909 – 1990s*. London, Philadelphia: UCL Press Ltd.

Donadio, Rachel (2006). "The Chick-Lit Pandemic." *The New York Times*, 19 March. www.nytimes.com/2006/03/19/books/review/19donadio.html (27.09.2015).

Dorney, Kate (2004). "Shop Boys and Girls! Interpellating Readers as Consumers in Chicklit and Ladlit." *Diegesis: Journal of the Association for Research in Popular Fictions*, vol. 8. 11-21.

drinkaware.co.uk (2015). "Alcohol Dependence." www.drinkaware.co.uk (27.08. 2015)

Driver, Felix (2001). *Geography Militant. Cultures of Exploration and Empire.* Oxford, Malden: Blackwell Publishing.

du Gay, Paul (1996). *Consumption and Identity at Work.* London, Thousand Oaks, New Delhi: Sage.

--- (1997). "Introduction." In du Gay et al., eds. *Doing Cultural Studies. The Story of the Sony Walkman.* London, Thousand Oakes, New Delhi: Sage. 1-5.

Dubino, Jeanne (1989). "The Cinderella Complex: Romance Fiction, Patriarchy and Capitalism." *Journal of Popular Culture*, vol. 27. 103-118.

Dudrah, Rajinder Kumar (2006). *Bollywood. Sociology Goes to the Movies.* New Dehli et al.: Sage.

Duff, Cameron (2014). "Accounting for Context: Exploring the Role of Objects and Spaces in the Consumption of Alcohol and Other Drugs." In Christopher M. Moreno and Robert Wilton, eds. *Using Space: Critical Geographies of Drugs and Alcohol.* Abingdon, New York: Routledge. 47-61.

Duffy, Francis "Frank" (1980). "Office Buildings and Organisational Change." In Anthony D. King, ed. *Buildings and Society. Essays on the Social Development of the Built Environment.* London et al.: Routledge & Kegan Paul.

--- (1997). *The New Office.* London: Conran: Octopus.

Dünne, Jörg ([2006] 2010). "Geschichten im Raum und Raumgeschichte, Topologie und Topographie: Wohin geht die Wende zum Raum?" www.uni-potsdam.de/romanistik/ette/buschmann/dynraum/pdfs/duenne.pdf (27.09.15).

Duyvendak, Jan Willem (2011). *The Politics of Home. Belonging and Nostalgia in Western Europe and the United States.* Basingstoke, New York: Palgrave Macmillan.

Earls, Nick ([1996] 1998a). *Zigzag Street.* London, Basingstoke: Pan Books.

--- (1998b). *Bachelor Kisses.* Ringwood et al.: Penguin Books.

--- ([2000] 2002). *Perfect Skin.* New York: St. Martin's Press.

--- ([2001] 2003). [*World of Chickens*] *Two to Go.* New York: St. Martin's Press.

--- ([2009] 2010). *The True Story of Butterfish.* Sydney: Vintage Books.

--- ([2011] 2012). *The Fix.* Sydney: Vintage Books.

Earnshaw, Steven (2000). *The Pub in Literature. England's Altered State.* Manchester, New York: Manchester University Press.

Ebert, Teresa L. (2009). *The Task of Cultural Critique.* Urbana and Chicago: University of Illinois Press.

Ezard, John (2001). "Bainbridge Tilts at 'Chicklit' Cult." *The Guardian*, 24 August www.guardian.co.uk/uk/2001/aug/24/books.generalfiction (27.09.2015).

Ekinsmyth, Carol and Pamela Shurmer-Smith (2002). "Humanistic and Behavioural Geography." In Shurmer-Smith, ed. *Doing Cultural Geography.* London, Thousand Oaks, New Delhi: Sage Publications. 19-27.

Ellegård, Kajsa and Bertil Vilhelmson (2004). "Home as a Pocket of Local Order: Everyday Activities and the Friction of Distance." *Geografiska Annaler. Series B, Human Geography*, vol. 86: 4. 281-296.

Emig, Rainer (2011). "Lost Places – Productive Spaces?" *Journal for the Study of British Cultures*, vol. 17: 2. 173-184.

Entrikin, J. Nicholas and John H. Tepple (2006). "Humanism and Democratic Place -Making." In Aitken and Valentine (2006). 30-41.

Farb, Peter and George Armelagos (1980). *Consuming Passions: The Anthropology of Eating*. Boston: Houghton Mifflin.

Farnham-Diggory, Sylvia (1966). "Self, Future, and Time: A Developmental Study of the Concepts of Psychotic, Brain-Damaged, and Normal Children." *Monographs of the Society for Research in Child Development*, vol. 31: 1. 1-63.

Featherstone, Mike (1998). "The *Flâneur*, the City and Virtual Public Life." *Urban Studies*, vol. 35: 5-6. 909-925.

Ferriss, Suzanne (2006). "Narrative and Cinematic Doubleness: *Pride and Prejudice* and *Bridget Jones's Diary*." In Ferriss and Young (2006). 71-84

Ferriss, Suzanne and Mallory Young, eds. (2006). *Chick Lit. The New Woman's Fiction*. New York, London: Routledge.

Ferriss, Suzanne and Mallory Young (2006a). "Introduction." In Ferriss and Young (2006). 1-28.

--- (2008). "Introduction: Chick Flicks and Chick Culture." In Ferriss and Young, eds. *Chick Flicks: Contemporary Women at the Movies*. New York, Abingdon; Routledge. 1-25.

Fest, Kerstin (2009). "Angles in the House or Girl Power: Working Women in Nineteenth-Century Novels and Contemporary Chick Lit." *Women's Studies*, vol. 38. 43-62.

Fielding, Helen ([1994] 2002). *Cause Celeb*. New York et al.: Penguin Books.

--- ([1996] 1998). *Bridget Jones's Diary*. London, Basingstoke, Oxford: Picador.

--- ([1999] 2004a). *Bridget Jones: The Edge of Reason*. London, Basingstoke, Oxford: Picador.

--- ([2003] 2004b). *Olivia Joules and the Overactive Imagination*. London, Basingstoke, Oxford: Picador.

--- (2013). *Bridget Jones: Mad about The Boy*. London: Jonathan Cape.

Fischer, Gustave-Nicholas ([1989] 1997). *Individuals and Environment. A Psychosocial Approach to Workspace*. Updated and revised translation. Transl. Ruth Atkin-Etienne. Berlin: Walter de Gruyter & Co.

Fisher, Alan G.B. (1936). "The Clash of Progress and Security." *Pacific Affairs*, vol. 9: 3. 494-496.

Fiske, John ([1989] 2011). *Understanding Popular Culture*. Second edition. London, Abingdon, New York: Routledge.

--- (1992). "Cultural Studies and the Culture of Everyday Life." In Lawrence Grossberg, Cary Nelson and Paula Treichler, eds. *Cultural Studies*. New York, London: Routledge. 154-173.

Forster, Marc and Maren Möhring (2009). "Introduction." In Forster and Möhring, eds. *Public Eating, Public Drinking. Places of Consumption from Early Modern to Postmodern Times. Food History*, vol. 7: 2. Turnhout: Brepols Publishers. 1-12.

Foucault, Michel ([1967] 2008). "Of Other Spaces (1967)." Trans. Lieven De Cauter and Michiel Dehaene. In Lieven De Cauter and Michiel Dehaene, eds. *Heterotopia and the City. Public Space in a Postcivil Society*. Abingdon, New York: Routledge. 13-29.

Fox O'Mahony, Lorna and James A. Sweeney (2011). "The Idea of Home in Law: Displacement and Dispossession." In Fox O'Mahony and Sweeney, eds. *The Idea of Home in Law. Displacement and Dispossession*. Farnham: Ashgate. 1-12.

Freeman, Hadley (2013). "Why Do We Expect So Much From Bridget Jones?" *The Guardian*, 8 October. www.theguardian.com/commentisfree/2013/oct/08/bridget-jones-helen-fielding-mad-about-boy (27.09.2015).

Gayle, Mike ([1998] 1999). *My Legendary Girlfriend*. London: Flame.

--- ([1999] 2000). *Mr Commitment*. London: Flame.

--- ([2000] 2001). *Turning Thirty*. London: Flame.

--- (2002). *Dinner for Two*. London: Flame.

--- (2005). *Brand New Friend*. London: Hodder.

--- (2007). *Wish You Were Here*. London: Hodder & Stoughton.

--- ([2010] 2011). *The Importance of Being a Bachelor*. London: Hodder.

--- (2013). *Turning Fourty*. London: Hodder & Stoughton.

Genoe, M. Rebecca, Douglas Kennedy and Jerome F. Singleton (2013). "History of Recreation." In Human Kinetics, ed. *Introduction to Recreation and Leisure*. Second Edition. Champaign et al.: Human Kinetics, Inc. 21-38.

Gilead, Sarah (1986). "Liminality, Anti-Liminality, and the Victorian Novel." *English Literary History*, vol. 53: 1. 183-197.

Gill, Rosalind (2003). "Power and the Production of Subjects: A Genealogy of the New Man and the New Lad." In Bethan Benwell, ed. *Masculinity and Men's Lifestyle Magazines*. Oxford: Blackwell Publishing Ltd. 34-56.

--- (2009). "Lad Lit as Mediated Intimacy: A Postfeminist Tale of Female Power, Male Vulnerability and Toast." In Gormley and Mills (2009). http://extra.shu.ac.uk/wpw/chicklit/gill.html (27.09.2015).

Gill, Rosalind and Elena Herdieckerhoff (2006). "Rewriting the Romance: New Femininities in Chick Lit?" London: LSE Research Online. http://eprints.lse.ac.uk/2514 (27.09.2015).

Glennie, Paul D. and Nigel Thrift (1996). "Consumption, Shopping, Gender." In Neil Wrigley and Michelle Lowe, eds. *Retailing, Consumption and Capital: Towards the New Retail Geography*. Harlow: Longman. 221-237.

Gold, John Robert (1980). *An Introduction to Behavioural Geography*. London: Oxford University Press.

Golledge, Reginald G. (1999). "Human Wayfinding and Cognitive Maps". In Golledge, ed. *Wayfinding Behavior. Cognitive Mapping and Other Spatial Processes*. London, Baltimore: The John Hopkins University Press. 5-45.

--- (2006). "Philosophical Bases of Behavioural Research in Geography." In Aitken and Valentine (2006). 75-85.

Golledge, Reginald G. and Aron N. Spector (1978). "Comprehending the Urban Environment: Theory and Practice." *Geographical Analysis*, vol. 10: 4. 403-426.

Goodman, Diane (1996). "What is chick-lit?" http://electronicbookreview.com/thread/writingpostfeminism/gutsy (27.09.2015).

Goodreads (2013). "Cheryl's Reviews > Turning Forty by Mike Gayle." www.goodreads.com/book/show/670973725?book_show_action=true (27.09. 2015).

Gormley, Sarah (2009). "Introduction." In Gormley and Mills (2009). http://extra.shu.ac.uk/wpw/chicklit/gormley.html. (27.09.2015).

Gormley, Sarah and Sara Mills, eds. (2009). *Chick Lit. Working Papers on the Web: Chick Lit*. http://extra.shu.ac.uk/wpw/chicklit. (27.09.2015).

Gottlieb, Robert (2007). *Reinventing Los Angeles. Nature and Community in the Global City*. Cambridge, London: MIT Press.

Gray, Paul (2000). "Publishing: Passion on the Pages." *Time Magazine*, 20 March. http://content.time.com/time/magazine/article/0,9171,996381,00.html (27.09. 2015).

Greenblatt, Stephen et al., eds. (2012). *The Norton Anthology of English Literature*, vol. 1. 9th edition. New York and London: W.W. Norton Company.

Greenlees, Donald (2008). "An Investment Banker Finds Fame Off the Books". *New York Times*, 26 March. www.nytimes.com/2008/03/26/books/26bhagat.html?_r=0 (27.09.2015).

Gregory, Derek (1978). *Ideology, Science and Human Geography*. London: Hutchinson & Co.

Gusfield, Joseph (1991). "Benevolent Repression: Popular Culture, Social Structure, and the Control of Drinking." In Susanna Barrows and Robin Room, eds. *Drinking. Behavior and Belief in Modern History*. Berkeley: University of California Press. 399-424.

Hägerstrand, Torsten (1985). "'Time-Geography: Focus on the Corporeality of Man, Society and Environment." In Shūhei Aida, ed. *The Science and Praxis of Complexity: Contributions to the Symposium Held at Montpellier, France, 9-11 May, 1984*. Tokyo: United Nations University. 193-216.

Hall, Stuart (1997). "Introduction". In Hall, ed. *Representation. Cultural Representations and Signifying Practices*. London, Thousand Oaks, New Delhi: Sage. 1-11.

Hall, Stuart and Alan O'Shea (2013). "Common-Sense Neoliberalism." In Hall, Massey and Rustin (2013). www.lwbooks.co.uk/journals/soundings/pdfs/Manifesto_commonsense_neoliberalism.pdf (28.08.15).

Hall, Stuart, Doreen Massey and Michael Rustin, eds. (2013). *After Neoliberalism? The Kilburn Manifesto.* (*Soundings. A Journal of Politics and Culture.*) www.lwbooks.co.uk/journals/soundings/manifesto.html (28.08.15).

Hall, Stuart, Doreen Massey and Michael Rustin (2013a). "After Neoliberalism: Analysing the Present." In Hall, Massey and Rustin (2013). www.lwbooks.co.uk/journals/soundings/pdfs/s53hallmasseyrustin.pdf (28.08.15).

Hameed, Amina and Shehla Amjad (2009). "Impact of Office Design on Employees' Productivity: A Case Study of Banking Organizations of Abbottabad, Pakistan." *Journal of Public Affairs, Administration and Management*, vol. 3: 1. 1-13.

Hardy, John (1984). *Jane Austen's Heroines. Intimacy in Human Relationships.* London et. al.: Routledge & Kegan Paul.

Hartley, John (2001). "Situation Comedy, Part 1." In Glen Creeber, ed. *The Television Genre Book.* London: BFI Publishing. 65-67.

Harvey, David ([1989] 1992). *The Condition of Postmodernity. An Enquiry into the Origins of Cultural Change*. Cambridge, Oxford: Blackwell.

--- (1997). "Contested Cities: Social Process and Spatial Form." In Nick Jewson and Susan MacGregor, eds. *Transforming Cities. Contested Governance and New Spatial Divisions*. London: Routledge. 17-24.

Harzewski, Stephanie (2006). "Tradition and Displacement in the New Novel of Manners." In Ferriss and Young (2006). 29-46.

--- (2011). *Chick Lit and Postfeminism.* Charlottesville, London: University of Virginia Press.

Heaven, Patrick C. L. (1994). *Contemporary Adolescence. A Social Psychological Approach.* Melbourne: Macmillan Education Australia PIY Ltd.

Hedge, Alan (1982). "The Open-Plan Office: A Systematic Investigation of Employee Reactions to Their Work Environment." *Environment and Behavior*, vol. 14. 519-542.

Heft, Harry (1988). "Review Essay: The Development of Gibson's Ecological Approach to Perception." *Journal of Environmental Psychology*, vol. 8. 325-334.

Heidegger, Martin ([1951] 2012). "Building, Dwelling, Thinking." In Chiara Briganti and Kathy Mezei, eds. *The Domestic Space Reader.* Toronto: University of Toronto Press. 21-26.

Heiss, Anita (2007). *Not Meeting Mr Right.* Sydney, Glenfield, London: Bantam.

--- (2008). *Avoiding Mr Right*. Sydney et al.: Bantam.

--- (2010). *Manhattan Dreaming*. Sydney et al.: Bantam.

--- (2011). *Paris Dreaming*. Sydney et al.: Bantam.

Heitman, Bethany (n.d.) "Good Girlfriend Behavior: Do This, Not That." http://www.cosmopolitan.com/sex-love/relationship-advice/be-a-good-girlfriend-test-6#fbIndex6 (27.09.2015).

Heller, Agnes (1984). *Everyday Life*. London: Routledge.

--- (1995). "Where are We at Home?" *Thesis Eleven*, vol. 41: 1. 1-18.

Hess-Lüttich, Ernest W. B. (2012). "Spatial Turn: On the Concept of Space in Cultural Geography and Literary Theory." *Journal for Theoretical Cartography*, vol. 5. 1-11.

Hirschon, Renée (1993). "Essential Objects and the Sacred: Interior and Exterior Space in Urban Greek Locality." In Shirley Ardener, ed. *Women and Space: Ground Rules and Social Maps*. Oxford: Berg. 70-86.

Hoffmann, Joan M. (2007). "'She loves with love that cannot tire': The Image of the Angel in the House across Cultures and across Time." *Pacific Coast Philology*, vol. 42: 2. 264-271.

Hollows, Joanne (2000). *Feminism, Femininity and Popular Culture*. Manchester: Manchester University Press.

Holmes, Oliver Wendell (1878). *Holmes's Illustrated Poems*. Revised edition. Boston: James R. Osgood and Company.

Hologa, Marie and Cyprian Piskurek (2013). "Building a Structure of Feeling: Raymond Williams and Millennium Architecture." In Marie Hologa et al., eds. *Cases of Intervention: The Great Variety of British Cultural Studies*. Newcastle upon Tyne: Cambridge Scholars Publishing. 83-101.

Homer ([720 B.C.?] 1990). *The Odyssey of Homer*. Trans. Allen Mandelbaum. Berkley et al.: University of California Press.

Hornby, Nick ([1995] 2010). *High Fidelity*. London, et al.: Penguin Books.

--- (1998). *About a Boy*. London: Victor Gollancz.

Horwitz, Jaime and Jerome Tognoli (1982). "Role of Home in Adult Development: Women and Men Living Alone Describe Their Residential Histories." *Family Relations*, vol. 31: 3. 335-341.

How To Write A Mills & Boon (2008). Dir. Claire Martin. Starring Stella Duffy. BBC DVD.

Howard, Matt (2004). *Street Furniture*. Kent Town: Wakefield Press.

--- (2008). *Taking Off*. Crows Nest: Allen & Unwin.

--- (2010). *Ethan Grout*. Millers Point: Pier 9.

Hubbard, Phil (2005). "Space/Place." In David Atkinson et al., eds. *Cultural Geography. A Critical Dictionary of Key Concepts*. London, New York: I.B. Tauris. 41-48.

--- ([2005] 2007). "The Geographies of 'Going Out': Emotion and Embodiment in the Evening Economy." In Joyce Davidson, Liz Bondi, Mick Smith, eds. *Emotional Geographies*. Aldershot, Burlington: Ashgate. 117-134.

Hubbard, Phil et al. (2002). *Thinking Geographically. Space, Theory and Contemporary Human Geography*. London, New York: Continuum.

Hui, Allison (2011). "Placing Nostalgia: The Process of Returning and Remaking Home." In Davidson, Park and Shields (2011). 65-84.

Illbruck, Helmut (2012). *Nostalgia. Origins and Ends of an Unenlightened Disease*. Evanston: Northwestern University Press.

Illouz, Eva (1997). *Consuming the Romantic Utopia. Love and the Cultural Contradictions of Capitalism*. Berkeley, Los Angeles, London: University of California Press.

India Tribune (2012). "Rape Statistics around the World." 29 December. http://www.indiatribune.com/rape-statistics-around-the-world/ (27.09.2015).

Iqbal Viswamohan, Aysha, ed. (2013). *Postliberalization Indian Novels in English. Politics of Global Reception and Awards*. London et al.: Anthem Press.

Iqbal Viswamohan, Aysha (2013a). "Marketing Lad Lit, Creating Bestsellers: The Importance of Being Chetan Bhagat." In Iqbal Viswamohan (2013). 19-29.

Isbister, Georgina (2009). "Chick Lit: A Postfeminist Fairy Tale." In Gormley and Mills (2009). http://extra.shu.ac.uk/wpw/chicklit/isbister.html (27.09.2015).

Jackson, Peter ([1982] 1992). *Maps of Meaning. An Introduction to Cultural Geography*. London, New York: Routledge.

--- (1999). "Consumption and Identity: The Cultural Politics of Shopping." *European Planning Studies*, vol. 7: 1. 25-39.

--- (2004). "Local consumption cultures in a globalizing world." *Transactions of the Institute of British Geographers*, vol. 29: 2. 165-178.

Jackson, Peter and Beverly Holbrook (1995). "Multiple Meanings: Shopping and the Cultural Politics of Identity." *Environment and Planning A*, vol. 27. 1913-1930.

Jackson, Phil (2004). *Inside Clubbing. Sensual Experiments in the Art of Being Human*. Oxford, New York: Berg.

Jameson, Fredric (1991). *Postmodernism, or, The Cultural Logic of Late Capitalism*. London: Verso.

Jayne, Mark (2006). *Cities and Consumption*. London, Abingdon, New York: Routledge.

Jayne, Mark, Gill Valentine and Sarah L. Holloway (2011). *Alcohol, Drinking, Drunkenness. (Dis)Orderly Spaces*. Farnham, Burlinton: Ashgate.

Jeffers McDonald, Tamar (2007). *Romantic Comedy: Boy Meets Girl Meets Genre*. London: Wallflower.

Jennings, Paul (2007). *The Local. A History of the English Pub*. Stroud: Tempus.

Jones, Peter and Andrew Lockwood ([1989] 2006). *The Management of Hotel Operations. An Innovative Approach to the Study of Hotel Management*. London: Thomson Learning.

Kala, Advaita ([2007] 2009). *Almost Single*. New York: Bantam Dell.

Kaltenborn, Bjørn P. (1997). "Recreation Homes in Natural Settings: Factors Affecting Place Attachment." *Norsk Geografisk Tidsskrift – Norwegian Journal of Geography*, vol. 51: 4. 187-198.

Kasbekar, Asha (2006). *Pop Culture India!: Media, Arts, and Lifestyle*. Santa Barbara, Denver, Oxford: ABC-Clio Inc.

Katz, Tamar (2010). "City Memory, City History: Urban Nostalgia, *The Colossus of New York*, and Late-Twentieth-Century Historical Fiction." *Contemporary Literature*, vol. 51: 4. 810-851.

Kaushal, Swati (2004). *Piece of Cake*. New Delhi: Penguin Books India.

Kerckhoff, Alan C. and Keith E. Davis (1962). "Value Consensus and Need Complementarity in Mate Selection." *American Sociological Review*, vol. 27: 3. 295-303.

Kershaw, Baz (2003). "Curiosity or Contempt: On Spectacle, the Human, and Activism." *Theatre Journal*, vol. 55: 4. 591-611.

Kiesow, Holger (2007). *Literature as a Mirror of Society. The Representations of Masculinity in Contemporary British Fiction*. Saarbrücken: VDW Verlag Dr. Müller.

Kießling, Tina (2012). *Nostalgie und Retro-Trends als Marketingchance. Eine Analyse der Ursachen für die Nachfrage nach vergangenheitsbezogenen Konsumangeboten*. Wiesbaden: Springer Gabler.

Kiley, Dan ([1983] 1984). *The Peter Pan Syndrome. Men Who Have Never Grown Up*. London: Transworld Publishers Ltd. Corgi Books.

Kinsella, Sophie ([2000] 2007). [*The Secret Dreamworld of a Shopaholic*] *Confessions of a Shopaholic*. Reissue. New York: Dial Press.

--- ([2001] 2004). [*Shopaholic Abroad*] *Shopaholic Takes Manhattan*. New York: Dell.

--- (2002). *Shopaholic Ties the Knot*. London: Black Swan.

--- (2003). *Can You Keep a Secret?*. London: Black Swan.

--- ([2005] 2006). *The Undomestic Goddess*. London: Black Swan.

--- (2008). *Remember Me?*. London: Black Swan.

--- ([2009] 2010). *Twenties Girl*. London: Black Swan.

--- (2012). *I've Got Your Number*. London:. Black Swan.

Kirk, William (1963). "Problems of Geography." *Geography: An International Journal*, vol. 48: 4. 357-371.

Klein, Naomi (2000). *No Logo*. New York: Picador.

Klimasmith, Elizabeth (2005). *At Home in the City. Urban Domesticity in American Literature and Culture, 1850-1930*. Hanover: University Press of New England.

Klinenberg, Eric ([2012] 2013). *Going Solo. The Extraordinary Rise and Surprising Appeal of Living Alone*. London: Duckworth Overlook.

--- (2012). "I Want to Be Alone: The Rise and Rise of Solo Living." *The Guardian*, 30 March. www.theguardian.com/lifeandstyle/2012/mar/30/the-rise-of-solo-living (27.09.2015).

Kneale, James (2001). "The Place of Drink: Temperance and the Public, 1856-1914." *Social and Cultural Geography*, vol. 2: 1. 43-59.

Knowles, Joanne (2004). "Editorial". In *Diegesis: Journal of the Association for Research in Popular Fictions: Chicklit*, vol. 8. 2-3.

--- (2004a). "Material Girls". In *Diegesis: Journal of the Asociation for Research in Popular Fictions: Chicklit*, vol. 8. 36-41.

Knox, Paul L. and Sallie A. Marston (1998). *Place and Regions in Global Context. Human Geography*. Upper Saddle River: Prentice-Hall, Inc.

Kobus, Kimberly (2003). "Peers and adolescent smoking." *Addiction*, vol. 98: supplement 1. 37-55.

Kraus, Richard (1978). *Recreation and Leisure in Modern Society*. Second Edition. Santa Monica: Goodyear Publishing Inc.

Krebs, Martina (2009). *Hotel Stories – Representations of Escapes and Encounters in Fiction and Film*. Trier: Wissenschaftlicher Verlag Trier.

Krinsky, Charles (2013). "Introduction: The Moral Panic Concept." In Krinsky, ed. *The Ashgate Research Companion to Moral Panics*. Farnham, Burlington: Ashgate. 1-14.

La'Brooy, Melanie (2003). *Love Struck*. Camberwell et al.: Penguin Books.

--- (2005). *The Wish List*. Camberwell et al.: Penguin Books.

--- (2010). *[Bittersweet] The Wedding Planner*. London: Piatkus.

Laing, Andrew (1997). "New Patterns of Work: The Design of the Office". In John Worthington, ed. *Reinventing the Workplace*. Oxford et al.: Architectural Press. 23-38.

Lal, Nandini (2004). "Single Game's Book Review: Swati Kaushal's Piece of Cake". *India Today*, 27 December. indiatoday.intoday.in/story/swati-kaushals-novel-titled-piece-of-cake-released/ 1/194855.html (27.09.2015).

Lando, Fabio (1996). "Fact and Fiction: Geography and Literature." *GeoJournal*, vol. 38: 1. 3-18.

Lanegran, David A. (2007). "Introduction." In Moseley, Lanegran and Pandit (2007). 181-184.

Langman, Lauren (1992). "Neon Cages. Shopping for Subjectivity." In Rob Shields (1992). 40-82.

Latour, Bruno (1996). "On Actor Network Theory: A Few Clarifications." *Soziale Welt*, vol. 47. 360-381.

--- (2005). *Reassembling the Social. An Introduction to Actor-Network-Theory*. Oxford: Oxford University Press.

Lee, So Young and Jay L. Brand (2005). "Effects of control over office workspace on perceptions of the work environment and work outcomes." *Journal of Environmental Psychology*, vol. 25. 323-333.

Lefebvre, Henri ([1974] 1991). *The Production of Space*. Trans. Donald Nicholson-Smith. Maldon, Oxford, Carlton: Blackwell Publishers.

Lenntorp, Bo (2004). "Path, Prism, Project, Pocket and Population: An Introduction." *Geografiska Annaler. Series B, Human Geography*, vol. 86: 4. 223-226.

Lenz, Christian (2013). "Let Love Lead the Way: Spatial Compatibility and Territories of Love in Chick- and Lad-Lit." In Brooke L. Rogers and Anna Sugiyama, eds. *Space and Place: Diversity in Reality, Imagination and Representation*. Oxford: Inter-Disciplinary Press. 199-210.

--- (2013a). "Spaces, Places and Bridget Jones." In Marie Hologa et al., eds. *Cases of Intervention. The Great Variety of Cultural Studies*. Newcastle: Cambridge Scholars Publishing. 123-141.

Lévi-Strauss, Claude ([1963] 1974). *Structural Anthropology*. Trans. Claire Jacobson. New York: Basic Books.

Little, Ben (2013). "Class and Generation under Neoliberalism." In Hall, Massey and Rustin (2013). www.lwbooks.co.uk/journals/soundings/pdfs/Manifesto_class_and_generation.pdf (27.09.2015).

Logan, Andy (1961). "Onward and Upward With the Arts: Building for Glory." *The New Yorker, 21 October*. www.newyorker.com/magazine/1961/10/21/building-for-glory *(27.09.2015)*.

Lotman, Jurij M. (1972). *Die Struktur literarischer Texte*. Trans. Rolf-Dietrich Keil. München: Wilhelm Fink Verlag UTB.

Lovatt, Andy (1996). "The Ecstasy of Urban Regeneration: Regulation of the Night-Time Economy in the Transition to a Post-Fordist City." In Justin O'Connor and Derek Wynne, eds. *From the Margins to the Centre*. Aldershot: Ashgate. 141-168.

Lunt, Peter K. and Sonia M. Livingstone (1992). *Mass Consumption and Personal Identity: Everyday Economic Experience*. Buckingham, Bristol (PA): Open University Press.

Lynch, Kevin (1960). *The Image of the City*. Cambridge, Massachusetts: MIT Press.

Lyotard, Jean-Francois (1984). *The Postmodern Condition: A Report on Knowledge*. Transl. Geoff Bennington and Brian Massumi. Minneapolis: University of Minnesota Press.

Maffesoli, Michel ([1988] 1996). *The Time of Tribes. The Decline of Individualism in Mass Society*. Trans. Don Smith. London, Thousand Oakes, New Delhi: Sage.

Malbon, Ben (1998). "Clubbing: Consumption, Identity and the Spatial Practices of Every-Night Life." In Tracey Skelton and Gill Valentine, eds. *Cool Places: Geographies of Youth Cultures*. London, New York: Routledge. 266-286.

--- (1999). *Clubbing. Dancing, Ecstasy and Vitality*. London, New York: Routledge.

Mallett, Shelley (2004). "Understanding Home: A Critical Review of the Literature." *The Sociological Review*, vol. 52: 1. 62-84.

Marapakwar, Prafulla (2012). "Will it soon be goodbye to 'babu' and 'babudom'?" *The Times of India*, 4 June. http://timesofindia.indiatimes.com/india/Will-it-soon-be-goodbye-to-babu-babudom/articlehow/13789075.cms (27.09.2015).

Massey, Doreen (1992). "A Place Called Home?" *New Formations: A Journal of Culture, Theory, Politics*, vol. 17. 3-15.

--- (1993). "Questions of Locality." *Geography*, vol. 78. 142-149.

--- (1994). *Space, Place and Gender*. Cambridge: Polity Press.

--- (2005). *For Space*. London, Thousand Oaks, New Delhi: Sage Publications.

--- ([1999] 2007). "Spaces of Politics." In Massey, Allen and Sarre (2007). 279-294.

--- (2013). "Vocabularies of the Economy." In Hall, Massey and Rustin (2013). www.lwbooks.co.uk/journals/soundings/pdfs/Vocabularies%20of%20the%20economy.pdf (28.08.15).

Massey, Doreen, John Allen and Philip Sarre, eds. ([1997] 2007). *Human Geography Today*. Cambridge, Oxford, Malden: Polity Press.

May, Paul (2003). "Why I Love... the Gherkin." *The Guardian*, 23 September. www.guardian.co.uk/theguardian/2003/sep/23/features11.g2 (27.09.2015).

Mazza, Cris (2006). "Who's Laughing Now? A Short History of Chick Lit and the Perversion of a Genre." In Ferriss and Young (2006). 17-28.

McAleer, Joseph (1999). *Passion's Fortune. The Story of Mills & Boon*. Oxford: Oxford University Press.

McCrum, Robert (2010). "Chetan Bhagat: The Paperback King of India." *The Guardian*, 24 January. www.guardian.co.uk/2010/jan/24/chetan-bhagat-robert mccrum (27.09.2015).

McDowell, Linda (1999). *Gender, Identity and Place. Understanding Feminist Geographies*. Cambridge: Polity Press.

Mehigan, Tim and Alan Corkhill (2013). "Vorwort." In Mehigan and Corkhill, eds. *Raumlektüren. Der Spatial Turn und die Literatur der Moderne*. Bielefeld: Transcript. 7-21.

Mezei, Kathy and Chiara Briganti (2002). "Reading the House: A Literary Perspective." *SIGNS: Journal of Women in Culture and Society*, vol. 27: 3. 837-846.

Miller, Daniel (1998). *A Theory of Shopping*. Cambridge: Polity Press.

Miller, Daniel et al. ([1998] 1999). *Shopping, Place and Identity*. London, New York: Routledge.

Mills & Boon Australia (n.d.). "About Us". www.millsandboon.com.au/about#history (27.09.2015).

Mills & Boon United Kingdom (n.d.). "About Us". www.millsandboon.co.uk/np/Content/ContentPage/5 (27.09.2015).

Mills, Jane (1989). *Womanwords. A Vocabulary of Culture and Patriarchal Society*. London: Virago Press.

Mitchell, Don (2000). *Cultural Geography: A Critical Introduction*. Oxford: Blackwell Publishers.

Modleski, Tania (1982). *Loving With a Vengeance. Mass-Produced Fantasies for Women*. New York, London: Routledge.

Moghe, Kiran and Mariam Dhawale (2003). "Anti-Dowry Convention in Maharashtra." *All India Democratic Women's* Association 12 October. http://aidwaonline.org/issues_of_concern/anti-dowry-convention-maharashtra (27.09.2015).

Montoro, Rocío (2007). "The Stylistics of Popular Fiction: A Socio-Cognitive Perspective." In Marina Lambrou and Peter Stockwell, eds. *Contemporary Stylistics*. London, New York: Continuum. 68-80.

--- ([2012] 2013). *Chick Lit. The Stylistics of Cappuccino Fiction*. London et al.: Bloomsbury.

Moore, Gary T. and Reginald G. Golledge (1976). "Environmental Knowing: Concepts and Theories." In Moore and Golledge, eds. *Environmental Knowing*. Dowden: Hutchinson & Ross. 3-24.

Morris, Pam, ed. (1994). *The Bakhtin Reader. Selected Writings of Bakhtin, Medvedev and Voloshinov*. London et al.: Edward Arnold.

Mort, Frank (1989). "The Politics of Consumption." In Stuart Hall and Martin Jacques, eds. *New Times. The Changing Face of Politics in the 1990s*. London: Lawrence & Wishart. 160-172.

Mortimer, Claire (2010). *Romantic Comedy*. London: Routledge.

Moseley, William, David Lanegran and Kavita Pandit, eds. (2007). *The Introductory Reader in Human Geography: Contemporary Debates and Classic Writing*. Oxford: Blackwell Publishing.

Moseley, William, David Lanegran and Kavita Pandit (2007a). "Introduction: Situation Human Geography." In Moseley, Lanegran and Pandit (2007). 1-9.

Muehlenhaus, Ian (2008). "Lecture Notes: Space and Place." 28 February. www.ian.muehlenhaus.com/muehlenhausCollege/Courses/Geog111/Lectures/Week3b.pdf (25.02.2014).

Muñoz González, Beatriz (2005). "Topophilia and Topophobia: The Home as an Evocative Place of Contradictory Emotions." *Space and Culture*, vol. 8: 2. 193-213.

Munro, Moira and Ruth Madigan (1999). "Negotiating Space in the Family Home." In Cieraad (1999). 107-117.

Murphy, Jonathan (2011). "Indian Call Centre Workers: Vanguard of a Global Middle Class?" *Work, Employment and Society*, vol. 25: 3. 417-433.

Musée du Quai Branly (n.d.) www.quaibranly.fr/fr/collections/les-collections-de-reference/presentation-des-collections-de-reference.html (27.09.2015).

Needleman, Sarah E. (2009). "Office Personal Space Is Crowded Out." *The Wall Street Journal*, 7 December. http://online.wsj.com/news/articles/SB10001424052748703735004574576510304934876 (27.09.2015).

Nieragden, Göran (2000). "'Cynical Young Men' – ein neues Paradigma für den englischen Roman der 1990er Jahre (?): Christopher Brookmyre, Nick Hornby, Irvine Welsh." In Ansgar and Vera Nünning, eds. *Klassiker und Strömungen des englischen Romans im 20. Jahrhundert.* Trier: Wissenschaftlicher Verlag Trier. 221-241.

Nixon, Sean (2001). "Resignifying Masculinity: From 'New Man' to 'New Lad'." In David Morley and Kevin Robins, eds. *British Cultural Studies. Geography, Nationality, and Identity.* Oxford: Oxford University Press. 373-385.

Norberg-Schulz, Christian (1982). *Genius Loci: Landschaft, Lebensraum, Baukunst.* Stuttgart: Klett-Cotta.

O'Keefe, John and Lynn Nadel (1978). *The Hippocampus as a Cognitive Map.* Oxford: Oxford University Press.

O'Sullivan, Ellen ([2006] 2013). "Power, Promise, and Possibilities of Parks, Recreation, and Leisure." In Human Kinetics, ed. *Introduction to Recreation and Leisure.* Second Edition. Champaign et al.: Human Kinetics, Inc. 3-20.

Oakes, Timothy and Patricia L. Price, eds. (2008). *The Cultural Geography Reader.* London, New York: Routledge.

Oakes, Timothy and Patricia L. Price (2008a). "Introduction". In Oakes and Price (2008). 1-8.

Ochsner, Andrea (2009). *Lad Trouble. Masculinity and Identity in the British Male Confessional Novel of the 1990s.* Bielefeld: Transcript.

Office for National Statistics (2015). "Families and Households, 2014." 28 January. www.ons.gov.uk/ons/dcp171778_393133.pdf (30.09.2015).

Oldenburg, Ray (1989). *The Great Good Place. Cafés, Coffee Shops, Community Centers, Beauty Parlors, General Stores, Bars, Hangouts and How They Get You Through the Day.* New York: Paragon House.

--- (2001). "Introduction." In Oldenburg (ed.). *Celebrating the Third Place: Inspiring Stories about the "Great Good Places" at the Heart of Our Communities.* New York: Marlowe & Company. 1-7.

Ommundsen, Wenche (2011). "Sex and the Global City: Chick Lit With a Difference." *Contemporary Women's Writing*, vol. 5: 2. 107-124.

Oxford English Dictionary (n.d.). www.oed.com (27.09.2015).

Page, Benedicte (2013). "Bridget Jones: First-Day Sales 'Topped 46,000'." *The Bookseller*, 14 October. www.thebookseller.com/news/jones-sales-top-46000.html (27.09.2015).

Paizis, George (1998). *Love and the Novel. The Poetics and Politics of Romantic Fiction.* Basingstoke, London: Macmillan Press Ltd.

Paling, Chris ([2004] 2007). "Dad-Lit in Decline." *Rationalist Association*, 31 May. http://rationalist.org.uk/articles/687/dad-lit-in-decline (27.09.2015).

Palmer, Jerry (1991). *Potboilers: Methods, Concepts and Case Studies in Popular Fiction.* London, New York: Routledge.

Park, Ondine, Tonya K. Davidson and Rob Shields (2011). "Introduction." In Davidson, Park and Shields (2011). 1-15.

Parker, Sharon K., Toby D. Wall and John L. Cordery (2001). "Future Work Design Research and Practice: Towards an Elaborated Model of Work Design." *Journal of Occupational and Organizational Psychology*, vol. 74: 4. 413-440.

Patterson, Christina (2013). "Bridget Jones: Mad About the Boy [sic] by Helen Fielding." *The Sunday Times*, 6 October. www.thesundaytimes.co.uk/sto/culture /books/fiction/article1321703.ece (27.09.2015).

Peet, Richard (1998). *Modern Geographic Thought*. Oxford: Blackwell Publishing.

Peitz, Annette (2009). *Chick Lit. Genrekonstituierende Untersuchungen unter anglo -amerikanischem Einfluss*. Frankfurt a. M. et al.: Peter Lang.

Pennartz, Paul J.J. (1999). "Home: The Experience of Atmosphere." In Cieraad (1999). 95-106.

Pérez-Serrano, Elena (2009). "Chick Lit and Marian Keyes: The Ideological Background of the Genre." In Gormley and Mills (2009). http://extra.shu.ac.uk/wpw/chicklit/perezserrano.html (27.09.2015).

Pini, Barbara and Josephine Previte (2013). "Bourdieu, the boom and cashed-up Bogans." *Journal of Sociology*, vol. 49: 2-3. 256-271.

Pocock, Douglas C. D. (1981). "Introduction: Imaginative Literature and the Geographer." In Pocock, ed. *Humanistic Geography and Literature. Essays on the Experience of Place*. London: Croom Helm. 9-19.

Porteous, J. Douglas (1976). "Home: The Territorial Core." *Geographical Review*, vol. 66: 4. 383-390.

Pred, Allan (1984). "Place as Historically Contingent Process: Structuration and the Time-Geography of Becoming Places." *Annals of the Association of American Geographers*, vol. 74: 2. 279-297.

Pronovost, Gilles (1998). *The Sociology of Leisure*. London, Thousand Oakes: Sage.

Purkayastha, Bandana et al. (2003). "The Study of Gender in India: A Partial Review." *Gender and Society*, vol. 17: 4. 503-524.

Putnam, Tim (1999). "'Postmodern' Home Life." In Cieraad (1999). 144-152.

Radford, Jean (1986). "Introduction." In Radford, ed. *The Progress of Romance. The Politics of Popular Fiction*. London, New York: Routledge & Kegan Paul. 1-20.

Radway, Janice A. ([1984] 1991). *Reading the Romance: Women, Partriarchy, and Popular Literature*. Chapel Hill and London: The University of North Carolina Press.

Rajan, Nandagopal (2012). "Love at First Site." *Business Today*, 23 December. http://businesstoday.intoday.in/story/india-new-love-interest-is-online-dating/1/190332.html (27.09.2015).

Rajashree (2006). *Trust Me*. New Delhi: Rupa & Co.

Ramesh, Babu P. (2004). "'Cyber Coolies' in BPO." *Economic and Political Weekly*, vol. 39: 5. 492-497.

Rask Knudsen, Eva (2004). *The Circle & the Spiral: A Study of Australian Aboriginal and New Zealand Māori Literature*. Amsterdam: Rodopi.

Reekie, Gail (1993). *Temptations. Sex, Selling and the Department Store*. Sydney: Allen & Unwin.

Regis, Pamela (2003). *A Natural History of the Romance Novel*. Philadelphia: University of Pennsylvania Press.

Reimer, Suzanne and Deborah Leslie (2004). "Identity, Consumption, and the Home." *Home Cultures*, vol. 1: 1. 187-208.

Rice, Maureen (2003). "Love in the 21st Century." *The Observer*, 20 April. www.therguardian.com/theobserver/2003/apr/20/features.magazine27 (27.09.2015).

Rief, Silvia (2009). *Club Cultures. Boundaries, Identities, and Otherness*. New York, London, Abingdon: Routledge.

Robinson, Kathryn (2009). "Why I Heart Chick Lit. Never Mind Doris Lessingit's [sic] the Ordinary Details That Count." *Seattle News Weekly*, 9 October. www.seattleweekly.com/2003-10-22/arts/why-i-heart-chick-lit (27.09.2015).

Rogers, Michelle K. (2007). "This is me only a lot worse – phew! (Review of *Confessions of a Shopaholic*)." 16 May. www.amazon.com/review/R1XDEXF7OUP99B (27.09.2015).

Rojek, Chris (1995). *Decentring Leisure. Rethinking Leisure Theory*. London, Thousand Oaks, New Delhi: Sage.

--- (2010). *The Labour of Leisure. The Culture of Free Time*. Los Angeles et al.: Sage.

Röll, Michaela (2002). *"No Place Like Home": Tendenzen zentrierter und dezentrierter Raumvorstellungen in den Romanen John Irvings und Margaret Atwood*. Dissertation. hss.ulb.uni-bonn.de/2002/0107.0107.pdf (27.09.2015).

Romance Writers of America (n.d.). "About the Romance Genre." www.rwa.org/p/cm/ld/fid=578 (27.09.2015).

Rostek, Joanna (2013). "Migration, Capital, Space: Econotopic Constellations in Recent Literature about Polish Migrants in Ireland." In Katrin Röder and Ilse Wischer, eds. *Anglistentag Potsdam 2012: Proceedings*. Trier: Wissenschaftlicher Verlag Trier. 47-60.

Routledge, Clay et al. (2011). "The Past Makes the Present Meaningful: Nostalgia as an Existential Resource." *Journal of Personality and Social Psychology*, vol. 101: 3. 638-652.

Rubinfeld, Mark D. (2001). *Bound to Bond: Gender, Genre, and the Hollywood Romantic Comedy*. Westport: Praeger.

Ruskin, John (1865). *Sesame and Lilies. Two Lectures*. London: Smith, Elder and Co.

Rustin, Michael (2013). "A Relational Society." In Hall, Massey and Rustin (2013). www.lwbooks.co.uk/journals/soundings/pdfs/Soundings%20Manifesto_Rustin.pdf (28.08.2015).

Saldanha, Arun (2002). "Music, Space, Identity: Geographies of Youth in Bangalore." *Cultural Studies*, vol. 16: 3. 337-350.

Saunders, Peter and Peter Williams (1988). "The Constitution of the Home: Towards a Research Agenda." *Housing Studies*, vol. 3: 2. 81-93.

Sayer, Andrew (2006). "Realism as a Basis for Knowing the World." In Aitken and Valentine (2006). 98-106.

Schein, Richard H. ([2004] 2008). "Cultural Traditions." In James S. Duncan, Nuala C. Johnson and Richard H. Schein, eds. *A Companion to Cultural Geography*. Oxford: Blackwell Publishing. 11-23.

Seamon, David and Jacob Sowers (2008). "Place and Placelessness (1976): Edward Relph." In Phil Hubbard, Rob Kitchin and Gill Valentine, eds. *Key Texts in Human Geography*. London et al.: Sage. 43-52.

Self, Will (1999). "Big Dome". In Ian Jack, ed. *London: The Lives of the City. Granta*, vol. 65. London: Granta Publication. 115-125.

Sewell Jr., William H. ([1999] 2008). "The Concept(s) of Culture." In Oakes and Price (2008). 40-49.

Shields, Rob (1992a). "Spaces for the Subject of Consumption." In Shields, ed. *Lifestyle Shopping. The Subject of Consumption*. London, New York. 1-20.

--- (1992b). "The Individual, Consumption Cultures and the Fate of Community." In Shields, ed. *Lifestyle Shopping. The Subject of Consumption*. London, New York. 99-113.

Shop a Man (n.d.). www.shopaman.de (30.09.2015).

Showalter, Elaine (2002). "Ladlit." In Zachary Leader, ed. *On Modern British Fiction*. Oxford: Oxford University Press. 60-76.

Shultz, Earle and Walter Simmons (1959). *Offices in the Sky*. Indianapolis: Bobbs-Merrill.

Shurmer-Smith, Pamela (2002). "Introduction." In Shurmer-Smith, ed. *Doing Cultural Geography*. London: Sage Publications 1-7.

Sibani (2013). "Efficiencies of Work Space – New Trends in Office Design in India." *Light Green*, 24 January. www.blog.idream.in/?p=91 (30.09.2015).

Silverstone, Roger (1994). *Television and Everyday Life*. London, New York: Routledge.

Singer, Ben (2001). *Melodrama and Modernity. Early Sensational Cinema and Its Contexts*. New York: Columbia University Press.

Singh, Rajiv (2013). "Fairness Creams' Segment Slows Down: Has the Nation Overcome Its Dark Skin Complex?" *The Economic Times (Times of India)*, 18 August. http://articles.economictimes.indiatimes.com/2013-08-18/news/41421066_1_fairness-cream-fairness-products-skin-colour (30.09.2015).

Skinner, Tim (2012). "A workspace is not a workplace: A mobility strategy is crucial." *City A.M.*, 28 June. *www.cityam.com/article/workspace-not-workplace-mobility-strategy-crucial* (30.09.2015).

Smith, Caroline J. (2008). *Cosmopolitan Culture and Consumerism in Chick Lit.* New York, London: Routledge.

Smith, Michael A. (1983). "Social Usages of the Public Drinking House: Changing Aspects of Class and Leisure." *The British Journal of Sociology*, vol. 34: 3. 367-385.

Smith, Susan J. ([1999] 2007). "The Cultural Politics of Difference." In Massey, Allen and Sarre (2007). 129-150.

Smyczyńska, Katarzyna (2007). *The World According to Bridget Jones. Discourses of Identity in Chicklit Fictions.* Frankfurt a.M. et al.: Peter Lang.

Snehanshu, Harsh ([2009] 2012). *Oops! 'I' Fell In Love! Just By Chance...* . New Delhi: Srishti Publishers & Distributors.

--- ([2011] 2012a). *Ouch! That 'Hearts'..* . New Delhi: Srishti Publishers & Distributors.

--- (2012b). *She Is Single I'm Taken and We're Committed...* . New Delhi: Srishti Publishers & Distributors.

---- (2013). *Because Shit Happened.* Noida: Random House India.

Soja, Edward W. (1996). *Thirdspace. Journeys to Los Angeles and Other Real-and-Imagined Places.* Cambridge, Oxford: Blackwell Publishers.

--- ([1999] 2007). "Thirdspace: Expanding the Scope of the Geographical Imagination." In Massey, Allen and Sarre (2007). 260-278.

Sparks, Richard, Evi Girling and Ian Loader (2001). "Fear and Everyday Urban Lives." *Urban Studies*, vol. 38: 5-6. 885-898.

Stacey, Jackie and Lynne Pearce (1995). "The Heart of the Matter: Feminists Revisit Romance." In Lynne Pearce and Jackie Stacey, eds. *Romance Revisited.* London: Lawrence & Wishart. 11-45.

Stallybrass, Peter and Allon White (1986). *The Politics and Poetics of Transgression.* London: Methuen.

Stea, David (1976). "Program Notes on a Spatial Fugue." In Gary T. Moore and Reginald G. Golledge, eds. *Environmental Knowing.* Dowden: Hutchinson & Ross. 106-120.

Stewart, Susan (1984). *On Longing. Narratives of the Miniature, the Gigantic, the Souvenir, the Collection.* Baltimore: The John Hopkins University Press.

Sumartojo, Rini (2004). "Contesting Place. Antigay and –Lesbian Hate Crime in Columbus, Ohio." In Colin Flint, ed. *Spaces of Hate. Geographies of Discrimination and Intolerance in the U.S.A.*. London, New York: Routledge. 87-107.

Sundstrom, Eric (1986). *Work Places. The Psychology of the Physical Environment in Offices and Factories.* Cambridge et al.: Cambridge University Press.

Taylor, Frederick Winslow ([1911] 1998). *The Principles of Scientific Management*. Mineola: Dover Publications.

Taylor, Ralph (1988). *Human Territorial Functioning. An Empirical, Evolutionary Perspective on Individual and Small Group Territorial Cognitions, Behaviors, and Consequences*. Cambridge: University Press.

Terkenli, Theano S. (1995). "Home as a Region." *Geographical Review*, vol. 85: 3. 324-334.

The Economist (2006). "A Guide to Womenomics." 12 April. www.economist.com/node/6802551 (30.09.2015).

--- (2013). "Rape and Murder in Delhi". 5 January. www.economist.com/news/leaders/21569031-horrible-attack-could-prove-turning-point-indias-women-rape-and-murder-delhi (30.09.2015).

The Hindu (2013). "India still second fastest growing economy: Chidambaram." 27 July. www.thehindu.com/business/Economy/india-still-second-fastest-growing-economy-chidambaram/article4959820.ece (30.09.2015).

The Independent (2003). "Helen Fielding: Beyond Bridget." 5 October. http://archive.is/Zriky (30.09.2015).

The Indian Express (2012). "Lonely Hearts in Britain Spend £3 Billion Looking for Love: Study." 29 January. http://archive.indianexpress.com/news/lonely-hearts-in-britain-spend--3-billion-looking-for-love-study/905199/ (30.09.2015).

The Times of India (2013). "India still second fastest growing economy, says Chidambaram." 27 July. http://timesofindia.indiatimes.com/business/indiabusiness/India-still-second-fastest-growing-economy-Chidambaram-says/articleshow/21399516.cms *(30.09.2015).*

The Times of Money (2007). "India Poised." http://www.timesofmoney.com/remittance/html/ip_remithome.htm *(30.09.2015).*

Thornton, Sarah (1995). *Club Cultures. Music, Media and Subcultural Capital*. Cambridge: Polity Press.

Trigg, Dylan (2006). *The Aesthetics of Decay. Nothingness, Nostalgia, and the Absence of Reason*. New York: Peter Lang Publishing.

Tuan, Yi-Fu (1974). *Topophilia. A Study of Environmental Perceptions, Attitudes, and Values*. New Jersey: Prentice-Hall.

--- (1977). *Space and Place: The Perspective of Experience*. London: Edward Arnold Ltd.

Turner, Gavin and Jeremy Myerson (1998). *New Workspace New Culture. Office Design as a Catalyst for Change*. Aldershot, Brookfield: Gower Publishing.

Turner, Janice (2005). "Dirty Young Men." *The Guardian*, 22 October. www.guardian.co.uk/theguardian/2005/oct/22/weekend7.weekend3 (30.09.2015).

Turner, Victor ([1969] 2008). *The Ritual Process: Structure and Anti-Structure*. Renewed Edition. Chicago: Aldine Publishing.

Uberoi, Patricia ([2006] 2009). *Freedom and Destiny. Gender, Family, and Popular Culture in India*. New Delhi et al.: Oxford University Press.

Umminger, Allison (2006). “Supersizing Bridget Jones: What’s Really Eating the Women in Chick Lit.” In Ferriss and Young (2006). 239-252.

Urry, John and Jonas Larsson (2011). *The Tourist Gaze 3.0.* Third edition. London: SAGE.

Van Slooten, Jessica Lyn (2006). “Fashionably Indebted: Conspicuous Consumption, Fashion, and Romance in Sophie Kinsella’s Shopaholic Trilogy.” In Ferriss and Young (2006). 219-238.

Vischer, Jacqueline C. (2005). *Space Meets Status. Designing Workplace Performance.* Abingdon, New York: Routledge.

Vnuk, Rebecca (2005). “‘Chick Lit’: Hip Lit for Hip Chicks.” *Library Journal*, 15 July. http://reviews.libraryjournal.com/2005/07/collection-development/chick-lit-hip-lit-for-hip-chicks-collection-development-may-2005 (30.09.2015).

Wacquant, Loïc ([2006] 2011). “Habitus”. In Jens Beckert and Milan Zafirovski, eds. *International Encyclopedia of Economic Sociology.* Abingdon, New York: Routledge. 317-321.

Walmsley, D.J. and G.J. Lewis (1993). *People* and *Environment. Behavioural Approaches in Human Geograhy.* Second Edition. Harlow: Longman Group UK Limited.

Wapner, Seymour, Bernard Kaplan and Saul B. Cohen (1980). “An organismic-developmental perspective for understanding transactions of men and environments.” In Geoffrey Broadbent, Richard Bunt and Tomás Llorens, eds. *Meaning and Behaviour in the Built Environment.* Wiley New York. 223-252.

Warner, Jessica and Frank Ivis (2000). “Gin and Gender in Early Eighteenth-Century London.” *Eighteenth-Century Life*, vol. 24: 2. 85-105.

Webb Johnson, Joanna (2006). “Chick Lit Jr.: More Than Glitz and Glamour for Teens and Twens.” In Ferriss and Young (2006). 141-158.

Wells, Juliette (2006). “Mothers of Chick Lit? Women Writers, Readers, and Literary History.” In Ferriss and Young (2006). 47-70.

Weston, Kath ([1991] 1997). *Families We Choose. Lesbians, Gays, Kinship.* New York, Oxford: Columbia University Press.

Whelehan, Imelda (2002). *Helen Fielding’s* Bridget Jones’s Diary. *A Reader’s Guide.* Continuum Contemporaries. London: The Continuum International Publishing Group Ltd.

--- (2004). “High Anxiety: Feminism, Chicklit and Women in The Noughties”. *Diegesis: Journal of the Association for Research in Popular Fictions: Chicklit*, vol. 8. 4-10.

--- (2005). *The Feminist Bestseller. From* Sex and the Single Girl *to* Sex and the City. Basingstoke, New York: Palgrave Macmillan.

Wildschut, Tim et al. (2006). “Nostalgia: Content, Triggers, Functions.” *Journal of Personality and Social Psychology*, vol. 91: 5. 975-993.

Williams, Raymond (1961). *The Long Revolution.* London: Chatto & Windus.

--- (1976). *Keywords: A Vocabulary of Culture and Society.* London: Fontana Press.

--- ([1983] 2008). "Culture." In Oakes and Price (2008). 15-19.

Williamson, Margaret (1986). "The Greek Romance." In Jean Radford, ed. *The Progress of Romance. The Politics of Popular Fiction.* London, New York: Routledge & Kegan Paul. 23-45.

Winkler, Kathrin, Kim Seifert and Heinrich Detering (2012). "Die Literaturwissenschaften im *Spatial Turn.* Versuch einer Positionsbestimmung." *Journal of Literary Theory*, vol. 6: 1. 253-269.

Wirth-Nesher, Hana (1996). *City Codes. Reading the Modern Urban Novel.* Cambridge: Cambridge University Press.

Wood, Helen (2004). "What Reading the Romance Did for Us." *European Journal of Cultural Studies*, vol. 7: 2. 147-154.

Yandell, James ([1995] 2006). "Foreword." In Clare Cooper Marcus. *House as a Mirror of Self. Exploring the Deeper Meaning of Home.* Berwick: Nicolas-Hays, Inc. xv-xvii.

Yardley, Cathy (2006). *Will Write for Shoes. How to Write a Chick Lit Novel.* New York: St. Martin's Press.

Young, Iris Marion (1997). *Intersecting Voices: Dilemmas of Gender, Political Philosophy, and Policy.* Princeton, Chichester: Princeton University Press.

Zelinsky, Wilbur ([1973] 1992). *The Cultural Geography of the United States.* Englewood Cliffs: Prentice-Hall.